CHAUCER STUDIES XXIV

Chaucerian Tragedy

CHAUCER STUDIES

ISSN 0261-9822

Previously published volumes in this series
are listed at the back of this book

Chaucerian Tragedy

HENRY ANSGAR KELLY

D. S. BREWER

First published 1997
D. S. Brewer, Cambridge
Reprinted in paperback 2000

ISBN 0 85991 505 0 Hardback
ISBN 0 85991 604 9 Paperback

D. S. Brewer is an imprint of Boydell & Brewer Ltd
PO Box 9, Woodbridge, Suffolk IP12 3DF, UK
and of Boydell & Brewer Inc.
PO Box 41026, Rochester, NY 14604–4126, USA
website: http://www.boydell.co.uk

A catalogue record for this book is available
from the British Library

Library of Congress Catalog Card Number: 96–31014

This publication is printed on acid-free paper

Printed in Great Britain by
Athanæum Press Limited, Gateshead, Tyne & Wear

For Marea, Sarah, and Dominic

The bad end unhappily, the good unluckily.
That is what Tragedy means.

Tom Stoppard

Tragedy was not in those times a poem of more general
dignity or elevation than comedy; it required only a calamitous conclusion, with which the common criticism of
that age was satisfied, whatever lighter pleasure it
afforded in its progress.

Samuel Johnson

Contents

Preface

I am grateful to friends and colleagues who have borne with me and encouraged me in my researches into the meanings of tragedy during the last two decades. The present volume is completely independent of my previous books and articles. But considerations of economy have prevented me from including full details when dealing with background materials, and I hope that I will be forgiven for referring to these studies or to other earlier treatments for supplementary texts and discussions.

A word on the cited texts of medieval works: since Latin was pronounced like the vernacular (see my essay on "Lawyers' Latin"), I treat it in the same way as the vernacular, distributing *i* and *j* and *u* and *v* according to modern (post-seventeenth-century) usage. I transliterate the obsolete English letters thorn and yogh into their modern values, and I de-classicize the archaic Latin diphthongs *æ* and *œ* to the simple medieval spelling of *e*, even in classical works when treated as sources, or possible sources, for medieval authors.

I feel free to translate all Christian names into English and, for the sake of convenience, to treat toponymic names as surnames, especially when the *topos* in question is small. Therefore, I say "William of Conches" and refer to him as either "William" or "Conches," rather than keeping his name in Latin, "Gullielmus Conchensis," or translating it into modern French, "Guillaume de Conches." We are used to treating place-names as surnames from Shakespeare, who says "Gaunt" for "John of Gaunt" and "Bolingbroke" for "Henry (of) Bolingbroke." We frequently omit the preposition of place in English even when it is present in Latin or French (or Norman French); thus we say "Thomas Becket" and not "Thomas from Becket," even though the Latin form is "Thomas a Becket" (the form "Thomas à Becket" retains an early modern diacritic signaling the one-syllable Latin preposition). In dropping prepositions, I am making no statement about the usage of the time or about whether the "surname" was hereditary. It is frequently thought that prepositions in English surnames did not begin to be dropped until the fourteenth century, but the practice can be found already in the eleventh century, with 163 examples in the Domesday Book (Reaney, *Dictionary of British Surnames*, p. xvi).

Abbreviations

EETS os, es, ss	Early English Text Society, original series, extra series, supplementary series (London)
LCL	Loeb Classical Library (London and Cambridge, Mass.)
MED	*Middle English Dictionary*
OED	*Oxford English Dictionary*
PL	Patrologiae latinae cursus completus, ed. J. P. Migne (Paris)

I will also employ the following abbreviated references to my previous studies on tragedy:

ARISTOTLE-AVERROES-ALEMANNUS: "Aristotle-Averroes-Alemannus on Tragedy: The Influence of the *Poetics* on the Latin Middle Ages," *Viator* 10 (1979) 161–209.

IDEAS AND FORMS OF TRAGEDY: *Ideas and Forms of Tragedy from Aristotle to the Middle Ages* (Cambridge 1993).

TRAGEDY AND COMEDY: *Tragedy and Comedy from Dante to Pseudo-Dante* (Berkeley 1989).

Introduction

"Tragedy" was a rarity in the Middle Ages. The word was not used much, and, to those that did use it, it had a wide variety of meanings. One of the more common interpretations of the term was that it designated a genre of poetry employed by the ancients but no longer practiced. This is what it meant to Boccaccio, for instance. A few writers were inspired to create tragedies of their own, but for the most part these were isolated efforts and not imitated. There was no felt need for a genre of tragedy, and no generic sense of "the tragic." I chronicle all of this in my study, *Ideas and Forms of Tragedy from Aristotle to the Middle Ages*.

Chaucer was unusual not only in being the first vernacular poet to write tragedies, but also in founding a genre that was taken up by others, specifically John Lydgate and Robert Henryson. Lydgate's example was imitated by the authors of *A Mirror for Magistrates*, which brings us to the era of Shakespeare.

The overall approach of this book can be characterized as "post-avant-garde"; for I see myself as forging (or foraging) ahead of the cutting edge of literary discourse and, at the same time, doing overlooked but necessary spadework behind the vanguard. Recent critical theory, varied and inventive as it is, has largely neglected genre-theory, even though historically it was one of the earliest subjects of theoretical discussion; it was the main topic of Aristotle's *Poetics*, with tragedy as the central focus of attention. The uses and misuses of Aristotelian notions constitute a large segment of the history of criticism. But postmodern theorists, it seems to me, are not much interested in tragedy or other generic concepts. Moreover, they are actively or even militantly uninterested in *criticism* itself, understood in its etymological and traditional meaning of "judgment" or "evaluation" of the artistic merits of literature or drama. This dislike of critical evaluation is shared by both structuralists and poststructuralists.

To use the distinction of Lubomír Doležel, Aristotle practiced both poetics (the scientific description of literary works) and criticism (the ranking of works according to effectiveness in achieving generic goals).[1] A constant problem in later times, particularly since the Renaissance, and particularly when dealing with tragedy, is that writers have not kept these functions separate but have imported evaluations into what should be objective exercises of poetics. A familiar example (which I will explain in more detail below) is the practice of importing one of Aristotle's "high-value" categories of tragedy

---

[1] Lubomír Doležel, *Occidental Poetics*, chap. 1: "Aristotle: Poetics and Criticism," pp. 11–32.

(the good-man-with-flaw plot) into his more general notions of tragedy and excluding from the genre of tragedy whatever works do not live up to this supposed prerequisite of the genre.

Tzvetan Todorov charges the New Critics with taking the evaluative process to extremes, but he analyzes their goal in terms of artistic *meaning* rather than value: they privilege interpretation over an analysis of structure.[2] His own goal, he asserts, is to redress the balance: but not, as one might think, by leveling out the structural and evaluative functions of analysis; rather, he wishes to eliminate evaluation altogether as a scholarly function. He is inspired to take this approach by Northrop Frye's call for a purely scientific poetics.[3] I wish to go beyond Frye and Todorov and set aside, at least as a general rule, not only evaluative criticism or interpretation but also scientific or structural poetics as well.

Rather than drawing on modern definitions or theories of genres, I restrict my consideration to medieval ideas of tragedy, setting my sight on Hans Robert Jauss's familiar "Horizont des Erwartbaren" ("horizon of the expectable"),[4] that is, the likely awareness that each author or reader in the Middle Ages would have of the classifications into which literature could fall. Todorov, in contrast, starts with theoretical generic notions. When he asks, "Are we entitled to discuss a genre without having studied (or at least read) all the works which constitute it?" he responds by saying, "One of the first characteristics of scientific method is that it does not require us to observe every instance of a phenomenon in order to describe it; scientific method proceeds rather by deduction." He concludes, "Let us leave exhaustiveness, then, to those who have no other recourse."[5]

In so saying, Todorov almost, but not quite, concludes that complete induction—that is, assessing as many instances of a phenomenon as possible—has no place in scientific procedure. He is speaking of his own peculiar purposes, which proceed from what can be called a "definitional" approach to genre. My own goals, of understanding authorial and audience intentions or meanings, derive from a "nominalist" or philological or contextual approach, which is, I maintain, the approach of Aristotle himself, one of the founders of scientific methodology, at the "fieldwork" or poetics phase of his enterprise. It means accepting everything that is called a tragedy as a tragedy, and accepting nothing as a tragedy that would not be considered such either by its author or by its readers or viewers. It does not proceed from an *a priori* definition but rather results in multiple *a posteriori* definitions or descriptions. I hope that Todorov would agree that for such a project exhaustiveness is indeed the only honorable recourse, and that it can be considered to partake of science.[6]

[2] Tzvetan Todorov, *Introduction to Poetics*, pp. 7, 12.

[3] Tzvetan Todorov, *The Fantastic: A Structural Approach to a Literary Genre*, pp. 8–10; Northrop Frye, *Anatomy of Criticism*, "Polemical Introduction," esp. pp. 8, 18–28.

[4] Hans Robert Jauss, "Theorie der Gattungen und Literatur des Mittelalters," p. 110; "Theory of Genres and Medieval Literature," p. 79. Cf. Paul Strohm, "Middle English Narrative Genres," pp. 385–88 (drawing on the incomplete French version of Jauss's essay).

[5] Todorov, *The Fantastic*, pp. 3–4.

[6] For further discussion of these matters, see my "Interpretation of Genres and by Genres in the Middle Ages."

When Aristotle concludes in chapter 5 that epics differ from tragedies only in lacking the staged elements,[7] one might wish to say that he is working from an *a priori* understanding of tragedy; if so, however, the priority of his understanding is of recent vintage, being based on his previous inductions, and his pronouncement about epics may be seen as an "interlocutory deduction." But in the definition that he gives of tragedy in chapter 6, as "a representation of an action which is serious, complete, and of a certain magnitude—in language which is garnished in various forms in its different parts—in the mode of dramatic enactment, not narrative—and through the arousal of pity and fear effecting the *katharsis* of such emotions,"[8] there seem to be genuinely *a priori* elements not based on previous inductions, in spite of his assertion that the definition "arises out of what has so far been said." Specifically, nothing has been said about pity and fear and its *katharsis*. It is likely that there was such a discussion in his original treatment and that it was subsequently omitted in the admittedly very defective text that survives to us. But even apart from this consideration, one can readily admit that there is a noninductive prescriptiveness about the definition, because Aristotle has entered into the critical or evaluative phase of his enterprise.[9] However, we should note that his definition is not as prescriptive as it has been made by the modern "vulgate" version, which includes a requirement that tragedy must deal with a protagonist who falls into affliction not because of wickedness but because of a certain failing or flaw (*hamartia*). This formulation comes from chapter 13, where Aristotle holds that a main character of this sort would best fulfill the emotional purposes of tragedy. He does not mean to exclude other kinds of tragedy from the category of tragedy, which includes anything called a tragedy and even embraces nondramatic narratives that tell a serious story. In fact, in the following discussion, in chapter 14, he concludes that a completely different kind of tragedy, one with a happy ending, like Euripides's *Iphigenia Among the Taurians*, is the best kind of tragedy.[10]

From a slightly different point of view, we can isolate two genres of genre theory, the subjective and the objective, or the idealistic and the historical.[11] Both approaches have been applied to medieval tragedy, with varying degrees of rigor. The practitioners of the first genre have their own idea of tragedy, or the tragic spirit, which is usually based in some way on a reading of Aristotle's *Poetics*, and they attempt to see whether or to what extent it is verified in the works of Chaucer and his contemporaries.[12] Practitioners of the second genre derive an idea of medieval tragedy from an examination of Chaucer's

---

[7] Aristotle, *Poetics*, chap. 5.

[8] Aristotle, *Poetics*, chap. 6, tr. Halliwell.

[9] For Doležel on Aristotle's presuppositions, see below, chap. 3, p. 142 n. 94.

[10] See IDEAS AND FORMS, pp. 1–5 ("Aristotle on Tragedy in General").

[11] The latter formulation of the distinction is made by Peter Haidu, "Romance: Idealistic Genre or Historical Text?" pp. 4–5.

[12] This genre of genre classification is familiar from literary handbooks, which, as Jauss points out, jumble classical and modern distinctions together with medieval understandings: "The generic divisions of the handbooks rest on a convention of the discipline that is scarcely called into question any longer, according to which one promiscuously uses original characterizations, classical genre concepts, and later classifications" ("Theory of Genres," p. 77).

(and sometimes others') uses of the term, and then interpret medieval works in its light.

The first genre of genre theory divides into two species, the descriptive and the critical (in Doležel's sense). The first species usually becomes an exercise in theoretical narratology, like Todorov's study of fantastic tales. Morton Bloomfield's analysis of Chaucer's *Man of Law's Tale* as a type of tragedy and a type of comedy can be mentioned as a well-executed example of this approach,[13] as can Piero Boitani's studies of tragedy in medieval literature, especially his analyses of Dante's and Chaucer's respective treatments of Hugolino of Pisa.[14] The critical subjective species has an impressionistic element to it, for it addresses the question, "Does this work strike me as tragic?" or, "Should that work be considered tragic?" In the chapter on *Troilus and Criseyde* we shall look at some examples of this enterprise, some overt, others not. Such an approach may seem hopelessly old-fashioned in our new *fin de siècle*, but we shall treat them from the postmodern perspective of reader reception—and perhaps even find a few signs of similar critical judgments still being made. Often such judgments involve what is known in the field of biblical hermeneutics as *eisegesis* (reading one's own ideas into a text), as opposed to *exegesis* (reading out of a text the meaning already contained in it).

As for the second genre of genre theory—the objective approach—those who have applied it to tragedy in the Middle Ages have mainly relied on Chaucer for their understanding of medieval tragedy. They have come up with widely differing notions of what Chaucer meant by tragedy, not all of which, of course, can be right. In most cases, the undertaking has also been flawed by misapprehensions of one kind or another: for instance, the assumption that "tragedy" was common in the Middle Ages—specifically, that Chaucer's understanding of tragedy was, at least in its broad outlines, widely shared by the literate populace—and the further assumption that other writers besides Chaucer thought of themselves as writers of tragedy.

In *Ideas and Forms of Tragedy*, I have shown, I hope, the following: (1) the word tragedy, in its various linguistic forms, was comparatively rare in the Middle Ages, and especially in England; (2) each of the few authors who are recorded as using it has a different understanding of it, and the various understandings often vary widely; (3) most users of the term considered it to be an obsolete genre; and (4) Chaucer is one of a minuscule number of authors who considered tragedy to be a living, or at least resurrectible, genre, and who actually self-consciously wrote tragedies. One conclusion from all this is that Chaucer's idea of tragedy can be applied strictly only to Chaucer and his imitators.

This last conclusion involves a presupposition that perhaps needs some defense, namely, that, practically speaking, one cannot have an idea of tra-

---

[13] Morton W. Bloomfield, "*The Man of Law's Tale*: A Tragedy of Victimization and a Christian Comedy."

[14] Piero Boitani, *The Tragic and the Sublime in Medieval Literature*; the essay on Dante and Chaucer is titled, "Two Versions of Tragedy: Ugolino and Hugelyn." This is also the approach of some of the essays, by Boitani and others, in *The European Tragedy of Troilus*, edited by Boitani (see my review in *English Language Notes*).

gedy without knowing the word tragedy or some recognizable equivalent. "Tragedy" is not like, say, "tree." One can get a respectable idea of a tree just by looking at a tree, whether it is called "tree" or "arbor" or "eert." But this is not the case with tragedy. Furthermore, one must know something of what others have meant by the word tragedy. A tree could be called a "tragedy," or "tragitree," and still mean only tree. If someone were to come upon the word "tragedian" totally unprepared, never having heard of tragedy, he or she might well conjecture that it meant "Trojan" or "tregetour." In fact, both of these conclusions seem to have been arrived at by medieval French writers, the first by Eustace Deschamps and the second by the translator of the most common French version of Boethius's *Consolation of Philosophy*.[15]

When a term is translated out of its lettered form, there are special problems. What if, for instance, William of Moerbeke had not used the form *tragodia* but rather, say, *aidomok* (the reverse of *komodia*) or *hircicantus* ("goat-song") in translating Aristotle's *Poetics*? An attentive reader would have a fairly good idea of what Aristotle meant by the idea of tragedy, but we cannot readily assume that he or she would identify it with what other writers meant by the word *tragedia*. When Herman Alemannus was translating Averroes's *Commentary on the Poetics*, he did not realize at first that the Arabic word *madik* ("encomium") corresponded to the Greek form of the Latin word *tragedia*, that is, τραγῳδία; and he could hardly have come to the realization without some specic help (say by nding a transliterated form in Al-Farabi or Avicenna). Averroes's idea of tragedy is so distorted by his idea of encomium that the connection of "the art of praise" with "tragedy" was completely unrecognizable to anyone who did not read far enough to see the glosses that Herman eventually began to add to his translation.[16]

In other words, every variation on the word-plus-concept of tragedy depends to some extent on tradition for its meaning. It can be modified by experience or by other ideas, but it cannot be wholly spontaneous and still serve any use for the history of ideas unless it is somehow connected to tradition. In all traditions of the word, tragedy is a certain kind of literary or dramatic category. As it is handed down, it can be affected by other generic ideas, and the result will be a new idea of tragedy. For instance, when the Arabs identified Greek tragedy with encomium, tragedy took on a completely new meaning, and encomium took on new dimensions.

It would be possible, I admit, for one traditional aspect of tragedy, say the emphasis on lamentation, to be singled out in such a way that it is clearly merged with another generic idea. This may have been the case with Deschamps, if he considered tragedy simply another word for the poetic complaint. But only when an author makes such an identification does the concept come within the scope of "the history of ideas of tragedy." However, I concede that anyone who knows about the complaint genre knows the equivalent of the Campestrian (Deschampsian) idea of tragedy, since for Deschamps tragedy would have been just a synonym for complaint—unless, of course, it was qualified by an idea that Trojans were particularly adept at it.

---

[15] IDEAS AND FORMS, pp. 176 (Deschamps), 160–61 ("vulgate" French Boethius).
[16] ARISTOTLE-AVERROES-ALEMANNUS.

One could also get a respectable idea of Senecan tragedy by reading several of the plays (or even by reading one and being told that there are others like it), without knowing that they are called tragedies. The idea would, of course, be quite different from the idea of "Seneca's tragedies" conjured up by persons who only had heard that the story of Nero in hell inviting lawyers to join him was taken from one of Seneca's tragedies.[17] One could have a distorted idea of the tragedies even after reading them, or in spite of reading them, if one is excessively swayed by an irrelevant or inappropriate definition of tragedy. Such is the case with Guido da Pisa when he indicates in his commentary on Dante's *Comedy*, followed by the *Epistle to Cangrande*, that Seneca's plays fit his characterization of tragedy, not only in having a fetid and horrible ending (which is certainly true of most of them) but also in having an admirable and pleasing beginning (which is true of none).[18]

But the question that concerns us now is this: could a person get a reasonably close equivalent of Chaucer's idea of tragedy, while knowing nothing of any tradition of tragedy, simply by writing or reading a story that Chaucer would consider to be a tragedy? I think it barely possible, but not likely; and I have not found any indication that it ever happened.

We shall conclude that Chaucer probably considered the *Thebaid*, the *Pharsalia*, parts of the *Aeneid*, and parts of the *Metamorphoses* to be tragedies, and most of the epistles of the *Heroides* to be suitable for making into tragedies. What chance is there that anyone else ever came up with a similar generic notion without being told of a class of poems like "tragedy" (as Chaucer uses it)? Let us take, for example, the *Heroides*. If a reader were asked to think up a generic description for them, under the name of tragedy, without having heard of the word before, she or he might well come up with this definition: "A tragedy is a poem written by Ovid in elegiac couplets in the form of a letter addressed by a woman to a man; the persons are usually Greek (never Roman), the man is usually a knave or a fool, and the woman has usually been left in the lurch."

But, one might ask, what about a narrative poem like the *Song of Roland?* If Chaucer knew it, he would perhaps have judged it at least to *contain* the tragedy of Roland, and perhaps others as well—for instance, the tragedy of Ganelon, when he is executed by Charlemagne—even though the poem ends with Charlemagne's triumph coupled with his lament that he must go on fighting. But would the author, or any auditor, consider the work to participate in a genre of poetry containing stories that begin in prosperity and end in adversity? No evidence is forthcoming that any such classification of poems existed or would have been thought of during the heyday of the chansons de geste. Such a genre is not likely to have been on anyone's horizon of expectations at the time. At the most, perhaps, one could have thought in categories of hero-subjects: "stories about Roland's final defeat," "stories of Charlemagne's vengeance on Ganelon," and so on.

On the other side, if one did have a notion of tragedy and applied it to such

---

[17] See below, chap. 2, p. 44.

[18] TRAGEDY AND COMEDY, p. 20. Guido's description of tragedy appears almost verbatim in the *Epistle to Cangrande*, which, as I try to demonstrate, is subsequent to Guido's work and dependent on it. See below, chap. 1, p. 20.

tales, the result would not necessarily correspond to Chaucer's concept, as can be seen with the French translators who interpreted the *tragediarum clamor* of Boethius as the chansons of jongleurs, including chansons of Roland.[19] The same is true of Aelred of Rievaulx and Peter of Blois when they referred to the similar Arthurian stories of heroism as tragedies.[20]

Chaucer clearly considered Roland's fall through the treason of Ganelon to be a suitable subject for tragedy, for he identifies the traitor in his *Tragedy of Pedro of Spain* with Ganelon.[21] Let us assume, for the sake of argument, that he knew the *Song of Roland* and considered it a tragedy. Would this fact have had any retroactive effect on the *Song of Roland*? Clearly not. But it might very well have affected Chaucer's understanding of the *Roland* and his understanding of tragedy, and also affected the way in which he composed tragedies.

Let me illustrate my point by supposing that William Butler Yeats believed that one of the medieval English cycle plays, say, the Chester *Play of Abraham*, was somehow inspired, whether through direct contact or through mystical forces, by the Japanese Noh play. Such a belief would clearly affect the way in which he viewed the *Play of Abraham*, but it would be meaningless for anyone who did not know about or believe in the Noh influences.

Since, however, there is no reason to believe that Chaucer knew the *Song of Roland*, and since the author of the *Song of Roland* was not consciously writing in a genre equivalent to Chaucer's genre of tragedy, I hope we can conclude that there is no reason to discuss the *Song of Roland*, or *Beowulf*, or similar works with sad endings, or sad episodes, as tragedies. (It is surprising, by the way, how few medieval narratives actually end unhappily—I mean, at the very end.) We can, however, discuss themes or motifs in such works which are connected to themes and motifs influencing Chaucer's theory and practice of tragedy. For instance, the motif of contrary Fortune is utilized in many narratives (some of which end unhappily, some of which do not) and in many lyrics, and the same motif is to be found in Chaucer's works; but only Chaucer's works are affected by a concept of tragedy.

The closest thing to a generic equivalent of Chaucerian tragedy in the Middle Ages can be found in Boccaccio's *De casibus*. Boccaccio may have been influenced by treatises or sermons on *contemptus mundi*, or lyrical or narrative laments on the theme of *ubi sunt*, or by historical works, especially the established genre, *De viris illustribus,* since many important men have in fact fallen suddenly and violently. Many of these works contained the same morals that Boccaccio uses, and the same figures, such as the play of Fortune. But Boccaccio was the first to make a deliberate collection of stories with disastrous endings.[22] However, he did not think of himself as contributing to a traditional genre, as did Chaucer, or of starting a new genre; though at one point, as we shall see, he recognized that the sort of events he was dealing

---

[19] IDEAS AND FORMS, pp. 160–64.

[20] Ibid., pp. 85–87.

[21] Chaucer, *Monk's Tale* 2386–90.

[22] In considering Boccaccio's compilation to be an original work without significant precedent, I agree with John S. P. Tatlock, *The Development and Chronology of Chaucer's Works*, p. 167, against the opposing view of R. W. Babcock, "The Mediaeval Setting of Chaucer's *Monk's Tale*."

with resembled the subject matter of the antique dramatic genre of tragedy. But he was not consciously writing or imitating tragedies, just as Petrarch was not alternating tragedies with comedies in his *De viris illustribus*, even though the first subject of his earliest version, Romulus, is carried off by a sudden eclipse of the sun and a horrible storm, while the second, Numa Pompilius, has a tranquil and quiet end to his life.[23] Petrarch's stated purpose was that of the historian: to choose details dealing with virtues and vices, providing a copious supply of illustrious examples to his readers of what to imitate and what to avoid.[24] It is precisely because Boccaccio did not have a clear generic idea in mind that the *De casibus* is, conceptually speaking, such a mess (as we shall see in chapter 1 below). Chaucer's *Monk's Tale,* on the other hand, though its stories might be judged to be no more skilfully told, does have a consistent framework, which is provided by his idea of tragedy.

As I have noted, there have been many differences of opinion about Chaucer's understanding of tragedy, and these disagreements have often come to the surface not in discussions of Chaucer but in speaking of other works, especially the *Alliterative Morte Arthure*, where it is thought to be relevant, on the assumption that Chaucer's idea of tragedy (as explained by each scholar) was a widely shared notion held by other authors of the Middle Ages.[25] There are two extreme positions that have been taken, both of which I believe to be misguided. One is the view that all of Chaucer's tragic protagonists bring disaster upon themselves by some sort of moral dereliction;[26] and the other is the view that Fortune (that is, external circumstances) is to be blamed for all of the falls, with little or no attention given to personal respon-

---

[23] Francis Petrarch, *De viris illustribus,* ed. Guido Martellotti, pp. 6–19. The contrast between the two lives is more striking in his *Compendium*, an abbreviated version of the original *De viris*, which he began to work on in the last years of his life. It was published under the title of *Vitarum virorum illustrium epitome* in his *Opera omnia* (Basel 1554). See Martellotti, pp. xiii, lii. Petrarch wrote his first series, mainly on early Roman figures, but including Alexander and Pyrrhus, between 1338 and 1343. The second series, beginning with Adam and going on to Noah, Nimrod, and other biblical figures, but including also Semiramis, Jason, and Hercules (unfinished), was composed between 1351 and 1353. His first and longer proem was also composed at this time. Martellotti did not complete his edition beyond the first series, but he did publish the proem and the Adam account in a volume of Petrarch's prose edited by him and others, *Prose*, pp. 218–228. The shorter proem, composed at the time of the *Compendium*, is given by Martellotti in *De viris*, pp. 3–5.

[24] Petrarch, early proem (*Prose*, p. 224): "Apud me ista frustra requiruntur, nisi quatenus ad virtutes vel virtutum contraria trahi possunt. Hic enim, nisi fallor, fructuosus historici finis est, illa prosequi que vel sectanda legentibus vel fugienda sunt, ut in utranque partem copia suppetat illustrium exemplorum" ("Such facts will not be found in my accounts, except insofar as they can be applied to virtues or their opposites. For, unless I am mistaken, this is the fruitful goal of the historian, to elaborate for his readers the things that they should follow and the things that they should avoid, so that there is a supply of illustrious examples on both sides"). Cf. the shorter proem, *De viris*, p. 4.

[25] The trend of applying Chaucerian notions of tragedy to the *Alliterative Morte Arthure* was started in 1960 by William Matthews, *The Tragedy of Arthur*, though he was anticipated in 1957 by Karl Josef Höltgen, "König Arthur und Fortuna." For other scholars who followed suit, see my "Non-Tragedy of Arthur," p. 92.

[26] The originator and main exponent of this view is D. W. Robertson, Jr., "Chaucerian Tragedy," which originally appeared in 1952.

sibility.[27] The truth of the matter, I claim, is that Chaucer's conception of tragedy allows for all kinds of falls, self-induced and other-induced, deserved and undeserved. When Tom Stoppard has his Player say, "The bad end unhappily, the good unluckily. That is what Tragedy means," he intends a witty oversimplification on the order of Miss Prism's account of her novel: "The good ended happily, and the bad unhappily. That is what Fiction means." But it very well epitomizes the generic common denominator of tragedy as Chaucer understood it, just as Miss Prism's summation could be taken as an accurate account of the double-plotted species of tragedy described by Aristotle.[28]

In the accounts that follow in this book, I will normally try to avoid critical evaluations based on either premedieval or postmedieval ideas of good tragedy or good literature, following the example of John Baldwin: "Aesthetic essentialism has attributed transhistorical value to works of art, and has undergirded literary criticism with ontological explanations of enduring beauty, but I shall not participate in these considerations."[29] I aim instead to follow what Otto Karl Werckmeister demonstrates to be the view of Karl Marx. Werckmeister takes the revolutionary approach of applying to art what Marx says about art, rather than what he says about everything else, or what communist philosophers, drawing on their Pickwickian forms of Marxism, wish he had said about art. Marx considered art to be just another ideology, like religion and metaphysics; from this it follows that no valid philosophy of esthetics is possible. Werckmeister concludes that it is not the business of art historians to make value judgments on what is beautiful and not beautiful. Instead, their efforts should be directed towards trying to determine the esthetic preoccupations of the artists and their patrons.[30] Just so, I shall feel free to speculate about the extent to which literary works are successful in terms of the expectations and standards of the authors themselves and projected or actual readers, and the extent to which certain pieces fail to conform to their authors' goals.

To sum up the plan of this study, I preface my account of Chaucer, Lydgate, and Henryson with a chapter on the "non-tragedies" of Boccaccio, in

[27] Larry D. Benson, "The Alliterative *Morte Arthure* and Medieval Tragedy," p. 79, comes close to this position, at least on a theoretical level; another example is Anke Janssen, "The Dream of the Wheel of Fortune," pp. 144–46, 151.

[28] Tom Stoppard, *Rosencrantz & Guiltenstern Are Dead*, Act 2; Oscar Wilde, *The Importance of Being Earnest*, Act 2. For Aristotle, see below, p. 89.

[29] John W. Baldwin, *The Language of Sex*, p. xxiii. Baldwin also dismisses other modern essentialisms, especially those of Sigmund Freud, "who postulated an unchanging psyche," and his French interpreter Jacques Lacan. See Jacques Bouveresse, *Wittgenstein Reads Freud: the Myth of the Unconscious*, for critiques of Freudian scientism by Wittgenstein and Bouveresse and by Vincent Descombes in his Foreword. Speaking of Lacan and what is considered "the true Freud," Bouveresse says, "We French are well known for our tendency to sometimes confuse the practice of philosophy with the practice of free association, and for our sovereign contempt for what Wittgenstein considered more important than anything else in philosophy, namely the recognition of differences" (p. xviii).

[30] Otto Karl Werckmeister, "Marx on Ideology and Art." See also his *Ende der Ästhetik* (Frankfurt 1971). For an example of the more usual kind of Marxist evaluations of art, see Werckmeister's comments on Meyer Schapiro during his Trotskyite phase (review of Schapiro's *Romanesque Art*).

order to define the achievement of the English authors more clearly. Lydgate's tragedies, to be found in his *Fall of Princes*, are elaborations of Laurence of Premierfait's expanded version of the life histories (or life-and-death histories) of Boccaccio's *De casibus virorum illustrium*. As I have noted above, Boccaccio did not consider these histories to be tragedies, and neither did his translator Premierfait, but Chaucer did, and Lydgate followed suit. A main concern of my study is to determine what difference this "genericizing," or "re-genericizing," of Boccaccio made to Chaucer and Lydgate. Many of the stories have the same "facts" in Boccaccio and Premierfait on the one hand and Chaucer and Lydgate on the other, and often the same or similar lessons are drawn. To what extent, if any, did classifying them as tragedies change them? To answer this question, we will first have to see what Boccaccio meant by tragedy, as far as possible, and to see how his understanding of the term would have precluded him from applying it to his Latin prose histories of illustrious men; and then we can try to see just what generic considerations he did bring to bear on the *De casibus*.

In chapter 2, I survey the ideas of tragedy to be found in fourteenth- and fifteenth-century England, apart from my three major authors, before discussing Chaucer's ideas of tragedy. Next, I analyze the earliest works that he designated as tragedies, namely, the seventeen narratives that he later assigned to the Monk in the *Canterbury Tales*. Finally, I broach the question of what he meant by comedy in contrast to tragedy. In chapter 3, I take up his major tragedy, *Troilus and Criseyde*. Chapter 4 is given over to discussing John Lydgate's changing notions of tragedy, with a glance at some related contemporary Continental ideas, and in chapter 5 we shall discuss the individual tragedies in the *Fall of Princes*. Finally, chapter 6 deals with Henryson's ideas of tragedy and his practice of tragedy in the *Testament of Cresseid*.

1

Background: Boccaccio's non-tragedies

Among the fourteenth-century commentators on Dante's *Comedy*, Giovanni Boccaccio is unusual in not discussing tragedy when he comments on the title of Dante's work.[1] But he has loomed large in the accounts of medieval tragedy, because it has been assumed, first, that he considered the falls described in his *De casibus virorum illustrium* to be tragedies, and, second, that he presented these tragedies with the primary intention of showing how they were caused by the fickleness of Fortune. For instance, Willard Farnham, in his influential book on the backgounds of Elizabethan tragedy, says: "Boccaccio's presupposition or working hypothesis amounts in its simplest terms only to this: All the notable tragedies which a diligent man can collect from literature, tradition, and observation show without exception that the mortal world (as distinct from Heaven) is ruled by Fortune, the irrational spirit of chance."[2] Neither of the above assumptions is true. Throughout the hundreds of "case histories" which Boccaccio recounts he refrains from calling the stories tragedies, and he shows little inclination to think of the accounts as conforming to an idea or form of tragedy. Moreover, his overriding purpose for telling them, as stipulated in his Preface, is to illustrate not the workings of Fortune (a misnomer for Providence) but the judgments of God on famous men and women, in order to persuade the eminent persons of his own day to reform their wicked lives.

It was Chaucer who hit upon the idea of calling these narratives tragedies, shortly after Boccaccio released the *De casibus* to the public, and Chaucer's example was followed by subsequent writers, notably Lydgate.[3] However,

---

[1] TRAGEDY AND COMEDY, pp. 44–48; cf. IDEAS AND FORMS, p. 154.

[2] Willard Farnham, *The Medieval Heritage of Elizabethan Tragedy*, p. 78. In this statement Franham also assumes that it was common to see events as tragedies, whereas in fact such a metaphorical use of the term was very rare; but we will see a Boccaccian example below. The unproved (and, as I will show, unlikely) notion, propagated by English literary scholars, that Boccaccio was drawing on a medieval idea of tragedy in narrating the falls of men has been taken up by Vittorio Zaccaria in the introduction to the edition of Text B (the second and final version, *c.* 1374), p. xlviii ("una serie di visioni storiche ... attuata secondo il canone retorico medievale della *tragedia*") and pp. l–li ("questo moralismo 'tragico' che infonde all' opera un flusso di grandiosità").

[3] Later in his book, at the end of his chapter on Chaucer and Lydgate, Farnham admits that Boccaccio does not call his stories tragedies, but he asserts that they quickly gained the name (p. 171, quoted below, in the Conclusion, p. 262). This is true only in the sense that Chaucer, and Chaucer alone, quickly considered them to be tragedies.

because of the influence that Boccaccio's work had upon the theory and practice of tragedy in medieval England, I wish to spend some time in analyzing first his ideas of genres and then the form and content of the *De casibus*.

TRAGEDY: AN OBSOLETE DRAMATIC GENRE

One of the few mentions of tragedy in the *De casibus* is taken from Valerius Maximus. In telling the story of Astyages, Boccaccio makes Valerius's point that great minds are not genetically limited, as can be seen from the examples of Euripides and Demosthenes:

> Sic nec Euripides nec Demosthenes, quorum ob generis vilitatem alterius mater, alterius vero pater, fuit incognitus, tragediarum clamores ingentes et eloquentie mellifluas suavitates ex muliercularum uteris eduxere.[4]

> (Just so neither Euripides nor Demosthenes, whose mother and father, respectively, were unknown because of mean birth, drew the great clamors of tragedies and the mellifluous sweetnesses of eloquence from the wombs of light women.)

Valerius speaks only of the *vis tragica* or "tragic force" of Euripides.[5] Boccaccio's phrase *tragediarum clamores ingentes* corresponds strikingly to Boethius's *tragediarum clamor*, as does another phrase in the *De casibus*, namely, *infinite clamitant tragedie*, in a passage that we will take up below.[6] We will also see indications in Boccaccio's conclusion at the end of his work that he is drawing on Fortune's monologue in Boethius where she asks her question about tragedy. But I do not see any other indication that the *Consolation of Philosophy* influenced the *De casibus*. Even when he describes Boethius's own fall, Boccaccio makes no reference to it.[7]

---

[4] Boccaccio, *De casibus illustrium virorum*, book 2, cited from "Text A," the early version, according to the edition of John Theodoric of Beauvais, published by John Gourmont and John Petit (Paris n.d.), fol. 19v = p. 64 of the facsimile reprint introduced by Louis Brewer Hall. Hall dates the edition *c.* 1520; Attilio Hortis, *Studi sulle opere latine del Boccaccio*, pp. 765–67, dates it "after 1507." Hall has also published an abridged translation, *The Fates of Illustrious Men*, but he does not indicate his excisions, and he sometimes changes the text. For instance, when Fortune presents five men to Boccaccio's attention at the beginning of book 6, Hall omits the second and third, and instead of calling Cicero the fifth, as in the text, he calls him the third (p. 142). For the "Text B" version of the cited passage, see Ricci-Zaccaria, p. 168: book 2, chap. 17, §9.

[5] Valerius Maximus, *Memorabilia* 3.4 ext. 2: "Quem patrem Euripides aut quam matrem Demosthenes habuerit, ipsorum quoque saeculo ignotum fuit. Alterius autem matrem holera, alterius patrem cultellos venditasse, omnium paene doctorum litterae loquuntur. Sed quid aut illius tragica aut huius oratoria vi clarius?" ("What father Euripides or what mother Demosthenes had was unknown in their own time. But the reports of almost all the learned say that the mother of the one sold vegetables and the father of the other sold knives. But what is more brilliant than the tragic force of the former and the oratorical force of the latter?"). Note that Boccaccio reverses the sex of the unknown parents.

[6] For Boethius's text, see chap. 2 below, p. 50.

[7] See below, chap. 5, p. 205.

If Boccaccio had already incorporated the above-cited allusion to Euripi-des's tragedies in the original text of the first version of the *De casibus*, which he finished around 1360, he would have known of the dramas only by hearsay; for it was in 1360 that he was first exposed to the actual texts of the Greek authors. But he could have added the Valerian reference to Euripides in 1360 or at any time during the subsequent decade, for he released the early *De casibus* to the public only in 1373 or so, after making some slight modifications around 1370. A second version, revised and expanded in 1373 or 1374, was dedicated to his friend Mainardo Cavalcanti. But it was the earl-ier form that was translated by Laurence of Premierfait and passed on to Lydgate.[8]

Boccaccio began his study of Greek, as I have said, in 1360, when he invited the Calabrian Greek scholar Leonzio Pilato to Florence. Among the works that Pilato brought with him were Homer's *Iliad* and *Odyssey* and the traged-ies of Euripides. Before he left Florence towards the end of 1362, he presented Boccaccio with a Greek copy of eight complete plays of Euripides, of which one, the *Hecuba* (which he called *Polydorus*), was provided with a Latin trans-lation and marginal notes. Boccaccio subsequently drew upon the *Hecuba* in the *Genealogia deorum gentilium*, the first version of which was produced between 1363 and 1366.[9]

It was in the *Genealogia* too that Boccaccio first began to cite the tragedies of Seneca by name. It has been deduced from a list of the holdings in the library of the Convent of Santo Spirito in Florence, to which Boccaccio willed his books, that he possessed not only his own copy of the plays, but also a copy of Trevet's commentary on them.[10] However, there is no certain trace of his use of Trevet, and his use of the plays is sparing, to say the least. His early works make no mention of the tragedies and do not quote from them, with the outstanding exception of the *Fiammetta* (written before 1345)[11]—though some readers see Senecan influences in early works, espe-cially the *Decameron*,[12] and also in the work written just after the *De casibus*, namely *De mulieribus claris*, which dates from 1361 or 1362.[13]

In the *De casibus*, Boccaccio speaks of Seneca in his account of Nero in book 7, but does not allude to his tragedies. We must remind ourselves that,

---

[8] See Vittorio Zaccaria, "Le due redazioni del *De casibus*." The dedicatory epistle to Mainardo Cavalcanti was written in 1373, and it is usually found in copies of the revised *De casibus*, but it is often attached to the first version as well, and it also circulated by itself.

[9] See Agostino Pertusi, "La scoperta di Euripide nel primo Umanesimo," pp. 145–51; he sums up this article in "Il ritorno alle fonti del teatro greco classico: Euripide nell' Umanesimo e nel Rinascimento"; see esp. 206–09. Pertusi points out that Boccaccio used Pilato's translation of Homer in the "vulgate" version of the *De mulieribus claris*, which was finished around the time of Pilato's departure, but did not use Pilato's translation of the *Hecuba*; for his histories of Hecuba and Polyxena in chaps. 33–34 he relies on Ovid, *Metamorphoses* 13. See the edition of *De mulieribus* by Vittorio Zaccaria. For Pilato's arrival in Florence, "probably at the beginning of the summer of 1360," see Vittore Branca, *Boccaccio: The Man and His Works*, p. 116.

[10] Antonia Mazza, "L'inventario della 'parva libraria' di Santo Spirito e la biblioteca del Boc-caccio," pp. 55–56, 60–61.

[11] See Mario Serafini, "Le tragedie di Seneca nella *Fiammetta* del Boccaccio," who finds para-phrases or echoes of passages from at least seven of the ten Senecan plays.

[12] Vittorio Russo, "Il senso del tragico nel *Decameron*," pp. 63–65, 74–75.

[13] See the discussion of Jocasta, below, p. 32.

to Boccaccio's way of thinking at this time, there was only one Seneca; he identified Seneca the Younger, Nero's counsellor, who wrote prose essays and letters and verse tragedies, with Seneca the Elder, author of rhetorical declamations. It was only around 1365 that he formed the theory of a separate Seneca Tragicus or Poeta, who, he believed, belonged to the same family but was slightly younger than the philosopher, Seneca Moralis.[14] But if he does not mention Seneca's tragedies in his account of Nero, he does speak of Nero's tragedies. He says that, after beginning his reign well,

> [Nero] sensim in miram et abhominabilem petulantiam decidit. Nam, posita imperatoria gravitate, absque rubore aliquo, velut maximum reipublice commodum peracturus, non solum coram cantavit atque cithara cum Greculis et Egyptiis histrionibus decertavit; quinimmo, quod turpius est, sepissime inter scorta totius urbis et lixas ganeonesque quam docte psalleret domonstravit; aurigavit et sepius; ac heroum tragedias fingens mimorum more saltavit in scena, plebe spectante romana.[15]

> (Nero gradually fell into a strange and abominable wantonness. For, putting aside his imperial gravity, without any shame, as if he were accomplishing the greatest good for the country, he not only sang openly and competed on the cither with Greek and Egyptian entertainers, but, what is more disgusting, he demonstrated how learnedly he could sing to an audience of prostitutes, servants, and debauchees; he also often drove a chariot; and he composed tragedies of heroes and danced them in the scene after the fashion of mimes, while the common people of Rome looked on.)

He based this account on the *Vita Neronis* of Suetonius,[16] who has this to say of Nero's heroic tragedies: "He also put on the mask and sang tragedies representing heroes and gods, and even heroines and goddesses, having the masks fashioned in the likeness of his own features or those of the women of whom he chanced to be enamored."[17] He mentions some of the roles he sang, namely, *Canace Giving Birth, Orestes the Matricide, The Blinded Oedipus,* and *The Mad Hercules*; and he tells the story of the soldier who ran to Nero's rescue when he was playing Hercules.[18] Suetonius does not make it clear that Nero was the composer as well as the performer of tragedies, but Boccaccio's inference to this effect is entirely correct. Suetonius does say that Nero was a

---

[14] See Guiseppe Billanovich, *Petrarca letterato: Lo scrittoio del Petrarca,* pp. 109–16, and Guido Martellotti, "La questione dei due Seneca, da Petrarca a Benvenuto," p. 152. Martellotti admits that Boccaccio may well be right in thinking that it was not the philosopher Seneca who wrote the plays.

[15] Boccaccio, *De casibus* A 7 (p. 176). Cf. B 7.4.21–22 (p. 606).

[16] Hortis, p. 43.

[17] Suetonius, *Nero* 21.3, tr. J. C. Rolfe; the Latin reads: "Tragoedias quoque cantavit personatus, heroum deorumque, item heroidum ac dearum, personis effectis ad similitudinem oris sui, et feminae prout quamque diligeret." Cf. Vincent of Beauvais's citation of Suetonius in his account of Nero, *Speculum historiale* 9.6. See IDEAS AND FORMS, p. 126.

[18] IDEAS AND FORMS, p. 18.

poet, and Boccaccio would know this too from Servius, at least by the time he wrote the *Genealogia*, where he gives Servius's account of Nero's *Troica*.[19]

In his remarks on Nero's dramatic career in the *De casibus*, Boccaccio says nothing of Nero's use of masks, perhaps because he understood *personatus* and *persona* as referring simply to impersonation or role-playing. He also ignores Suetonius's statement that Nero sang his tragedies. Rather, he says that he danced them like a mime. That is to say, if we can judge his meaning from his later accounts of the performance of comedy (which I will detail below), he acted them out in pantomime. Perhaps Boccaccio had in mind Livy's rather obscure account of Livius Andronicus, who acted out the sung parts of his plays in silence, while a boy sang the text.[20] He knew Livy well: he translated his third and fourth Decades much earlier (around 1338–46),[21] and drew heavily upon him for the *De casibus*.[22]

In his later works, namely, the *Genealogia* and the commentary on the *Inferno*, Boccaccio gives a basically Isidorian picture of the ancient theater, according to which the role of the poet was not to act but to sing (Boccaccio says recite) his poetry while mimes pantomimed the action: "Scelestis compositis fabulis, eas mimis introductis recitabant in scenis" ("Having composed wicked fables, they recited them in the scenes, while mimes were brought on").[23] He is speaking here in the *Genealogia* of *poete comici inhonesti,* among whom he includes Ovid, at least sometimes. He wishes to discredit them, while defending the *comici honestiores,* like Plautus and Terence, and the *poete heroici* such as Vergil and Homer.[24] One should think that the reputable comedians as well as the *poete tragici,* whom he does not mention in this context, would also stage their plays in the way just described. But he is at pains to put the theater in a bad light, and he seems never to have considered the words of the authors he admires as meant for the stage. Plautus and Terence used the same kind of storytelling as Vergil and Homer, he says, and the works of these latter poets were closer to history than to fiction. The aim of the good comic playwrights was to *describe* the characters and words of men and thereby to teach their *readers* and make them cautious.[25]

---

[19] Boccaccio, *Genealogia deorum gentilium* 6.22 (p. 303). See Hortis, pp. 404, 457, and my "Tragedy and the Performance of Tragedy in Late Roman Antiquity," pp. 30–31. There is a brief Servian account of Nero's *Troica* in the Third Vatican Mythographer, Alberic, whom Boccaccio cites by name elsewhere (see *Genealogia*, p. 867, note by the editor, Vincenzo Romano). But Boccaccio may have used the Second Vatican Mythographer, that is, Remigius of Auxerre, who gives a fuller account. Remigius ends with the detail that Paris was received by Priam: "et a patre in fratrum consortia receptus." Cf. Boccaccio: "Et sic videtur quod cognitus receptus fuerit in domum patriam." For Remigius, see Georg Heinrich Bode, *Scriptores rerum mythicarum latini tres*, 1:139 (chap. 197); for Alberic's account, ibid., 1:242 (book 11, chap. 23).

[20] IDEAS AND FORMS, chap. 3.

[21] Maria Teresa Casella, "Nuovi appunti attorno al Boccaccio traduttore di Livio."

[22] Hortis, pp. 419–20.

[23] Boccaccio, *Genealogia* 14.19 (p. 743). For an English translation of books 14 and 15 of the *Genealogia*, see Charles G. Osgood, *Boccaccio on Poetry.*

[24] Ibid. 14.9 (p. 707); 14.19 (743).

[25] Ibid. 14.9: "Volentes tamen arte sua diversorum hominum mores et verba describere, et interim lectores docere et cautos facere."

In Boccaccio's last work, the text of the lectures on Dante which he delivered in 1373–74, he expands upon his picture of the comic stage:

> Comedians [that is, poets who composed comedies] call the separate sections of their comedies "scenes," because, when they recited them in the place called the scene in the middle of the theater, each time that they introduced various persons to speak, mimes would come forth from the scene. The mimes would have transformed themselves from the characters whose words and actions they had spoken and performed before, and would appear as those who were now supposed to speak; they would come before the people, who were looking on and listening to the comedian speaking the lines.[26]

This is the procedure of "dumbshow with voice-over" which Isidore of Seville described for both comedies and tragedies in the theatrical section of his *Etymologies*.[27] We might think from this passage that the actors as well as the poet had speaking parts; but when Boccaccio a little later expands upon his defense of poetry from the *Genealogia*, he shows that this is not the case. Once again, he is speaking of the bad comic poets, in whose comedies various adulteries and other shameful deeds were perpetrated by men whom the stupidity of that age counted among the gods.[28] He says: "Then they recited these comedies in the scene, that is, in a little house set up in the middle of the theater, around which scene all the people of the city, both men and women, stood to listen."[29] But the audience, he says,

> were not so much attracted by the desire to listen as to watch the horse-play that the recitation of the comedian gave rise to; that is to say, certain buffoons called "mimes," whose business it was to know how to imitate the actions of men, would come out from the scene, having been instructed by the comedian, in dress appropriate to the persons whose actions they were to imitate, and they would perform all the actions, whether decent or shameful, that corresponded to the words of the comedian.[30]

[26] Boccaccio, *Esposizioni sopra la Comedia di Dante*, Accessus, section 23, pp. 5–6: "Chiamano ... i comedi le parti intra sé distinte delle loro comedìe 'scene,' per ciò che, recitando le comedi quelle nel luogo detto scena, nel mezzo del teatro, quante volte introduceano varie persone a ragionare, tante della scena uscivano i mimi trasformati da quegli che prima avevano parlato et fatto alcuno atto, e, in forma di quegli che parlar doveano, venivano davanti dal popolo reguardante e ascoltante il comedo che racontava."

[27] Isidore, *Etymologiae* 18.42–50; see IDEAS AND FORMS, pp. 41–49.

[28] Boccaccio, *Esposizioni* 1.1.84 (p. 37).

[29] Ibid. 1.1.85: "E queste cotali comedie poi recitavano nella scena, cioè in una piccola casetta, la quale era constituita mel mezzo del teatro, stando dintorno alla detta scena tutto il popolo, e gli uomini e le femine, della città ad udire."

[30] Ibid. 1.1.86: "E non gli traeva tanto il disiderio di udire quanto di videre i giuochi che dalla recitazione del comedo procedevano; li quali erano in questa forma: che una specie di buffoni, chiamati 'mimi,' l'uficio de' quali è sapere contrafare gli atti degli uomini, uscivano di quella scena, informati dal comedo, in quegli abiti ch'erano convenienti a quelle persone gli atti delle quali dovevano contrafare, e questi cotali atti, onesti o disonesti che fossero, secondo che il comedo diceva, facevano."

We might think that Boccaccio knows what an ancient theater looks like when he speaks in the *Decameron,* at the conclusion of the sixth day, of seeing the steps in theaters ranged in tiers from top to bottom.[31] But he is clearly referring here, as in the *Teseida,* to the circular amphitheaters of Roman times, in which the gladiatorial games took place.[32] In a gloss to the *Teseida,* he defines the term theater, as used in ancient times, in a more general sense: it was any public place, like the balconies and *ridotti* ("drawing rooms") of his own day, though some places because of their "excellence" had a special claim to the name—for instance, the Colosseum at Rome, which was a theater for all the people.[33]

Boccaccio could have found an accurate discussion of ancient Roman and Greek drama-theaters in Vitruvius's *Architecture,* which he cites several times in the *Genealogia,* but he obviously did not avail himself of the opportunity.[34] He could also have drawn directly on Isidore, whom he cites much more frequently than he cites Vitruvius. Isidore describes the theater as half of an amphitheater;[35] and he characterizes the scene as a house, by which he means the large stage building, in front of which, on the stage itself (which he calls the pulpit or orchestra), the poet's chanting and the pantomimed acting took place.[36] However, Nicholas Trevet's interpretation of Isidore seems closer to Boccaccio's understanding. According to Trevet's *Commentary on Seneca* (which, as I have noted, Boccaccio may have possessed), the scene was a little house: in it, or on it, was a pulpit used by the poet to pronounce the text while mimes acted it.[37]

There is nothing in Trevet's account, or in Vitruvius's, for that matter, to suggest Boccaccio's altogether accurate notion of the scene building as a "tiring-house" for the actors.[38] It is not until the fifteenth century that we will encounter a similar idea, in connection with the plays of Terence.[39] Of Boccaccio's fellow-commentators on Dante, only one, Pietro Alighieri, knew of a staged dimension of tragedy, and his idea may have been based on Trevet.[40] Another fourteenth-century interpretation of Trevet's work can be

[31] Boccaccio, *Decameron* 6.C.21 (pp. 764–65).

[32] Boccaccio, *Teseida* 7.108–10.

[33] Gloss to *Teseida* 2.20. See Mary Hatch Marshall, "*Theatre* in the Middle Ages: Evidence from Dictionaries and Glosses," pp. 371 and 384–85 n. 115.

[34] Leon Battista Alberti, writing in the middle of the fifteenth century, seems to have been the first to study Vitruvius on the theater. See Robert Klein and Henri Zerner, "Vitruve et le théâtre de la Renaissance italienne," pp. 294–95.

[35] Isidore, *Etymologiae* 18.52.2.

[36] Ibid., 18.42–49; see IDEAS AND FORMS, pp. 42–48.

[37] Nicholas Trevet, *Expositio super tragedias Senece,* commentary on *Hercules furens,* ed. Vincenzo Ussani, pp. 5–6; IDEAS AND FORMS, pp. 133–34. Trevet composed his commentary between 1314 and 1317.

[38] On the scene building as changing room in the ancient theaters, see Margarete Bieber, *The History of the Greek and Roman Theater,* pp. 57–59, 67, 173, 193, 200, 201, 205, 208. Vitruvius *De architectura* 5.9.1, says that there is usually a colonnade behind the *scaena* where the people can take refuge from the rain, and also *choragia* (rooms) where the *laxamentum* (stage machinery) is prepared.

[39] See below, chap. 4, p. 159. Claudia Villa, *La "Lectura Terenti,"* p. 249, says that the idea is very common in Terence manuscripts, but she gives no details.

[40] Pietro Alighieri, *Super Dantis ipsius genitoris Comediam commentarium,* p. 9; TRAGEDY AND COMEDY, p. 27.

seen in the splendid illustration showing the artist's conception of the performance of *Hercules furens*, which serves as a frontispiece of the Urbino codex
of Seneca.[41] The poet, wearing a crown like those worn by Juno and King
Lycus, stands inside a small structure like a castellated telephone booth (it
has four parapet teeth with a trapezoidal dome above). Against the left wall
stands a lectern, which holds the book from which the poet is reading, his
finger marking his place. His feet, however, are pointed towards the "open
wall." No doubt he is meant to be in full view of the audience, labeled *populus
expectans*, who sit, and gesticulate in response to the action, outside the semicircular stage of the "theater." This conception agrees with Boccaccio's in
having the poet recite in the scene building. But there seems to be no question
of the poet's sharing of the structure with any of the actors, since he barely
fits in it himself. One half of the stage is occupied by the chorus, consisting of
seven members, who are holding hands. The other half contains the other
characters. Juno, in accord with her opening speech, points to the constellation Bear (seven stars are grouped together at the top of the illustration) with
one hand, and to the Furies with the other. The Furies appear on stage, sitting
in the midst of flames, each with a dog-eared (and apparently winged) serpent
on her head. Amphitryon, Hercules's putative father, is shown talking to his
daughter-in-law Megara. King Lycus, scepter in hand, looks on at Hercules,
who is completely covered in his lion skin and brandishes a club in one hand
while holding a bow and arrows in the other. In a fourth scene portrayed on
the same half-stage, a clearly older Amphitryon, with beard and longer hair,
is talking to Theseus.

Boccaccio has other observations about the bad comic poets, which he took
over from a letter addressed to him on 2 February 1372 by Pietro Piccolo de
Monteforte and incorporated into the *Genealogia* and the Dante commentary.[42] They include his remarks on "the enormities sung in the scenes and
theaters by mimes, histrions, parasites, and suchlike"[43] (which indicates that
Pietro at least conceived of actors with vocal roles), and on the decree of
Roman law labeling as infamous all those who entered into the scene to perform the acting or speaking parts.[44] Also from Pietro is the comparison of
Christ's parables to the comic style, and His use of a line from Terence to
rebuke Paul on his way to Damascus ("Durum est tibi contra stimulum calci-
trare," Acts 9.5).[45] The chapter dealing with the objection that Boethius

---

[41]   Vatican Library MS Urb. lat. 355, fol. 1v, reproduced in color in the edition of Trevet's *Expositio Senece* on *Hercules furens*, facing p. 1, and in black and white in IDEAS AND FORMS, Frontispiece (and see p. 134).

[42]   Giuseppe Billanovich, "Pietro Piccolo da Monteforte tra il Petrarca e il Boccaccio," in *Medioevo e Rinascimento: Studi in onore di Bruno Nardi* (Florence 1955), pp. 1–76, esp. 32–43; Pietro's
letter is given on pp. 44–58, and Boccaccio's reply on 59–65. The portions of the *Genealogia*
which were revised to take in Pietro's ideas are given on pp. 65–72, and relevant passages of Boccaccio's *Esposizioni sopra la Comedia* on 72–76 (corresponding to sections 1.1.71–72, 83–88, 92–
111 in Padoan's edition).

[43]   Boccaccio, *Genealogia* 14.14 (p. 724): "que in scenis atque theatris a mimis et histrionibus
atque parasitis et hujusmodi hominibus enormia canebantur."

[44]   Ibid.: "qui artis ludrice [i.e., ludicre] pronuntiandive causa in scenam prodirent, ipso facto
haberentur infames" (cf. Justinian, *Digest* 3.2.1).

[45]   Ibid. 14.18 (p. 737); see Billanovich, "Pietro Piccolo," p. 37 n. 121. The text of Terence that
Pietro had in mind was *Phormio* 77–78: "Inscitiast / Adversum stimulum calces" ("It is madness

called the Muses theatrical harlots, *meretricule scenice*, is also inspired by Pietro, who said it was to be understood only of *scenica et theatralis poesis*. Boccaccio decides that just as there are two kinds of poets, good and bad, so too there are in the one genus of Muses two species: the good group inhabits pastoral places like the Castalian spring, whereas the others, who are those of the shameful comic poets, inhabit the scenes and theaters and crossroads.[46] Once again, therefore, he would seem to leave no room in the theater for the good dramatists. He is, however, speaking here of the places where the poets are inspired, as he was in an earlier chapter.[47] In another passage taken over from Pietro, dealing with the mythical poetry fit for the *comedi* and theaters, which is deplored even by poets, Boccaccio adds that famous poets deplore it, "because of the filthy things acted in the scenes."[48]

In the Dante commentary, Boccaccio qualifies his interpretation of Boethius's words. He says that, rather than understanding Boethius to mean two sets of Muses, those of Philosophy on the one hand and those of the *comici disonesti* and *elegiaci passionati* on the other, one can take him as simply referring to poets of different qualities.[49]

When discussing the title of Dante's *Comedia*, unlike other commentators Boccaccio does not define tragedy, but simply says that there are various kinds of poetic *narrazioni*, among which are tragedy, satire, comedy, the bucolic, elegy, the lyric, and so on.[50] He then proceeds to discuss the ways in which the term comedy is not appropriate to Dante's work,[51] without ever returning to the subject of tragedy. But we can infer some of his ideas of tragedy, or at least raise some questions, from what he says about comedy. For instance, when he says that, unlike Dante, the poet of comedy does not introduce himself into any of the acts to take on a speaking role, but always presents other persons to carry on dialogue,[52] the same would be true of tragedy. And just as Boccaccio concludes that Dante cannot be called a comic poet in this sense, he would also have to conclude that he cannot be called a tragic poet from this point of view. It is also clear, by the way, that the term "narration" in Boccaccio's vocabulary is not restricted to narrative works, but can also include works entirely in dialogue, and, presumably, in other poetic forms as well.[53]

[to kick] your heels against the goad"), at which point Boccaccio in his copy of Terence noted "hinc Paulus." See plate 3 in Billanovich (facing p. 48) for the manuscript page of the *Genealogia* on which Boccaccio added Pietro's remarks in the margin.

[46] *Genealogia* 14.20.

[47] Ibid. 14.11 (p. 712): Poets seek solitude, for they cannot compose their verses in the greedy forum or in pretoria or theaters or capitols or squares.

[48] Ibid. 15.8 (pp. 767–768): "Mythica . . . comedis, de quibus supra, et theatris accomoda est, que ob turpia in scenis actitata ab illustribus poetis etiam improbatur." Pietro's letter reads (p. 52): "Mythicon . . . ad theatrum accommodatur: hec a poetis etiam improbatur." For this notion of mythical poetry, Pietro and Boccaccio cite Varro as quoted by Augustine, *City of God* 6.5. Trevet used the same passage at the beginning of his *Expositio Senece* (ed. Ezio Franceschini, pp. 5–6); see IDEAS AND FORMS, p. 130.

[49] Boccaccio, *Esposizioni* 1.1.111.

[50] Ibid., Accessus 17.

[51] The text of Boccaccio's discussion is given in TRAGEDY AND COMEDY, pp. 45–47.

[52] Boccaccio, *Esposizioni*, Accessus 20.

[53] Trevet too speaks of what is "narrated" in Seneca's plays (ed. Franceschini, p. 8); see IDEAS AND FORMS, p. 132.

When Boccaccio says that the events of comedy are possible but not necessarily true,[54] our first inclination is to infer that tragedy is to be contrasted with comedy, and that it deals primarily or entirely with true events. We know for a fact that he considered most of Seneca's and Euripides's characters to be historical, from his treatment of the same figures in the *De casibus* and the *De mulieribus*; and it is also clear that Dante's poem deals with real persons and events. Are we then to conclude that Boccaccio would, or could, have considered Dante to be a tragic poet, from this aspect?

Boccaccio accepts the characterization of comic style as humble and "remiss," given by what I call the *Proto-Accessus* (that is, the original form of the Accessus of the *Epistle to Cangrande*, which Boccaccio used before the letter was compiled by Pseudo-Dante),[55] but he decisively rejects its conclusion that Dante's work fits the characteristic of remiss language. For even though the poem is in the vernacular, in which insignificant women communicate (Boccaccio translates *muliercule* as *feminette*), and even though he knew that Dante himself had characterized the vernacular as comic in his eclogue to Giovanni del Vergilio,[56] he nevertheless maintains that the language of the poem is "ornate e leggiadro e sublime."[57] Is he thereby claiming tragic style for Dante, the *modus elate et sublime loquendi* specified by the *Proto-Accessus* for tragedy? Is he suggesting something similar when he contrasts the base material of the comic poet with Dante, who writes of excellent persons, the outstanding and noteworthy deeds of vicious and virtuous men, the effects of penitence, the characteristics of angels, and the divine essence?[58] It is this point that Guido da Pisa hit upon when characterizing Dante as a tragic poet. But though it has been claimed that Boccaccio used Guido's commentary, I can see no clear sign of his influence in Boccaccio's accessus.[59]

Boccaccio rejects two other aspects of comedy as inapplicable to Dante's work: comedies do not use similes and examples, whereas Dante does;[60] and the divisions of comedy are called scenes, whereas the parts of Dante's poems are cantos.[61] We can ask no significant question about his presumed ideas of tragedy from these two points, but we can do so from the last characteristic of comedy that he names, where he finally finds some reason to apply

---

[54] Boccaccio, *Esposizioni*, Accessus 22.
[55] The *Epistle to Cangrande* was known only to Filippo Villani, at the end of the fourteenth century. See TRAGEDY AND COMEDY, pp. 11–18, 35–41, 61–111, for discussions of its composite authorship, sources, and dating. My thesis has been well received by some Dantists: see Zygmunt G. Barański, "*Comedia*: Notes on Dante, the Epistle to Cangrande, and Medieval Comedy," pp. 27–33, and see the reviews of Steven Botterill, Deborah Parker, Lino Pertile, Madison Sowell, and John Took. Robert Hollander, *Dante's Epistle to Cangrande*, has made a concerted attack on it, to which I reply in "*Cangrande* and the Ortho-Dantists." See also Botterill's review of Hollander, and Ruggero Stefanini, "Tenzone sì e tenzone no," p. 125.
[56] In his own gloss to the eclogue (*Eclogue* 1.52), Boccaccio interprets *comica* as *vulgaria* (TRAGEDY AND COMEDY, p. 47; cf. p. 5 n. 21).
[57] Boccaccio, *Esposizioni*, Accessus 19.
[58] Ibid., 18.
[59] For Guido's doctrine, see his *Expositiones et glose super Comediam Dantis*, and see TRAGEDY AND COMEDY, pp. 19–23. His influence on Boccaccio has been alleged by Francesco Mazzoni, "Guido da Pisa interprete di Dante e la sua fortuna presso il Boccaccio," pp. 106–28.
[60] Boccaccio, *Esposizioni*, Accessus 21.
[61] Ibid., 23.

the term to Dante's poem. He admits that there must be a reason, since Dante himself calls his work a comedy in canto 21 of the *Inferno*. Dante, he concludes, must have been speaking figuratively ("figurativamente parlando"), because of the poem's overall similarity to comedy, which can be seen from the works of Plautus and Terence. Comedy has a beginning that is turbulent and full of uproar and discord, while it ends in peace and tranquillity. Dante's work begins in the sorrows and tribulations of hell and ends in the repose, peace, and glory enjoyed by the blessed in eternal life.[62]

When Boccaccio comments on Dante's reference to "Seneca morale" in canto 4, he distinguishes him from the "poeta tragedo" who wrote the tragedies, and then goes on to describe Moral Seneca's writings. He adds a note about a work that is dubiously ascribed to him, which "is more poetic than moral." He is speaking of the *Apocolocyntosis divi Claudii* ("Pumpkinification of the Divine Claudius") or *Ludus de morte Claudii*, which, he says, "is in prose and verses, in form of tragedy" (*è in prosa ed in versi, in forma di tragedia*), in which it is described "how Claudius was driven from paradise and led to hell by Mercury." Even though it does not seem to be in Moral Seneca's style, he says, it does fit his hatred of Claudius, for the whole little book (*quello libretto per tutto*) makes jokes about him and his unpraiseworthy life.[63]

Some readers of this passage assume without question that Boccaccio is calling the *Ludus* a tragedy.[64] It is no doubt true that he accepted the idea (found in the *Proto-Accessus* and elsewhere) that tragedy had a movement opposite from comedy, and if he is saying that the whole *Ludus* is "in form of tragedy," it may be for this reason; for though the Senecan tragedies do not fit the progression from tranquillity to horror, as I have noted, Guido da Pisa and the *Proto-Accessus* say that they do. He can hardly be taken to say that its prosimetrical form was that of tragedy, since he knew that this was not the form of the Senecan tragedies.

However, given Boccaccio's acknowledgment of the crudely jocose subject matter of the *Ludus* (for instance, the emperor's last words are, "Oh my, I think I've beshit myself!" ["Vae me, puto concacavi me"]),[65] it is doubtful that he considered the *libretto* to be a tragedy, even though he may have thought that it shared the form of tragedy in some way. Even so we may be reading too much into his words. In citing the passage above, I have given the punctuation of Padoan's edition, with a comma after *versi*, but it may be that *in forma di tragedia* is restrictive, modifying *versi*, so that he would be saying that the *Ludus* "is in prose, with verses in tragic form." Of the six sets of verses in the *Ludus*, four are dactylic hexameters, which of course would not be appropriate to tragedy, but the fifth, a funeral dirge for Claudius in anapestic tetrapodies or dipodies,[66] is suggestive of a tragic chorus, and the fourth is in iambics and is spoken by Hercules, who is said to become a *tragicus* in order to appear the more terrible.[67]

---

[62] Ibid., 24–25.
[63] Ibid., Canto 4, 1.333, 337–38.
[64] So Renate Haas, "Chaucer's *Monk's Tale*," p. 49.
[65] Seneca, *Apocolocyntosis*, chap. 4.
[66] Ibid., chap. 12.
[67] Ibid., chap. 7.

Boccaccio did not get to the line in the *Inferno* where Vergil calls the *Aeneid* a high tragedy.[68] If he had done so, he would no doubt have decided that it was another example of the figurative use of a dramatic term. However, it could not be the same figure that he saw Dante using in calling his own work a comedy because of its turbulent beginning and peaceful end, since the *Aeneid* in this respect is just as much a comedy as Dante's poem, at least from the protagonist's point of view. He would perhaps have to say, like Nicholas Trevet, that Vergil is a tragic poet because he deals with tragic subject matter,[69] or because he uses tragic style.

Boccaccio himself seems to have used the term comedy in imitation of Dante much earlier in his career, in a work written in 1341–42, which he titled *The Comedy of the Florentine Nymphs*—if it is true that this was indeed his title.[70] The piece is composed of passages of *terza rima,* alternated with prose passages, like Boethius's *Consolation of Philosophy* and other prosimetrical works. Perhaps he meant nothing more by this title than to acknowledge that he was using the meter of Dante's *Comedy,* for his composition resembles Dante's in no other way. According to his listing of types in the *Esposizioni,* he would have to classify it as bucolic; but in a simpler system, it could well be classified as comedy because of its humble style and "private deeds."

Boccaccio never duplicated this figurative application of dramatic terminology to narrative discourse. He did not do so in the *Decameron* (written between 1349 and 1353), and those who wish to discuss the comic and tragic aspects of that work are using language, if not concepts, that find no echo in his pages.[71] One of the stories therein is based on *Lidia,* an example of narrative comedy from twelfth-century France, which is given the title of comedy in extant manuscripts of the fourteenth century.[72] But if it was so called in Boccaccio's copy, he made no use of the idea.[73]

In addition to the reasons he was to give for the inapplicability of the term comedy to Dante's work, Boccaccio could have given another for the *Decameron*: He thought of comedy only as a form of versified composition, whereas the *Decameron* is in prose. The same reason would apply in forbidding the name of tragedy to be attached to the *De casibus,* for tragedy too was considered a verse form.

But Boccaccio could have applied at least one aspect of tragedy to the *De casibus* in a figurative sense, if he had wished; or, if he did not wish to go so far as to call his stories of falls tragedies, he could at least have called them tragic, if that word had been an active part of his vocabulary. For the progression of the stories is, in the main, the opposite to what he said was the characteristic movement of comedy, and it fulfills a common definition of tragedy.

---

[68] Dante, *Inferno* 20.113.

[69] Trevet, *Expositio super tragedias*, ed. Franceschini, pp. 6–7; text in IDEAS AND FORMS, pp. 130–31.

[70] Boccaccio, *Comedia delle ninfe fiorentine*. The editor of the 1964 edition, Antonio Enzo Quaglio, maintains that this was Boccaccio's original title, which the printed editions abandoned in favor of *Ameto* (p. 670). But he does not discuss the point further, or offer documentation.

[71] See the *Concordanze del Decameron*.

[72] *Lidia*, ed. Edmond Lackenbacher, p. 225.

[73] Boccaccio, *Decameron* 4.9.

The Accessus section of the *Epistle to Cangrande* makes this explicit: "Tragedia in principio est admirabilis et quieta, in fine seu exitu est fetida et horribilis."[74] Boccaccio even points out something of the sort for the *De casibus* as a whole, when apologizing for ending with the story of the lowborn Philippa of Catania:

> In order that the whole of the work should to some extent seem to conform to its parts, which begin in joy and end in misery, it seemed fitting that, as we began with the noblest of men [that is, Adam], we should end thus with a plebeian and degenerate woman.[75]

Given the similarity of this language to some definitions of tragedy,[76] it is all the more noteworthy that Boccaccio does not make any reference to the tragic nature of his stories, either here or throughout his work.

He does, however, at one point apply the term tragedy in a figurative sense to certain stories of misfortune:

> Mellita verba et bilinguium suasiones injectas credulis ruinas urbium et incendia regionum, populationes et regnorum subversiones sive exitia stulte credentium eduxisse fere per omne trivium infinite clamitant tragedie.[77]

> (Countless tragedies keep shouting at almost every crossroad that honeyed words and the urgings of the double-tongued which are passed on to the credulous have led to the ruin of cities and the conflagration of countries, and to the devastation and subversion or destruction of the kingdoms of those who stupidly put credence in them.)

> (Or, to keep the word-order: That honeyed words and double-tongued persuasions poured into the ears of the credulous have caused the ruination of cities and conflagration of countries and the devastation and subversion or destruction of the kingdoms of those who stupidly put credence in them, countless tragedies keep shouting out at almost every crossroad.)

It is important to emphasize that Boccaccio's rhetorical figure of speech here is clearly based on his notion of the antique classical dramatic genre: he envisages tragic poets presenting their plays in public squares (which would doubtless qualify as theaters in his general definition of the word) and declaiming about the sort of catastrophes that he writes of in the *De casibus*; and perhaps he is even thinking of them as accompanied by the mimic dancing

---

[74] *Epistle to Cangrande* 10.29; see the edition in TRAGEDY AND COMEDY, pp. 102–111, esp. 105.

[75] Boccaccio, *De casibus* A 9 (p. 237): "Ut scilicet opus totum suis partibus in aliquo videretur esse conforme, in quibus cum exordiatur a letis et in miseriis finiatur, visum est uti a nobilissimo homine operi initium datum est, sic in plebejam degeneremque feminam finis imponeretur." Also in Lydgate, *Fall of Princes*, 4:390; cf. B 9.25.2 (p. 854).

[76] Pointed out by Monica E. McAlpine, *The Genre of Troilus and Criseyde*, pp. 93–94. I disagree, of course, with her conclusion that Boccaccio "regards his entire collection as a single tragedy of the conventional type."

[77] Boccaccio, *De casibus* A 1, rubric *Adversus nimiam credulitatem* (p. 38); cf. B 1.11.12 (p. 62).

of tragedians like Nero. We noticed earlier that the last words of this passage, *clamitant tragedie*, recall Boethius's *tragediarum clamor*. The similarity goes further, for Boccaccio, like Boethius, is speaking of lamentations over large-scale disasters. But whereas Boethius is primarily referring to undeserved misfortunes caused by the haphazard blows of Fortune, Boccaccio is thinking of falls that are to some extent deserved. However, his emphasis here is not on divine punishments brought on by sin, but on self-inflicted disasters, disasters brought on by a lack of caution.

Boccaccio's outburst comes after telling the story of Theseus, and he is perhaps influenced not only by Fortune's question in Boethius but also by his recollection of Seneca's *Phaedra*, also called *Hippolytus*, viewed not as the tragedy primarily of one or the other of these two eponymous characters, but rather as the tragedy of Theseus. If so, however, he must not have refreshed his memory of the play, or else he was thinking of similar dramas that could be written about such circumstances; for, although the disaster in Seneca's tragedy is to a large extent caused by Theseus's credulity, it does not contain an outcry against credulity, appropriate as it might have been.

Seneca's tragedies might have inspired Boccaccio to cast his stories in the same form, following Albertino Mussato's example of a Senecan imitation in his mainly dialogical *Ecerinis* (*c.* 1315). The form is described by Trevet in his characterization of Seneca's book (drawing on Isidore): "It contains mournful poems (*carmina*) about the falls of the great (*de casibus magnorum*), in which the only speakers are introduced persons, and never the poet himself."[78] In the event, Boccaccio wrote prose rather than verse, but the subject matter and the mood (as epitomized by Trevet) are appropriate; and though he uses the mixed mode rather than the purely dramatic form of the dialogue of characters, he does sometimes speak as a *persona introducta* (like Seneca in the *Octavia*) as well as a narrator—something (but not quite) like what Dante does in his *Comedy*.

But there is no indication that Boccaccio knew of Mussato's tragedy until he mentioned it in his Dante commentary.[79] And it was only after Boccaccio's death that Coluccio Salutati's championship of Seneca and Mussato began to inspire a few other tragedies.[80] Furthermore, it seems clear that Seneca's tragedies were not fresh in Boccaccio's mind when he wrote the *De casibus*; and by the time that he refamiliarized himself with them shortly afterwards, his career as a literary author was effectively at an end. The *De casibus* itself marks the transition between his works of fiction and his works of scholarship: the stories he relates in the *De casibus* are meant to be historically accurate for the most part, but he allows himself some imaginative license in presenting them.

In sum, Boccaccio could not have considered the *De casibus* a tragedy or a series of tragedies in the strict sense of the word. For he knew that a tragedy was a drama composed entirely in dialogue. But he could have applied the

---

[78] Trevet, *Expositio Senece*, Introduction (Franceschini, p. 7).

[79] Boccaccio, *Esposizioni* 12.1.99: "*Azolino*: costui chiama Musatto padovano in una sua tragedia 'Ecerino.'"

[80] See Wilhelm Cloetta, *Die Anfänge der Renaissancetragödie*; IDEAS AND FORMS, pp. 185–94: "Italian Latinists."

term figuratively to the work, if he had wished to do so, as he had apparently done with "comedy" in calling the *Ameto* the *Comedy of the Florentine Nymphs*. At the end of his life he came to believe that Dante had similarly made a figurative use of comedy for his poetic treatment of hell, purgatory, and heaven, and at the same time he noted that the Senecan *Ludus de morte Claudii* had the form of tragedy in some way, or contained some verses in tragic meters—without however declaring it to be a tragedy like those written by the other Seneca. But there is no indication that he intended either a figurative or attributive connection between tragedy and his narratives of falls. However, as I said earlier, since Chaucer and Lydgate did consider the *De casibus* to be a series of tragedies, an analysis of Boccaccio's work is not only appropriate but essential for this study.

EXAMPLES OF ILLUSTRIOUS MEN

William Baldwin and his committee of fellow authors titled their continuation of Lydgate's *Fall of Princes* (itself a translation of Boccaccio's *De casibus*) thus: *A Mirror for Magistrates, Wherein May Be Seen by Example of Other with How Grievous Plagues Vices Are Punished, and How Frail and Unstable Worldly Prosperity Is Found, Even of Those Whom Fortune Seemeth Most Highly to Favor.*[81] In so doing they expressed very well the purpose that Boccaccio gave for the *De casibus* in his Preface. But they were acting largely on instinct; for though Lydgate included the message of Boccaccio's Preface in his rendition, he inverted the hierarchy of themes therein expressed by giving his attention first to the instability of earthly things for all men, and only then stressing the providential retribution visited upon the vicious in high places. It seems likely, however, that Baldwin did not avail himself of the opportunity to be misled by Lydgate, for he and his fellow tragedians give little sign of having paid their English predecessor much note. It is rather Lydgate's printer, John Wayland, the man who first proposed the idea to Baldwin, who articulated the themes as they appear in the *Fall of Princes*. In Baldwin's preface to the reader, he says that Wayland was counseled by many of his associates "to procure to have the story continued from whereas Bochas left unto this present time, chiefly of such as Fortune had dallied with here in this island; which might be as a mirror for all men, as well noble as others, to show the slippery deceits of the wavering lady and the due reward of all kind of vices."[82]

---

[81] William Baldwin *et al., A Mirror for Magistrates*, p. 62: title page of the first edition of 1559. Lydgate's *Fall of Princes* was published twice shortly after Mary Tudor became queen in 1553, first by Richard Tottel in 1554 and then by John Wayland, the queen's printer, in the same year or the next. Wayland already had in hand and intended to publish all of the *Mirror* materials, which he had commissioned from Baldwin, George Ferrers, and five other gentlemen-poets; but publication was forbidden by Mary's chancellor, Bishop Stephen Gardiner, and it was only after Elizabeth ascended to the throne in 1558 that it was allowed to appear.

[82] Ibid., p. 68 (cf. pp. 5–10). See below, chap. 5, p. 213, and, for Lydgate's *fortuna*, see A. S. G. Edwards, "The Influence of Lydgate's *Fall of Princes*, c. 1440–1559: A Survey."

If Boccaccio had read and understood Averroes's *Commentary on the Poetics*, he might have intended his *De casibus* to be a series of narrative tragedies describing the undeserved falls of virtuous men.[83] But he had never so much as heard of Averroes's treatise; and in fact his primary purpose in the *De casibus* was to show the judgments of God to high-ranking knaves and fools. Of course, he did not always stick to this narrow schema, as we shall see. We often find him telling of disasters with no sin or stupidity in sight, sometimes with the explicit admission that the misfortunes were undeserved.

Since Boccaccio's chief goal, of providing object lessons to the wicked, has been so often ignored or misunderstood by his modern readers, I will give here a translation of his entire Preface:[84]

(1) As I was casting about for a means of doing some service to public government with my scholarly labors, I was particularly struck by the way in which great men conducted themselves. I saw how immoral they were and how vile they had become through filthy lust; they carried on without check, acting as if they had drugged Fortune into a lasting sleep by herbs or incantations, and as if they had anchored their princedoms with iron supports to an adamantine rock. I saw that their attitude not only caused them to oppress other men with all their might, but also led them to rise up with a foolish kind of temerity even against the very Creator of all things. When I beheld all this I was stupefied.

(2) And, while I condemned their madness and marvelled at the long-suffering patience of our loving Father, there occurred to me what I was seeking. For what could be more useful to the eager craving of mortal men and to their perpetual salvation than this charity: to lead back the erring, if you could, to the right path?

(3) Even though in the past many eloquent men outstanding for their holy piety have often given themselves with great effort to this purpose, I think it will be not unhelpful if I myself, though unequal to their powers, should try to rouse the watch, in order to summon these men from their deadly sleep. However, since such people, being accustomed to their obscene pleasures, usually reveal minds not easily receptive to intellectual argument—but nevertheless minds that can sometimes be held by the delights of history—I decided that it was necessary to make use of examples.

(4) I intend to tell them what God (or, to use their mode of expression, Fortune) can do to those who are in high place; and, to prevent any objections on the score of time or sex, I also intend to give a succinct account of fallen leaders and of the falls of other famous persons, both men and women, from the beginning of the world up to our own age. But far be it from me to speak of them all; for what mortal man could

---

[83] For a full account, see Aristotle-Averroes-Alemannus, pp. 163–72; for a summary, Ideas and Forms, pp. 119–23.

[84] I follow Text A, the first version of *c.* 1360, as given in the Paris edition reprinted by Hall, p. 25; it is also printed, with some errors, by Henry Bergen in his edition of Lydgate's *Fall of Princes*, 1:xlvii.

command the resources to meet an infinite labor of this kind? It will be enough to select from the famous some of the most famous.

(5) So that when men see princes old and frail, and kings cast to the ground by the judgment of God, they might acknowledge God's power, their own frailty, and the slipperiness of Fortune, and learn to place a limit upon their joys; and thus by the danger that has occurred to others they will be able to take counsel for their own profit.

(6) But lest a continuous series of histories should give rise to tedium, I will attempt, thinking it both pleasurable and useful, to insert every now and then attacks on vice and exhortations to virtue. I humbly pray that He to whom belongs all power will be favorable to the undertaking and success of such a sublime project; and may He preserve to the glory of His name what He has allowed to be written.[85]

To sum up: Boccaccio wishes to address great men and women who are defiled by filthy lust, who show no restraint in their actions in oppressing

---

[85] Here is the original text from the Paris edition, but divided into the above sections and repunctuated:

(1) Exquirenti mihi quid ex labore studiorum meorum possem reipublice utilitatis adferre, mores hominum illustrium maxime obtulere sese obviam—quos dum illecebres turpique libidine fedos intuerer, effrenesque non aliter quam si Fortunam in so[m]pnum perpetuum soporassent herbis aut cantato carmine suosque principatus ferreis uncis adamantino in scopulo firmassent adverterem, nec ob id solum ceteros pro viribus premere, quinimmo et in ipsum rerum omnium opificem stulta quadam temeritate consurgere cernerem, obstupui.

(2) Et dum damnarem dementiam longamque pii patris patientiam admirarer, ecce in mentem incidit quod querebam. Quid enim hac charitate aviditati mortalium et saluti perpetue utilius quam oberrantes, si possis, in rectum tramitem revocare?

(3) In quod etsi hactenus eloquentissimi et sacra pietate conspicui viri persepe conatu maximo elaboraverunt, non inofficiosum existimo si, ut ipse, quamvis par viribus non sim, eos a sopore letifero invitarem, vigiliam excussisse tentaverim. Sane cum tales, oscenis voluntatibus adsueti, difficiles animos demonstrationibus prestare consueverint et lepiditate historiarum capi nonnunquam, exemplis agendum ratus sum.

(4) Et quid Deus, sive, ut eorum more loquar, Fortuna, in elatos possit, describere, et, ne in tempus aut sexum cadat objectio, a mundi primordio in nostrum usque evum consternatos duces illustresque alios tam viros quam mulieres passim disjectos in medium succincte deducere mens est. Absit tamen ut omnes dixerim; quis enim mortalium tanti foret, ut infinito posset labori sufficere? Set ex claris quosdam clarissimos excerpsisse sat erit.

(5) Ut dum senes fluxosque principes et Dei judicio quassatos in solum reges viderint, Dei potentiam, fragilitatem suam, et Fortune lubricum noscant, et letis modum ponere discant; et sic aliorum periculo sue possint utilitati consulere.

(6) Porro ne continua historiarum series legenti possit esse fastidio, morsus in vitia et ad virtutem suasiones inseruisse quandoque, tam delectabile quam utile arbitratus, adnectam. Cui tam sublimi cepto ac successui is quem penes potestas est omnis, supplex precor, favens adsit, et in sui nominis gloriam quod scripsisse dederit, ipse conservet.

Note that in §1, he has *illecebres* rather than the second-declension form, *illecebros*. He uses the third-declension form in other places as well; see, for instance, *Genealogia* 14.14 (p. 724, lines 9–11): "Actus vero deorum gentilium illecebres, quocumque modo a poetis (a comicis potissime) descriptos, nec laudo nec commendo" (he added *a comicis potissime* later, under Pietro Piccolo's inspiration).

others and who even challenge God in their madness. He will try to rescue these erring persons from their obscene pleasures by showing them the troubles that the judgment of God has brought upon princes and kings in the past, so that they can change their ways and profit from the dangers that have occurred to others.

His only stated objective for his narratives, then, is that they are to serve as *exempla* of the disasters that have befallen conspicuous men and women as divine punishment, which is what *Dei judicium* should mean, and the punishment should be for acting sinfully, like his sinful readers; otherwise there would be no point to the stories. When, however, he goes on to say that the stories are intended to show his readers not only the power of God and their own frailty but also the slipperiness of Fortune (even though he has just identified Fortune as their way of talking about God), he could be taken to mean that life is not fair and that disasters can occur even to the innocent and virtuous. But if so, he would be violating the logic of his moral. For the disasters he recounts are to teach his readers that if they place a *modus* upon their pleasures they will be able to profit by avoiding similar dangers, by renouncing vices and embracing virtues.

He introduces his work as a sort of "casuistic" treatise, that is, as a study of cases of conscience, like St. Raymund of Pennafort's *Summa de casibus*—a work that may have influenced Boccaccio in choosing his title, since *casus* means both "case" and "fall." His stories of misfortune are designed to impel men to the practice of virtue, as are the ideal tragedies described by Averroes, which also resemble Boccaccio's work in containing encomiums of virtue. But according to Averroes, as noted above, the effect of inciting men to virtue is best attained by the presentation of undeserved misfortunes. Moreover, the audience to be influenced is not restricted to great men, and the same is true of the men whose misfortunes are described. In contrast, the ostensible object of Boccaccio's work resembles the implicit purpose of Lorens of Orleans's *Somme le roi*, a manual for diagnosing vices and encouraging virtues composed at the request of King Philip III of France in 1279.[86] But just as Lorens must have intended his work not only for the king but also for the people at large, so too Boccaccio undoubtedly did not wish his stated purpose to be taken so literally as to make his work a mirror for major magistrates alone. In fact, he may not have seriously intended it for their eyes at all, in view of the insulting and condescending terms of his Preface, for he says that magnates are so besotted by their vicious pursuits that they need stories to get their attention and to keep them interested. Or perhaps he thought of his princely readers as the sort of people who, though they had enough Latin to handle his rather difficult style, would skip over his Preface, thinking it to consist of dull preliminaries, and move on at once to the historical delights that awaited them!

When, more than a decade later, he came to dedicate the revised version of his work (which he characterizes as "dealing with the falls and usually also the deaths of illustrious men"), he maintained that he could think of no prince worthy of it, and to prove his point he proceeded to run through his

---

[86] W. Nelson Francis, *The Book of Vices and Virtues*, p. xi.

objections to a sampling of them. He decided instead to dedicate it to a friend, Mainardo Cavalcanti, who, though born of a *clara familia* of Florence and having the rank of a knight, did not perhaps reach the level of illustriousness referred to in his original Preface.[87] The Preface to the revised edition remains unchanged in its statement of purpose, though in his description of the vices of governors he is much more detailed: he speaks of "their obscene lusts, violent slaughters, profligate leisures, insatiable avarice, bloody hatreds, armed and headlong revenges, and many other wicked crimes" which "defile all public honesty, dissolve the most sacred laws of justice, cause all virtues to fall, and, what is unspeakable, drag the minds of the ignorant multitude into impious habits by their detestable example."[88] He did not, of course, think that the ignorant would be able to profit from his book, but clearly he did look forward to its being read with edification by literate non-magnates.

Any prince, vicious or otherwise, who did take up Boccaccio's Prefaces with a humble will to be directed along the right path stood in danger of being seriously misled. For, as noted above, it is clearly stated that by observing the judgment of God on others, they should learn to moderate their own joys and thereby profit from the dangers encountered by others. Is not Boccaccio promising, in effect, that the rich and powerful who live moderately and virtuously will be able to put Fortune to sleep, so to speak, and to prevent the sort of disasters that befall the wicked? Such a generalization is nonsensical, of course, but it and others like it are constantly found in the *De casibus* and similar works of exemplary moralizing.[89]

A sensible, that is, noncontradictory, moral could be stated thus: without a direct revelation from God (which, of course, Boccaccio could actually claim in his biblical stories), one cannot know the reason, or set of reasons, in the divine mind for a given disaster; the disaster may be providentially arranged for purposes of punishment, for trial or temptation, or for discipline and the exercise of virtue, or for reasons not primarily concerned with the "protagonist" of the disaster; one can only say that sometimes it seems appropriate that a certain person should fall because of his sins.[90] One cannot, however, say that such sinful persons will always receive a blow to their good

---

[87] Boccaccio, *De casibus* B, pp. 2–6; also given by Bergen, *Fall of Princes*, 1:xlix–l.

[88] Boccaccio, *De casibus* B, pp. 8–10; Bergen, 1:xlviii, from Ziegler's Augsburg 1544 edition. Ziegler reads Boccaccio as saying that he saw the crimes *cum ductu caelestium*, "by heavenly guidance," that he realized the import of all these misdeeds, and believed himself led by Fortune to his project of attacking those who committed them; but Ricci reads *cum ductu scelestium*, taking the phrase to mean that the misdeeds were committed "with the guidance of the wicked." In this second version Boccaccio also omits the conceit that the princes acted as if they had put Fortune to sleep, though he keeps the notion that it is really the princes who are caught in a deadly sleep. Towards the end, he speaks of princes who are *segnes fluxosque*, "sluggish and frail," rather than *senes fluxosque*, "old and frail," as in §5 of the first version.

[89] See my *Divine Providence in the England of Shakespeare's Histories*, pp. 163–82, for some of the moralistic fallacies to be found in *A Mirror for Magistrates*. For other instances of the sort of conceptual collisions that moralistic and hortatory generalizations give rise to, see also my *Love and Marriage in the Age of Chaucer*, Index, s.v. "contradictions." For narrative and thematic clashes, see the discussion on disjunctions in chap. 6 below, pp. 222–25.

[90] See the summary of various ideas on this subject in the Judeo-Christian tradition in my *Divine Providence*, pp. 1–5.

fortunes. Nor can one say that the sinless man will never fall in such a way. One can only say that, if an innocent man should fall, it would not be due to any personal guilt.

In other words, the vigilance and moderation and reform that Boccaccio urges upon his readers will at least prevent punitive falls for future conduct (though there is no guarantee that punishment will not overtake them for their past sins). Perhaps the *modus* or moderation he speaks of reflects the Boethian notion (that is, the notion of Boethius's Fortune) that higher status brings greater dangers; as the maxim puts it, "The higher you go, the harder you fall." The fallacy behind this notion can be exposed by another equally facile maxim: "The lower you sink, the more you are oppressed." We remember that one of the crimes of modern princes singled out by Boccaccio was their oppression of others. Nevertheless, vigilance remains a good idea for good and wicked alike, since it can obviously prevent falls caused by lack of vigilance! And, finally, the vigilance inspired by historical catastrophes may help his readers by making them better able to cope with their troubles if and when Fortune does make them slide. This last idea especially will often be implicit and sometimes explicit in the material that he presents, but not particularly aimed at his primary audience of high-class malefactors.

The first of the historical examples given is the fall of Adam and Eve. Boccaccio introduces them in the "dramatic" fashion that he will consistently use in the course of his long treatise: that is, as he runs through the lamentable falls of the great men who have gone before him, the "victims" of the falls actually materialize before him, and, with the signs of their earthly misery about them, they tell their story or demand that Boccaccio tell it. In this first instance, Adam and Eve appear, so old and feeble that they can scarcely move their limbs, and Adam begins to recount what happened to them: "By the devil's urging we experienced the slipperiness of Fortune," and so on; but Boccaccio himself soon takes over and finishes the story of this original fall from which all the subsequent troubles of mankind proceeded.[91] Then, after detailing the story of Cain, he inserts the first of his moralizing sections, *Adversus inobedientiam.* He ends it by urging obedience: let us, he says, dedicate the few days remaining to our life to Him by whose merit we ourselves may merit the eternal glory in heaven, which the disobedience of our first parents took from us.[92]

The main lesson of the first *casus*, therefore, has nothing explicit to do with the prevention of falls in this world, but tells us how to achieve the happy ending of eternity. We are left to draw for ourselves the conclusion that obedience to God will keep us from experiencing the kind of punitive fall that Adam and Eve suffered, but will not guarantee our freedom from other kinds of falls, given the fallen condition that we have inherited from our first parents.

The second major story is of Nimrod and the Tower of Babel; Nimrod in his pride rebels against God himself, and the divine reprisal is clearly manifested in the confusion of tongues that overtakes the builders of the Tower. Nimrod's

---

[91]   Boccaccio, *De casibus* A 1 (pp. 25–26); cf. B 1.1 (pp. 10–16).
[92]   Ibid., A 1 (p. 27); cf. B 1.2 (pp. 16–20).

final fall comes when Fortune changes her course: "variante Fortuna vices."[93] Boccaccio then gives us two moral discourses, one an attack on the proud (*In superbos*) and the other a meditation on Time the devourer of all (*Nihil non absumit Tempus*). The lesson of the latter homily is simply that the passage of time has left small record of those cast down by Fortune in this early age. The moral of the former is that the humble will win out in the end. He does not quite tell us, however, how this works out in practice, and one gets the uneasy suspicion that the humble will have to wait until eternity for their victory, like most of the rest of us who are notable neither for our humility nor for any advanced degree of illustriousness.

Let us analyze the movement of Boccaccio's thoughts in the first of these exhortations. He starts with a consideration of high status in the world and the inflated self-esteem or pride that often accompanies it; but then he moves on to a contemplation of this prideful state alone, with no thought now of worldly success. To pride of soul he opposes humility of soul, which no attack of a savage spirit can cast down.[94] In other words (we must add), if a ruler is humble, a savage attack may indeed strike him down from his worldly power, but he will not feel too depressed about it. This, however, is advice for illustrious losers, not for winners—that is, not for those princes who wish to avoid falls by the proper exercise of their responsibilities. Once again, therefore, Boccaccio has failed to address himself to his expressed purpose of showing magistrates how they can maintain their posts by the exercise of virtue. In fact, the thrust of his discourse would seem to be, "Resign from office before you are thrown out."

The next significant casualty on Boccaccio's list is Cadmus, King of Thebes. He seems to have been a harmless enough ruler, with no vices to speak of. When therefore he goes from bad to worse, Boccaccio does not blame it on him but attributes it to the unknown purposes of God: "Sane, cum Cadmus undiquaque factus miserior, vitam non opinione sua sed forsan divina dispositione ad miseriora reservat" ("But when Cadmus was made more miserable on all sides, he preserved his life for still greater misery not by his own intention but perhaps because of the divine disposition").[95] Why, then, we might ask, does Boccaccio include the story in his collection? He did indeed promise to tell us of the power of God or Fortune to bring down the exalted, the *elati*, but they were to be suitable examples for readers who were swollen with pride and other vicious habits, in order to bring them to a reformed state.

He has no treatise on morality to offer at this point, but merely moves ahead in time: now the whole earth is populated, and Fortune through the course of her numerous revolutions has manifested herself, in the misery of many men, as the mistress of all things that are to perish. In so saying, however, he implicitly acknowledges the chestnut that Fortune has an animus against all men, both good and bad. This moral fits in not only with the story of Cadmus but with those that follow as well, inspired by another vision of weeping has-beens. One of them is Aeetes, Medea's father, who rapidly tells of the misery

[93] Ibid., A 1 (p. 29); B 1.3.10 (pp. 22–24).
[94] Ibid., A 1, *In superbos* (p. 29); cf. B 1.4.(pp. 24–26). The next chapter in B is called *De Saturno* rather than *Nihil non absumit tempus*.
[95] Ibid., A 1 (p. 31); cf. B 1.6.7 (p. 32).

caused to him, through no fault of his own, by Jason's coming. Boccaccio himself then tells the story of the figure standing next in line, namely Minos, King of Crete, who was noted for his justice. Once again, no sin is singled out; his fall is simply the occasion for an outburst about the passing of power: "O instabilis mortalium gloria!" No moral at all is drawn for Sisera, chieftain of the Canaanites; his ignominious end at the hands of a pair of women is allowed to speak for itself.[96]

Boccaccio then reaches down the line of suppliants, past other kings from Israelite history, to tell of the disasters of Thebes; he is moved at the insistent demand, not of Oedipus as we might expect, but of Jocasta, Queen of Thebes. However, after the episode in which Laius orders the infant Oedipus to be thrown to the wild beasts, the story shifts to Oedipus's point of view, until the time of his marriage to Jocasta. Boccaccio tells the tale methodically, without a glimmer of suspense. Jocasta's suicide is postponed until after her sons Eteocles and Polynices kill each other in their struggle for power.[97] This ending is in accord with the account in Statius's *Thebaid*, which Boccaccio had long been familiar with.[98] He does not allude to the Sophoclean ending followed in Seneca's *Oedipus*, according to which Jocasta killed herself as soon as Oedipus put out his eyes. But he seems to have renewed his acquaintance with Seneca later, for he follows the Senecan version of the story in *De mulieribus*,[99] and in his revised *De casibus* he says that "there are those whom it pleases to say that she ended these miseries with a noose."[100]

The moral of Jocasta's fall in the *De casibus* centers around the evanescence of all earthly beauty, splendor, and joy. Boccaccio ends his summary of Oedipus's losses, none of which are blamed on any sin of his, by saying that he does not remember reading how he died.[101]

Next, Boccaccio starts to respond to Theseus's request that his story be told, but he is interrupted by Thyestes, who gives a long self-serving account of the horrors he endured at the hands of his brother Atreus. Atreus then makes a rebuttal: he admits his crimes, but says he was provoked by those that Thyestes committed against him. Thyestes hastens to respond, but Boccaccio turns with disgust from their inhuman and bestial conduct and takes up again with Theseus.[102]

This shouting match might be considered a little drama, perhaps, but it is closer to the genre of the debate. For though Atreus speaks directly to Thyestes at first, his defense itself is addressed to Boccaccio, as is that of Thyestes. Their arguments have little similarity to the dialogue at the end of

---

[96]   Ibid., A 1 (pp. 31–32); B 1.7 (pp. 34–36).

[97]   Ibid., A 1 (pp. 32–34).

[98]   For Jocasta's death, see *Thebaid* 11.634–637. Boccaccio relied heavily on the *Thebaid* for his *Teseida*, written *c.* 1339–41.

[99]   Boccaccio, *De mulieribus* 25: he says that there are those who report that she killed herself immediately after the revelation of Oedipus's identity, because she could no longer endure her *noxii errores*. Zaccaria in his edition, p. 109, translates this as "colpevoli errori," in spite of the fact that Jocasta is not said to have been at fault.

[100]   Boccaccio, *De casibus* B 1.8.24 (p. 44).

[101]   Ibid., A 1 (p. 34); B 1.8.27 (p. 44).

[102]   Ibid., A 1 (pp. 34–35); B 1.9 (pp. 44–50).

Seneca's *Thyestes*, in the scene in which the two brothers confront one another.[103]

In allowing Thyestes and Atreus to present their cases, Boccaccio returns us to the subject of evil rulers, but not explicitly to the theme that such men were meant to illustrate, according to the Preface; and the same is true of the story of Theseus. For though he mentions various sins that contribute to Theseus's downfall, such as his killing of his wife Hippolyta out of anger, his abandonment of Ariadne, and his wrath against Hippolytus, the emphasis is upon Fortune and her arts, and the inability of earthly power or even glory virtuously sought (*virtute fulgores quesiti*) to have any effect against stepmothering Fortune.[104] In the homily against facile belief that follows, *Adversus nimiam credulitatem*, he singles out Theseus's chief failing as a kind of intellectual defect rather than any moral failing. For, though he was otherwise a prudent man, he should have known better than to believe Phaedra, since he had experienced what a lying and lustful lot women were, especially Cretans like Pasiphäe and Ariadne.[105] But in the story of Ariadne as Boccaccio has just told it, it was Theseus, not Ariadne, who was the liar and luster.

It is in *Adversus nimiam credulitatem* that Boccaccio imagines the disasters brought about by credulousness as having been incorporated into tragedies and proclaimed at the crossroads of the world. And it is here for the first time in the *De casibus* that he gives some practical advice to princes on how to avoid destruction. But it is not only princes that he is advising. As in his essay on disobedience, he resorts to the first person plural and thereby includes himself and all of his readers in his exhortation. His advice for once has nothing to do with Fortune, religious piety, or divine punishment. Now it is Credulity rather than Fortune who is Mother and Stepmother; and she is to be combated by imitating the caution of the legal codes:

> Let us, however, since quick Credulity is the mother of error, a stepmother in her counsels, the source of animosity, a precipice to those who follow her, ever the near kin to Repentance—let us, if we are men, if we have eyes, if we are prudent, imitate the authority of the venerable laws, which hold the haste of Credulity in such abhorrence that they specifically command their executors to believe nothing rashly, to do nothing on the spur of the moment, and always, if at all possible, to hear the other side before coming to a decision: lest while we express our disapproval of Theseus we find ourselves rushing into his misfortunes.[106]

Next Boccaccio passes quickly over a large company of Greek complainers, including Hercules, who says that in spite of his great "virtue" in overcoming

---

[103] When he tells the story of Atreus and Thyestes in *Genealogia* 12.5, Boccaccio cites both Seneca and Lactantius Placidus's commentary on the *Thebaid* (he identified Lactantius with Lactantius Firmianus, the Church Father; see Hortis, p. 473). Zaccaria, p. 920, sees some influence from Seneca in the *De casibus* account of Thyestes, especially in the the imagery of B 1.9.9 (p. 46), which is identical in the A version.

[104] Boccaccio, *De casibus* A 1 (p. 37); B 1.10.30 (p. 58).

[105] Ibid., A 1 (p. 38); B 1.11.7 (p. 60).

[106] Ibid., A 1 (p. 39); B 1.11.17 (pp. 62–64).

the pests of the world, he was himself overcome by one, namely, lust (*cupido*) for Iole. Boccaccio refrains from telling his story for fear of defiling his glory, which the *clamor* of all the more glorious poets tries to extol even above the stars.[107] He could have given a better reason: namely, that it is hardly consonant with his purpose to spend time glorifying heroes. The sort of *clamor* that he should be drawing on is the *tragediarum clamor* of Seneca, who devoted two tragedies to Hercules. Another reason for omitting his story will appear later: Hercules is perhaps to be historically identified with Samson.[108]

He moves on to Priam and Hecuba, whose fate he considers an outstanding *spectaculum* of the revolutions of Fortune.[109] Priam's faults were not the worst; but he had an *elata mens*, and plump Fortune reminded him of what she had previously made him forget when she was slender, namely the thought of his disgraced sister Hesione. This led to Paris's rape of Helen; and, when Priam neglected to return her, all Greece mobilized against him. After years of siege, Troy was captured and Priam was finally given a fatal wound, through which he sent forth his *superba anima*, weary with years and miseries. Hecuba too went from glory to misery, to suffer all the injuries of a savage Fortune.[110] But Hecuba seems to have been an entirely faultless victim.

Boccaccio takes the fall of Troy as signal for another tirade, *Contra superbos*, "Against the Proud"—against those, that is, who place their hope in what must fall away, and who take pride in their lineage and wealth. Such things did not prevent Priam and his family from falling. But the idea that they fell because God was punishing them for their pride and misplaced confidence is not at all to the fore here, nor is there any suggestion at this point that a moderation of excesses and a resort to prudent policy (which would have dictated a prompt return of Helen, for example) will prevent disasters of this kind. On the contrary, it is clear that falls will come in any case, and Boccaccio can only suggest that we be ready for them by adhering to Christ the cornerstone, in whom alone is true strength and stability and eternal life.[111]

Agamemnon is then offered as another great argument of *Fortuna instans*. However, there is no word of his pride or trust in glory, but only of his inability to restrain the lust of his wife.[112] This leads to a discourse on the cares of kingship and an apostrophe to Poverty (*Paupertati applaudit*): cold comfort for illustrious men.[113] He does not, of course, have in mind the sort of miserable penury that many of his exalted victims have fallen into. A side note in the sixteenth-century Paris edition of the first version rightly defines it as *mediocris paupertas*.[114] Fortune despises Poverty, and this sort of Poverty contemns Fortune; but if Fortune were to make her really poor, below the median-income line, she would no doubt be less defiant.

[107]   Ibid., A 1 (p. 39); B 1.12.3 (p. 64).
[108]   Ibid., A 1 (p. 45); B 1.17.8 (p. 86).
[109]   Ibid., A 1 (p. 39); B 1.12.9 (p. 66).
[110]   Ibid., A 1 (pp. 39–41); B 1.13 (pp. 66–74).
[111]   Ibid., A 1 (pp. 41–42). B 1.14 (pp. 74–76).
[112]   Ibid., A 1 (pp. 42–43); B 1.15 (pp. 76–82).
[113]   Ibid., A 1 (pp. 43–44); B 1.16.(pp. 82–84). Zaccaria gives the verb of the rubric as *applaudet*, noting that Boccaccio mistakenly took it as second conjugation.
[114]   Ibid., A1 (p. 44): "Mediocris paupertas optanda."

Next Samson comes, *exclamitans* ("persistently shouting out") against the perfidy shown by women to those who love them. Boccaccio rushes to take up the theme, though he admits that Samson should have known better. He was deceived once by his wife; but, after overcoming the danger in which she put him, and after having his thirst appeased by God's intervention, he nevertheless proceeded to confide too much in himself and to give his love to the harlot Delilah, who got from him the secret of his strength. Boccaccio does not think to chide Samson specifically for his rather curious taste in choosing his female confidantes, but instead lashes out against all trust in women: "Sic adversa credulitas, sic amantis pietas, sic muliebris egit inclyta fides!" ("Thus did adverse credulity act, thus the affectionate loyalty of a lover, thus the renowned faith of woman!"). Fortune too had a role in the action: "Lubricum Fortune ludum sistere non potuit" ("He could not make the slippery game of Fortune stand still"), and "agente Fortuna" ("with Fortune taking charge"). Samson became an object of play to his enemies; and though he had the satisfaction of taking his tormentors with him, he brought upon himself an unworthy death.[115]

The longest moral discourse encountered so far now follows, consisting of an attack on women: *In mulieres*. He starts with the theme, "Woman is a flattering and destructive evil." He ends with the concession that some few women are good, and in fact such women are more praiseworthy than virtuous men, because they have had to overcome their weaker character.[116] At the end of the discourse, he asserts that he had not written enough against women, but was forced to interrupt himself by the *clamor* of more weeping figures. But he realized that he was tired, and he decided to put an end here to the first book. He wants to make it clear, however, that the division into books does not signal any variation in the overall intention of his work.[117]

But our suspicions that he himself has forgotten the scope of his *summaria intentio*, or even that his Preface was an afterthought and that the intention expressed therein did not in fact govern the form of his work, are justified further in the opening words of book 2: "Perhaps there will be those who will say that enough examples have already been given to show what are the powers of Fortune, what instability there is in mortal things, and how fallacious is the hope and how empty the glory of the happiness of this world."[118] It is true that such a theme of *contemptus mundi* might be of service in waking princes from their sleep and showing them that they are mistaken in thinking that they have put Fortune to sleep, but this purpose was supposed to be subordinated to the demonstration that it is God, not Fortune, who causes falls, and that His judgments have nothing to do with the arbitrariness attributed to Fortune but rather are dictated by the the norms of just retribution.

Boccaccio has not neglected the latter perspective altogether, however, and it is an exaggeration to say that he first faces the idea of men causing their

---

[115] Ibid., A 1 (pp. 44–45); cf. B 1.17 (pp. 84–90).
[116] Ibid., A 1 (pp. 46–48); B 1.18 (pp. 90–100). The whole treatise is given by Bergen in Lydgate, *Fall of Princes*, 4:161–163.
[117] Ibid., A 1 (p. 48); B 1.19 (pp. 100–102).
[118] Ibid., A 2 (p. 49); B 2.0.1 (p. 104).

own falls only at the beginning of book 3, when he tells the story of the encounter between Fortune and Poverty,[119] and that he finally makes a full confession of this truth only at the end of book 9, at the close of the work.[120] We may agree, however, that his conclusion is noteworthy in pulling together most of his themes into a fairly coherent whole and placing them in the perspective of his Preface. Here is how he does it: After humbly relinquishing his work to wise men to correct any errors that might be in it, he gives thanks to God if it should lead anyone to self-knowledge and humility. He then delivers a direct address to those of high estate, finally giving them some truly practical advice, not merely from the perspective of prudence, as in his treatise *Adversus nimiam credulitatem*, but from the providential point of view as well:

> You, however, who hold high command, open your eyes and unlock your ears. Be vigilant lest a deadly sleep come upon you, and observe the javelins [*tragule*] of Fortune to which you expose your breasts, how great they are, and how human counsel cannot resist their force. All that is strong is broken, and what is most illustrious is obscured under an indissoluble cloud. Recognize from the falls of others what a slippery place you stand upon. Do away with avarice, lust, rage, boasting, and ambition, and learn to place a limit upon your joyful condition [*letis modum ponere*]. Remember while you fill your minds with rejoicing, or while you are irritated by some circumstance and a great temptation comes upon you, that you have ascended to the apogee [*aux*] in accord with the same law as others: that is, you are poised to fall in an instant, if it should please Fortune, to suffer the punishment of your offenses. And lest it happen that you be deceived by some judgment about the stability of her play, fix this in your minds: every time it appears that revolving Fortune is permitting some estate to stand, she is preparing a trap for the miserable people who place their trust in her. And the more you seem to be lifted to the stars, the more carefully must you set your desires upon humble place.[121]

There are, perhaps, echoes of the monologue of Fortune in Boethius, in which she asks her question about the *tragediarum clamor*.[122] But the idea of falls

---

[119] Farnham, *Medieval Heritage*, p. 86: "At last it seems to him (if his judgment is to be trusted) that these people who have fallen into misery have provoked their own misfortunes."

[120] Ibid., p. 102: "Here, without that equivocation to which he descends in the story of Fortune and Poverty, Boccaccio is finally constrained to recognize for tragedy a certain measure of human responsibility which he has actually discovered in his stories." Farnham's thesis is that there was an evolutionary movement from tragedy of Fortune (or Fate) to tragedy of character in the period from Boccaccio to Lydgate. See below, chap. 5, p. 214. He neglects the Preface, in which, as we have seen, Boccaccio implicitly attributes all misfortunes to human responsibility.

[121] Boccaccio, *De casibus* A 9 (pp. 240–241); cf. B 9.27.8–9 (p. 868).

[122] Compare Boethius, *De consolatione Philosophiae*, book 2 pr. 2, "Ascende, si placet, sed ea lege: ne utique, cum ludicri mei ratio poscat, descendere injuriam putes" ("Ascend, if it pleases you, but with this law, that you do not really think it an injury to descend when the reason of my game demands it"), with Boccaccio's language: "Memorantes . . . ea vos lege augem conscendisse qua ceteri, ruituros scilicet si lubuerit in puncto, . . . ne . . . ludi stabilitate decipi forte contingat" ("Remembering . . . that you have ascended to the apogee by the same law as others, that is, to

as punishment for offenses, and of Fortune as motivated by an intention to punish, is foreign to the main point of the Boethian passage. Boccaccio continues:

> In order that you may have something to rejoice over when lifted up, and so that you may have no cause for sadness when you fall, worship God with the greatest devotion and love Him with your whole affection. Follow wisdom, take hold of the virtues, honor the deserving, protect friends with the utmost fidelity, obey the counsels of the prudent, and deal kindly with those who are less great. Seek honor, praise, glory, and fame by abounding in humanity and justice, and show yourselves worthy of the height you have attained. And if you should happen to fall, let it appear not that it has occurred because of a crime that you have committed, but rather that it was done by the impudence of Fortune, who overturns all things.[123]

In the end, then, it all comes down to this point: not of preventing the falls that may come because of external circumstances and the general mutability of the world, but of practicing virtue and avoiding sin, so that the fortunate ones of this world will not precipitate their own misfortunes, and, just as important, so that they will not give any excuse to critics like Boccaccio to blame them for bringing destruction upon themselves. There is no question now of their voluntarily embracing poverty or humility in the sense of giving up most of their goods and their high position, but only of recognizing that such goods and status, while not incompatible with true happiness, are not of its essence and are not necessary to it.

To return to the Preface to book 2: Boccaccio goes on to admit that even one example should be sufficient to move "generous" minds *in rectum*, to the right path. But others, he says are so far gone in their attachment to perishable things that they need more examples to soften their adamantine hearts.[124]

However, we ourselves, whatever the moral texture of our hearts, need not continue along with him further at this point. Eight more books of the same sort of thing follow, but we have seen enough examples from the *De casibus* for the purposes of our study of tragedy. Since Boccaccio was not writing tragedies but histories of a specialized kind, it will be better to put off further consideration of his narratives until we come to those who regarded them as tragedies, namely Chaucer and Lydgate.

We have also seen enough to be able to make some assessment (with due Werckmeisterian caution) of Boccaccio's themes, and of his skills and short-comings. He was by no means a brilliant thinker (though much ahead of a writer like Chaucer in matters of learning and scholarship), and his artistic powers often flagged. He talks too much and tells too many stories for most modern tastes, I suspect—though not, it seems, for the taste of his own time.

---

fall in an instant if it should please her, ... lest ... it happen that you be deceived by the stability of her game").

123 Boccaccio, *De casibus* A 9 (p. 241); cf. B 9.27.9–10 (pp. 868–70).
124 Ibid., A 2 (p. 49); B 2.0.2–3 (p. 104).

But his Latin is more concise than his Italian (almost in the same way that the tightness of Chaucer's verse lacks the prolixity and formlessness of his prose), and this feature can be admired as a virtue. For instance, if I may be allowed one further example from the *De casibus,* as Dido is about to leap onto the funeral pyre of her dead husband, rather than marry again, she says simply, "Cives optimi, ut jussistis, ad virum vado" ("Good citizens, as you bade me, I go to my husband").[125] If her story had been told in the *Decameron,* she would doubtless have expressed the same message in a page or so of the sort of turgid rhetoric that is a feature of much of the dialogue in Boccaccio's vernacular prose. (It has been suggested, by the way, that some aspects of this rhetoric were inspired by Seneca's tragedies.)[126]

On the other hand, much of Boccaccio's compression comes from his desire to treat a great many subjects. One story carefully told is normally more moving to both generous and ungenerous minds than a hundred delivered on the run. He gets carried away with the urge to tell the history of the world, which makes him include incidents not relevant to his purpose; and his interest in relieving monotony by inserting a variety of hortatory essays encourages a scattergun moralizing or rhetorical overkill that often misses the right targets and leaves innocent victims covered in blood. His exaggerated diatribe against women is only one of the more obvious examples of this tendency. But it is a tendency that was widely shared by the men of his time, and we will see more examples of it below, especially in our analysis of the *Fall of Princes*, Lydgate's version of the *De casibus*.

In many ways the *De casibus* resembles the sort of *De viris illustribus* collections that he refers to at the beginning of his next work, *De mulieribus claris,* and it also resembles the *De mulieribus* itself. He says in the Prologue to that work that the definition of illustriousness or *claritas* that he and others have followed in choosing subjects for inclusion refers not to glory but to notoriety: persons who are well known to history, whether they are good or bad, are treated, Crassus as well as Cato, Medea along with Penelope.[127] And, I conclude, since all famous people die, like everyone else, before they are ready to die, except for saints and those to whom death seems a blessed relief from other miseries, most of the accounts in the *De mulieribus* could be added to the *De casibus*, as could most lives in *De viris illustribus* collections; and the lessons that he draws and the homilies that he preaches in the one book can find echoes and duplications in the other. In both cases, he would seem to be not so much inventing a new genre as contributing to the existing genre of moral exempla, which, when they involve unfortunate outcomes, fall into the subgenre of cautionary tales.

---

125   Ibid., A 2 (pp. 57–58); B 2.10.29 (p. 142).
126   Russo, "Il senso del tragico nel *Decameron*."
127   Boccaccio, *De mulieribus*, Proemio §§ 5–6 (pp. 24–26).

2

Chaucer on tragedy

Though both Dante and Boccaccio conceived of themselves as writing comedies, Chaucer seems to have been the first major author of postclassical times who considered himself to be a composer of tragedies, at least *avant la lettre*—that is, before he wrote them. Earlier on, Dante did come to consider some of his works to be tragedies, but only after he had composed them. He classified his own love lyrics, and lyrics by other poets on a range of noble topics, as tragedies when he composed his *De vulgari eloquentia*.[1] Chaucer was anticipated by at least two lesser lights who wrote not in the vernacular but in Latin. A century and a half before his time, around 1220, his fellow countryman John Garland claimed that only two tragedies had ever been written in Latin: Ovid's *Medea*, which was lost, and his own.[2] But Garland himself had been anticipated in the previous century by the tragedies written by William of Blois (according to his brother Peter), one of them called *Flaura et Marcus*.[3] Chaucer, however, doubtless knew nothing of these works, which were the victims of unfortunate *fortunae*, or reader-nonreceptivity: William of Blois's tragedies were lost entirely, Garland's *Poetria* was unknown in England (and in most other places as well), and even Dante's Italian commentators were unfamiliar with the *De vulgari eloquentia*.

I assume Chaucer's probable nonreception of, or insulation from, other pertinent developments as well. For instance, he does not seem to have been aware of Seneca's tragedies, which had been resurrected in Padua around the turn of the fourteenth century and commented on by an Oxford professor, Nicholas Trevet (1314–17),[4] and it is unlikely that he had heard of Mussato's

---

[1] Dante, *De vulgari eloquentia* 2.4–12; see TRAGEDY AND COMEDY, pp. 3–4; IDEAS AND FORMS, pp. 144–46.

[2] John Garland, *Parisiana poetria* 7.4–6 (p. 136); IDEAS AND FORMS, p. 100.

[3] Peter of Blois, Epistles 76 and 93 (PL 207:235A, 291–93).

[4] A younger Dominican colleague of Trevet's at Oxford, Robert Holcot, was undoubtedly somewhat familiar with another tradition of tragedy, namely, Averroes's interpretation of Aristotle's *Poetics*, as translated into Latin by Herman Alemannus, according to which tragedy is the praise of virtue and virtuous men. He quotes from Averroes-Alemannus in his commentary on the Book of Wisdom (written in the 1330s) to repeat a statement twice cited earlier by Thomas Aquinas, that men naturally take delight in representation. This comes from Averroes's excerpts from chap. 4 of the *Poetics*, well before the point at which Alemannus gets around to mentioning that Aristotle is dealing with tragedy (midway through chap. 6). See ARISTOTLE-AVERROES-ALEMANNUS, p. 174, and, for Holcot's text, Beryl Smalley, *English Friars and Anti-*

Paduan imitation of Seneca, which was given its first public hearing while
Trevet was at work on his commentary. Chaucer may well have become
aware, towards the end of his life, of a tendency in France to call laments tragedies, evidenced in the works of Philip Mézières and Eustace Deschamps;[5]
but no evidence is yet forthcoming that this usage existed when Chaucer
came up with his own different idea of tragedy and began to put it into practice.

In other words, Chaucer was doing something very original when he started
to compose tragedies, in spite of the fact that he himself did not consider it to
be new or unusual. Rather, he doubtless thought of himself as adding to a
long list of such works, which included the *Filostrato* (the story of Troiolo
and Criseida), the *De casibus*, and at least parts of the *De mulieribus claris*,
all composed by an author whose name Chaucer never mentions and whose
identity he may not have known. He seems to attribute one or both of the
two last-named compilations to Petrarch,[6] and, when adapting the *Filostrato*
in his *Troilus*, he deliberately omits reference to it, referring instead to an
invented Latin source allegedly written by a historian named Lollius.[7]

"TRAGEDY" IN LATE-MEDIEVAL ENGLAND

Before we consider Chaucer's tragedies, we shall examine his idea of tragedy. Chaucer is credited with introducing the word "tragedie" into the English language, but even scholars who know about this credit assume that
there was widespread knowledge of the Latin word *tragedia* and perhaps its

quity in the Early Fourteenth Century, p. 159 n. 4. But Holcot also draws on the commentary on
chap. 16 for illustrations of prosopopeia and metaphor (Smalley, pp.159, 169–70, 379–80). I
shall suggest below, chap. 3, pp. 119–20, that the example of prosopopeia, *O domus egregia*, may
have influenced Chaucer in having Troilus address Criseyde's empty palace.

[5] IDEAS AND FORMS, pp. 176–84; see especially Mézières's *Oracio tragedica seu declamatoria
Passionis domini nostri Jhesu Christi*, 1389–90.

[6] Chaucer, *Monk's Tale* 2325.

[7] John Lydgate knew well enough that Chaucer's *Troilus* was "translated" from an Italian
source, which he identifies as "a book which callid is *Trophe* / In Lumbard tunge"—*Fall of Princes*
1.284–85. Chaucer cites a person named "Trophee," presumably an author, as a source for the
story of Hercules, *Monk's Tale* 2117. The name could conceivably refer to someone connected
with the episcopal see of Tropea in southern Italy (Calabria), for instance, James Dardani,
canon of Tropea, who was appointed papal nuncio and collector for England in 1388; he can be
seen operating there as such from 1391 to 1397, during which time, or part of it, he was archdeacon
of Norfolk. See *Calendar of Entries in the Papal Registers Relating to Great Britain and Ireland:
Papal Letters*, 4: 267, 280, 294–295; John Le Neve, *Fasti ecclesiae anglicanae*, 4:29. For other con-
jectures, see the *Riverside Chaucer* note to this line, p. 931. Skeat and others suggest that since
the Pillars of Hercules were called *Tropaeae*, or in the medieval spelling *Tropee* or *Trophee*,
Guido of Le Colonne (in Latin, de Columnis, "of the Pillars") might have been called "de Tro-
pheis," hence "Tropheus." We might suppose that Lydgate heard of Guido's *Historia destructionis Troje* at second hand under this title and conjectured that it was the name of the book that
Chaucer used. Lydgate of course knew the book at first hand, since it served as the basis of his
Troy Book. But although he knew that John Bochas, the author of the *De casibus*, was also a celebrated poet, he did not know any of his poems; and in fact he does not indicate whether he thinks
Trophe was in verse or in prose. Even if he had seen a copy of the *Filostrato*, he would not have
been able to read it, since he did not know Italian.

French reflex as well, and that it was understood to signify a fairly uniform concept. I have been at pains to deny such assumptions of familiarity and uniformity for Europe as a whole;[8] and I wish to show here that, if they are not true of the Continent in general and of England in the earlier Middle Ages, they are even less true of England in the fourteenth and fifteenth centuries.

An early-fourteenth-century author who knew of the word *tragedia* was Ranulph Higden: he uses the term in telling of the death of Prince William by shipwreck in 1120. He says that a survivor of the accident "narrated the entire tragedy" ("totam tragediam enarravit").[9] He is drawing on a still earlier historian, William of Malmesbury, who says that the man "expressed the act of the entire tragedy."[10] But in taking over Malmesbury's expression, Higden was aware that *tragedia* was more than a simple synonym for "disaster," being well acquainted with John of Salisbury's *Policraticus*, where a clear understanding of ancient tragedy in its literal and metaphorical uses is set forth. But John Trevisa, in translating this passage around 1387, seems to have been less knowledgeable, for he renders the phrase as: "tolde alle the geest how it was byfalle." A fifteenth-century translator puts, "rehersede of this processe."[11] Similarly, when Higden repeats from Orosius that Nero at the burning of Rome "sang the *Iliad* with tragic bellowing," Trevisa says, "He gan to yelle and songe the gestes of Troye," and the other translator simply says, "He songe a songe of Troy."[12] Again, when Higden, drawing on Eutropius, says that the emperor Titus composed poems and tragedies in Greek, Trevisa has "poysies and gestes," and the other translator omits the passage.[13] These examples indicate that *tragedia* was unfamiliar to both translators, or at least that it had no generic signification for them. As far as Trevisa is concerned, we may see confirmation of this conclusion when he passes on Higden's list of the works of Seneca, which includes "tragedias." Trevisa keeps the Latin, including the accusative case, perhaps in the distorted form "tregideas."[14] It would seem also that Trevisa saw no difference in content between tragedy and comedy, for he defines comedy as "a song of gestes."[15]

Another contemporary of Chaucer's, the surgeon John Arderne, writing

---

[8] IDEAS AND FORMS, *passim*.

[9] Ranulf Higden, *Polychronicon* 7.16 (7:460).

[10] William of Malmesbury, *Gesta regum Anglorum*, 2:653–54.

[11] Higden, *Polychronicon* 7.16, tr. Trevisa and Anon. (7:461).

[12] Ibid. 4.9 (4:394–95).

[13] Ibid. 4.11 (4:458–59).

[14] Ibid. 4.9 (4:402–03). In my "Non-Tragedy of Arthur," p. 93, I mistakenly indicate that Higden is citing Jerome; he actually cites John of Salisbury at this point, namely, *Policraticus* 8.13 (PL 199:764B), but John's list of Seneca's works does not include the tragedies. The later translator (in MS Harl. 2261) translates Seneca's titles, rendering *tragedias* as "tragedies." Higden himself must have had some access to Trevet's commentary on Seneca, since in book 3 chap. 34 he records Trevet's explanation of the theater and the scene, which he attributes to *auctores* (4:98–100). He adds to Trevet's account only the point that *carminatores* as well as poets recited their *carmina* on the pulpit. Trevisa elaborates as follows: "In that hous poetes and gestoures upon a pulpet rehersede poysees, gestes, and songes, and withoute were mynstralles that counterfeted the doynge and the dedes that they speke in her gestes and songes, with bendynge and wyndinge and settynge and styntynge of here lemes and here body" (p. 101).

[15] Ibid., 1.30, tr. Trevisa (1:315). He is translating Higden's citing of Isidore's statement in *Etymologies* 14.6.33 that in Sicily "primum inventa fuit comedia" (p. 314). See below, p. 152 n.10.

around 1379, speaks of "the Bible and other tragedies" as sources for humorous stories of a good and decent kind that doctors can use to provoke their patients to laughter.[16] He clearly takes *tragedia* to mean nothing more than "book." The same meaning was attached to the word by a reader of Chaucer's *Troilus and Criseyde* in 1442, namely, the translator of the rules for Whittington's College and Almshouse, who concluded his prosaic task with the following rhyme-royal stanza:

> Go, litel boke, go, litel tragedie,
> Thee lowly submitting to al correccion
> Of theym beyng maistres now of the Mercery,
> Olney, Feldyng, Boleyne, and of Burton,
> Heartily theym besekyng with humble salutacion
> Thee to accepte and thus to take in gre
> For ever to be a servant within theire cominalte.[17]

The little tragedy in this case is a twelve-page booklet of regulations.

Later in the century, in 1486, the author of the second continuation of the Croyland Chronicle, whom I identify as Dr. Richard Lavender, chief ecclesiastical judge of the diocese of Lincoln,[18] takes the word *tragedia* to mean "book" or "chapter," that is, part of a larger work. He uses it to refer both to secular history (the reigns of Edward IV and Richard III) and to the history of Croyland Abbey. I speculate that he could have derived this definition from a reading of Lydgate's *Fall of Princes*, where tragedies seem to be the subdivisions of the nine books that comprise the work.[19]

A reader of Lydgate who composed a poem in the 1460s on the fall of Humphrey of Gloucester and his duchess and the duke of Suffolk[20] seems to have concluded that Boccaccio's work was "a tragedy" or was titled *Tragedy*:

[16] John Arderne, *Practica*, fol. 65v (=25v), Latin text in "Non-Tragedy," p. 93 n. 17; for an early fifteenth-century English translation, see John Arderne, *Treatises of Fistula in ano*, etc., ed. D'Arcy Power, EETS os 139 (1910), p. 8. When Peter Murray Jones, "Four Middle English Translations of John of Arderne," p. 64, says that there is no certain record of Arderne's life after 1377, he overlooks Power's note on p. 107: Arderne was writing after the death of his former patient Adam Everyngham, which occurred on 8 February 1379. A later medical author, John Metham, in his *Physiognomy,* preserved in a manuscript from the middle of the fifteenth century, may also be using tragedy to mean book when he refers to a conclusion made about a point of physiognomy by "doctour Palemon . . . in hys tragedy, the thyrd metyr, upon Herculys, qwere he begynnyth, 'In aladis oculis.'" See Hardin Craig, ed. *The Works of John Metham*, EETS os 123 (1916), p. 128. Craig identifies Palemon as Marcus Antonius Polemon, author of a work on physiognomy in the second century A.D. (p. xxix). I am grateful to Lister M. Matheson for giving me this reference and several of those following from the files of the *MED*. See now fasc. T8 (1996) s.v. "Tragedie."

[17] I have slightly edited the stanza from the edition of Jean Imray, *The Charity of Richard Whittington*, p. 121. Reginald Pecock was Master of the College at this time (p. 39 n. 1).

[18] See my "Last Chroniclers of Croyland" and "Croyland Observations." I am speaking of the so-called "Second Continuation," which extends from 1459 to the end of April, 1486. I argue that the third and final continuation, a brief supplement written in May, 1486, is by Lavender's superior, John Russell, bishop of Lincoln.

[19] *Croyland Chronicle*, ed. William Fulman, pp. 564, 569; ed. Nicholas Pronay and John Cox, pp. 152, 166–68; see my "Croyland Chronicle Tragedies."

[20] Titled *Examples of Mutability* by Rossell Hope Robbins, *Historical Poems of the Fourteenth and Fifteenth Centuries*, pp. 184–86 (no. 74).

> Wee nede not nowe to seke the cronicles olde
> Off the Romans, nor Bockas *Tragedye*,
> To rede the ruyen and fallys manyffolde
> Off pcynces grett, putt to dethe and miserye
> In sondry landes.   (9–13)

A poem of the fifteenth century, the *Vision of Philibert Regarding the Body and the Soul*,[21] may be using tragedy in the sense of "account" or "narrative," when referring to the "dreadful tragedy" of a soul that has gone to hell. The pertinent lines are:

> Consydure, O frendys, in yowre presense,
> Of this speryte the dredfule tragedye,
> And in specyal ye that have no concyanse,
> Lete this a storry be byfor youre eey.   (p. 37 vv. 1–4)

Tragedy is here identified with story, and later the account is called a "dredful storrye" (p. 39 v. 18). If dreadfulness is assumed to be part of the connotation of tragedy, then a close-to-Chaucerian meaning is intended.

The Augustinian friar John Capgrave provides other instances of odd understandings of tragedy. In his *Abbreviation of Chronicles*, compiled in the middle decades of the fifteenth century, he draws on a version of Isidore of Seville's *Chronicles* to say that Sophocles (which comes out "Sophodes") and Euripides were poets who were called "tragedies," which is how he renders Isidore's *tragedi*. He then defines tragedy: "Trajedi is as mech to sey as he that writith eld stories with ditees hevy and sorowful."[22] He has clearly heard something about a connection between tragedy and sad poetry. But a bit later on, though he now takes tragedies to mean the poems rather than the poets, he makes Terence the author of such works and thereby attributes to tragedy Terence's themes: the manners of young and old men, female treachery, the deceit of avarice, and (in the Latin), the trickery of bawds.[23]

Another author of Capgrave's time, Thomas Norton, in a poem on

---

[21] *The Vision of Philibert*, ed. J. O. Halliwell; the last two stanzas in this edition are mistakenly attached to the next piece, as is pointed out by Auvo Kurvinen, "MS Porkington 10," p. 46.

[22] John Capgrave, *Abbreviation of Chronicles*, ed. Peter J. Lucas, p. 40; Isidore, *Chronicorum epitome,* no. 11 (p. 446): "Sophocles et Euripides tragoedi celebrantur insignes" (variants: tracoedi, traguedi, tragodii, tragoedia, tracoediae). Lucas refers instead to the full text in Isidore's *Chronica maiora,* no. 174 (ibid.): "Aeschylus, Pindarus, Sophocles, et Euripides tragoediarum scriptores celebrantur insignes" (variants: tracoediarum, traguediarum, traguendiarum, tragoedarum, tragohereditarum, trogoediarum); one MS abbreviates thus: "Soflodes et Euripides tagedi celebrantur." Lucas, p. 259, rightly objects to the *MED*'s interpretation of Capgrave's "ditee" (and other citations under "dite" 1c) to mean "drama."

[23] Capgrave, p. 45: "Undir his tyme deied the noble poete Terrencius, that wrote so many trajedies, whose grave was wrytin with these vers:

> Natus in excelsis tectis Cartagenis alte,
>   Romanis ducibus bellica preda fui.
> Descripsi mores hominum, iuvenumque senumque,
>   [Qualiter et servi decipiant dominos,]

alchemy,[24] uses the word "tregedy" to mean trickery or treachery. He is speaking of false "multipliers," who deceive people:

> Of whose deceptis moche can y reporte,
> But I darre not, lest I gife conforte
> To such as be disposide to tregedie,
> For so moche hurte myghte growe therbye.   (341–44)

In a fifteenth-century manuscript in the Huntington Library, an astrological-medical compilation, tragedy (*tregedia*) is also applied to a person—not an author of tragedies, however, but someone who lives out a tragic sequence, who begins joyfully and ends sorrowfully. In contrast, a *commeda* follows the opposite sequence, and a *demogogus* goes his own way, while a *satera* is a thing (rather than a person) that remains good from beginning to end.[25]

Perhaps Arderne got his notion of tragedies as a source for funny stories from an English version of an exemplum of James of Vitry which was attributed to one of Seneca's tragedies, namely, the anecdote of Nero in hell inviting lawyers into the bath of molten gold reserved for them.[26] The association of this kind of story with a tragedy of Seneca's may have been influenced by the identification of the scurrilous *Ludus de morte Claudii* as a tragedy (I argued

> Quid meretrix, quid leno dolis, quid fingat avarus.
>   Hec quoque qui legit, sic, puto, cautus erit.

Thus thei mene in Englisch:

> Born in the toures hy in the cite of Cartage,
> To the dukes of Rome pray of bataile was I.
> I have descrived the maneris of men both eld and yong,
> What gile in woman is, what feyning in covetise.
> He that redith al this, the betyr he may be war.

The entry in Isidore's *Chronica majora* (no. 214a, p. 451), reads simply: "Terentius comicus claruit." I complete the second distich of Terence's epitaph from the version given by Vincent of Beauvais, *Speculum historiale* 5.72 (see below, p. 82). In the last line, Vincent has "Hic quicunque" for "Hec quoque qui."

[24]   Thomas Norton, *Ordinal of Alchemy*. The work was begun in 1477 (p. lii).

[25]   San Marino, Huntington Library MS 64, fol. 14v. I owe this reference to Dr. Mark Infusino. The complete text is as follows:

Satera is a thyng that bygynnethe goodely and so endithe.
Commeda is he that begynnythe laborusly and wickidly and endithe joyfully.
Tregedia is he that begynnythe joyfully and endithe sorowfully.
Demogogus is he that folowithe his owne wille and all waye demythe his owne will beste.

[26]   Besides the *Liber exemplorum*, p. 43, mentioned in IDEAS AND FORMS, p. 134, see J. A. Herbert, *Catalogue of Romances in the Department of Manuscripts in the British Museum*, 3:135 no. 136, where the story appears in a late fourteenth-century manuscript, Royal 7 C.i, fols. 93–121v, a series of moral exhortations probably by Robert Holcot (d. 1349): "Narrat Seneca in quadam tragedia" (fol. 120v). It also appears in the *Speculum laicorum*, a work by an English cleric in the latter part of the thirteenth century; Herbert describes an early-fourteenth-century copy, British Library Additional MS 11284, where the story comes on fol. 4 (p. 374 no. 18). It is also in another fourteenth-century manuscript, Additional 18364, fol. 87b (Herbert, p. 621 no. 197). It can be found as well in a later-fourteenth-century manuscript of the *Alphabetum narrationum* (probably compiled in 1308 by Arnold of Liège), Harley 268, fol. 55 (Herbert, p. 431 no. 7), except that here *tragedia* is corrupted to *cracedio*.

in the previous chapter that Boccaccio did not make such an identification,[27] but other writers may have).

The Scottish chronicler Walter Bower, writing in the 1440s, continuing the *Scotichronicon* of John Fordun (d. *c.*1385), indicates that tragedies could well be considered the source not of good and decent stories, as for Arderne, but of bad and indecent jokes and humorous escapades. He is referring to the 1260s, noting the emergence of "that notorious homicide Robin Hood and Little John" and their followers, but he seems to be talking of his own day when he says that the foolish common people avidly make bawdy festivity about these figures in comedies and tragedies, and they take delight in mimes and bards who sing of them in other romances.[28]

One other unusual usage of tragedy which at least preserves the notion of sadness can be found in the English version of Charles of Orleans's poems.[29] He is addressing Death, who has taken his beloved from him:

> But syn thou hast biraft me my maystres,
> Take me, poore wrecche, hir cely serviture,
> For levyr had y hastily forto dy
> Than langwysshe in this karfulle tragedy
> In payne, sorwe, and woofulle aventure.   (1998–2002)

"In this karfulle tragedy" corresponds to *en tourment* in the French original.[30] This correspondence and the context of the English text show that "tragedy" is taken to mean something like "condition" or, to use the formulation of Chaucer's Theseus, "prison of this life."[31]

After this survey of bizarre and benighted uses of the term tragedy, let us look at a learned contemporary of Chaucer's who also considered himself to be an author of tragedies—of sorts. I refer to Thomas of Walsingham, the great Benedictine chronicler of the Benedictine abbey of St. Albans, just north of London. To judge from the evidence of his chronicles, tragedy for him seems to mean an account of a great crime or crimes, and it is contrasted with comedy. He usually writes comedy, he says, but he interrupts his narrative of 1378 to tell of "a more than tragic matter," a murder in Westminster Abbey. In recounting the events of the Peasants' Revolt, he calls his narration of the crimes committed at London a tragedy, and he refers to the whole account as a tragic history. Later on, in a chronicle written around 1420, the *Ypodigma Neustriae*, he tells readers "who wish to see the rustic tragedy" to go to his earlier account.[32]

---

[27] Above, p. 21.

[28] Walter Bower, *Scotichronicon* 10.20 (2:104): "Hoc in tempore de exheredatis et bannitis surrexit et caput erexit ille famosissimus sicarius Robertus Hode et Litill Johanne cum eorum complicibus, de quibus stolidum vulgus hianter in comediis et tragediis prurienter festum faciunt, et super ceteras [*sic*] romanciis mimos et bardanos cantitare delectantur" (the meaning of the last clause is uncertain). Bower goes on to say that there are also commendable things reported of Robin Hood, specifically his devotion to the Mass. See R. B. Dobson and J. Taylor, *Rymes of Robyn Hood*, pp. 4–5.

[29] *The English Poems of Charles of Orleans*, p. 68.

[30] Charles d'Orléans, *Poésies*, 1:81.

[31] Chaucer, *Knight's Tale* 3061.

[32] Thomas Walsingham, Long History: *Chronicon Angliae*, pp. 206, 301, 312 (see also the

Walsingham's reference to "seeing" the tragedy may indicate that he was aware of the dramatic nature of tragedy in antiquity, such as could be gathered from reading Isidore's theatrical definitions.[33] If so, he may simply have been applying the term metaphorically to his prose accounts. It is even possible that he used the term metaphorically to refer to the events themselves as well as to his account of the events.[34] In other words, he would have considered himself to be an author of tragedy and comedy only figuratively.

But we have more to go on, because Walsingham was the author of literary works as well as of histories: he composed a commentary on Ovid's *Metamorphoses,* the *Archana deorum,* and he compiled an account of the lives and works of poets, which he called *Prohemia poetarum,* "Prologues of the Poets." In the *Archana,* compiled at the turn of the fifteenth century,[35] the subject of tragedy comes up only at the end of the discussion of the nine Muses. Walsingham gives all three standard explications of these figures: the first refers them to the organs of speech; the second account distributes them among the modes of teaching and knowledge, according to which Melpomene is explained as meaning "meditationem faciens"; and the third explanation assigns them to various arts, as illustrated by the Catonian verses on the Muses. In the last-named explanation, Melpomene represents tragedy, which brings forth mournful subjects with tragic bellowing, and Talia, as the representative of comedy, rejoices in lascivious speech.[36]

The *Prohemia* may date from around 1380,[37] which would make it earlier than the *Archana.*[38] Tragedy is dealt with not only in the treatment of

equivalent sections of his revised Long History for this period, *Historia Anglicana*); Late Short History: *Ypodigma Neustriae,* p. 335. Texts in "Non-Tragedy," pp. 94–95 nn. 21–24. "Tragedy" does not appear in the Early Short History for this time, which is not by Walsingham himself. For more on Walsingham's historical works, see V. H. Galbraith's Introduction to *The St. Albans Chronicle,* esp. pp. ix–x, xlvi–xvii, and see my *Divine Providence,* pp. 11–14, 23–26, 35–38, 335.

[33] See above, p. 16; two such definitions, of *tragoedi* and *comoedi,* are given below, n. 45.

[34] See "Non-Tragedy," p. 95 n. 24.

[35] Thomas Walsingham, *Archana deorum,* ed. Robert A. van Kluyve, *De archana* [sic, for *archanis*] *deorum*); he dates the work to the first decade of the fifteenth century; it was dedicated to Simon Southerey when he was prior of St. Albans, therefore after 1396 and before *c.* 1420.

[36] Walsingham, *Archana* 1.9 (pp. 16–17): The cited entries are: "Melpomene, id est, tragedia. Versus: 'Melpomene tragico proclamat mesta boatu.' Talia, id est comedia. Versus: 'Comica lascivo gaudet sermone Talia.,'" citing lines 4 and 3, respectively, of Pseudo-Cato, *Nomina Musarum.* See IDEAS AND FORMS, p. 90.

[37] *Prohemia poetarum Fratris Thome de Walsingham,* London, British Library MS Harley 2693, fols. 131–202v. The script is English, datable to the second half of the fourteenth century, according to my colleague Richard Rouse. Of the examples given by Malcolm B. Parkes, *English Cursive Book Hands, 1250–1500* (Oxford 1969), it most closely resembles no. 5.1, which is dated 1380. I have consulted also with Professors A. S. G. Edwards and Ralph Hanna III, who confirm the general time and English provenance of the script. I should note that the designation "Frater" in Latin and "Brother" in English was given not only to the mendicant friars or brothers but also to members of other religious orders, specifically monks, canons regular, and knights hospitaler. See the *Dictionary of Medieval Latin from British Sources,* fascicle 4 (F-G-H) s.v. *frater,* and *MED* s.v. "brother."

[38] In the brief chapter on Ovid in the *Prohemia,* fols. 175v–176v, the *Metamorphoses* is explained as a work designed to draw men from the immoderate love of temporal things to the worship of God. As van Kluyve notes, this approach is not followed in the *Archana ;* but he also notes that the *Prohemia* follows two different accounts of Statius (p. xiii). Both *Prohemia* and

Seneca, which is by far the largest section of the work, but also in the chapter on Terence. In the latter, he first takes up the subject of comedy. He points out that Terence's fables were not recited by Terence himself in the Senate (somehow the unfamiliar term *scena* has been "corrected" to *senatus*), but were instead recited by his learned supporter Calliopius. Flaccus was the modulator, who had to be present whenever they were recited. And others "spoke," that is, performed, the same attitudes and emotions as the recitor, but by means of bodily gestures.[39] This account reflects the "Isidorian" method of stage presentation, which we have already seen described by Boccaccio, and it draws on the Carolingian tradition of Calliopius as reciter of Terence's comedies.[40]

Under the rubric, "Effects of Comedy," Walsingham comments that comedy is so constructed that it does not narrate events in the manner of histories, but rather an event is put together from the "collocution" (dialogue) of persons, as if happening among them at that moment.[41] After giving summaries of Terence's comedies, he draws directly on the dictionary of Papias (compiled around A.D. 1045) and gives his various accounts, including the historical development by which comedians came to bring the actions and faults (*delicta*) of everyone onto the scene, and the observation that comedy is written in not as high a style as tragedy, but rather in a middle and sweet style, dealing as it does with humble persons (this is taken from the grammarian Placidus);[42] however, it also often deals with grave persons and historical truth (here Papias has confused what Donatus says not about comedy but tragedy).[43] Then he gives the differences between tragedy and comedy:

Archana draw extensively on Papias, but *Archana* makes no allusion to Seneca's tragedies, which are very fully summarized in *Prohemia*.

[39] Walsingham, *Prohemia*, fol. 156r–v: "Istud etiam advertendum: has fabulas non ab ipso esse recitatas in senatu, sed a Calliopio, viro clarissimo satisque erudito, cui ipse precipue adherebat cujusque ope sustentabatur et auctoritate audiebatur. Modulator autem harum fabularum fuit Flaccus. Quocienscumque enim recitabantur erat presens modulator, et alii qui gestu corporis eosdem affectus ajebant [Gloss: *id est, faciebant*]." Earlier he notes Terence's sources: "Imitatur autem Nevium, Plautum, Ennium, veteres comicos, precipueque Menandrum" (fol. 156). In TRA-GEDY AND COMEDY, p. 44 n. 4, where Guglielmo Maramauro's list of comic poets is given, "Enie-vio" should be emended to "e Nevio," that is, "and Naevius." Naevius was known as an author of both tragedies and comedies.

[40] See IDEAS AND FORMS, pp. 53–54.

[41] Ibid., fol. 156v, margin: *"Effectus comedie"*; text: "Comedia enim ita constat ut non res gestas more historiarum narret, sed ex collocucione personarum res gesta comprehenditur, quasi inter eos tunc agatur." Under another rubric it is explained why Terentian illustrations have a turgid and inflated mouth: "Hoc quidem notandum, quod non sine causa ymagines teren-ciane turgido et inflato ore pinguntur. Facundia enim et eloquium affluens comicorum per hoc intuitur, quia fastuose loquuntur. *Unde Oracius:* 'Iratusque Chremes tumido dilitigat ore' [*Ars poetica* 94]."

[42] Placidus, *Glossae* S 21 (p. 34). See IDEAS AND FORMS, p. 7. Placidus flourished around the year 500.

[43] Walsingham, *Prohemia.*, fols. 161v–162: "Comedi dicti sunt quia prius post commessacio-nem ad eos audiendos homines venire solebant, sed ex post aggressi, gesta universorum et delicta corripientes in scena proferebant. Comedia est que res privatarum et humilium personarum comprehendit, non tam alto stilo ut tragedia, sed mediocri et dulci; que sepe et de historica fide et de gravibus personis tractat. Comedia dicitur villanum carmen. Nam *comos* grece "villa" dici-tur. Comedia in quatuor partes dividitur: in prologum, prothesin, epithasin, et cathastrophen.

Tragedi differunt a comedis. Nempe tragediarum exitus semper debet esse luctuosus, cum comedia semper jocundos exitus habere debeat. Etiam sicut comedia res comprehendit privatarum et humilium personarum, sic tragedia demonstrat antiqua gesta et facinora sceleratorum regum et tirannorum.[44]

(Tragedic poets differ from comedic. For the end of tragedies should always be mournful, while comedy should have happy endings. Furthermore, just as comedy comprises the affairs of private and humble persons, so tragedy shows the old deeds and crimes of wicked kings and tyrants.)

The bipartite structure of this characterization may be due directly to Isidore of Seville's similar distinctions,[45] though some of the Isidorian language is in Papias's form, and the Donatian reference to *jocundi exitus* is also from Papias. But neither source accounts for the mention of tyrants. Some of this language recurs in his characterization of Seneca's tragedies:

Scripsit autem Seneca multos libros, inter quos etiam scripsit tragedias decem, in quibus fedos actus et scelera quam turpis sequatur exitus luculentissime demonstravit, per has cupiens Romanos, scilicet Neronem precipue, a dolis et fraudibus atque facinoribus revocare. Tragedia erat quicquit luctuosis cantibus antiqui tragedi describebant de gestis regum vel tirannorum sceleratorum; que quamvis inchoabatur jocunde, luctuose tamen continue terminabatur.[46]

Prologus est prefacio fabule, in qua licet absque argumento aliquid ad populum loqui ex comodo poete vel recitatoris. Prothesis est primus actus et inicium dragmatis, id est, fabule, cujus prothesis persona postea non apparet in fabula; et semper aperit in principio maximam partem. Epithasis est incrementum turbacionum in fabula. Catastrophen est custodia turbacionum ad jocundos exitus. Comediarum nomina ex quatuor rebus sumuntur, a loco, ut *Andria*, a facto, ut *Eunuchus*, ab eventu, ut *Adelphe*, a nomine, ut *Phormio*," repeating Papias, *Elementarium doctrinae rudimentum*, s.v. *comedi* and *comedia*. In Bonino Mombrizio's edition of Papias, *rectoris* appears where Walsingham has *recitatoris*. Papias is drawing on Donatus's *Commentum Terenti*, which in turn draws on Evanthius, *De fabula*, where the text reads, "aliquid ad populum vel ex poetae vel ex ipsius fabulae vel actoris commodo loqui." I have suggested that Papias's presentation of comedy mixed with features of tragedy may lie behind Dante's singular notions of comedy. See TRAGEDY AND COMEDY, pp. 7–8; IDEAS AND FORMS, pp. 11–12, 64–66, 148.

[44] Walsingham, *Prohemia*, fol. 162.

[45] Isidore treats of tragedy and comedy in two places of his *Etymologiae*: in book 8, comic and tragic poets do not deal with wicked subjects and their poetry has no theatrical dimension: "Comici privatorum hominum praedicant acta; tragici vero res publicas et regum historias. Item tragicorum argumenta ex rebus luctuosis sunt; comicorum ex rebus laetis (8.7.6)." In book 18, in contrast, "Tragoedi sunt qui antiqua gesta atque facinora sceleratorum regum luctuosa [or: luctuoso] carmine spectante populo concinebant" (18.45), and "Comoedi sunt qui privatorum hominum acta dictis aut gestu cantabant, atque stupra virginum et amores meretricum in suis fabulis exprimebant" (18.46). The specification of sinful subject matter in the chapters of book 18 is taken from Lactantius, *Diuinae institutiones* 6.20.27–30; see IDEAS AND FORMS, pp. 20–23, 46–49.

[46] Walsingham, *Prohemia*, fol. 178. Cf. Papias s.v. *Tragoedi*: "Qui antiquitus gesta et facinora sceleratorum regum concinebant"; s.v. *Tragedia*: "quidquid luctuosis carminibus describebant." He goes on to modify Papias's citing of Isidore 8.7.5 on the etymology of *tragedi*, as follows: "Tragedi autem dicti sunt eo quod cum primo inceperunt officium tragicum dabatur illis pro premio hircus, quem Greci *tragos* vocant. Sed ex post tragedi multum honorem adepti sunt qui excellu-

(Seneca wrote many books, among which he wrote ten tragedies, in which he very clearly demonstrated how foul an ending follows upon filthy acts and crimes, desiring by their means to summon the Romans, that is, especially Nero, from deceits and frauds and crimes. Tragedy was whatever the ancient tragedic poets wrote in mournful songs about the deeds of kings or wicked tyrants, which, even though beginning happily, would always end mournfully.)

Walsingham was obviously an unusually learned man for his time, demonstrating that a wide range of authorities was available in England, at least in some circles. The slightly later example of a literary monk, John Lydgate, will show a similar range of available sources.

It may be useful to list here some of the characteristics that Walsingham attributes to tragedy before looking at Chaucer's understanding of the genre. First, there are the aspects explicit in the Papias definitions:

(1) focused on criminal activity (Papias/Isidore 18/Lactantius)
(2) restricted to persons of high standing (Papias/Isidore 8 & 18)
(3) written in high style (Papias/Placidus)
(4) ending in sorrow (Papias/Donatus)
(5) containing lamentations (Papias/Isidore 8 & 18)
(6) practiced only in ancient times (Papias/Isidore 8 & 18)
(7) a kind of poetry, written in verse (Papias/Isidore 8)

Then there are features deducible from Papias on comedy:

(8) restricted to the speeches of characters
(9) intended for public recitation
(10) intended for multiple actors

There is one characteristic not derivable from Papias:

(11) may begin happily

The notion that a tragedy could, or regularly did, begin happily is contradicted by Seneca's tragedies, all of which begin disastrously. But Walsingham may have been drawing on the later dictionary of Huguccio of Bologna (*c.* 1165) or the still later dictionary of John Balbus (1286), who repeats Huguccio: tragedy, being the contrary of comedy, begins in joy and ends in sadness.[47] Let us give this absolute rule as a variant characteristic:

(11a) begins happily

---

runt in in argumentis fabularum" Fols. 178–201v, contain the summaries of eight of the Senecan tragedies, ending with an announcement of a ninth play, "Incipit *Octavia*," but with no summary; instead a second account of Claudian is given in another hand (fols. 201v–202v). The tenth play, *Hercules ætaeus*, is not mentioned at all.

[47] Huguccio, *Magne derivationes*, Oxford, Bodleian MS Laud Misc. 626, s.v. *oda*, fol. 124r–v: "Et differunt tragedia et comedia, quia comedia privatorum hominum continet acta, tragedia regum et magnatum. Item comedia humili stilo scribitur, tragedia alto. Item comedia a tristibus incipit set in letis desinit, tragedia e contrario." Taken over by John Balbus Januensis, *Catholicon*, s.v. *tragedis*. For Huguccio's whole entry on *oda*, see TRAGEDY AND COMEDY, pp. 6–7 n. 27.

Finally, let us list two figurative meanings derivable from Walsingham's chronicles:

(12) a writing describing events like those of tragedy
(13) real events suitable for treatment in a tragedy

We shall find that Chaucer's idea of tragedy shares some of these character-istics while others are foreign to it. In addition, three aspects are peculiar to Chaucer's notion and are not in Walsingham's:

(14) featuring unexpected or undeserved misfortunes
(15) consisting of a narrative account
(16) a present-day genre

A NARRATIVE GENRE

It is clear that Chaucer's primary source for his understanding of tragedy was Fortune's rhetorical question in Boethius's *Consolation of Philosophy*: "Quid tragediarum clamor aliud deflet nisi indiscreto ictu Fortunam felicia regna vertentem?" In his translation he renders it thus: "What other thynge bywaylen the cryinges of tragedyes but oonly the dedes of Fortune, that with an unwar strook overturneth the realmes of greet nobleye?"[48] This question, or a declarative statement derivable from it ("The shout of tragedies con-stantly bewails the unforeseen destruction of prosperous kingdoms"), pri-marily satisfies, out of the above-noted characteristics of tragedy, those of lamentation (5) and unexpected bad fortune (14). The characteristic of public recitation (9) is no doubt also indicated by the term *clamor*, Chaucer's "cryinges," which would of course be at least potentially true of all forms of medieval verse. But then it is not clear that we are dealing primarily or exclu-sively with verse (7). When we consider the context of Boethius's prose chap-ter, it is clear that tragedy deals with men and nations of great nobility (2) and involves a beginning in happiness (11a) and an ending in misery (4). How-ever, Fortune's words speak only to a potential narrative account: for one can bewail overturned happiness without telling the story of how it happened (15). In other words, the resulting form could be lyrical rather than narrative, a complaint or elegy rather than a story. As such, it would begin in misery and stay there, except perhaps for plaintive or mournful flashbacks to happier times. One can imagine Eustace Deschamps, for instance, arriving at his notion of "tragedian" from this passage: that is, a poet brought in to give vent to sorrow and mourning.[49] I have noted that Philip de Mézières had a similar understanding of tragedy.

[48] Chaucer, *Boece*, book 2 pr. 2, *Riverside Chaucer*, p. 409. The editors of the *Riverside Boece*, Ralph Hanna III and Traugott Lawler, follow Robinson in taking MS C1 (Cambridge University Library Ii.1.38) as their base text. The other Cambridge manuscript, C2 (Cambridge University Library MS Ii.3.21), which I call the Croucher Manuscript (see below), has a similar reading, except that "the" before "realmes" is omitted (fol. 38).
[49] Deschamps, *Oeuvres* no. 206 (2:27–28): "Picardie, Champaigne, et Occident / Doivent pour plourer acquerre / Tragediens" (lines 15–17). See IDEAS AND FORMS, p. 176.

There is widespread scholarly agreement nowadays that Chaucer made thorough and consistent use of Nicholas Trevet's commentary on the *Consolation of Philosophy* when he worked on his translation. If so, he would have learned of other characteristics of tragedy from Trevet's gloss on Fortune's question. According to him, tragedies were doleful poems that contained nothing but the uncertain mutability of Fortune; they were recited in the theater by the poets themselves in front of spectators, as pointed out by Isidore of Seville when defining the *ludus scenicus*. The poets sang of the ancient deeds and misdeeds of wicked kings. Tragedy therefore is a poem about great iniquities beginning in prosperity and ending in adversity. The word itself means goat-song, which refers to the prize of a goat that used to be given to the poets on such occasions.[50]

The chief additions to the Boethian text supplied by Trevet's explanation are the Isidorian subject matter of crime (1) and the supplementary notions of poetic form, that is, verse (7), and a clear specification of public recitation (9). It also clarifies the narrative aspect of the form, the sequence from good to bad (11 and 4). Left unmentioned is the Placidian requirement of high style (3), and also the characteristics of dramatic or dialogic mode (8) and mimetic production (10). Most of Trevet's account would indicate that tragedy is a form of poetry that was practiced only in antiquity (6), but his definition is given in the present tense, which suggests, whether he intended it or not, that tragedy is a current genre (16). No doubt he was simply copying William of Conches, who says: "Tragedia enim est scriptum de magnis iniquitatibus a prosperitate incipiens et in adversitate desinens."[51] Trevet's version is: "Tragedia est carmen de magnis iniquitatibus a prosperitate incipiens et in adversitate terminans."

Chaucer's own gloss on the Boethian passage is nothing more than a translation of Trevet's definition, with one extraordinarily important modification: he omits the phrase *de magnis iniquitatibus* (or as one manuscript has it, *de magnis criminibus vel iniquitatibus*).[52] The result reads as follows: "Tragedye is to seyn a dite of a prosperite for a tyme, that endeth in wrecchidnesse."[53] Therefore, in Chaucer's explanation there is no focus at all on criminal activity, which is true also of the passage being glossed in Boethius's *Consolation*.

The idea of tragedy as dealing with vicious protagonists whose misdeeds deserved and invited their downfall is quite foreign to the Boethian context, where the emphasis is rather upon unexpected misfortunes that come upon innocent persons like Boethius himself. There is no wrongdoing mentioned on the part of the fallen king of the Persians named by Fortune before she asks her question. The king may or may not have been at fault in his actions, but the matter is irrelevant to the subject at hand. The same is true of Chaucer's own tragedies. Granted, sometimes the adversities of the *Monk's Tale*

---

[50] Nicholas Trevet, *Expositio super librum Boecii de consolatione*, book 2, prose 2, text in IDEAS AND FORMS, p. 128; see also the unpublished edition by Edmund Taite Silk, p. 200.

[51] William of Conches, *Glose super librum Boecii de consolacione*, Vatican MS lat. 5202, fol. 13v; complete text in IDEAS AND FORMS, p. 69 n. 6.

[52] Trevet, *Expositio super librum Boecii*, Vatican MS lat. 562 (14 c.), fol. 29.

[53] Chaucer, *Boece*, book 2 pr. 2 (*Riverside Chaucer*, pp. 409–10).

are brought about by the wickedness of the protagonists, but sometimes they are not. It is also true that when the protagonist is blameless, his fall is usually (but not always) precipitated by the wickedness of a human antagonist. But for Chaucer, as for Boethius, the primary lesson is the randomness of misfortune. Chaucer's choice of the word "unwar" to translate Boethius's *indiscretus* is brilliant: it gives both the active and passive sense of the term. Fortune's blow is both undiscerning (it comes for no logical or just reason) and undiscerned (no one can predict it).

In view of this, we might be inclined to hold that it was a great inspiration on Chaucer's part to eliminate the *magne iniquitates* (and *magna crimina*, if present) from Trevet's definition, thereby rejecting the Patristic slur upon the genre that was passed on by Isidore.[54] But more likely, in my opinion, our conclusion should be that Chaucer's definition was not due to his insight but to a stroke of good fortune that occurred to him. I suggest that his definition appeared ready-made in his immediate source, which was not Trevet's commentary, but a copy of Boethius's text lightly furnished with glosses taken mainly from Trevet. Most of the glosses that he gives in his translation are preserved in their original Latin form in one of the Cambridge manuscripts of Chaucer's *Boece,* which contains not only Chaucer's translations, but also, before each meter and prose, a glossed text of the Latin original. The gloss on Fortune's question reads as follows: "Tragedia dicitur carmen de prosperitate incipiens et in adversitate terminans."[55] Quite clearly, Chaucer's explanation is a direct translation of this gloss. Let us consider the implications of this fact.

The manuscript in question, Cambridge University Library Ii.3.21, was given to the library by one John Croucher sometime before 1424; it is known as C2, to distinguish it from the other Cambridge manuscript of the *Boece,* Ii.1.38, but I will also call it the Croucher Manuscript. Walter Skeat was of the opinion that the Latin portions of the manuscript represented Chaucer's own glossed text of the *Consolation,* but he added the admonition that the manuscript "can only be a *copy* of the Latin, and the scribe can err."[56] Skeat was unaware of the connection of the apparatus with Trevet's commentary, and he was inclined to think that Chaucer had no help from a French translation. Later scholars claimed that Chaucer was dependent on Trevet and on Jean de Meun's French version, but no one considered the question of how the Croucher Manuscript related to these sources until E. T. Silk took up the matter in his dissertation of 1930.[57]

Silk concludes that Chaucer did make some use of Jean de Meun, but that his principal guide was a Latin text of Boethius, of the sort that Trevet used, and that Chaucer also used Trevet's commentary. He assumes, that is, that Chaucer used a text of Boethius that was glossed with Trevet's complete com-

---

[54] IDEAS AND FORMS, pp. 20–23, 46–47. Perhaps "slur" is the wrong word here, since the Lactantian-Isidorian characterization of tragedy seems a fair enough assessment of Seneca's tragedies.

[55] Croucher Manuscript: Cambridge, Cambridge University Library MS Ii.3.21, fol. 37, p. 142 in Edmund Taite Silk's edition, *Cambridge MS Ii.3.21.*

[56] Walter W. Skeat, *Complete Works of Geoffrey Chaucer,* 2:xl.

[57] Silk, *Cambridge MS Ii.3.21*; he gives the conclusions of his predecessors on pp. 2–3.

mentary. Chaucer's copy of Boethius-Trevet, he thinks, was then used as the basis of the Latin section of the Croucher Manuscript; but not all of Trevet's commentary was copied into it, because there was not sufficient room in the margins and interlinear spaces.[58]

However, Silk's reconstruction of events is unacceptable, in light of what we have seen of the Latin and English glosses on tragedy. According to his schema, Chaucer would first have made his very selective excerpt from Trevet's gloss on tragedy, and then the compiler of the Croucher volume would have made the *identical* selection and modification from Trevet. The compiler would also have made the same selection of unmodified glosses as Chaucer had made from Trevet's full commentary. It is too much to be believed.

It seems, then, that we must return to Skeat's thesis. Silk mentions it: "He believed that the Latin portion of Ii.3.21 was a copy of the very manuscript that Chaucer consulted, and that the whole thing had been put together for the express purpose of preserving in one book all the apparatus connected with Chaucer's *Boethius*."[59] However, for some reason Silk does not test Skeat's theory in the course of his study, but only takes it up in a paragraph that he seems to have included at the last minute on an added page.[60] He finds it disturbing that the Croucher Manuscript "does not always contain enough Trivet." He gives only one example of extra Trevet material in Chaucer, in the long paraphrase of the first part of book 3 meter 11, where, for instance, Chaucer's "false proposiciouns" corresponds to Trevet's *falsis propositionibus* rather than to Croucher's interlinear *falsis opinionibus*, which matches Conches's *opinionibus falsis*.[61] But Chaucer's next gloss in the same meter shows a clear dependence on the Croucher modification of Trevet rather than on Trevet's text.[62]

Silk concludes, "If Chaucer used an incomplete copy of Trivet, there was nevertheless more of the commentary in his copy than there is in MS Ii.3.21." But he prefers to believe that Chaucer used the entire commentary.[63] However, it is possible that both hypotheses are correct: that is, he may have used the full commentary as well as the excerpted commentary. This seems to be the view of Ralph Hanna and Traugott Lawler, the *Riverside Chaucer* editors of *Boece*, who say, "Like C2, which contains an abbreviated copy of Trivet but other glosses as well, Chaucer's Latin text gave eclectic annotation of Boethius."[64] But in practice they assume that Chaucer used only the complete commentary, for they never consult the Croucher glosses as possible sources for Chaucer's comments.

If Chaucer's copy-text of Boethius had a fuller apparatus than appears in

---

[58] Silk, pp. 42–43 n. 2.

[59] Silk, p. 2.

[60] The paragraph appears on pp. 7 and 7a.

[61] Chaucer, *Boece*, book 3 m. 11 (*Riverside* p. 437 lines 13–27); Silk, p. 5 (Conches and Trevet); pp. 339–41 (Croucher).

[62] Details are given in my "Chaucer and Shakespeare on Tragedy," pp. 203–04 n. 15.

[63] Silk, pp. 7–7a.

[64] Hanna and Lawler, p. 1004. In contrast, Alastair Minnis, " 'Glosynge Is a Glorious Thyng': Chaucer at Work on the *Boece*," p. 122, does not think that there were any Trevet glosses in Chaucer's copy-text of Boethius, but he speculates that there were some glosses derived from Remigius of Auxerre.

the Croucher Manuscript, it may be that some of the glosses were lost because of negligent copying. Silk concludes that there were three main scribes employed on the Croucher production, one for the Latin text of Boethius, one for the glosses, and one for the English translations.[65] Perhaps the English scribe was Adam the Scrivener, whom Chaucer rebuked in these terms:

> Adam Scriveyn, if ever it thee bifalle
> *Boece* or *Troylus* for to wryten newe,
> Under thy long lokkes thou most have the scalle,
> But after my makyng thou wryte more trewe.[66]

But Silk shows that it was not only the English translation but also the Latin text and especially the glosses that were defective in the Croucher Manuscript, and that many of the faults were remedied by the efforts of at least one corrector. The corrector usually supplies the missing glosses himself,[67] but on one occasion he complains that material on Nero is missing: "Hoc deficit de Nerone, etc."[68] On one occasion the corrector refers to Trevet: "See Alfred on free will in Trevet on the first meter, near the end of the meter."[69] But it need not mean that either the corrector or Chaucer was familiar with Trevet's commentary; he may simply have been reproducing an instruction in the glossed text that Chaucer used. The latter possibility seems especially likely because the rubric was garbled in transmission: instead of "super p° metro," it should read "super hoc metro," or "super ij° metro," or the like, since Trevet's citation of King Alfred on free will occurs at the end of the meter under consideration, which is not the first but the second meter of the fifth book.[70] There is another similar reference to Trevet in a gloss written by the original scribe.[71]

In my view, then, the conclusion is inescapable that Chaucer's copy-text of Boethius contained many of the Latin glosses that appear in Croucher. The fact that Chaucer's translation contains much more of Trevet's commentary than is to be found in Croucher can be explained in a number of ways: his copy-text may have had more Trevet in it than the Croucher scribe copied; or Chaucer may have consulted a complete Trevet for his additional glosses; or his copy-text may have resembled Croucher and a collaborator supplied the additional glosses from Trevet as Chaucer labored on his translation: "philosophical Strode" immediately comes to mind as a candidate. To indulge this last scenario for a moment, we can think of Chaucer's friend Strode, whom he addresses as expert in philosophy and whom he invites to

---

[65] Silk, p. 52.

[66] *Chaucer's Words unto Adam, His Own Scriveyn (Riverside Chaucer*, p. 650).

[67] Silk, pp. 58–60.

[68] Croucher MS, fol. 75v, on Boethius, book 3 m. 4 (Silk, p. 267; cf. p. 51).

[69] Croucher MS, fol. 154v, on Boethius, book 5 m. 2 (Silk, p. 484, and see the facsimile, pl. 6, after p. 60): "Vide in Trivet super primo metro in fine metri Alvredum de libero arbitrio."

[70] Trevet, *Expositio super librum Boecii*, book 5 m. 2 (ed. Silk, pp. 694–95). See the edition of the passage by B. S. Donaghey, "Nicholas Trevet's Use of King Alfred's Translation of Boethius, and the Dating of His Commentary," pp. 29–30.

[71] Croucher MS, fol. 24v on Boethius, book 1 m. 5 line 10 (ed., Silk, p. 108): "Vide Trivet pro septem partibus noctis." See Trevet, *Expositio super librum Boecii*, book 1 m. 5 (ed. Silk, p. 128).

correct the *Troilus*,[72] as responsible for compiling all of the Croucher glosses as well as for supplying others not found there.[73]

It does not seem at all likely to me that the author of the Croucher glosses could have been Chaucer himself. They were compiled by a more learned Latinist than Chaucer ever manifests himself to be. The glossator not only made intelligent summaries of Trevet's material, but also gave other explanations in his own words. Chaucer never seems to have been at home writing another language, whether Latin or French—in spite of the unsubstantiated speculations that have been made about him as an author of French verse. If, then, when Chaucer set about translating Boethius he had in front of him not only the Latin text but also a comparatively small number of Latin glosses already in place in his copy-text of Boethius, it still remained for him to find the appropriate words in English, or to go to another authority (for instance, Jean de Meun's translation) for guidance or inspiration. And it also remained to his discretion whether to use a gloss or not. It is to his sole credit that he translated the phrase *ictu indiscreto* as "with an unwar stroke," and further that he chose not to use the gloss attached to the phrase, which would have placed an undue restriction on the meaning of the text. Trevet's gloss reads, "id est, eventu incerto,"[74] which I take to mean, "that is, with an uncertain outcome." In the Croucher Manuscript, the gloss originally read, "id est, in certo adventu" ("that is, in a certain arrival"), but *in certo* was corrected to *incerto*, making the gloss mean, "with an uncertain arrival." In whatever form, the gloss does not do justice to the fullness of Boethius's meaning. Nor does Jean de Meun's translation: "par coup despourveu" (with an unforeseen blow").[75]

Granted (if only hypothetically) that Chaucer relied primarily on the glosses already at hand in his copy of Boethius, but also kept an eye on Jean de Meun's version, let us consider what other sources he could have used to reinforce his idea of tragedy. First of all, he could have drawn on other passages in the *Consolation*. For instance, at one point Philosophy says (in Chaucer's version): "The olde age of tyme passed, and ek the present tyme now, is ful of ensaumples how that kynges han chaungyd into wrecchidnesse out of hir welefulnesse."[76] Later she speaks specifically of the wicked: "The grete hope and the heye compassynges of schrewednesses is ofte destroyed by a sodeyn ende, or thei ben war."[77] Moreover we must acknowledge the possibility that Chaucer would have been able from time to time to consult Trevet's

---

[72] Chaucer, *Troilus* 5.1856–59. See the next chapter, p. 133, where I bring up the possibility that Strode was at least partially responsible for the addition of Boethian materials to the *Troilus*.

[73] For this hypothesis, see my "Chaucer and Shakespeare," pp. 194, 204 n. 16; I should, however, say a word about my argument there that Chaucer drew on Latin glosses which were added to his English translation. This conclusion seemed plausible from Silk's transcription of book 3 m. 4. But the layout of the meter in the manuscript itself suggests a different explanation. The text of the poem is given at the bottom of fol. 75v and Chaucer's translation appears at the top of fol. 76r. It could be that all of the Latin glosses, even those that appear next to Chaucer's translation, appeared in the original copy-text, but that the Croucher scribe did not have room to put them all next to the Latin meter, and simply carried them over to the next page, setting them next to Chaucer's translation.

[74] Trevet on Boethius, book 2 pr. 2, ed. Silk, p. 200.

[75] Jean de Meun, trans. of Boethius, book 2 pr. 2, p. 189.

[76] Chaucer, *Boece*, book 3 pr. 5 (*Riverside Chaucer*, p. 426).

[77] Ibid., book 4 pr. 4 (pp. 446–47).

complete commentary or other commentaries on points that interested him. One example of a commentary that may have been available to him is that of William of Aragon, which is contained in the second part of the Croucher volume. Aragon characterizes comedy as rejoicing in banquets and delights, and tragedy as lamenting over misfortunes that occur.[78]

If Chaucer did seek further information on tragedy and did read all of Trevet's gloss, he could have gathered that the poets of tragedy shouted, recited, or sang their poems before a watching audience in the theater. This account, however, need not have suggested to him anything more than a vigorous public recitation of the sort that he himself must have engaged in. If Chaucer had been able to see the frontispiece illustration of the *Troilus* manuscript at Corpus Christi College, Cambridge, which seems to have been executed a few years after his death, he would no doubt have approved of it not only as an ideal portrayal of his own performance of his tragedy, but also as conforming to the ancient method of tragic recitation (we are still supposing his knowledge of Trevet on the point). The illustration shows a man, presumably meant to represent Chaucer, standing in a wooden pulpit and addressing an audience of men and women, most of whom are watching as well as listening; in the background can be seen a meeting of two retinues, and other people on other business. This open-air setting might have qualified as a theater, in Chaucer's mind (as we shall see below when discussing Chaucer's translation of *scenice meretricule*); and while he may not have known of any traditional association of the tragic poet with a pulpit, such as could have been derived from a reading of Isidore, he might well have considered its use appropriate.

The illustrator himself need not have been familiar with any such tradition. It has been suggested by Derek Pearsall that he is simply drawing upon the standard method of portraying preachers preaching their sermons;[79] and Elizabeth Salter points to precedents in the prefatory illustrations of William of Deguileville's *Pèlerinage de vie humaine*, in which the poet addresses a mixed audience from his pulpit.[80]

Furthermore, Chaucer would doubtless have concluded (rightly) that Trevet interpreted Boethius's shouting and Isidore's singing to mean recitation. One need only think of the opening of the *Aeneid*, "Arma virumque cano," for a precedent. Chaucer's own *Troilus* is a song that is spoken.[81] When he paraphrases Fortune's rhetorical question at the end of the *Monk's Tale*, he makes the point that tragedies, of the sort that have just been spoken, are "cried," "bewailed," and "sung":

---

[78] William of Aragon, *Commentum in Boethii Consolationem*, Cambridge Univ. Lib. MS Ii.3.21, part 2, fol. 29v, on book 2 pr. 2: "Sicut enim comedia gaudet de commessacionibus et deliciis, ita tragedia dolet de infortuniis que contingunt." In chap. 6 below, p. 220 n. 11, I note a similarity between Chaucer's citing of the verse of the *tragicus* (Euripides) and Aragon's text on fol. 54 (but Aragon gives the poet's epithet as *trahicus*). When treating of the scenic whores of book 1 pr. 1, Aragon interprets *scenica* as *sordida* (fol. 13v). In his edition of the first part of the Croucher MS, Silk says that he has found no sign of Chaucer's knowledge of Aragon's commentary (p. 5).

[79] Derek Pearsall, "The *Troilus* Frontispiece and Chaucer's Audience"; idem, *The Life of Geoffrey Chaucer*, p. 179.

[80] M. B. Parkes and Elizabeth Salter, *Troilus and Criseyde: A Facsimile of Corpus Christi College Cambridge MS 61* (Cambridge 1978), pp. 15–23.

[81] Chaucer, *Troilus* 3.1814; cf. *Book of the Duchess* 471–72, 1181–82.

Tragedies noon oother maner thyng
Ne kan in syngyng crie ne biwaille
But that Fortune alwey wole assaille
With unwar strook the regnes that been proude.   (2761–64)

Is the "singing" to be taken as proof that Chaucer has read Trevet's complete gloss? Or, in view of the common occurrence of the conceit of singing poetry, can it be easily accepted as a coincidence? Perhaps neither choice is correct, for we will see below that Chaucer had another source that spoke of singing tragedies, that is, Vincent of Beauvais's account of Nero. Let me only note here that when Chaucer incorporated his series of tragedies into the *Canterbury Tales*, he had no difficulty in allowing his Monk simply to recite tragedies: "tragedies wol I telle" (1971). Furthermore, the characterization of tragedy given in the first stanza of the series follows the Croucher Manuscript gloss (and Chaucer's own gloss) rather than Trevet, for there is no mention of "great iniquities":

I wol biwaille, in manere of tragedie,
The harm of hem that stoode in heigh degree,
And fillen so that ther nas no remedie
To brynge hem out of her adversitee.   (1991–94)

The same is true of the definition that Chaucer gave later to the Monk:

Tragedie is to seyn a certeyn storie,
As olde bookes maken us memorie,
Of hym that stood in greet prosperitee,
And is yfallen out of heigh degree
Into myserie, and endeth wrecchedly.   (1973–77)

We have seen that Chaucer need not have interpreted the Trevet gloss, if he saw it, as anything other than a normal poetry recital; this is another way of saying that there is nothing in Trevet's gloss to suggest to Chaucer that tragedies were in any way acted out. Chaucer knew nothing of the ancient stage. I have claimed earlier that he did not know, or even know about, the tragedies of Seneca; and I hold that the same is true of the comedies of Plautus and Terence, and *a fortiori* of Greek drama.[82] He could have learned that Seneca, Aeschylus, and Sophocles were authors of tragedies from Vincent of Beauvais's *Speculum historiale*,[83] though not that their tragedies were dramas or written entirely in dialogue; but there is no reason to think that he consulted these sections of Vincent's work. If he had known Vincent's *Speculum doctrinale*, he could have found support for his crime-free idea of tragedy in book 3, partially based in Isidore's book 8, and Trevet's crime-oriented view in

[82] Extensive claims for Chaucer's knowledge of the Roman dramatists have been made by John Norton-Smith, *Geoffrey Chaucer*, esp. pp. 162–72, but I find his arguments unpersuasive.

[83] Vincent of Beauvais, *Speculum historiale* 3.33 (Aeschylus); 3.40, 42 (Sophocles); 8.102–04, 113–14 (Seneca), see IDEAS AND FORMS, p. 126.

book 1, based on Isidore's book 18.[84] Anyone who thinks that Chaucer was familiar with Horace's *Ars poetica* must rely on wishful thinking more than on proof.[85] Horace was almost entirely unread in northern Europe after the twelfth century.

The main kind of "theatrical" activity Chaucer knew was the sort of mummings, interludes, and other court entertainments described in the *Franklin's Tale*:

> For ofte at feestes have I wel herd seye
> That tregetours, withinne an halle large,
> Have maad come in a water and a barge,
> And in the halle rowen up and down;
> Somtyme hath semed come a grym leoun,
> And somtyme floures sprynge as in a mede,
> Somtyme a vyne and grapes white and rede,
> Somtyme a castel al of lym and stoon.   (1142–49)

He also knew the biblical plays of his time, to which he refers in the *Miller's Prologue and Tale*: the Miller crying out in Pilate's voice (3124), Absalom Heroding Herod on a scaffold high (3384), and perhaps Nicholas's allusions to the problems of Noah and his wife (3534–43).

There remains the question of what Chaucer would have made of Trevet's report of Isidore's *De ludo scenico*, where he says that tragedies were sung in the theater. A ready answer is to be had by looking at Chaucer's translation and explanation of Boethius's *scenice meretricule*: "Thise comune strompettis of swich a place that men clepen the theatre."[86] His phraseology makes it seem that the term theater is new to him, and that he is not quite sure about what goes on in "such a place," except that prostitutes are there. It is in fact one of the words that Chaucer introduced into the English language. What he did in this case was to combine Jean de Meun's "ces communes putereles abandonees au peuple"[87] with the gloss of the Croucher Boethius:

> Scenicas eo tamen dicitur a *scena* grece, quod est "obumbracio" latine; et dicuntur scenice quia in scenis, id est, in teatro, fiebant.[88]
>
> (The word "scenic" comes from the Greek *scena*, which means "shade" in Latin; and they are called scenic because they used to become such in the scenes, that is, in the theater.)

Chaucer clearly assumed that *meretricule* was the subject of *fiebant*—these women became whores in the theater—which shows that he did not read or absorb Trevet's commentary on the point. Trevet says that the Muses are called prostitutes for one reason (because poets wrote about any subject not

---

[84] Vincent of Beauvais, *Speculum doctrinale* 3.109–10 and 1.76; see below, pp. 81–82.
[85] See Richard L. Hoffman, "The Influence of the Classics on Chaucer," p. 186.
[86] Chaucer, *Boece*, book 1 pr. 1 (*Riverside Chaucer*, p. 398).
[87] Jeun de Meun, translation of Boethius, book 1, pr. 1, p. 173.
[88] Croucher MS, fol. 10v (Silk, p. 67). I have emended Silk's reading of *ea* to *eo*.

for love of knowledge but for praise or gain) and scenic for another (because poems used to be recited in the scenes). He goes on to quote Isidore: the scene was a place within the theater built like a house, with a pulpit. He then gives the etymology and the Latin meaning of shade, which he explains by the fact that it served as a hiding place for persons singing tragic and comic poems.[89]

When Chaucer comes to the expression *in hanc vite scenam*, he translates it, "into the schadowe or tabernacle of this lif."[90] Once again, he draws both on Jean de Meun and on his glossator. Jean provides "shadow": "en la cortine et in l'ombre de ceste vie,"[91] and the glossator, "tabernacle":

> Id est, mundum; scena est habitacio transitoria, et dicitur a *scenos*, quod est "tabernaculum."[92]
>
> (That is, the world; for a scene is a temporary dwelling. The word comes from *scenos*, meaning "tent.")

In this case, Trevet's gloss is much the same.

Later on in the *Boece*, Chaucer translates the word *tragicus* as "tragedien, that is to seyn, a makere of dytees that highten tragedies."[93] It is curious that there is no comment by the Croucher glossator on this unusual word. Perhaps there was one in Chaucer's copy-text, and the scribe of the Croucher volume neglected to include it. Trevet explains it as "quidam poeta grecus qui tragedias composuit," and refers back to his earlier explanation of tragedy.[94] John of Meun translates it as "ung poetez tragiciens."[95] This would account for Chaucer's text, except for the form "tragedien"; but then Trevet's gloss would not provide the form either. Machaut's "tragediennes" would have struck Chaucer as ludicrously inappropriate (they were minor goddesses whose function it was to make sacrifice to the gods and perform the divine office),[96] while Deschamps's mention of "tragediens" in his ballade on the death of Bertrand de Guesclin (d. 1380)[97] may have been too late to have influenced him.

Chaucer could have seen the term *tragedus* in Trevet's full commentary on prose 4 of book 3, where he tells of the Emperor Nero: he quotes the account of Freculph of Lisieux, which was taken verbatim from Orosius, of Nero's tour of the theaters of Italy and Greece, where he was frequently seen to have

---

[89] Trevet, *Expositio super librum Boecii*, book 1 pr.1 (ed. Silk, p. 35), drawing in Isidore, *Etymologiae* 18.43; text in IDEAS AND FORMS, p. 127.

[90] Chaucer, *Boece*, book 2 pr. 3 (*Riverside Chaucer*, p. 411).

[91] Jean de Meun, translation of Boethius, book 2 pr. 3, p. 191. Cf. the woodsy setting of *Aeneid* 1.164–65, where *scaena* is associated with *umbra*. The passage is cited by Norton-Smith, pp. 163–64, along with other texts in an attempt to show that *scena* would suggest the theatrical to Chaucer. I would say that his relevant evidence suggests the opposite.

[92] Croucher MS, fol. 40 (Silk, p. 152).

[93] Chaucer, *Boece*, book 3 pr. 6 (*Riverside Chaucer*, p. 426).

[94] Trevet, *Expositio super librum Boecii*, book 3 pr. 6 (ed. Silk, p. 349).

[95] Jean de Meun, translation of Boethius, book 3 pr. 6, p. 214.

[96] Guillaume de Machaut, *La prise d'Alexandrie*, lines 11–25; text in IDEAS AND FORMS, p. 176 n. 13.

[97] Cited above, n. 49.

overcome heralds, citharists, tragedians, and charioteers.[98] This gloss may have been in Chaucer's own text of Boethius, if it was contained in the material on Nero that the corrector of the Croucher Manuscript notes is missing (his note comes at the following meter).[99]

Chaucer seems definitely to have read another account of Nero, at the time that he first compiled his tragedies, namely, Vincent of Beauvais's excerpt from Suetonius in the *Speculum historiale*.[100] There, Nero is said to have participated with "scenics" even in private spectacles, and, while "personated" (*personatus*), to have sung tragedies. But this is a detail that Chaucer did not take over in his *Tragedy of Nero*. Perhaps he omitted it because, unlike Boccaccio, he did not consider the presentation of tragedies to be a particularly horrible example of the emperor's corrupt ways. But it may also be the case that Chaucer was puzzled about the meaning of the passage. What would he have understood by *personatus* (the sense of which seems to have eluded even Boccaccio)? And would he think of the *scenici* as somehow connected with Boethius's *scenice meretricule*? Vincent reports that while Rome burned Nero sang "in that scenic habit of his,"[101] which would present Chaucer with another puzzle.

There is no way of telling whether Chaucer read Boccaccio's chapter on Nero in the *De casibus*, but one wonders how he would have interpreted the statement, "Making tragedies of heroes, he leaped around (*saltavit*) in the scene like a mime." Would he have had any notion of the technical meaning of *saltatio* as the art of the pantomime or balletic acting? The question of how Chaucer would have understood theatrical terminology is important in connection with Ovid's works as well. Equally important, of course, is whether Chaucer knew the relevant portions of those works. Familiarity with all of Ovid's major poems could easily be assumed with an accomplished Latinist like John Gower, who actually borrows from them all in the *Vox clamantis*,[102] whereas in Chaucer's case we cannot assume a thorough knowledge of anything but the *Metamorphoses* and *Heroides* (and perhaps only parts of them).

It is probable that Chaucer considered the *Metamorphoses* as well as the classical epics to consist of, or at least to contain, tragedies. Since the *Heroides* is made up entirely of epistles, it would not, of course, fit under his strict definition of tragedy, even though it could supply the subject matter for many tragedies. Chaucer may be telling us something about his views of tragedy and the classics in his address to his *Book of Troilus*:

---

[98] Trevet, *Expositio super librum Boecii*, book 3 pr. 4 : "Petulancia percitus (id est, allectus), omnia pene Ytalie et Grecie theatra perlustrans, assumpto eciam varii vestitus decore, cericas [= ceryces], citharistas, tragedos, et aurigas sepe sibi superasse visus est" (ed. Silk, p. 338). Cf. Freculph, *Chronicon* 2.1.16 (PL 106:1131) = Orosius, *Historiae* 7.7 (PL 31:1076). These texts read *dedecore* rather than *decore*.

[99] See p. 54 above.

[100] See Pauline Aiken, "Vincent of Beauvais and Chaucer's *Monk's Tale*."

[101] Vincent of Beauvais, *Speculum historiale* 9.8: "In illo suo scenico habitu" (p. 325).

[102] See Eric W. Stockton, *The Major Latin Works of John Gower*, Index s.v. Ovid.

Go, litel bok, go litel myn tragedye,
Ther God thi makere yet, er that he dye,
So sende myght to make in some comedye!
But, litel book, no makyng thow n'envie,
But subgit be to alle poesye;
And kis the steppes, where as thow seest pace
Virgile, Ovide, Omer, Lucan, and Stace.   (5.1786–92)

Since, however, he moves in this stanza from considering the *Troilus* a tragedy to considering it under the category of all "making" or all poetry, the poets he names may not be intended as examples of tragic authors; they could just as well be authors of comedy (I will speculate later on what Chaucer meant by comedy). But the Monk's Prologue would seem to confirm the generally tragic content of the works we nowadays designate as epics:

[Tragedies] ben versified communely
Of six feet, which men clepen *exametron*.
In prose eek been endited many oon,
And eek in meetre in many a sondry wyse.   (1978–81)

Skeat rightly assumes that the second line must refer to the dactylic hexameter (the six iambs of the standard dramatic line were usually analyzed not as a hexameter but as a trimeter, consisting of three double iambs). Vergil's *Aeneid* is in dactylic hexameters (as are the *Georgics and Eclogues*, though Chaucer seems not to have known them); so are Lucan's *Pharsalia* and Statius's *Thebaid*; and Chaucer would no doubt have guessed that Homer also used this meter. Of Ovid's works, only the *Metamorphoses* is in hexameters, while the *Heroides* and everything else is in elegiac couplets (hexameters alternating with pentameters). But the Monk does take note that tragedies can be in other meters, as well as in prose. Perhaps Chaucer felt it necessary to include works in prose in order to account for Boccaccio's *De casibus* and Guido of Le Colonne's *Historia destructionis Troje*, but in doing so he went beyond the *carmen* of Trevet's definition, taken over in the Croucher modification, a term that Chaucer translated by "dite." But William of Conches's more general term, *scriptum*, readily allowed for prose works to be designated as tragedies.

Of the classical works that Chaucer might be thinking of as tragedies from his own firsthand knowledge, the *Pharsalia* and *Thebaid* end unhappily, the *Metamorphoses* is riddled with unhappy endings along the way, and the *Aeneid* tells of the fall of Troy and Dido's misfortunes, among other disasters.[103] If Chaucer read in the *Tristia* that Ovid gave a regal writing to the tragic cothurns (buskins),[104] and understood him to mean that he wrote a

---

[103] Charles Blyth, "Virgilian Tragedy and *Troilus*," notes that Gavin Douglas in his translation of the *Aeneid* considers the accounts of book 2 (fall of Troy) and book 4 (Dido) to be tragedies. See below, chap. 3, p. 112 n. 35, for an indication in the *Man of Law's Tale* that Chaucer considered Vergil's account of Turnus at the end of the *Aeneid* to be a tragedy.

[104] Ovid, *Tristia* 2.553. See IDEAS AND FORMS, pp. 19–30, for this and the following Ovidian passages, where I analyze them from Ovid's point of view. Neither "cothurn" nor "buskin" is medieval, and *cothurnus* is very rare in post-Conquest insular Latin.

tragedy, he would doubtless have thought of the *Metamorphoses*—especially since he would hardly have heard of Ovid's *Medea*. He would also think of the *Metamorphoses* if he read of Ovid's conversation with Roman Tragedy in the *Amores*.[105] Shortly before this in the *Amores*, Ovid tried to write a tragedy while holding a scepter and wearing cothurns (the same garb that Roman Tragedy wears); Chaucer could easily have understood him to mean that the subject of his tragedy was the same as the subject his friend Macer was dealing with, namely, wrathful Achilles and the Trojan War. When Love laughs at him and prevents him from continuing, Ovid says he can only write the *artes Amoris* or else the words of Penelope to Ulysses, the tears of abandoned Phyllis, miserable Dido with her drawn sword, and so on.[106] Now since the Dido and Phyllis stories and several other subjects of the *Heroides* were suitable for tragedy in Chaucer's view, he might have interpreted Ovid to be saying that he was forced to compromise: by writing, if not tragedies that dealt with love, then at least epistles dealing with tragic love.

This understanding of Ovid's meaning could have been confirmed by Chaucer's reading in the *Tristia* of how the exiled poet defends his preoccupation with love: he says that tragedy is the most serious form of writing and that it has always been concerned with love. Just before this, he gives examples of love themes from the *Iliad* and *Odyssey*, including the *flamma Briseidos*; and now, when he goes on to detail *tragici ignes*, Chaucer could be forgiven for thinking that he is continuing to draw on Homer—when for instance he refers to the episode of Achilles's becoming soft for love to illustrate his assertion that "tragedy is also mingled with lewd laughter, and contains many words of past shame."[107] This last passage in fact looks like a recipe for turning Boccaccio's Pandaro into Chaucer's Pandarus by adding jovial ribaldry.

Just after addressing his book as a tragedy, Chaucer resumes his narrative thus:

> The wrath, as I bigan yow for to seye,
> Of Troilus the Grekis boughten deere.   (5.1800–01)

Whether or not he could have heard indirectly of Homer's opening announcement that the *Iliad* is about the wrath of Achilles, he could have learned from the *Remedies of Love* that wrath befits the tragic cothurns,[108] if he knew Ovid's work. He may be referring at least to its title when saying of the Wife of Bath in the *General Prologue*, "Of remedies of love she knew per chaunce" (475), but in this line he clearly is thinking of homeopathic medicine rather than Ovid's heteropathic formulas.[109]

---

[105] Ovid, *Amores* 3.1.

[106] Ibid., 2.18.

[107] Ovid, *Tristia* 2.371–412. The lines quoted in translation (411–12) read in Latin (with medieval spelling):

> Est et in obscenos commixta tragedia risus,
> Multaque preteriti verba pudoris habet.

[108] Ovid, *Remedia amoris* 375: "Grande sonant tragici: tragicos decet ira cothurnos" ("Tragic poets resound with power; wrath becomes the tragic cothurns").

[109] See my *Love and Marriage in the Age of Chaucer*, p. 73; cf. p. 36 n. 13. I am more skeptical now about Chaucer's acquaintance with all of Ovid's works than I was earlier on.

Chaucer could have found out something about the theater from the *Tristia*. Ovid says that though his poems have been reportedly "leaped" in the theater, he did not compose anything for theaters and has no desire for applause.[110] It would be natural for Chaucer to read this to mean that Ovid did not want his poems recited in the theater. Ovid says elsewhere that he did not write *mimi* with their obscene jests and "scenic adulteries."[111]

In the *Fasti*, Flora is associated with the "lightweight scene" (*scena levis*) and the "prostitute crowd" (*turba meretricia*), and dissociated from the buskined goddesses (*dee coturnate*).[112] In the *Ars amatoria*, Ovid described the "curved theaters" as the happy hunting ground for woman-chasers.[113] It has been suggested that when Chaucer interpreted the scenic prostitutes as the common strumpets of the theater, he was drawing on the old identification of the theater with the brothel, which was passed on by Isidore of Seville.[114] If so, Chaucer's reading of these portions of Ovid would have supported the idea.

Chaucer's only other use of the term theater came some time after his translation of Boethius, in the *Palamon and Arcite* (which I assume had the same basic form and content as it does when told by the Knight in the *Canterbury Tales*). Here Chaucer has simply taken the word from the *Teseida*, in his description of the huge amphitheater or tournament stadium built by Theseus.[115] Chaucer omits Boccaccio's earlier use of the word: ladies are said to appear in the theaters, balconies, and streets to display their beauty.[116] If Chaucer had a copy of the *Teseida* containing Boccaccio's gloss, which he probably did not,[117] he could have seen theater defined as any public gathering place.[118] This was also a fairly common meaning of the word *theatrum* in some documents of fourteenth-century England, especially taken in the sense of a public square or marketplace.[119]

When Chaucer was working on the *Canterbury Tales*, he could hardly have avoided seeing what St. Jerome had to say about tragedy in his *Against Jovinian*. He may have found there for the first time that Euripides was an author of tragedies, if not a dramatist. Jerome says, "All the tragedies of Euripides are curses against women."[120] Chaucer may at this time have identified the author in question with "my Euripides" cited by Philosophy in Boethius's *Consolation*. But it is also possible that he would not have connected the two names. He probably found the name as Europides in his text of Jerome.[121] In

---

[110] Ovid, *Tristia* 5.7.25–28; cf. 2.519–20.

[111] Ibid., 2.497–518.

[112] Ovid, *Fasti* 5.347–50. Ovid's spelling, of course, would be *deae cothurnatae*.

[113] Ovid, *Ars amatoria* 1.89–134.

[114] Marshall,"*Theatre* in the Middle Ages," p. 39 n. 86; Isidore, *Etymologiae* 18.42.2; IDEAS AND FORMS, p. 49.

[115] Chaucer, *Knight's Tale* 1885; Boccaccio, *Teseida* 7.108.

[116] Boccaccio, *Teseida* 2.20.

[117] See my *Chaucer and the Cult of St. Valentine*, pp. 101–02.

[118] See above, chap. 1, p. 17.

[119] Marshall, pp. 381–82.

[120] Jerome, *Adversus Jovinianum* 1.48 (PL 23:292); IDEAS AND FORMS, pp. 31–32.

[121] See John Patrick Brennan, Jr., *The Chaucerian Text of Jerome, Adversus Jovinianum*, pp. 229–30: "Tote Europidis tragedie in mulieris [*sic*] maledicta sunt."

the Latin text of the Croucher Manuscript it appears as Euripidis, genitive form of Euripides; the glossator takes from Trevet the explanation that Philosophy calls him hers because he studied philosophy,[122] and also gives Trevet's citation of the historian Eutropius, as if he were the author Boethius meant. Chaucer renders the phrase as "my disciple Euripidis."[123]

Chaucer would certainly have found Jerome's comment to be a much sourer assessment of the subject matter of tragedy than that provided by Boethius and the Croucher gloss. Whereas Boethius characterizes all tragedies as outcries against the disasters caused by Fortune, Jerome says that all tragedies are bursting with the disasters caused by women: "Everything in swollen tragedies, everything that subverts honor, cities, and kingdoms, is connected with disputes over wives and whores. The hands of parents are armed against their children, unspeakable meals are prepared, and because of the rape of one light woman Europe and Asia fight a ten-year war."[124] A reader could easily conclude that Jerome is speaking, like Isidore after him, principally of "the crimes of scelerate kings" who came to destruction, even though he lays the chief blame upon the provocation of women. Some of Chaucer's early tragedies in the *Monk's Tale* would have confirmed the saint's satirical hyperbole, to some extent—say, those of Samson and Hercules. But Chaucer knew how to take grumpy moralizing with a grain of salt when it suited him, and Jerome's remarks would no doubt have confirmed Ovid's observation (if Chaucer knew it) that love is an inevitable component of tragedy. Jerome's example of the world war fought over Helen might have reminded him of his own Trojan tragedy, *Troilus and Criseyde*. But his attitude towards love and women in this tragedy, in spite of what the God of Love might imply in the *Legend of Good Women*, or of what later moralizing critics might allege, is sympathetic rather than satirical, and compassionate rather than disdainful.

Jerome deflates his tragic theme to a ridiculous level when he tells of Philip of Macedon's domestic woes: the mighty monarch was reduced to quoting lines from tragedies to cheer himself up when his wife shut him out of his own bedroom. A different reduction of the scale of tragedy is to be seen in a section of John of Salisbury's *Policraticus* that Chaucer may have used for *The Wife of Bath's Prologue*: namely, the story of the Widow of Ephesus who murdered her husband, which John says was told by a *tragicus*.[125] But it would hardly have shaken his view that the prosperity preceding tragic adversity normally entailed high social standing.

In summary: whatever additional material Chaucer is likely to have read on the subject of tragedy, there is no reason to think that he ever appreciably altered his original view, which he derived from his glossed copy of the *Consolation of Philosophy*. Tragedy was normally, though not always, written in

---

[122]   Croucher MS on Boethius, book 3 pr. 7: "*Euripidis mei*, scilicet quia philosophiam studuit" (fol. 80, ed. Silk, p. 281).

[123]   Chaucer, *Boece*, book 3 pr.7 (*Riverside Chaucer*, p. 427).

[124]   Jerome, *loc. cit.*

[125]   John of Salisbury, *Policraticus* 8.11 (cols. 753B–55A); IDEAS AND FORMS, p. 81; see Robert A. Pratt, "A Note on Chaucer and the *Policraticus* of John of Salisbury." Cf. Amnon Linder, "The Knowledge of John of Salisbury in the Late Middle Ages," pp. 911–12.

verse (no. 7 of the characteristics of tragedy outlined above), and could be recited like other verse (9); it was a narrative account (15) that usually dealt with persons of high standing (2) and began in joy (11a) and ended in sorrow (4); and there was emphasis on Fortune, that is, the unexpected (14), and on lamentation (5).

There is no sign that he knew of or subscribed to other possible characteristics. Tragedy was by no means restricted to dialogue (8), or acted out (10); it was not obsolete (6) but current (16); it was not necessarily limited to stories of crime (1), or written in high style (3). I have not yet dealt with the last point, but it should be obvious. Chaucer's only discussion of high style seems to have come from a misreading of *stilo alio* as *stilo alto* in his copy of Petrarch's retelling of Boccaccio's story of Griselda.[126] Originally, Chaucer interpreted Petrarch to be saying that he wrote the whole tale in high style: "Therfore Petrak writeth / This storie, which with heigh stile he enditeth" (1147–48). But he takes a different view when he comes to incorporate it into the *Canterbury Tales*. Now he believes that only Petrarch's introduction is written in high style. This is evident from the exchange between the Host and the Clerk in the Prologue. The Host contrasts high style with plain style, high style being the sort of thing one uses when writing a letter to a king; it is filled with rhetorical terms, colors, and figures, and has no place in a story dealing with "som murie thyng of aventures" (line 15). The Clerk agrees that high style should have no part in his story (which in general is quite serious and could easily have had a tragic ending); but he asserts that Petrarch has used high style only at the beginning of his work, in the prologue where he describes northern Italy. He gives a brief summary of the prologue, but says he will not repeat it in full. In his opinion, it is not essential to the narrative, but simply serves as a means of introducing it:

> And treweley, as to my juggement,
> Me thynketh it a thyng impertinent,
> Save that he wole conveyen his mateere.   (53–55)

Chaucer probably believed that high style was not a necessary ingredient for any form of poetry, tragedy included.

THE LESSONS OF TRAGEDY

Let us now examine the *Monk's Tale* more closely, to see how Chaucer first put the concept of tragedy into practice. It is generally thought that Chaucer wrote the tragedies he gave to the Monk at a date earlier than the period of the *Canterbury Tales*, say around 1374, after his first trip to Italy, when he would have acquired the Italian sources he draws upon.[127] If so, this would

---

[126] This misreading is preserved in a marginal excerpt in some copies of the *Clerk's Tale*; see the *Riverside Chaucer* notes to lines 41 and 1142 (pp. 880, 883).

[127] See the discussion of the *Riverside Chaucer* editor, Susan H. Cavanaugh, pp. 929–30, following F. N. Robinson. Noel Harold Kaylor, Jr., "Chaucer's Use of the Word *Tragedy*: A Seman-

mean that Chaucer acquired, or saw, a copy of the *De casibus* only months after Boccaccio first released it, according to Vittorio Zaccaria's chronology. Only the stanza on Bernabo Visconti, who died at the end of 1385, would have had to be written later. The protagonists of two of the other "Modern Instances," Peter of Spain and Peter Lusignan of Cyprus, both died in 1369, and the fourth instance, Hugelino, is much less modern.

The main reason for such an early assignment to the tragedies seems to be a perception of extreme simplemindedness in the stories, a judgment that Chaucer was clearly not working at the full artistic level of his later period. Yet he was doing sophisticated things in the 1370s as well as later. More important than the time in which he wrote the tragedies, one could argue, is the way in which he wrote them. Chaucer has almost always been found to be much less interesting when he abridges than when he expands, since the need for compression allegedly restricted his powers as a creative translator. A similar judgment normally holds for the "chapters" of the *Legend of Good Women*, all or most of which must have been written in the late 1380s, between the *Troilus* and the *Canterbury Tales*. These stories of disappointed love have generally not been well received in our time as artistic successes, in spite of some revisionist attempts at revaluation.[128] Whether or not Chaucer recognized shortcomings in them, he made fun of them through the mouthpiece of the Man of Law in the Introduction to his tale; similarly, as we shall see, he has another confident critic, Harry Bailly, give voice proleptically to the usual present-day assessment of the tragedies.

The format of the *Monk's Tale* could be justified from that of the *De casibus*: Chaucer was simply keeping within the same elementary limits set up by Boccaccio. (We should note that modern-day reception of the *De casibus* has generally been no warmer than that given to the *Monk's Tale*.)[129] At any rate, whatever our opinion, or even Chaucer's later opinion, of the artistic quality of the tragedies, such judgments are not a good basis for a chronological placement of the series.

The *Boece* is usually assigned to 1380 or later, since Chaucer's use of the

tic Analysis," p. 444, makes the interesting suggestion that the early set of stories were not conceived of as tragedies but only *De casibus* accounts, and that Chaucer added the material on tragedy to the first and last stanzas only at the time that he wrote the Monk's Prologue, intending his audience to recognize that the Monk was drawing on a very limited and superficial notion of tragedy (as compared to the tragedy of *Troilus and Criseyde*).

[128] Robert W. Frank, Jr., *Chaucer and the Legend of Good Women*, started the revisionism by arguing for Chaucer's skilful use of *abbreviatio* and other rhetorical strategies. More recently the legends have received renewed attention from the perspective of gender studies, but with varied conclusions. For instance, Carolyn Dinshaw, *Chaucer's Sexual Poetics*, argues that Chaucer's narrator "produces a dull text and wearies of it. . . . The narrator's excising of the women's acts of honor and virtue, or recrimination and revenge—his rendering of all the fables as 'the same old story'—constitutes this masculine narrative strategy of weariness: he makes his heroines and the fables boring because they would otherwise terrify" (p. 86). Elaine Tuttle Hansen, "Irony and the Antifeminist Narrator in Chaucer's *Legend of Good Women*," p. 29, makes a similar argument. In contrast, Jill Mann, *Geoffrey Chaucer*, argues for "a groundswell of seriousness" beneath the mannered surface of the work (p. 32); "Chaucer does not simply slant the old stories so that they favour women; he also makes them into expressions of a peculiarly female ethos, based on the 'pite' to which Criseyde had given such a bad name" (p. 39).

[129] See specifically the judgments of Hortis and Koeppel, given in chap. 5 below, p. 213.

Consolation is particularly noticeable in the works conjecturally dated to that time; and, as we have seen from his admonition to Adam the Scribe, it was being copied at the same time as the *Troilus*. But we have also seen that Chaucer must have had his glossed copy of Boethius close at hand when he wrote the first of the "*Monk's Tale* stanzas," since it relies on the glossator's unique definition of tragedy. The similar definition in the Monk's Prologue could, of course, be based on the first stanza rather than upon a re-reading of his glossed text or prose translation.

Insofar as the list of tragic media contained in the Prologue applies to the tragedies that follow, the hexametric form would apply to Ovid's *Metamorphoses*, which Chaucer is probably referring to in the Hercules account ("somme clerkes," line 2127), and to Lucan's *Pharsalia*, cited in the tragedy *De Julio Cesare* (2719). He found stories in other meters in the *Roman de la Rose* and the *Inferno*, and he was no doubt thinking of *Heroides IX*, that is, *Dejanira Herculi*, as well as the *Metamorphoses*, in his *Tragedy of Hercules*. The prose works upon which he draws are mainly the Latin Vulgate Bible (used directly or indirectly), Boethius's *Consolation*, Vincent's *Speculum historiale* (or, to judge from the title that he gives Vincent's work in the *Legend of Good Women*, namely, *Estoryal Myrour*, which seems to have the French prosthetic *e*, he may have been using John de Vignay's translation, completed in 1333),[130] and Boccaccio's *De casibus* and *De mulieribus*. Only the last stanza of the Zenobia tragedy can be traced with certainty to the *De casibus*, the rest of it being taken from the *De mulieribus*; however, the influence of the *De casibus* should probably be recognized in other of the tragedies, notably those of Hercules and Hugelino. But it is probable that Chaucer did not read widely in Boccaccio's "Book of Falls." The Italian author's Latin is difficult, and Chaucer's mastery of the tongue would in my view frequently not have been equal to it. Nevertheless, Chaucer was obviously impressed by the idea of the work, and it seems that he gave its title to his own series: *Heere bigynneth the Monkes Tale de casibus virorum illustrium.*[131] The Monk is probably referring to Boccaccio's work when he says he has a hundred tragedies in his cell, and also when he apologizes for not telling the stories "after hir ages" (1987), in view of the determinedly chronological order of the *De casibus*. In Chaucer's original series, he was fairly chronological up through Zenobia, though unlike Boccaccio he places Samson before Hercules. But then he moved from Zenobia's third-century Christian era back to the first with Nero, and then back to the sixth century before Christ with Holofernes, a general of Nabuchodonosor. He ended in the same century with Croesus, following upon Antiochus, Alexander, and Julius Caesar, who date from the

[130] See Claudine A. Chavannes-Mazel, *The Miroir historial of Jean le Bon: The Leiden Manuscript and Its Related Copies.* Dr. Chavannes-Mazel tells me that none of the thirty-eight surviving manuscripts of Vignay's work has a title corresponding to Chaucer's, and none is of English provenance; but we will see below in chap. 6 that Caxton did draw on Vignay a hundred years after Chaucer's time, presumably using a copy that has not survived.

[131] This designation of the tale as *De casibus* appears to have been Chaucer's own doing, for, though it appears in only fifteen of the fifty-one manuscripts, it is not restricted to a single manuscript type. See Robert K. Root, "The Monk's Tale," p. 615. The late-fifteenth-century Huntington Library MS 144 (formerly Huth) has no rubric or title at the beginning of the *Monk's Tale*, but on subsequent pages it has the running title of *The Fall of Princes.* See below, chap. 4, p. 150.

second, third, and first centuries before Christ, respectively. It would therefore not be incongruous for Chaucer to have placed the Modern Instances
between Zenobia and Nero, where most manuscripts put them. I accept the
argument that the longer version of the Nuns' Priest's Prologue (which I take
to be the final version), where the Host clearly refers to the ending of the *Tragedy of Croesus*, proves that this tragedy continued to be the ending of the
Monk's Tale after the Modern Instances were added.[132]

Let us discern, as a working hypothesis, four chronological stages in the
composition of the *Monk's Tale* and its links. First, Chaucer composed the
original thirteen tragedies in the early 1380s; then, in 1386, when he was com-
pleting the *Troilus*, he added the Modern Instances; next, he gave the set of
tragedies to the Monk, introduced by the Monk's definition of tragedy and
"interrupted" by the Host's complaint; and, finally, the Knight was made
the interrupter (as we shall discuss below).

We know by now that it is not true that "Chaucer adds nothing important to
Boccaccio's conception of tragedy."[133] It was Chaucer's idea to add the very
notion of tragedy to Boccaccio's collection of stories, and to compose a
series of his own in accord with his understanding of tragedy. And, unlike
Boccaccio, he enunciates at the very beginning a pair of universally valid lessons. He first explains the tragic mode, which is lamentation over the fallen
great:

> I wol biwaille, in manere of tragedie,
> The harm of hem that stoode in heigh degree,
> And fillen so that ther nas no remedie
> To brynge hem out of hir adversitee.   (1991–94)

He then draws the lessons:

> For certein, whan that Fortune list to flee,
> Ther may no man the cours of hire withholde.
> Lat no man truste on blynd Prosperitee;
> Be war by thise ensamples trewe and olde.   (1995–98)

It is true that Boccaccio often preaches on these themes in the *De casibus*, but
they are meant to be subordinate to his chief purpose, of making vicious
leaders fear the judgments of God by seeing historical examples. As we saw,
Boccaccio's implied moral, that the wicked in high places will invariably
receive their just deserts, is not a valid generalization. Sometimes great men
suffer falls that can be attributed to their vices, sometimes not. But one
cannot argue against Chaucer's maxim that when one is going to fall, one
will fall; or his warning that Prosperity, especially when she is blind, is
worthy of no greater confidence than Fortune herself. Apart from lamentation, the proper reactions to these situations are, respectively, resignation (of
the sort that Theseus preaches at the end of the *Knight's Tale*) and caution.

---

[132] See *Riverside Chaucer*, pp. 930, 1132.
[133] Farnham, *Medieval Heritage*, p. 131.

The second lesson is contained in the last line: "Beware." The first lesson is well expressed by Walter in the *Clerk's Tale*:

> No man may alwey han prosperitee.
> With evene herte I rede yow t'endure
> The strook of Fortune or of Aventure.   (810–12)

Another characterization of tragedy comes in the last stanza of the tragedy of Croesus, which is clearly meant to close the compilation; in the Ellesmere manuscript, it is followed by the rubric *Explicit Tragedia*. As we have seen, Chaucer is drawing on Fortune's rhetorical question in the *Consolation of Philosophy*. But he has changed the question to a statement, and he draws a lesson not present in the Boethian passage:

> Tragedies noon oother maner thyng
> Ne kan in syngyng crie ne biwaille
> But that Fortune alwey wole assaile
> With unwar strook the regnes that been proude;
> For whan men trusteth hire, thanne wol she faille,
> And covere hir brighte face with a clowde.   (2761–66)

We can infer Boethius's meaning to be that Fortune frequently overthrows happy kingdoms, and that this is the constant subject of lamentation in tragedies. But there is no suggestion that Fortune will invariably act this way, for it is her nature to be unpredictable, not only as to *when* she will strike, but also *whom* she will strike and *if* she will strike. In fact, just before asking her question about tragedies, Fortune gives Croesus as an example of how she sometimes unexpectedly rescues a person who has suffered a fall and lost all hope.

One might think, however, that Chaucer has altered the Boethian frame of reference at the end of his tragic sequence by substituting "proud" for "happy." It has usually been assumed that he has thereby injected the idea of sin into his definition of tragedy. But it may be that he chose the word proud mainly for the sake of the rhyme, and that he meant it to mean no more than "noble," as in his prose translation of Boethius's Latin: "realmes of greet nobleye." If so, he would not be designating primarily the vice of pride, though it certainly could be included in its connotation, but rather a condition of magnificence and high standing. This is a sense of the word common in Chaucer's time as well as our own, as when one speaks of a proud horse or a proud castle.[134] The same is true of the Latin *superbus*, which (for example) Benvenuto da Imola applies to tragedy: "Tragedia est stilus altus et superbus."[135] But we must also look to the context of Chaucer's *Tragedy of Croesus* for the specific flavor of the word. The pride that goes before Croesus's fall does not seem to be the sort of capital sin that is defiant of God and

---

[134] See *MED* s.v. "proud," 4a: "noble, excellent, splendid"; 4b: "noble in bearing or appearance."

[135] TRAGEDY AND COMEDY, p. 49 n. 21.

punished by God, as is that of Antiochus.[136] Rather, it is the foolish and misplaced confidence in Fortune and Prosperity warned against in the opening
stanza of the series, and versified in the final couplet: reigns are proud when
they put their trust in Fortune, and it is then that she will be found wanting—
if not always, at least often.

After Croesus was caught "amyddes al his pryde" (2729), he was delivered
from the stake by a sudden rain. This is the event referred to by Fortune in
Boethius, and Chaucer indicates that Croesus himself was aware that he
owed his escape to Fortune; but this thought only led him to believe that her
favor made him invincible. He has a dream,

> Of which he was so proud and eek so fayn
> That in vengeance he al his herte sette.   (2741–42)

We get the impression that Croesus is not so much morally at fault as intellectually derelict. Military vengeance on the part of a ruler is not automatically
sinful and not necessarily wrong on the level of policy unless it is ill-timed.
We must remember that Croesus's foe is a secular king, Cyrus, and not the
people of God, as in the case of Antiochus.[137]

Croesus's pride increases (2746), at least until his daughter Phanye explains
to him the significance of the dream; then, for all we know from Chaucer's
account, he realizes the worst: Fortune is on the move against him, and nothing can stop her. In Chaucer's other major source for this tragedy, the
Roman de la Rose, after the daughter interprets his dream, she gives him a
rather confused moral instruction: he is to leave his pride and become courte-
ous and kindly, and then he will apparently be in line for Fortune's gift of her
daughter Nobility. But whether or not such a conversion on Croesus's part
would make Fortune revise her plans to ambush him, as indicated by his
dream, is not made clear. In any case, he does not humble himself in any way,
but, full of pride and folly, he thinks all his deeds wise, no matter what great
outrages he commits. Even so, however, his pride is not the sort that directly
challenges the divine power, for he is confident that all the gods are on his
side, as indicated by his own interpretation of his dream.[138]

Chaucer reduces the viciousness of Croesus's pride, whether by design or
simply as a result of his abridgment, and brings it into line with the Boethian
context of Fortune's discourse. After recounting Phanye's prediction, he
simply shows how it was verified:

> Anhanged was Cresus, the proude kyng;
> His roial trone myghte hym nat availle.   (2759–60)

---

[136] He speaks of Antiochus in these terms: "His hye pride, his werkes venymus" (2577); "Fortune hym hadde enhaunced so in pride" (2583); "wenynge that God ne myghte his pride abate"
(2590); "God daunted al his pride and al his boost" (2609); "swich gerdoun as bilongeth unto
pryde" (2630).

[137] William C. Strange, "The *Monk's Tale*: A Generous View," p. 170, rightly stresses the ambiguity of Croesus's condition.

[138] Jean de Meun, *Roman de la Rose* 6483–6589. See Richard A. Dwyer, *Boethian Fictions*, pp.
35–49, esp. 42.

This statement is followed by the general characterization of tragedy quoted above.

It is clear from Chaucer's version of *De casibus* that sin sometimes brings about one's fall, but not always. Whereas Boccaccio's faulty introductory admonition was, "Moderate your prosperity, and thereby profit from the falls of others," with the implied promise: "Stop sinning and you will be all right," Chaucer's is: "Falls can come to anyone; do not trust in prosperity." Boccaccio's rule is faulty because often contrary to fact: villains can go through life without a fall, and falls can befall the repentant and even those who have never sinned. Chaucer simply tells us to become aware of the facts of life. But he does not leave us there. He enunciates a corollary, a plan of action, namely, "Beware." That is, by taking precautions against falls, one may sometimes avoid or prevent them. Precautionary measures include not only refraining from sin (thereby preventing punitive falls organized by God), but also by following the counsels of ordinary prudence. At times, of course, neither virtue nor alertness suffices to prevent disaster; such is Zenobia's case, for, as far as we are told, she did not put a foot wrong. Fortune simply had had enough of her (2347, 2367). Or, translated into plain unmetaphorical English, external obstacles became insuperable and she was defeated, through no fault or defect of her own.

Let us do a census of the Monk's tragedies, or, rather, Chaucer's early tragedies, which I assume were given to the Monk virutally unchanged from their original form.[139] Personal sin is clearly a causal factor in the falls of Lucifer, Adam, Nabuchodonosor, Balthasar, Nero, Holofernes, and Antiochus; it is not so in the tragedies of Zenobia, Pedro of Spain, Pierre of Cyprus, Hugelino, Alexander, Caesar, or the subtragedy of Pompey (2687–94). Samson and Hercules fall not because of sin but because of the fault of "unwariness," and Croesus falls because of foolish overconfidence. Chaucer does not know why Bernabo was slain; but there is clearly betrayal involved, as there is in several other cases: Samson, Pedro, Pierre, Hugelino, Alexander, Caesar, perhaps Hercules. Holofernes is an evil man rightly deceived by a good woman; the term "betrayal" would be inappropriate in this case.

The stories of Samson and Hercules are particularly interesting. Chaucer was well aware of sins for which they could be punished, but he does not mention them. Like Boccaccio, he uses the Samson story as an excuse to attack women and the folly of placing one's trust in them. (Surprisingly, Chaucer does not touch on this theme in the one-stanza *Tragedy of Adam*; but it, like the *Tragedy of Lucifer*, may have been added at the last minute to fill out the series.) Chaucer also parallels Boccaccio by noting that Samson's thirst was satisfied through divine aid (2039–46).[140] But unlike Boccaccio Chaucer deliberately mutes Samson's sinfulness, specifically his lechery. He does not mention the *meretrix* of Gaza with whom Samson slept before carrying off the city gates (2047–51), and he identifies the *mulier* Dalida whom he later

---

[139] I will discuss this point below. My classification of the tragedies draws on that given by Paul G. Ruggiers, "Towards a Theory of Tragedy in Chaucer," pp. 90–91.

[140] See Aiken, "Vincent of Beauvais," pp. 57–58, for other indications of Boccaccio's influence.

loved[141] not as a *meretricula*, Boccaccio's term, but as his second wife.[142] It is true that Chaucer also calls her Samson's "lemman" (2063), but though this term can mean the male or female equivalent of "whore" at times, as it does for the Manciple, at other times it means nothing more than "sweetheart," as when Absalom uses it repeatedly to Alison or when Sir Thopas, who "was chaast and no lechour," wants an elf-queen as his lemman, since no woman in the world is worthy to be his "make."[143] The word was also widely used in Chaucer's day in highly spiritual senses.[144]

In the next tragedy Chaucer uses lemman once again to refer to a wife, namely, Hercules's wife Dejanira.[145] Chaucer first blames her for Hercules's fate, but then ostentatiously makes a point of not accusing her, since, as he says, some clerks (notably Ovid, of course) excuse her (2127). But he quietly refrains from mentioning Hercules's illicit love for Iole and Omphale, which was a material cause of his downfall; and he indicates by indirection that the only contributory failing of his own, apart from trust in Fortune, was a lack of self-knowledge:

> Thus starf this worthy, myghty Hercules.
> Lo, who may truste on Fortune any throwe?
> For hym that folweth al this world of prees,[146]
> Er he be war, is ofte yleyd ful lowe.
> Ful wys is he that kan hymselven knowe!   (2135–39)

Alexander is another great conqueror and ruler, who had a weakness for women (like Samson) and for wine (unlike Samson):

---

[141] See Judges 16.1 for the *meretrix* of Gaza, also mentioned by Boccaccio, and 16.4 for Dalida (this rather than "Dalila" is the usual spelling in the late medieval copies of the Vulgate Bible that I have checked): "Post hec amavit mulierem que habitabat in valle Sorech."

[142] See line 2063, "To his wyves toolde he his secree"; cf. lines 2091–94, where he draws the lesson that men should not confide in their wives.

[143] *Manciple's Tale* 204–39; *Miller's Tale* 3278, 3280, 3700, 3705, 3719, 3726; *Thopas* 745, 788–92.

[144] For instance, in *Piers Plowman*, Poverty is "a lemman of alle clennesse" (B 14.300), and Peace speaks of "Love that is my lemman" who commissioned her and her sister Mercy to save mankind (B.18.182–83). The *MED* cites Chaucer's use of the term for Dalida as an example of its meaning of "wife" (sense 1d).

[145] Chaucer may have been inspired to follow Samson with Hercules by Boccaccio's mentioning of authorities who identify the two figures, saying, for instance, that the Nemean lion is to be understood as the beast that Samson killed, though Boccaccio himself refuses to assert or deny the identification: "Nec defuerunt qui leonem ab eo occisum Nemeeum dicerent, et Herculem arbitrarentur Samsonem. Quod etsi non affirmo contradicere tamen nescio quid prohibet." *De casibus* A 1 (p. 45); cf. B 1.17.8 (p 86) (I should note that Robert K. Root, "The Monk's Tale," *Sources and Analogues*, pp. 626–28, claims to have corrected the B text to A, which Chaucer would have used; but in the case of the second sentence quoted here, he gives the B wording). But the notion may have added to his earlier determination not to include a history of Hercules in his collection (see above, chap. 1, pp. 33–34). Boccaccio considered Hercules to be a real enough Greek hero earlier still when he related his rescue of Theseus from the lower world: A 1 (p. 37); B 1.10.17 (p. 54), and later, when he repeatedly mentions him, usually in close association with Samson, as the victim of women, in his homily *In mulieres*: A 1 (pp. 46–47); B 1.18 13–14, 17, 19, 25 (pp. 94–98).

[146] This line means: "For he whom all this world of turbulence follows."

> Save wyn and wommen, no thing myghte aswage
> His hye entente in armes and labour,
> So was he ful of leonyn corage.   (2644–46)

But these peccadilloes are in no way signaled as reasons for his being poisoned by his own people; rather they are mentioned as slightly crimping his praiseworthy (and not sinful) feats as a conqueror of the wide world.

After the tragedies of Samson and Hercules come those of Nabuchodonosor and Balthasar. In each, pride is clearly portrayed as a sin against God (2167–69, 2212, 2223–25), and as cause of the respective falls. Nabuchodonosor's divine restoration is a clear contradiction of Chaucer's definitions, which limit him to falls for which there is no remedy; but his recovery serves to accentuate Balthasar's guilt and folly. Nero's pride is similar; but his fall is attributed to the whim of a suddenly moral Fortune (2519–26), whereas in the next tragedy, Holofernes, than whom no one was more "pompous in heigh presumpcion," was lecherously kissed by Fortune (2556–58). He was later done in by wine and woman: one night while he was drunk, Judith smote off his head. With Antiochus we are presented with the case of a sinner punished by God whose efforts to repent (2621–22) were of no avail,[147] whereas in the case of Nabuchodonosor God intervenes without any previous sign of repentence.

According to the Monk's Prologue, tragedy is the story of a person who falls from great prosperity and high degree into misery and suffers a wretched end. It is the end that counts, and though Chaucer normally describes the period of high estate, he does not do so for Hugelino, but simply lingers over his fallen state, much as we shall see Robert Henryson doing in his Chaucer-inspired tragedy, *The Testament of Cresseid*. Chaucer's account lacks all reference to Hugelino's own crimes and their terrible repercussions on earth and in hell. Rather than grieving over any faults of his own, Hugelino sounds like a completely innocent man who laments against the unfairness of Fortune: "Allas, Fortune, and weylaway! / Thy false wheel my wo al may I wyte" (2445–46); and: "From heigh estaat Fortune awey hym carf" (2457). Is this just another instance of Chaucer's arbitrary suppression of evidence of wrongdoing in a protagonist? Perhaps, but I suspect that in this case there is a different reason for his silence, which is that he did not know exactly what Hugelino's faults were. For though he advises those who wish to "hear" a longer version of the story to "read" Dante (2459–2462), he was probably inspired to limit the story as he does by Boccaccio's brief account:

Venientem Hugolinum Pisarum comitem vidi, amplissimo fletu civium suorum sevitiam ac inediam qua cum filiis perierat deflentem.[148]

(I saw Hugolinus, Count of Pisa, approaching, with abundant weeping bewailing the savagery of his people and the starvation by which he and his children perished.)

---

[147] This is in keeping with 2 Maccabees 9.12–27.
[148] Boccaccio, *De casibus* A 9 (p. 227); B 9.20.1 (p. 820).

If Boccaccio's Latin is often tortuous (it is not so in the present instance), Dante's Italian presents many more problems, and it is doubtful that Chaucer could follow very much of his more allusive and densely textured passages. His treatment of Hugelino consists of 105 lines, of which Chaucer translates only five.[149] Chaucer's forms of the count's name, Hugelinus and Hugelyn,[150] are closer to Boccaccio's Hugolinus than to Ugolino, the usual form that appears in Dante manuscripts—though it is clearly possible that Chaucer's source copy of the *Comedy* had the Hugolino spelling.

The single-stanza *Tragedy of Lucifer* resembles the treatment of Hugelino in having no formal "prosperity section"; Chaucer simply conjures up the evil spirit's former high estate in a brief flashback: "O Lucifer, brightest of angels alle" (2004). This kind of after-the-fall lament might almost be defined as "tranquillity recollected in emotion." Chaucer brings this aspect of tragedy to its height, as we shall see, in the fifth book of the *Troilus*, when Troilus revisits the places where he and Criseyde enjoyed their love. The emotional power of summoning up remembrance of things past in this way is expressed by Boethius in his objection to Philosophy: "In omni adversitate Fortune infelicissimum est genus infortunii fuisse felicem," which Chaucer translates, "In alle adversites of Fortune the moost unzeely kynde of contrarious fortune is to han ben weleful."[151] Pandarus expresses this sentiment to Troilus (3.1625–28) when he is urging one of the main lessons of the *Monk's Tale*, that falls from good fortune are often brought about through rashness and neglect. Troilus recalls Pandarus's words later, when he is on the point of losing Criseyde (4.481–83), after Pandarus has made an awkward attempt to console him over his loss (something that never happens in the *Monk's Tale*) and has unthinkingly suggested that the memory of his happiness should be enough for him.

We saw above that the lessons at the end of Chaucer's early series of tragedies (Fortune will *always* assail proud realms, and fail when men trust her) are expressed in a more absolute way than those at the beginning (when Fortune flees, she flees; don't blindly trust in prosperity). We will find that something similar happens at the end of the *Troilus*. The tragedies of the *Monk's Tale* might seem to give the impression that evil men always fall because of their evil, but this is true only of the protagonists who have been singled out, not of their antagonists. However, one would no doubt be justified in thinking that it could easily happen to these antagonists as well. As for the idea that the foolish inevitably fall because of their foolishness, it is, of course, an exaggeration: a generalization rhetorically elevated to the status of a universal truth. The foolish are clearly more likely to end with a bang as time goes on

---

[149] See the analysis of Piero Boitani, "The *Monk's Tale:* Dante and Boccaccio," p. 54. Boitani also argues for the influence of Boccaccio's sentence on Chaucer's tragedy, but he assumes that Chaucer could read Dante's whole account perfectly, and therefore he sees a different rationale for Chaucer's omissions of Ugolino's faults and other discrepancies from Dante. See also his "Two Versions of Tragedy: Ugolino and Hugelyn," which I mentioned above in the Introduction as a good example of treating tragedy from a modern perspective.

[150] The Ellesmere and Hengwrt rubrics, *De Hugelino Comite de Pize,* give a correct Latin form for Hugelinus but not for Pisa. The other four texts of the six-text group have similar forms.

[151] Chaucer, *Boece,* book 2 pr. 4 (*Riverside Chaucer*, p. 411); Croucher MS, fols. 41v–42, 44r–v (ed. Silk, pp. 159, 166–67).

than are the prudent; but then time will bring everyone to some kind of adversity, for everyone must die.

An obvious difference between the *Monk's Tale* and the *Troilus* is that in the latter we have a sad story touchingly elaborated, whereas in the former there are mere sketches of stories hardly more moving or interesting than bare "arguments" of plays, such as those that Trevet supplies for each of Seneca's tragedies. Nevertheless, as in the case of Boccaccio's repetitious *casus virorum*, it is possible that some people might have found his set of miniature tragedies impressive. Chaucer himself must have thought them effective when he first compiled them. But when it came time to insert them into the *Canterbury Tales*, he clearly had second thoughts. He could, of course, afford to take his early efforts at tragedy lightly, since in the meantime he had written a masterful example of the form.

At first, Chaucer seems to have ruled out entirely the effectiveness of the early series, by having the Host interrupt the Monk and urge him to change to something more interesting. But on further second thoughts, Chaucer gave the function of interrupter to the Knight and portrayed the Monk's performance as badly received for two completely different sets of reasons. The reactions of the Knight and the Host, respectively, resemble those of the trial readers of Petrarch's experiment in reader response: he gave his history of Griselda to two friends, and the first, a Paduan, was so overcome by the account of her sufferings that he could not stop weeping, whereas his Veronese colleague found her unbelievable and was totally unmoved.[152] Similarly, the Knight is distressed by the Monk's stories, whereas the Host is bored.

[152] Petrarch, *Epistola senilis* 17.4, pp. 170–71: "Dicam tibi quid de hac historia, quam fabulam dixisse malim, mihi contigerit. Legit eam primum communis amicus Patavinus, vir altissimi ingenii multiplicisque notitie, et cum epistole medium vix transisset, subito fletu preventus substitit. Post modicum vero, cum in manus eam resumpsisset, firmato animo perlecturus, ecce iterum, quasi ad condictum rediens, lecturam gemitus interrumpit. Fassus itaque se non posse prodesse, eam uni suorum comitum docto satis viro legendam tradidit" ("I shall tell you what happened to me concerning this history, or fable, as I would prefer to call it. The first to read it was a common friend of ours in Padua, a man of the highest wit and varied accomplishments, and when he had barely got through the middle of the epistle, he was overcome by sudden weeping and stopped. But after a while, when he had taken it into his hands again and was set to read it through to the end with confirmed purpose, almost as if by prearrangement, his groaning interrupts the reading. Confessing therefore that he could not do it, he gave it to one of his companions, a man of good education, to read"). After commending this friend for his great sensitivity, Petrarch goes on to tell of another mutual friend, a man of much more limited capacities, who, hearing of what had happened to the Paduan, wanted to read it for himself: "Legit eam totam, nec alicubi substitit, nec frons obductior, nec vox fractior, nec lachryme nec singultus intervenere. Et in finem, 'Ego etiam,' inquit, 'flessem, nam et pie res et verba accommodata fletum suadebant, nec ego duri cordis sum, nisi quod ficta omnia credidi, et credo. Nam si vera essent, que usquam mulier, vel romana vel cujuslibet gentis, hanc Griseldim equatura sit? Ubi, queso, tantus amor conjugalis? Ubi par fides? Ubi tam insignis patientia atque constantia?' " ("He read all of it without stopping at any point, with no additional knitting of his brow or cracking of his voice, and no tears or sobs intervened. And at the end he said, 'I too would have wept, for the pitiful subject matter and the words in which it is fittingly told were conducive to tears, and I am not hard-hearted, except that I believed that the whole thing was sheer invention, and I still believe it. For if it were true, what woman of any time or place, whether Roman or of any other race, would be equal to this Griselda? Where, I ask you, is there such great marital love? Where the like fidelity? Where such outstanding patience and constancy?' "). There is a looser translation in Robert P. Miller, *Chaucer: Sources and Backgrounds*, p. 139.

However, though the Knight has clearly been greatly moved by the stories, he finds the experience unpleasant. The Monk has failed both to instruct and to please: the Knight takes no notice of the lessons set forth, but instead complains of the depressing effect of the stories:

> "Hoo!" quod the Knyght, "good sire, namoore of this!
> That ye han seyd is right ynough, ywis,
> And muchel moore; for litel hevynesse
> Is right ynough to muche folk, I gesse.
> I seye for me, it is a greet disese,
> Whereas men han been in greet welthe and ese,
> To heeren of hire sodeyn fal, allas!"   (2767–73)

The last two lines constitute yet another definition of tragedy, to which the Knight opposes his preference for stories in a rags-to-riches genre.

The Host, for his part, is also clearly disappointed in the Monk, whom he had thought of earlier as the best person to match the Knight's story.[153] He gives several reasons for approving of the Knight's interruption:

> Ye seye right sooth: this Monk, he clappeth lowde;
> He spak how Fortune covered with a clowde
> I noot nevere what; and als of a tragedie
> Right now ye herde; and, pardee, no remedie
> It is for to biwaille ne compleyne
> That that is doon; and als it is a peyne,
> As ye han seyd, to here of hevynesse.   (2781–87)

He includes himself along with the Knight in the number of those who find sad endings painful. He too ignores the Monk's exemplary purposes in telling his tale: he considers it merely a matter of crying over spilled milk. But it is evident that he has not been very attentive to what the Monk was saying; he missed the point of the last image, of Fortune covering her face: he does not connect it with the theme of tragedy, and he seems to think that the Monk has spoken of a single tragedy. Our suspicions are soon confirmed: like Petrarch's friend from Verona, Harry has been untouched by the Monk's tales of woe. In fact, he was stupefied into a state of unwariness and was in imminent danger of suffering a fall:

> For sikerly, nere clynkyng of youre belles,
> That on youre bridel hange on every syde,
> By hevene Kyng that for us alle dyde,
> I sholde er this han fallen doun for sleep,
> Althogh the slough had never been so deep;
> Thanne hadde your tale al be toold in veyn.
> For certeinly, as that thise clerkes seyn,

153   *Miller's Prologue* 3118–19.

Whereas a man may have noon audience,
Noght helpeth it to tellen his sentence.
And well I woot the substance is in me,
If any thyng shal wel reported be. (2794–04)

The Monk's main problem, then, Harry tells him as diplomatically as he can, centers not so much upon the subjects and themes of his stories, but upon their execution: he has not reported them well. A tale of hunting would be better suited to his talents (2805).

The Host's assessment is of the utmost importance for our study, for it provides us with a qualitative criterion for Chaucerian tragedy. Chaucer's general category of tragedy, like Aristotle's, is nonqualitative. As we noted in the Introduction, for Aristotle, any serious story, whether dramatic or narrative, falls into the category of tragedy. For Chaucer, tragedy is any written or recounted story that begins happily and ends sadly. In the course of the *Poetics* Aristotle gives various considerations for ranking examples of tragedy as good, bad, or in-between. Chaucer does not discuss his criteria, but instead provides examples. He gives seventeen examples of short tragedies, which attracted the praise of some early readers, notably Lydgate, but which most recent readers have evaluated as bad—agreeing with the judgment of the Host rather than with that of the Knight. Chaucer also designated a longer work, *Troilus and Criseyde*, as a tragedy, and it has in general been consistently well received. We shall try to deduce both his and others' criteria for excellence when we take up the *Troilus* in the next chapter, by using the Aristotelian method of examining the work and assessing its intended and perceived effects.

The simple but universally valid lessons of caution when appropriate and resignation when hope is gone, which we distilled from the first stanza of the *Monk's Tale*, have not been profound enough for some readers to take seriously. D. W. Robertson came up instead with a formula for Chaucerian tragedy that is much like Boccaccio's view of what he was doing with his falls of great men, that is, telling how they had gone astray. The subjects of Chaucer's tragedies, he postulates, are always morally at fault: "The tragic 'hero' turns from the way and seeks false worldly satisfactions, abandons reason and becomes subject for Fortune. In short, through some sort of cupidity the protagonist loses his free will so that when adversity or 'evil' fortune strikes, his doom has a certain inevitability."[154]

Robertson does not admit the conclusion that we reached above, that some of the tragedies told by the Monk do not fit this moral pattern. Robert Kaske does admit it, but he concludes that the tales are faultily told and that the fault is with the Monk, not Chaucer; that is, he believes that Chaucer deliberately made the Monk's morals superficial: some are facile examples of falls through pride and the other vices, while others show only "the workings of a traditionally fickle Fortune," a viewpoint that "is at best equally facile and is even more limited, in that it ignores also the ordered role of Fortune in the Boethian hierarchy." He admits that not every story "is bound to explore the

---

[154] Robertson, "Chaucerian Tragedy," p. 91.

universal design, much less according to the plan of the *De consolatione*,"[155] but he paves the way for the idea that Chaucer himself would have had a more sophisticated and philosophical notion of tragedy than he gives to the Monk. Robert Lumiansky develops this idea: not only Chaucer but every "right-thinking" audience would realize that "tragedy cannot lie in loss of earthly goods or position or even in death." He holds that the well-educated author of the *Alliterative Morte Arthure* not only, like Chaucer, excavated Fortune's remark on tragedy from Boethius, but also enlarged it to fit the whole *Consolation* and applied it to his poem about the death of Arthur: he composed it as a deliberate non-tragedy, because Arthur is saved from a tragic end by exercising the virtue of fortitude.[156] Monica McAlpine applies both the Kaske and Lumiansky trains of thought to *Troilus and Criseyde*: the narrator, another limited character like the Monk, thinks of the story of Troilus as a tragedy of Fortune; but for Chaucer himself it is not only a deliberate non-tragedy, it is a comedy, of the "Boethian" sort; and only the story of Criseyde is a tragedy of this philosophical kind: that is, it conforms to tragedy as Lady Philosophy might have defined it rather than the way that her whimsical colleague Fortune deals with it.[157]

These and similar speculations,[158] though often accompanied by interesting and valid insights into Chaucer's works, are flawed by the mistaken assumptions noted in the Introduction: that tragedy was a widely known and uniform concept in the Middle Ages, and that it was common for authors to think of themselves as writing tragedies; or, to put it another way, they are insufficiently grounded in actual traditions and practices, such as those we have surveyed above. Most often they overlook the fact that Chaucer gives a

[155] R. E. Kaske, "The Knight's Interruption of the *Monk's Tale*," pp. 263–64. Another recent assessment of the Monk's tragedies as deliberately "banalized" is that of Winthrop Wetherbee, "The Context of the *Monk's Tale*." He finds another deliberate banalization in the account of the death of Hector in *Troilus* 5.1541–57, 1562–68 (pp. 172–74), apparently (though he is not clear on this point) because Chaucer wishes to draw attention away from Hector and back to Troilus. Cf. Renate Haas, "Chaucer's *Monk's Tale*: An Ingenious Criticism of Early Humanist Conceptions of Tragedy," who hypothesizes that Chaucer deliberately made the Monk a blunderer who takes up "the fashionable tragedy" and performs in such a way as to constitute a comment on discussions of tragedy by Petrarch and other contemporary Italians. But she is vague both on where these humanist ideas of tragedy were to be found and how Chaucer and his audience could have learned about them. See Larry Scanlon's critique, *Narrative, Authority, and Power*, pp. 218–19.

[156] Robert M. Lumiansky, "The Alliterative *Morte Arthure*, the Concept of Medieval Tragedy, and the Cardinal Virtue Fortitude," pp. 98–99, 101, 117. See my "Non-Tragedy of Arthur," p. 108.

[157] Monica E. McAlpine, *The Genre of Troilus and Criseyde*, chap. 4: " 'Litel myn tragedye': The Narrator of *Troilus and Criseyde* (pp. 116–47); chap. 5, "The Boethian Comedy of Troilus" (pp. 148–80); chap. 6, "The Boethian Tragedy of Criseyde" (pp. 182–217). Compare Ruth Morse, "Absolute Tragedy: Allusions and Avoidances," p. 10: "The poem may be a literary creation called 'tragedy,' but from within it denies not only its own tragic content, but the idea of tragedy itself."

[158] See, for instance, Farnham, *Medieval Heritage*, pp. 409, 446–47; Joseph J. Mogan, *Chaucer and the Theme of Mutability*, pp. 126–28; and Andrea Clough, "Medieval Tragedy and the Genre of *Troilus and Criseyde*," esp. p. 215. Compare Kaylor, "Chaucer's Use of the Word *Tragedy*," who, after criticizing Robertson's and McAlpine's notions of Chaucerian tragedy (pp. 435–37), interprets the statement of Paul Ruggiers, "Notes Towards a Theory," that we must look to Latin, French, and Italian sources for "the softer, more domestic aspects of tragedy in Chaucer" (p. 93), as a call to find softer tragedies that contrast with "the pessimistic tragedies told by the Monk," to account for the achievement of the *Troilus* (p. 438).

serious definition of tragedy that is secure from possible contamination, whether by Fortunal fickleness or by Monkish shallowness, in his gloss to Fortune's rhetorical question in *Boece*.

We shall examine the *Troilus* as a tragedy in the next chapter, but first let us attend to the question of what Chaucer is likely to have meant by "comedy."

FROM DYSTOPIA TO EUTOPIA

In contrast to the Monk's tragic formula, the Knight presents his own recipe for an entertaining story:

> The contrarie is joye and greet solas,
> As whan a man hath been in povre estaat,
> And clymbeth up and wexeth fortunat,
> And there abideth in prosperitee.
> Swich thyng is gladsom, as it thynketh me,
> And of swich thyng were goodly for to telle.   (2774–79)

Many readers have assumed that Chaucer is here presenting a definition of comedy, one that is based on one or other historical definition.[159] But since the Knight does not mention comedy, Chaucer may be doing nothing more than reversing the definition of tragedy he inherited from his glossed Boethius, book 2, prose 2, without recognizing that such a reversal could, or did, constitute a definition of comedy. If so, he may have been inspired by other glosses in his text. He in fact added a reverse-of-tragedy gloss to the preceding prose, where he forces the text to mean that wisdom can see happy turns of events beyond the menaces of Fortune:

> Wisdom loketh and mesureth the ende of thynges. And the same chaungynge from oon into another (*that is to seyn, fro adversite into prosperite*) maketh that the manaces of Fortune ne ben nat for to dreden, ne the flaterynges of hir to ben desired.[160]

Chaucer deviates here from the gloss that appears in the corresponding Latin section of the Croucher Manuscript, which gives the more likely interpretation that wisdom foresees changes for the worse as well as for the better: "in prosperitate et adversitate."[161] It may be that in Chaucer's original copy-text (of which, as we have noted, Croucher is only a copy) the gloss at this point was longer, like the one that appears a bit further on: Fortune is moved "de adversitate in prosperitatem, vel econtra."[162]

---

[159] For outlines of the variety of different understandings of comedy antedating Chaucer, see the analytical indexes of TRAGEDY AND COMEDY and IDEAS AND FORMS, s.v. "comedy."

[160] Chaucer, *Boece*, book 2 pr. 1 (*Riverside Chaucer*, p. 408).

[161] Croucher MS, gloss to book 2 pr. 1 fol. 34 (ed. Silk, p. 132); cf. Trevet: "tam in prosperitate quam in adversitate" (ed. Silk, p. 187).

[162] Croucher MS, gloss to book 2 m. 1, fol. 35v (ed. Silk, p. 138); cf. Trevet: "de adversitate in prosperitatem vel e converso" (ed. Silk, p. 192)

However, we know from the end of the *Troilus* that Chaucer was aware of the term comedy and of its meaning as a contrasting form to tragedy. After addressing his book of Troilus as a tragedy, he says that he hopes to be able "to maken in som comedye" before he dies (5.1787–88). The unusual expression "make in" probably means simply "compose."[163] Any suggestion that the line refers to Chaucer's hope of adding some humor to the *Troilus*, must surely be rejected, both because it was rare in the Middle Ages to associate humor with comedy (a point I will return to below) and also because Chaucer regards the *Troilus* as finished, except for whatever corrections Gower and Strode may suggest. He addresses it, "Go, litel bok."[164]

How would Chaucer have known that comedy was a traditional opposite to tragedy? Comedy is not mentioned in the Croucher Manuscript nor in Trevet's commentary on Boethius, nor in any of the other possible sources noted above for Chaucer's knowledge of tragedy. If he knew that Boccaccio's *Ameto,* which he seems to have drawn on for the *Franklin's Tale*, was called *Comedy of the Florentine Nymphs*, he could not have guessed that it was the opposite number to his notion of tragedy. If he registered that Dante called his *Inferno* a comedy, or knew that the whole work was called a comedy, or was named *Comedy*, or was identified as a series of three comedies,[165] he would have been no more enlightened. If he already had some idea of what a comedy was (the opposite of tragedy) when he encountered Dante's *Comedy*, he could easily have been just as mystified about the significance of the name as Petrarch was, who said he had no idea why Dante chose the title.[166] Boccaccio, as we have seen, rejected several characteristics of comedy as irrelevant to Dante's poem, and he gives the impression of clutching at the last remaining straw when he finally accepts, in a figurative sense, the turbulence-to-tranquillity criterion.[167] But the criterion is not an obvious fit. The plot-definition of comedy, like the plot-definition of tragedy, does not normally refer to a protagonist who simply witnesses some persons experiencing adversity and others experiencing prosperity, but rather to a protagonist like Aeneas who passes from adversity to prosperity in his own experiences. The *Aeneid* fulfills this definition of comedy, yet Dante in the *Inferno*, clearly operating under different notions of tragedy and comedy, calls it a tragedy in contrast to his own comedy.

Lydgate considered the *House of Fame* to be an imitation of Dante's poem: he calls it *Dante in English*.[168] If Chaucer likewise considered his work in

---

[163] So Stephen Barney, the editor of *Troilus* in the *Riverside Chaucer*, who likens it to the similar "make on" at the end of the Prologue of the *Legend of Good Women*, F 579: "And ryght thus on my *Legende* gan I make" (p. 1056).

[164] This latter consideration applies also to the interpretation that Chaucer wanted to make the *Troilus* more like Dante's *Comedy* (see below, chap. 3, p. 137 n. 85).

[165] One traditional set of rubrics identified each major section of Dante's poem as a comedy; see Lino Pertile, "*Canto-cantica-Comedia* e l'Epistola a Cangrande." This is the tradition known to Dante's son Pietro and justified by him; see TRAGEDY AND COMEDY, pp. 31–32; IDEAS AND FORMS, pp. 154–56, 204–08; "*Cangrande* and the Ortho-Dantists," p. 79.

[166] Francesco da Buti, *Commento sopra la Divina comedia*, 1:543, cites a lost letter of Petrarch's to this effect.

[167] See above, chap. 1, pp. 19–21.

[168] Lydgate, *Fall of Princes* 1.303.

such terms, he could hardly have thought of himself as writing the same kind of comedy as Dante; for one thing, the *House of Fame* has a great deal of humor, which is an ingredient only fleetingly present in the *Comedy*. Most medieval definitions of comedy either ignore the attribute of humor or at most only imply it. This would doubtless be true of any definition that may lie behind the Knight's words. Specifically, it has been noted that there is a similarity between what the Knight says and the definition of comedy given by William of Conches.[169] Conches was the source of Trevet's definition of tragedy, but Trevet did not repeat the accompanying characterization of comedy. It is entirely possible, as I suggested above, that, even if Chaucer used his mini-glossed text of Boethius almost exclusively, he occasionally consulted another commentary. If he had Conches's commentary at hand when he came to Fortune's question about tragedy, he might very well have looked up what Conches had to say. There he would have found a statement that "tragedy is a writing about great iniquities beginning in prosperity and ending in adversity; it is contrary to comedy, which begins with some adversity and ends in prosperity."[170] If Chaucer did see this gloss, he was not moved to insert the phrase about great iniquities into the definition that he found in his glossed text and which he faithfully translates. But he need not have considered Conches's definition to contradict his text definition, since he could have interpreted *iniquitates* as "inequities" as well as "iniquities." Or, if the biblical identification of *iniquitates* with *peccata* was too strong for such etymologizing,[171] it could be taken to refer to sins inflicted upon tragic protagonists rather than evils committed by them.[172] For, unlike Trevet, Conches does not bolster his definition with Isidore's statement about criminous kings, where it is clear that the protagonists are the malefactors. But Conches's further statement about tragedy containing the fetor of vices would have been harder to read away.

It may be, however, that Chaucer found comedy defined as the opposite of tragedy in some source that did not compromise his own definition of tragedy, and which did not tell him more about tragedy and comedy than he gives evidence of knowing. One such source would be Osbern of Gloucester's dictionary: "Tragedy is a mournful poem, because it begins in joy and ends in sadness; comedy is its contrary, because it begins in sadness and ends in joy."[173] Similarly, Vincent of Beauvais in book 3 of the *Speculum doctrinale* says: "Comedy is poetry changing a sad beginning to a joyful end; but tragedy is poetry with a joyful beginning that comes to a sad end." And in the next chapter he gives the nonincriminating characterizations of tragedy and comedy from book 8 of Isidore: comedy deals with private persons and joyful matters; tragedy with public affairs, histories of kings, and sorrowful

---

[169] Minnis, "Aspects," p. 359 n. 82.

[170] For the Latin text, see IDEAS AND FORMS, p. 69 n. 6.

[171] See, for instance, the *Miserere* (Psalm 50), vv. 3–5: "Dele iniquitatem meam; amplius lava me ab iniquitate mea, et a peccato meo munda me, quoniam iniquitatem meam ego cognosco, et peccatum meum contra me est semper."

[172] Compare *Miserere* v. 7: "Ecce enim in iniquitatibus conceptus sum, et in peccatis concepit me mater mea."

[173] Osbern of Gloucester, *Liber derivationum*, p. 593; text in IDEAS AND FORMS, p. 104 n. 180.

matters.[174] This would doubtless have confirmed the reference that Chaucer may have seen in Macrobius's *Commentary on the Dream of Scipio* to the comedies of Menander and his imitators as examples of fables that delight the ear.[175]

Vincent gives much different accounts of comedy in the *Speculum historiale*, which, as we have seen, Chaucer definitely did use. If he had consulted it for his *Tragedy of Antiochus* (the indications are that he used nothing more than the Second Book of Maccabees), Chaucer could have found that Plautus, a *poeta comicus* according to the rubrics, was an extremely eloquent writer of fables. From among all of his comedies, Vincent chooses to give a selection of brief moral *sententie* from the *Aulularia* (really the pseudo-Plautine *Querolus*), such as: "Sibimet esse sufficientem, primum bonum est" ("To be self-sufficient is the first good").[176]

Further on, just before telling of the death of Judas Maccabeus, Vincent cites Eusebius's *Chronicles* as noting the death of Terence of Carthage, writer of comedies. Vincent then gives Terence's auto-epitaph,[177] in which he describes the morals of people both young and old, showing how servants deceive their masters and how whores and avaricious pimps engage in trickery—all of which should make his readers cautious. In the prose account of comedy that follows, Vincent says that among the writers of comedy, Plautus and Terence are held to be the chief. Comedy means *villanus cantus*, "rustic song," but from its original rustic beginnings its cheap and lowly material was eventually formed into art by means of witty sayings (*facetie*) and an artful manner of speaking. Whence Horace's comment about the alternating "Fescennine" verses that poured forth rustic reproaches (*opprobria rustica*) (*Epistles* 2.1.145–46). There were two kinds of native Latin comedy: the *togata*, which was only about the deeds of ignoble persons, and the *pretextata*, which dealt with the deeds of noble persons; Horace reprehended both in *Ars poetica* (288). A third kind, the *palliata*, named after the *pallium*, which is the philosopher's garb among the Greeks, refers to comedies translated from the Greek into Latin, like those of Plautus and Terence. The author of comedy needed three persons other than himself to produce his work, namely, the corrector, the defender, and the reciter, and those whom Terence had were excellent: Titus Livius, who was a writer of tragedies, was his corrector, Domicius was his defender, and Calliopius his recitor. Therefore, Vincent says in his next chapter, he has decided to excerpt some brief moral sentences from Terence's comedies.[178]

---

[174] Vincent, *Speculum doctrinale* 3.109–10.

[175] Macrobius, *Commentarii in Somnium Scipionis* 1.2.8.

[176] Vincent, *Speculum historiale* 5.55 (p. 152).

[177] *Epitaphium Terentii*, edited in *Anthologia latina*, no. 487c (part 2, p. 40); attributed to Sulpicius Appollinaris (second century A.D.), teacher of Aulus Gellius, by Curt Richard Opitz, "De argumentorum metricorum latinorum arte et origine," pp. 200–01. For the text as given by Vincent and by John Capgrave, see above, p. 43, n. 33.

[178] Vincent, *Speculum historiale* 5.72–73 (pp. 158–59); most of chap. 72 is reproduced and annotated in Wilhelm Cloetta, *Komödie und Tragödie im Mittelalter*, pp. 34–35. The historian Titus Livius (Livy) is here confused with the early dramatist Livius Andronicus. In chap. 75, Vincent notes the death of a genuine author of tragedies, "Pacuvius Brundusinus, tragediarum scriptor clarus."

Lee Patterson cites Vincent's account of comedy along with characterizations by Donatus-Evanthius, Placidus, and Isidore, to suggest that "comedy is typically understood by the Middle Ages as a socially antithetical form," that is, "socially humble, realistic in its mode of representation, and festive in its occasion; and its subject matter is the private person." It is opposed to tragedy, which, as Donatus says, "aspires to historical truth"; and it is this sort of thing that Chaucer has in mind when he contrasts comedy to tragedy at the end of the *Troilus*, and when, after the noble discourse of the *Knight's Tale*, he turns to "the highly politicized *cantus villanus* of the *Miller's Tale*."[179] But this picture, intriguing as it is, depends on too unitary a notion of comedy, and it makes Chaucer too inventive in applying it.

Donatus, Placidus, and even Isidore were outside Chaucer's ken, except indirectly, and then sometimes in distorted form. Donatus would not be recovered until later, and would not surface in England until the sixteenth century;[180] but we have seen above that Donatus's statement about tragedy and historical truth was applied to comedy in Papias, whence it was cited by Walsingham. The account that Vincent transmits mixes Donatian material on tragedy with comedy in a similar way. *Fabulae praetextae* were not comedies but tragedies on Roman themes, like the *Octavia* ascribed to Seneca.[181] In the line cited from *Ars poetica* (288), Horace was actually praising such dramas.

It is doubtful that Chaucer ever saw Vincent's account of Terentian comedy; but if he did, what, can we suppose, did he make of it? Would he conclude that even after the crude rusticity of the original mode gave way to a literary form applicable to characters of both low and high estate, it was still unacceptable to a critic like Horace? That the more sophisticated Greek comedies translated by Plautus and Terence were mainly moral or philosophical discourses? That the genre was now obsolete? That, as Paul Theiner says of the medieval reader-reception of Terence, "he is an authority to be cited on the subject of human nature and the mores of men, an authority who does not suffer even in juxtaposition to biblical commentary and, in some cases, to the Scriptures themselves"?[182] We do not know. He may well have considered the account to be dealing with an archaic understanding of the term, certainly much different from comedy seen as the reverse of tragedy. It is highly unlikely that Chaucer would have been so theoretically adventurous that, of the three chronological periods of obsolete Latin comedy, which moved from crude to less crude and finally to sophisticated forms, he would have identified the French and other vernacular fabliaux with Vincent's first generation, "villainous chant" (*cantus villanus*), and his own reworkings of them as the second-generation but still declassé *comedia togata*.

[179] Lee Patterson, *Chaucer and the Subject of History*, pp. 242–43.

[180] See below, chap. 4, p. 157; and see my "Chaucer and Shakespeare on Tragedy," pp. 197–98.

[181] See Donatus 6.1: "Fabula generale nomen est; eius duae primae partes, tragoedia et comoedia; [tragoedia,] si latina argumentatio sit, praetexta dicitur; comoedia autem multas species habet: aut enim palliata est aut togata aut tabernaria aut Atellana aut mimus aut Rinthonica aut planipedia." The loss of the second *tragoedia* from the text (it has been restored by editorial conjecture) was doubtless the first step in the evolution of Vincent's statement: "Tria vero sunt genera comediarum: togata, pretextata, palliata."

[182] Paul Theiner, "The Medieval Terence," p. 244.

The question arises whether Chaucer could have considered fabliaux to be not old-style but new-style comedies, perhaps relying on Geoffrey of Vinsauf. If Chaucer did not have the advantage of knowing what Geoffrey says in his *Documentum de arte versificandi*, that the sort of comedy that Horace spoke of was no longer practiced, and that he will deal instead with *jocosa materia*,[183] he was familiar with the *Poetria nova*, where Vinsauf identifies *res comica* with *res jocosa*.[184] But even though Vinsauf illustrates it with a humorous story, contrasting *sermo jocosus* with *sermo serius* and associating *jocus* with *jocundus*,[185] it may be that "joy" rather than "joke" was the the prevailing connotation of the terms, both in Vinsauf's intention and in his readers' interpretation. John Garland for one seems to have read Vinsauf in this way,[186] and perhaps Chaucer would have done the same. We must remember that "joke" and "jocose" did not arrive in the English language until the latter part of the seventeenth century, and that in the fourteenth century *jocari* meant not "to jest" but "to rejoice,"[187] and a *joculator* was not a stand-up comedian but a *jongleur*. In any case, no writer in Chaucer's time or before seems to have thought that vernacular fabliaux were comedies, and such a conclusion on Chaucer's part would be unlikely, if only because it would clash with his understanding of comedy as the opposite of tragedy—unless, of course, both terms were to be taken in a satirical or mocking sense.

We have seen that Chaucer's notion of tragedy included the aspect of high social or political estate in the initial prosperity; similarly, the Knight's reference to poor estate may also include a social dimension. But let us assume for now that the sequence-of-events criterion takes precedence over all else, even social class, in Chaucer's understanding of comedy as well as tragedy, so that Egeus's line in the *Knight's Tale*, "Joye after wo, and wo after gladnesse" (2841), could be taken to summarize both genres.[188] On this basis, one could almost divide all of Chaucer's works into comedies and tragedies, as John Lydgate seems to do in the *Fall of Princes*:

> My maister Chaucer, with his fresh comedies,
> Is ded, allas, cheeff poete off Bretenye,
> That whilom made ful pitous tragedies:
> The fall of pryncis he dede also compleyne.   (1.246–49)

In order to avoid the sense that "the fall of princes" is to be distinguished from "tragedies," I interpret the fourth line as explaining the third. Accordingly, Lydgate is saying that Chaucer wrote not only comedies but tragedies, for Chaucer too composed complaints of the fall of princes. But he need not be interpreted as saying that only princes' falls can qualify as tragedies.

Even so, some of Chaucer's tales would fall between the two stools. We can hardly classify as comedies the life of St. Cecilia in the *Second Nun's Tale* and

---

[183]   Geoffrey of Vinsauf, *Documentum de arte versificandi* 2.3.162–63 (p. 317).

[184]   Geoffrey of Vinsauf, *Poetria nova* 1885–87 (p. 255).

[185]   Ibid., 1888–1919 (pp. 255–56).

[186]   John Garland, *Parisiana poetria*, pp. 80–82; see IDEAS AND FORMS, p. 101.

[187]   *Revised Medieval Latin Word-List*, p. 262.

[188]   So Robert A. Pratt, " 'Joye after Wo' in the *Knight's Tale*," p. 421.

the story of the murdered boy in the *Prioress's Tale*, though they end happily enough from a martyr's point of view. Lydgate probably considered the *vite sanctarum secularium* of the *Legend of Good Women* to be tragedies, since he deals with some of the stories—for instance, those of Lucretia and Dido—in the *Fall of Princes*. These histories would also fulfill Chaucer's definitions of tragedy, especially since they draw so heavily upon Ovid's "tragic" works; but for the purposes of his context, Chaucer treats them as examples of the genre of "sacred legend," as Lydgate acknowledges.[189] The stories are not designed to stress the Monk's primary lesson of the inconstancy of Fortune, but rather the constancy and virtue of women—and, usually, the inconstancy of men.[190]

The *Physician's Tale* of Virginia is closer to the spirit of the *Monk's Tale*, both in the Physician's moral, which is irrelevant to the story as told:

> Beth war, for no man woot whom God wol smyte,
> In no degree, ne in which manere wyse.
> The worm of conscience may agryse
> Of wikked lyf, though it so pryvee be
> That no man woot therof but God and he,   (278–82)

and in Harry Bailly's more pertinent reflections: after wishing a similar death upon all wicked jurists, he points out that Virginia was killed because of what Fortune gave her:

> Algate this sely mayde is slayn, allas!
> Allas, to deere boughte she beautee!
> Wherfore, I seye al day that men may see
> That yiftes of Fortune and of Nature
> Been cause of deeth to many a creature.
> Hire beautee was hire deth, I dar wel sayn.   (292–97)

The question of class clearly is important in the *Friar's Tale* and the *Pardoner's Tale*. The damnation of the low-life protagonists in these stories can hardly be perceived as tragic by any standards, except perhaps those of John Arderne and anyone who believed that Seneca's tragedies contained stories like that of Nero in hell inviting lawyers to join him in his bath of molten gold. The Pardoner does maintain that his tale has a moving effect on his congregations; but the movement is doubtless only to fear of a non-Aristotelian sort and not to Aristotelian pity or Chaucerian lamentation.[191]

---

[189] Lydgate, *Fall of Princes* 1.331: He calls Chaucer's work "a legend off parfit hoolynesse." In 2.980, speaking of Lucretia, he says that Chaucer "wrot off hir liff a legende soverayne."

[190] Renate Haas, "'Kissing the steppes of Uirgile, Ouide,' etc. and *The Legend of Good Women*," analyzes the *Legend* as an experimental crossing of tragedy with legend, in which many of the usual aspects of the legend are missing—for instance the public repercussions and veneration that follow on the death of the protagonist. In Chaucer's collection this feature is to be found only in the *Legend of Lucrece* (p. 299).

[191] In *Poetics* 13, Aristotle says that the most untragic kind of tragedy shows wicked men passing from affliction to prosperity, but the reverse, in which the wicked fall from prosperity to affliction, seems little better, "for such a plot-structure might move us [*philanthropon echoi*, "might

As for the fabliaux of the *Canterbury Tales*, all have endings that are happy (in the sense of amusing) for the audience, but some of them can hardly be classified as happy for the principal characters.[192] The *Miller's Tale* and *Reeve's Tale* can be regarded as stories of men suffering falls from relatively high positions (I refer to John the Carpenter and Simon the Miller). Absolon comes to a bad end, but then, like Samson, he rises to the occasion of making Nicholas's end bad as well; whereas the Cambridge clerks John and Alan rise from poor estate to a certain prosperity.

Granted that there are others besides the Monk in the Canterbury pilgrimage who favor heavy endings, they are clearly in the minority. For although some of the other tales contain heaviness, some lightening of effect is usually achieved in the conclusion. From this aspect, even the *Parson's Tale*, which ends with a description of the glorious life of heaven, merits the teller's description of it in his Prologue as "a myrie tale in prose" (46).

It will not be doing the modest Knight an injustice to suppose that, if asked, he would have exemplified his formula for entertaining tales by pointing to the story that he himself has told. The *Knight's Tale* deals with two knights who have fallen from rich estate to poor.[193] They work their way back to material prosperity, and each of them succeeds in his amatory pursuit. But Arcite's success lasts only for an instant, and his fall is told with much Monkish heaviness and pseudo-Boethian "sentence." However, the Knight goes beyond the *memento cadere* of Egeus, with its rest-in-oblivion lesson that "deeth is an ende of every worldly soore" (2849), to Theseus's more cheerful postmortem: the good Arcite has departed with honor from the foul prison of this life (3059–61), and his soul lives on (3065, cf. 2809–15). Palamon's joy, though briefly told, makes life's prison seem noticeably less foul. It is of more than sufficient lightness to outweigh the heaviness. The Knight speaks of him in the present tense and prays to God for His blessing on him, which seems to be given:

> And God, that al this wyde world hath wroght,
> Sende hym his love that hath it deere aboght.[194]
> (3099–3100)

possess philanthropy," that is, evoke human feelings or a sense of poetic justice], but would not arouse pity or fear, since pity is felt towards one whose affliction is undeserved, fear towards one who is like ourselves."

[192] See Paul G. Ruggiers, "A Vocabulary for Chaucerian Comedy: A Preliminary Sketch," p. 195. In this essay, and in "Some Theoretical Considerations of Comedy in the Middle Ages," Ruggiers is mainly concerned not with medieval meanings of *comedia* and its cognates, but rather with what we today understand by comedy, especially its humorous aspect (but based on what Aristotle, Donatus, and others have said). This is also the focus of Thomas J. Garbáty's essay, "Chaucer and Comedy."

[193] Pratt, "'Joye,'" dates the *Knight's Tale* shortly after the *Troilus* and suggests that it "may be the comedy he had looked forward to writing" at the end of the *Troilus*. I, however, agree with those who date the original version to before the *Troilus*. I have suggested that it was the second anniversary tribute to Richard II's engagement to Anne of Bohemia on May 3, 1381, dating therefore to 1383, with the *Parliament of Fowls*, which also uses Boccaccio's *Teseida*, being the first, written in 1382, and the *Troilus* the fourth, for 1385. See my *Chaucer and the Cult of St. Valentine*, p. 127.

[194] In this reading the lines are to be understood as in Tatlock's translation, "And may God That wrought all this wide world send him the joy of love that has paid for it so dear," speaking

Or "Sende" could have been intended as past tense,[195] which would make the historical reference to Palamon clear. The Knight continues in the present tense (or moves to the present tense), but then switches to the past, to assure us that the newlyweds lived happily ever after:

> For now is Palamon in alle wele,
> Lyvynge in blisse, in richesse, and in heele.
> And Emelye hym loveth so tendrely,
> And he hire serveth so gentilly,
> That nevere was ther no word hem bitwene
> Of jalousie or any oother teene.
> Thus endeth *Palamon and Emelye*.   (3101–07)

In the last line, Chaucer seems to title the whole work after the happy ending, as I indicate by my italics, thus removing Arcite from consideration.[196] Boccaccio did the same thing, at the request of Fiammetta, calling his poem *Teseida di nozze d'Emilia*, that is, *Theseid of Emily's Wedding Feast*.[197]

When Theseus proposes the marriage between Palamon and Emily, he says,

> I rede that we make of sorwes two
> O parfit joye, lastynge everemo.   (3071–72)

His optimism might strike us as extreme, given the human condition and the world as it is—and was—in spite of the Knight's assurances that it was borne out in this case. This optimism might be adduced as another reflection of the plot-criterion of comedy; it can be compared with the exaggerated pessimism at the end of the *Monk's Tale*, where a medieval Murphy's Law is enunciated ("Whatever can go wrong will").[198]

---

of Palamon; but one could conceivably take him to be praying for the redemptive love of Christ to be given proleptically to him: "May God who created the world send to Palamon the love of Him who redeemed the world." Pratt's interpretation, that the Knight is praying for God to reward whatever man who has paid dearly for his love, seems forced in light of the explanatory "For" of the next line (3101, cited above).

[195] As in *Reeve's Tale* 4136: This millere into toun his doghter sende." Fisher notes that the *hath* in 3100 is "omitted in Ellesmere and placed variously in other manuscripts—evidently a marginal insertion." A past-tense reading would most logically take *hadde* in both lines, but the sequence of tenses was not yet hidebound in Chaucer's day.

[196] This accords with A. C. Cawley's interpretation of the line: "So ends the story of Palamon and Emily." Tatlock's interpretation, "Thus end Palamon and Emily," is possible, but less likely, in my opinion, given the penultimate position of the line as a virtual *explicit*. Later on, when referring to the work in the *Legend of Good Women*, Chaucer calls it *The Love of Palamon and Arcite* (G 408), now mentioning Arcite but putting him after Palamon.

[197] See the final *sonetto*, the *Riposta delle Muse*. The *nozze* of the title does not refer in any way to Emilia's marriage to Arcita, who died after the *sposalizie* were celebrated and before the *nozze* or wedding festivities could take place. See my *Love and Marriage*, pp. 180–81, 194–95.

[198] There is another context known to Chaucer in which exaggerated pessimism has a standard place, namely, that of *contemptus mundi*; for Chaucer's use of it, see below, chap. 3, p. 112. We should remember that Aristotle would have had to put the *Knight's Tale* into the category of tragedy, because of its "spudean" characters and events; but he would also have to say, at least in the context of the thirteenth chapter of the *Poetics*, that its effect is more suitable to comedy, as he observes of the tragic plot of the *Odyssey* (see below, p. 89).

We do not know for sure whether Chaucer had a criterion of social rank for comedy, but if he did it no doubt took second place to the plot-criterion. If the Knight's reference to "poor estate" is taken as a status-criterion for comedy, as in Lydgate:

> [Comedie] the dedis only doth expres
> Of swiche as ben in povert plounged lowe,[199]

the initial poverty need not preclude noble blood and eventual rescue from poverty in the ensuing prosperity.

Chaucer may have had second thoughts about the *Palamon*, just as he did about his *de casibus* tragedies. It presents an easy target for mockery in many ways, at least from the point of view of a churl like the Miller. From a higher perspective, one curious aspect of it is that, though it preaches resignation, there is no stress on personal merit as the "specific difference" distinguishing human from animal and vegetable life in the sublunary cycle of generation and corruption, whether in Theseus's speech at the end or in the earlier action: for instance, Arcite is not held to account for betraying his oath of blood brotherhood by anyone but Palamon, and there is no consideration of which knight is the better man. This "moral absence" might seem to call into question Robert Kaske's suggestions "that the *Monk's Tale* is in Boethian terms a philosophically inadequate representation of 'evil' fortune; that the *Knight's Tale* (so far as this pattern is concerned) is a philosophically true representation of good fortune apparently evil; and that the Knight's interruption is a protest against the philosophical limitations of the *Monk's Tale*, as well as a reminder that philosophical truth may also be found in works dealing with obvious good fortune."[200] If one had to make a choice between the *Knight's Tale* and the *Monk's Tale*, one might well hold that it is the latter that is much closer to true Boethian "indifference." For though the stress of the tragedies is upon the transience and unpredictability of worldly fortune, human responsibility is often brought into the center of the picture, as it is not in the story of Arcite and Palamon; and at least on one occasion, in the *Tragedy of Nabuchodonosor*, we see how bad fortune can be turned to good. The *Knight's Tale* ignores in effect the existence of moral evil, whereas in the *Monk's Tale* God appears as punisher of evil deeds and intentions and the rewarder of repentance.

---

[199] Lydgate, *Troy Book* 2.850–51.

[200] R. E. Kaske, "The Knight's Interruption of the *Monk's Tale*," p. 261. I concur with James Smith, "Chaucer, Boethius, and Recent Trends in Criticism," p. 22, in considering the Monk's "matter" morally and intellectually superior to the Knight's; see also Douglas L. Lepley "The Monk's Boethian Tale." However, I do not share Smith's low opinion of the character of the Knight and of his tale, which he considers designed for the Knight. This is also the working assumption of Terry Jones, *Chaucer's Knight: The Portrait of a Medieval Mercenary*, and H. Marshall Leicester, Jr., *The Disenchanted Self: Representing the Subject in the Canterbury Tales*, who seems willing to accept Jones's conclusions, or at least his general outlook (p. 223 n. 2). In his two chapters on "The Knight's Critique of Genre" (pp. 221–66), Leicester holds that the Knight is criticizing the genres of epic and romance, without saying how Chaucer could have gained his knowledge of them; as discussed here, they seem to be the sort of unhistorical amalgams criticized by Jauss (see above, p. 3 n. 12).

It may be, then, that the Nuns' Priest is poking fun at the *Knight's Tale* as well as at the *Monk's Tale*, and that we should read his mock-romance as a send-up of the Knight's pretentiousness. As for the "tragic" qualities of the *Nuns' Priest's Tale*, many of them have been pointed out by others.[201] In confirmation of the gloomy generalizations that "evere the latter ende of joye is wo" and "God woot that worldly joye is soone ago" (3205–06), we are given the story of the cock and the fox, which is as true as the *Book of Launcelot de Lake* (3212). When Russell seizes Chanticleer, the latter's wives are said to cry out in the way that other females have done in bewailing remediless falls: the Trojan ladies at the death of Priam, Hasdrubal's wife at her husband's death, the wives of senators lost in Nero's burning of Rome (3355–73).[202]

But in order to fulfill the Host's injunction, "Telle us swich thyng as may our hertes glade" (2810), Sir John arranges a rescue for his protagonist. He turns his tale into what Aristotle would call, if it were treated on a more spudean level, a second-grade tragedy, like the tragedy or two that could be hewn out of the *Odyssey*: a tragedy, that is, with a double plot, entailing victory for the good and defeat for the bad.[203] In so doing, the Nuns' Priest has had to sacrifice verisimilitude, for his characters must suddenly act out of character: the cock becomes foxy and the fox cocky. But the tale is nevertheless able to leave the doctrine of Fortune intact:

> Lo, how Fortune turneth sodeynly
> The hope and pryde eek of hir enemy!   (3403–04)

And the fox adds his own "sentence" concerning *indiscretio*, if not of Fortune's *ictus indiscretus*, of himself as a *gubernator indiscretus*:

> "Nay," quod the fox, "but God yeve hym meschaunce,
> That is so undiscreet of governaunce
> That jangleth whan he sholde holde his pees.
> Lo, swich it is for to be reccchelees
> And necligent, and truste on flaterye."   (3433–37)

The last lines are usually given to the narrator (that is, the Nuns' Priest, Sir John), and thereby applied to both Chanticleer and Russell. But they are equally appropriate for the fox, and in his mouth the words gain a special

---

[201] See especially Samuel B. Hemingway, "Chaucer's Monk and Nun's Priest"; Charles S. Watson, "The Relationship of the *Monk's Tale* and the *Nun's Priest's Tale*"; and Strange, "The *Monk's Tale*," pp. 178–79. Nancy Dean, "Chaucerian Attitudes Toward Joy with Particular Consideration of the *Nun's Priest's Tale*," sees the Nuns' Priest as espousing a humane and moderate view that avoids the extremes of both Monk and Knight. See also Derek Pearsall's Variorum Chaucer edition of the *Nuns' Priest's Tale*.

[202] Elsewhere, namely, *Boece*, book 2 m. 6 (*Riverside Chaucer*, p. 417), and *Monk's Tale* 2479–81, the burning of Rome and the slaying of the senators are treated as separate atrocities.

[203] Aristotle, *Poetics* 13: "The second-best pattern [of tragedy] (which some hold to be the best) is the kind which involves a double structure (like the *Odyssey*) and contrasting outcomes for good and bad characters. . . .But this is not the proper pleasure to be derived from tragedy—more like that of comedy." Compare chap. 23: "The *Iliad* and *Odyssey* provide material for only one or two tragedies each."

poignance: for the cock has already learned this lesson, and he has turned it to advantage against the fox.

The *Nuns' Priest's Tale* satisfies more of the traditional requirements of comedy than does the *Knight's Tale*. The *dramatis personae* are of sufficiently low estate, being not only private but rustic; if the style is elevated at times, it is so in accord with the permissiveness of Horace (whom Chaucer, of course, did not know); the story has an unquiet and turbulent beginning, in Chanticleer's uneasy state of mind, and it ends in a condition of tranquillity. But in being "comic" in the modern sense, that is, "humorous," it violates the spirit of comedy understood as the opposite of tragedy, and therefore it should doubtless be thought of as a mock-comedy. Even Osbern of Gloucester, who gives *facetus* as one of the meanings of *comicus*, was probably thinking of "urbane" rather than "amusing."[204] For when comedy is defined as differing from tragedy only in having a sad beginning and joyful ending, it is a question of "serious comedy," which could be transformed into a tragedy by putting the ending first and the beginning last. To put it another way, it would be theoretically awkward for the ending of a comedy, which corresponds to the beginning of tragedy, to be thought of as humorous as well as joyful, since humor would seem to be inappropriate in a tragedy even before disaster strikes. (When Ovid in the *Tristia* speaks of obscene humor in some love-tragedies about Achilles, he is not saying that such an ingredient is appropriate, but rather that, in spite of its inappropriateness it is tolerated, whereas his own lighter works of love have been banned.)

We see, then, that Chaucer has followed the tragedies of the *Monk's Tale* with a comedy. What of his earlier desire to follow the *Tragedy of Troilus* with "some comedy"? Perhaps he had the *Canterbury Tales* in mind as the sequel to his tragic masterpiece. Or if, as is more likely, he had not as yet conceived his grand plan, perhaps he eventually came to see the *Tales* in this light.[205] For this work could be considered a linked series of comedies just as the *Monk's Tale* is a series of tragedies. In fact, one might even consider the *Monk's Tale* itself as one of the component comedies and mock-comedies. Chaucer was doubtless being intentionally droll in giving these tragic and world-contemning stories to the worldly Monk and in having them interrupted by the austere Knight, thus putting an end to the audience's misery and lamentation.[206] The humor of this collocation would not turn the individual tragedies into comedies, since humor was not a note of comedy, but into mock-tragedies. From the Monk's point of view, of course, his tale is a tragedy of sorts, since he comes to a bad end, just as the Pardoner does at the end of his tale. But in the case of the Pardoner, the Knight's intervention restores tranquillity to the adversity brought on by the Host.

In so fashioning the context of the *Monk's Tale*, Chaucer has managed to salvage the chaff as well as the fruit. He has taken these "miserable" stories and given them a dramatic function in his work, though at the same time he allows anyone who is so moved, as he himself must have been at one time, to take them seriously and derive moral sustenance from them.

204 Osbern, *Liber derivationum*, pp. 111, 143, in IDEAS AND FORMS, p. 103.
205 See Watson, "Relationship."
206 See Kaske, "Knight's Interruption," pp. 251–58.

Let me summarize what has been said about Chaucer thus far. Before Chaucer's time, concepts of tragedy were rare. Rarer still was the notion that tragedy was not an obsolete genre, but was applicable to modern works. Rarest of all was the idea of writing tragedies.

The most common concept of the subject matter of tragedy restricted it to criminal activities. Chaucer was fortunate in being guided by an unknown glossator to accept a wide-open definition of tragedy, in keeping with the Boethian characterization of the genre. As a result, Chaucer considered all kinds of disasters and all kinds of protagonists eligible for tragedy. The innocent, the guilty, the betrayed, the punished, and the merely unfortunate, all find a place in his early series of tragedies. The same variety of stories appears as well in one of Chaucer's models, Boccaccio's *De casibus*; but Chaucer transformed Boccaccio's idiosyncratic exercise into a new genre, that of tragedy, which he proceeded to exemplify. And, unlike Boccaccio, he formulated a universally verifiable and valid moral rationale for himself and his followers. The stories that he considers to be tragedies teach the ever-present possibility of misfortune. Within the stories themselves, he offers no advice other than, "Beware." Chaucer, or his Monk, has been criticized for not drawing a profounder moral. Even the Marquis Walter, one might allege, did better in his advice to Griselda, which I repeat here:

> No man may alwey han prosperitee.
> With even herte I rede yow t'endure
> The strook of Fortune or of Aventure. (*Clerk's Tale* 810–12)

But Chaucer doubtless felt obliged to work within the limits of his new genre. "Bewailing" rather than "advising" or "consoling" is the principal business of tragedy. We will find the same priority in Chaucer's large-scale tragedy, the *Book of Troilus*. It is on the level of generic theory that we can distinguish between Chaucer's tragedies and some of his other sad stories, specifically his legends of good women. These latter are modeled on the genre of the *vita sancti*, in which the main purpose is not to lament disasters that befall the protagonists but to rejoice in their virtue under the most daunting of conditions, even in death, and to urge emulation. Therefore, even when the *curriculum vitae* of the saint might seem to resemble that of the tragic protagonist, it is generically different. In Chaucer's secular adaptation of this sacred genre, his featured women lament mistreatment, and he as narrator joins them, but their constancy is held up for imitation; and their stories need not end sadly: the account of Alcestis, which is told in the Prologue, ends happily, and so does the story of Penelope, one of the projected legends.[207]

---

[207] I am speaking here only of the formal or structural elements of the legends, and not addressing questions of Chaucer's conscious or unconscious motivations.

3

The tragedy of Troilus

It might seem, at first glance, that Chaucer's *Troilus and Criseyde* does not fit his definition of tragedy as a story that begins in prosperity and ends in adversity, since he describes it at the beginning as the story of Troilus's double sorrow; that is, it starts out sadly as well as ending sadly. It will not do to speak of "the familiar rise-and-fall sort of tragedy" that was connected with the wheel of Fortune,[1] since there was no such formulation of tragedy in the Middle Ages.[2] There was, indeed, the widespread motif of Fortune's wheel, which in its full turning described a cyclical plot. But it was Chaucer's idea to compose tragedies in conjunction with this motif, and in his early series he limited himself to the "disaster arc" of Fortune's revolutions: that portion, namely, that answers precisely to the dictates of the tragic sequence of events. There is rarely any notion of an antecedent climb to prosperity in the *Monk's Tale*, whether with or without Fortune's help. Most of the characters seem to have started out in life on a high plain of prosperity. It is true that we read of Antiochus, "Fortune hym hadde enhaunced so in pride" (2583); but we are given no details of his enhancement, and we have no reason to think that it was a Horatio Alger ascent from hard times.[3] The same is true of Julius Caesar, whom Fortune helps until she becomes his enemy. Even in the case of Zenobia, who perhaps corresponds most closely to Troilus as a tragic protagonist, there is no real sense of adversity overcome. Though the greater part of the story is spent in detailing her expanding prosperity, she seems to have acted effortlessly, with no anguish or emotional upheaval, and with no growth or other change in character: her virtues, martial and other, were well developed from the beginning.

If we accept *Troilus* as a Chaucerian tragedy, then, we must consider the first part of the work to deal with the protagonist's prosperity; I shall argue that his troubles in this part (specifically, books 1–3) are a function of his prosperity. I shall also argue that Troilus's release from his earthly sorrows at the

---

[1] See McAlpine, *The Genre of Troilus and Criseyde*, pp. 16, 73.

[2] IDEAS AND FORMS, pp. 221–22.

[3] Horatio Alger is a byword in America, but for readers abroad who are not familiar with him, I recommend *Struggling Upward; or, Luke Larkin's Luck*, as a good example of the sort of story he produced; it was first published serially in 1886 and in book form in 1890; see the introduction by Ralph D. Gardner in the 1984 reprinting, and see also Gardner's *Horatio Alger; or, The American Hero Era*, and Bob Bennett, *Horatio Alger, Jr.: A Comprehensive Bibliography*.

end of the poem is primarily a part of Chaucer's lamentation over his adversity. It is possible, of course, that, since Chaucer calls the *Troilus* a tragedy only at the end, his classification of the work was an afterthought. But we shall assume that he intended it from the beginning, and try to see what light can be thrown upon the poem by analyzing it from the viewpoint of his understanding of tragedy. Our focus will necessarily be rather narrow, and we will not be able to do justice to other genres that may have had an influence upon its content and tone, but I do not mean to deny such dimensions. I refer my readers to Barry Windeatt's excellent survey of generic possibilities.[4]

ESTABLISHING PROSPERITY

We saw in the last chapter that Chaucer allowed his early tragedies, which he wrote to the double formula of Fortune's rhetorical question and his glossator's definition, to be criticized by Harry Bailly, who says that they were not well told, and did not engage his attention. We concluded that Chaucer himself had come to have second thoughts about them, for we can conjecture some disenchantment on his part without being overly reliant on the Host as a literary judge. One reason that may have occurred to him, which would account both for the Host's lack of interest and the Knight's excessive depression, is that they tell nothing of the protagonists' struggle for prosperity and therefore give little cause to engage one's sympathies when they come to lose it. It may be, then, that Chaucer came to realize that a full-cycle story would make a better tragedy than a half-cycle plot. He could have found some justification for this expansion of the scope of tragedy by going back to his main source in the *Consolation of Philosophy*. For shortly before Fortune speaks of the clamor of tragedies, she says, in Chaucer's translation:

> I torne the whirlynge wheel with the turnynge sercle; I am glad to chaungen the loweste to the heyeste, and the heyeste to the loweste. Worth up yif thow wolt, so it be by this lawe, that thow ne holde nat that I do the wroong, though thow descende adown whan the resoun of my pley axeth it.[5]

At the beginning of this passage, she could be taken to be speaking of separate comic and tragic movements, if the persons she lifts up are different from those whom she drops. But she goes on to speak of the same person—someone like Boethius himself—being raised and then lowered. In such a case the whole movement, the *totius vitae curriculum*, would have to be interpreted

---

[4] See Windeatt's Oxford Guide to *Troilus*, pp. 138–79; but one must be cautious about some of the generic categories, especially epic, which , I believe, was not an identifiable genre in Chaucer's experience. For Windeatt's assumption that Chaucer uses Clio as the Muse of epic poetry, see below, pp. 107–08.

[5] Chaucer, *Boece*, book 2 pr. 2 (*Riverside Chaucer*, p. 409).

tragically, rather than comico-tragically. But even here Fortune's language gives the impression of an effortless rise to prosperity, whereas the distinctive aspect of Troilus's rise is that it is accompanied with great effort and a certain kind of sorrow; and the very fact of this first sorrow increases our appreciation of his second sorrow. His ultimate adversity is all the more painful to us because we have seen the suffering caused by his being without Criseyde at the beginning.

It is possible, of course, that Chaucer did not have a theoretical justification in mind for the form of his tragedy, at least not at the beginning, but that, rather, he was simply confronted with Boccaccio's story of Troilus in the *Filostrato*, and saw no reason to change the main outline of the events. In fact, he clearly saw reason to enlarge upon it, because that is what he did. As we have already noted, the most striking difference between the *Troilus* and the tragedies of the *Monk's Tale* is the great length at which Chaucer tells the story. No other self-professed tragedy has ever reached such proportions, I suppose, except for Goethe's *Faust* and Dreiser's *American Tragedy*. We must ask ourselves what effect Chaucer's choice of a long story, which he made even longer, had upon his concept of tragedy.

To judge from my own experience of reading the work, I can say that one major effect of the poem's expansiveness is to lull the audience into the same sense of trust in prosperity that the Monk's tragedies are meant to caution us against. In spite of warnings at the beginning of the poem that things will end badly, the campaign of Pandarus and Troilus for Criseyde is so prolonged and absorbing, and the account of their union so full of present joy, that it is difficult to take thought for the future. Chaucer makes their happiness so memorable and totally consuming that its loss becomes all the more painful, to us as well as to Troilus. His achievement in creating this effect is remarkable. It would be an almost comparable achievement for his Pardoner to convince his fellow-pilgrims of the genuineness of his relics after his confession of fraud. Let us see how he does it.

He makes no attempt—at the beginning—to disguise the overall nature of the story he is about to tell. Though he refrains from calling it a tragedy, he does say that it is "a sorwful tale" which must be told, and heard, with "a sory chere" (1.14). He twice speaks of Troilus's double sorrow, and specifies what the sorrows consisted of: "in lovynge of Criseyde, /And how that she forsook hym er she deyde" (55–56). He expects his audience to respond sympathetically to both of these sorrows, which correspond to two kinds of "adversite / Of othere folk" (25–26): the first can be ended by Love bringing them "in hevene to solas" (31); the other has no remedy and they can only hope, by God's permission, "soone owt of this world to pace" (41). Presumably such a "passing" is to be to another kind of heaven, one that is open even to those who are "despeired out of Loves grace" (42).

But after these gloomy forecasts of the ultimate downturn of events, Chaucer avoids referring to it again and immerses us in the present. Even in the midst of his warnings, we might be inclined not to take him altogether seriously because of the hints of self-mockery in his role as narrator. He puts himself forward as a servant of Love's servants, but he falls into a third category of sufferers: those who despair of Love's grace but who are content to help more likely lovers. Pandarus, who is to play the role of "hermeneut" in the story, will soon emerge as another example of this type.[6]

It is common for literary critics to detect and praise "thematic continuities" as a sign of artistry in a work. But sometimes one can argue for still greater artistry when an author restrains himself from signposting his themes. In the *Troilus*, Chaucer does something even more interesting. He manages to avoid underlining the nature of the work as a whole in the first three books, not by steering clear of all "tragic indicators"—that is, various kinds of gloomy thoughts—but rather by subordinating such things to the more hopeful context of immediate concerns.[7] For instance, at the very beginning of the action we are told that Calkas "knew wel that Troie sholde destroied be" (1.68); and we could easily be made to recall the national tragedies that Boethius refers to (happy kingdoms suddenly overturned by Fortune); but instead we focus upon Calkas's treachery and the plight of his daughter Criseyde.

A bit later Chaucer speaks of the equal combat between the Greeks and Trojans, with both sides being wheeled up and down in turn by Fortune (1.134–40). Perhaps we cannot avoid thinking of such vicissitudes as mere epicycles on the larger orbit of Greek ascendance and Trojan ruin; but Chaucer cuts the idea short by saying that the story of the fall of Troy would be "a long digression / Fro my matere" (1.143–44). He recommends a few authors to those who are interested in pursuing the question, and proceeds to tell the story that concerns him. Although the Greeks are just outside the walls, they are henceforth out of sight and largely out of mind until Troilus's fortunes take a turn for the worse.[8]

When the God of Love strikes Troilus with his arrow, Chaucer goes on for a half dozen stanzas to elaborate the theme of pride going before a fall, and he points to Troilus as an exemplum:

> Forthy, ensample taketh of this man,
> Ye wise, proude, and worthi folkes alle,
> To scornen Love, which that so soone kan
> The fredom of youre hertes to hym thralle. (1.232–35)

But his jovial tone shows that his message is more of a promise than a warning: people who scorn love are likely to be caught up in it themselves. Such a comeuppance would serve them right. But it would also serve them well:

---

[6] The Greek word *hermēneus* (or *hermēneutēs*) includes the meanings of "matrimonial agent," "go-between," "broker" as well as "interpreter," "expounder."

[7] As John Ganim says in the chapter on "Consciousness and Time in *Troilus and Criseyde*" in his *Style and Consciousness in Middle English Narrative*, p. 80, Chaucer "warns but does not convince us" that the story will not have a happy ending. Paul Strohm, *Social Chaucer*, sees the situation in terms of a flexible audience: "Privy at the outset to the knowledge that Troilus's love will fail, the audience is then treated as a group of accomplished lovers who hope for his success" (p. 63); and Leonard Michael Koff, "Ending a Poem Before Beginning It, or The 'Cas' of Troilus," sees it as a matter of the narrator's loss of control: "We are witnessing the confident thread with which Troilus was explained in the proem to book 1 unravelling *for the narrator*, and seeing Troilus deepen as a 'cas' *for himself and for us*" (p. 177).

[8] See John P. McCall, "The Trojan Scene in Chaucer's *Troilus*," p. 265: all mentions of Troy in this part of the poem are favorable. Cf. Ganim, *Style*, pp. 94–95.

> And trewelich it sit wel to be so.
> For alderwisest han therwith ben plesed;
> And they that han ben aldermost in wo,
> With love han ben comforted moost and esed.   (1.246–49)

Such a state, he says, not only brings happiness but is irresistible as well, and morally enhancing; and we, the readers, or listeners, should put up no resistance: "Refuseth nat to Love for to ben bonde" (1.255).

Students of the *Troilus* have reacted in various ways to Chaucer's wholehearted endorsement of love at this point. Some have praised his subtlety in parodying and thereby foreshadowing the tragic outcome. Others have seen his approval of love as an ironic condemnation of it. Some readers have been inclined to criticize him for becoming so simple-mindedly absorbed in his story that he is oblivious to the tragic outcome, while others have chosen to praise him for producing this state of mind in his *persona*-narrator. But if we try to look at the poem from the viewpoint of his understanding of tragedy, we may well conclude that his narratorial obliviousness is designed to make his audience forget about the final outcome rather than to alert them to it by various hints: that he wishes, in other words, to "detoxify" the sorrows and distresses of love. One could postulate a similar intention in the first *Canticus Troili*, where it is stated: "Every torment and adversity / That cometh of [Love] may to me savory thinke" (1.404–05).

It is both a matter of consent (1.413–14) and necessity that the high-ranking Troilus is held as Love's thrall "lowe in destresse" (439). He tells himself that he is forced to love by his destiny (520); but he can also ask what "cas" or "aventure" has guided Pandarus to find him languishing (568–69)—a chance occurrence, of course, being the opposite of a destined occurrence. Troilus professes to wish for death to relieve him of his sorrow and languishing (526–29) and despair (605–06). But Pandarus points out to him that a certain amount of such suffering is a necessary ingredient of true happiness, because we know things by contraries (638–41). A somewhat similar point is made, in Criseyde's hearing, by Antigone in her song: "No wele is worth that may no sorwe dryen" (2.866): that is, one does not deserve happiness if one is not able or willing to suffer for it.

Pandarus succeeds in convincing Troilus that his present course of suicidal inaction is both unmanly and sinful (1.820–24). When Troilus takes a pessimistic view of Fortune (837–40), Pandarus tells him, "Lat be thy wo and tornyng to the grounde" (856); he recalls to him the full picture of Fortune's workings: her wheel has ups as well as downs; if her joys pass, so do her sorrows ("in one way or another," he should add, but does not); and it may well be that "she be naught fer fro thyn helpynge" (853). Pandarus's further generalizations, that the rose is next to the nettle, and so on (950–52), are of course too optimistic for life as a whole, but not for the present context; and when he goes on to say, "I hope of this to maken a good ende" (1.973), we know he is right and we are eager to see how he will bring it about.[9]

---

[9] For an excellent analysis of Pandarus's techniques as adviser and consoler of Troilus, especially as they relate to the *Consolation of Philosophy*, see Martin Camargo, "The Consolation of

I argued earlier that Chaucer shows Troilus's initial sufferings in order to increase our sympathy for him later. But though the sympathy then will be a deep compassion, at the moment it is more of an amused understanding that comes close to impatience or exasperation: for we recognize that the barriers to his immediate success are not at all formidable. And, of course, it is Chaucer's intention that none of his audience would want him not to succeed.

Chaucer reinforces these attitudes by directing our attention, in the prologue to the second book, to the impractical or puzzling aspects of Troilus's campaign for Criseyde, while taking for granted our approval of his goal:

> And forthi if it happe in any wyse
> That here be any lovere in this place
> That herkneth, as the storie wol devise,
> How Troilus com to his lady grace,
> And thenketh, "So nold I nat love purchace,"
> Or wondreth on his speche or his doynge,
> I noot; but it is to me no wonderynge.   (2.29–35)

He also continues his practice of defusing tragic motifs. In the opening stanza of the prologue, the Calends of hope replace the tempestuous matter of despair. The ponderous storm metaphor, ponderously explained, seems to be deliberately overdone, and to be scarcely appropriate to Troilus's self-manufactured tempest in a teapot. The tragedy of Procne is recalled when the swallow wakens Pandarus; she sings of "how Tereus gan forth hire suster take" (2.69). But no one would think of classifying Troilus with Tereus, or with the sort of husbands that Criseyde thinks of: "Either they ben ful of jalousie, / Or maisterfull, or loven novelrie" (2.755–56).[10] When Criseyde continues to meditate on the wretchedness that untrue men cause women by their treason (786–93), it is obvious that she is simply thinking in the abstract, and does not seriously include Troilus in her generalizations. We know even better than she that he will never fall short in any of the ways she has listed.

It never enters Criseyde's mind, as Chaucer portrays her here, that she is the one who will be found lacking, since she believes that women are always the victims and never the traitors. Chaucer already has distracted his audience from thinking such thoughts by bringing up, and refuting, a different kind of possible objection against Criseyde, namely, that her love for Troilus was too sudden (666–79).

In sum, Chaucer indicates, in book 2, the successful outcome of Troilus's quest by introducing negatives that are instantly negated or shown to be negligible. But he does the same thing by means of positive formulations of human possibilities. Pandarus tells Criseyde:

Pandarus." He says, on p. 225, "It is possible to see the positive, life-affirming dimension of Pandarus's optimism without ever forgetting that Philosophy's detachment is safer."

[10] I have heard it stated that "there are pretty good grounds for comparing Pandarus to Tereus," but I confess that I cannot think of them: Pandarus strikes me as loving and well-intentioned toward both his friend and his niece, while Tereus is one of the most brutal characters in all of classical literature.

> To every wight som goodly aventure
> Som tyme is shape, if he it kan receyven;
> But if he wol take of it no cure,
> Whan that it commeth, but wilfully it weyven,
> Lo, neyther cas ne Fortune hym deceyven,
> But ryght his verray slouthe and wrecchednesse;
> And swich a wight is for to blame, I gesse.   (2.281–88)

And he adds:

> Good aventure, O beele nece, have ye
> Ful lightly founden, and ye konne it take;
> And, for the love of God, and ek of me,
> Cache it anon, lest aventure slake!   (289–92)

In this interesting account of the interplay of destiny, chance, and free will, Pandarus says that the occurrence of good opportunities is predestined, but it remains up to us to take advantage of them or to neglect them. Neglect of offered opportunities is caused by our own internal wretchedness, and not by Fortune.

Chaucer himself says something similar of chance and destiny. Commenting on the fact that Troilus comes riding along the street after Pandarus has left Criseyde alone with her thoughts, he says that Troilus's appearance just now is a piece of good fortune that was inevitable:

> Right as his happy day was, sooth to seyne,
> For which men seyn, may nought destourbed be
> That shal bityden of necessitee.[11]   (2.621–23)

This is almost to see things from the viewpoint of Providence, who predestines all events as "happy." But it is easier to take this view when our notions of good fortune coincide with God's. There is perhaps a suggestion in this "prosperous" part of the poem that Pandarus plays a providential role. The day after Troilus's destined fortunate appearance outside Criseyde's house, Pandarus shapes another such "coincidence," which Troilus willingly executes.

Criseyde has her own ideas about the limits of free will. She will be able to go against her inclinations and be pleasant to Troilus: "I wol doon my peyne, / I shal myn herte ayeins my lust constreyne" (2.475–76). However, she cannot change her inclinations at will:

> But that I nyl nat holden hym in honde,
> Ne love a man ne kan I naught, ne may,
> Ayeins my wyl.   (2.477–79)

---

[11] Compare what Troilus says to his letter: "Lettre, a blisful destine / The shapyn is: my lady shal the see!" (2.1091–92).

The *alpha* text of the last two lines reads instead:

> Ne love no man, that can no wight, ne may,
> Ayeins his wil.[12]

In this confused statement, whether in its original or modified form, "wyl" seems to be doing service both for free will and unfree appetite: she *cannot* love a man whom she does not in fact love, for love is not simply a matter of willing it; and she *may not* pretend to love him (hold him in hand). She *could* pretend love, but it would be wrong, and Pandarus should not expect it of her. The former "action" (loving Troilus) she cannot help but refuse; the latter (showing signs of love) is within her power to refuse, and she fully determines to do so:

> Though al the world on o day be my fo,
> Ne shal I nevere of hym han other routhe.   (2.488–89)

But of course even firm resolves are not always in one's power to keep, as Criseyde will find out, first to her joy and then to her sorrow. In another context (Criseyde's complaint about the difficulty of writing to Troilus), Pandarus aptly remarks, "God woot, of thyng ful often looth bygonne / Comth ende good" (2.1234–35). What one is not able to like at first and what one does unwillingly often ends well (and, presumably, one ends up liking it). But part of Criseyde's difficulty comes not from an unwillingness to love Troilus but from her sympathy for him, which is increased by the planned repetition of his chance appearance in the street. Chaucer prays that her distress will end well (for her as well as for Troilus):

> To God hope I, she hath now kaught a thorn,
> She shal nat pulle it oute this nexte wyke.
> God sende mo swich thornes on to pike!   (2.1272–74).

In keeping with Pandarus's overall plan of augmenting Criseyde's pity, Troilus is to speak to her of his state in person, and it will help much if he believes in the efficacy of such an approach:

> Somtyme a man mot telle his owen peyne.
> Bileve it, and she shal han on the routhe;
> Thow shalt be saved by thi feythe, in trouthe.   (2.1501–03)

Perhaps the last line should be punctuated, as Root and Windeatt have it, "Thow shalt be saved by thi feyth in trouthe," in view of the *alpha* text, "Thow shalt be saved by thi feyth and trouthe." Taken by itself, in any of these forms, it could be seen as a striking statement of Troilus's ultimate fate of eschatological salvation, which is brought about by his fidelity.[13] But the

---

[12] For textual variants, see the editions of Robert Kilburn Root and B. A. Windeatt.
[13] See the discussion below about the salvation of the Trojan Ripheus, pp. 134–35.

immediate picture the words were likely to conjure up in the minds of Chaucer's audience is quite different: namely, a Gospel cure. Faith and confidence in Jesus make one whole.[14]

In the context of the smooth-running farce at Deiphebus's house, optimism has full sway. Chaucer inserts an address to Venus into its midst, in the prologue to the third book, in which everything connected with love receives a good interpretation, even the stories of Jove's philanderings and the "ese or adversite" that Venus gave him in love (3.19). Adversity can only lead to ease, it seems, for the goddess's influence is aimed at virtue and joy and unity; only those who resist her will come to grief:

> Ye folk a lawe han set in universe
> And this knowe I by hem that lovers be,
> That whoso stryveth with yow han the werse.[15]   (3.36–38)

Criseyde effects the desired cure of Troilus when she visits him in his sick-room, and she promises him full recompense for his sufferings:

> I shal trewely, with al my myght,
> Youre bittre tornen al into swetenesse;
> If I be she that may yow do gladnesse,
> For every wo ye shal recovere a blisse.   (3.178–81)

Later, when Pandarus talks to Troilus alone, he speaks in almost the same terms: all of his efforts have been "to brynge the to joye out of distresse" (3.245). But he wants to make sure that the "business" does not end badly for Criseyde—which would also, of course, be a bad end for Troilus: "She forlost, and thow right noght ywonne" (280). Pandarus is thinking of standard love-tragedies (as Chaucer would conceive them):

> I koude almoost
> A thousand olde stories the allegge
> Of wommen lost through fals and foles bost.   (3.296–98)

By Pandarus's own testimony, there is ample support for the fears voiced by Criseyde in her monologue: no wonder that women fear to deal with us men (321–22). As before, however, we are well assured of Troilus's exceptional character and "gode governaunce" in spite of his burning desire (425–27).

As Pandarus goes about binding up "al this heigh matere" (3.516), Chaucer indulges in some cosmological apostrophes, followed by an explication:

---

[14] See Luke 8.48: "Fides tua te salvam fecit" (var. "salvam te"), and cf. 18.42; cited by Root in his edition. Barbara Newman, "'Feynede Loves,' Feigned Lore, and Faith in Trouthe," p. 264, while noting the rich ambiguity of the line, says that as far as Pandarus is concerned, he is simply telling Troilus to take it on faith that his guileful plan will work.

[15] For Chaucer's richly positive treatment of Venus in the *Troilus*, see Theresa Tinkle, *Medieval Venuses and Cupids*, pp. 199–201.

> But O Fortune, executrice of Wierdes!
> O Influences of thise Hevenes hye!
> Soth is, that under God ye ben oure hierdes,
> Though to us bestes ben the causez wrie.
> This mene I now: for she gan homward hye,
> But execut was al bisyde hire leve
> The Goddes wil; for which she most bleve.   (3.617–23)

By this confused conjunction of Fortune, Weirds, Influences, Heavens, God, and Gods—among whom must be included the Moon, Saturn, and Jupiter, from the next stanza:

> The bente Moone with hir hornes pale,
> Saturne, and Jove, in Cancro joyned were—   (624–25)

Chaucer gives the initial impression of another unforeseen happy coincidence; but Pandarus's pleased reaction suggests that he is not one of the beasts from whom the causes of such events are hidden, and we may easily suspect that Chaucer is being playfully pompous.

Troilus, however, also takes up the cosmological motif, as he prays to six of the seven planetary gods. He omits Saturn (of whose cooperation we, the readers, have had some indication because of his participation in the conjunction), but does pray to Mars, asking him only not to interfere, for love of Venus.[16] However, in his initial prayer to Venus, he seeks her intercession against the bad aspects of both Saturn and Mars (3.715–32). Later, he thanks them all, "the blisful goddes sevene" (3.1203). He even asks for help from the three Fates, which is somewhat illogical, for he knows that they have long since predetermined what will happen:

> O Fatal Sustren, which, er any cloth
> Me shapen was, my destine me sponne,
> So helpeth to this werk that is bygonne.   (3.733–35).

Chaucer risks breaking the euphoric spell he has cast by having Criseyde speak realistically, for four stanzas, on false felicity and the "condicioun of veyn prosperitee" (3.817). Knowledge of the transitory nature of worldly joy, she says, must naturally cast a pall over one's happiness. She also denies that ignorance is bliss; but here she is less convincing, because people who are unaware of the fleeting nature of happiness are *temporarily* happy—which is the most that one can expect in a world where everyone must die.

But any uneasiness that might infect us from Criseyde's musings is quickly dispelled. We know that the "wikked serpent Jalousie" (3.837) is, in this instance, imaginary. It causes true distress in Criseyde, and Troilus prolongs her distress, considering this course to be the lesser of two evils: "For the lasse harm, he moste feyne" (1158); but it is soon over. Furthermore, both Troilus and Criseyde go on to experience more joy than they have ever

---

[16] An echo of Chaucer's prayer to Venus: "Ye fierse Mars apaisen of his ire" (3.22).

experienced before, which, for the moment at least, exhausts all of their potentialities for happiness. Troilus thanks Love in terms similar to those of Christian justification: grace exceeds his merits. Troilus has been "bistowed in so heigh a place / That thilke boundes may no blisse pace" (1271–1272); and Criseyde calls Troilus her "suffisaunce" (1309). Chaucer says they both had "as muche joie as herte may comprende" (1687), which exceeded not only scholarly definitions of felicity but also "al that herte may bythynke" (1694). In this sense, therefore, they enjoy perfect happiness.

These expressions of rapture may be extreme, but they are not given an entirely unrealistic setting. The heights of joy are not constantly maintained; they are cut short by "cruel day" (3.1695), and put in perspective by Pandarus's practical reminders. In keeping with his earlier admonitions to Criseyde about the perils of delay,[17] he warns Troilus that, since "worldly joie halt nought but by a wir" (3.1636), he not only must not cause it to fail himself, but also take great care to preserve it. Troilus responds that he will never knowingly be responsible for its loss: "in my gylt ther shal nothyng be lorn" (3.1641). This, of course, is the most that anyone can do.

In the midst of his warning, Pandarus sums up in Boethian terms[18] the pain in which a personal tragedy must chiefly consist:

> Of Fortune's sharpe adversitee
> The worste kynde of infortune is this,
> A man to han ben in prosperitee,
> And it remembren, whan it passed is.   (3.1625–28)

This is the viewpoint of *Locksley Hall*: "A sorrow's crown of sorrow is remembering happier things," rather than that of *In memoriam*: " 'Tis better to have loved and lost / Than never to have loved at all."[19] But something of the latter view as well can be seen in *Troilus*, in the stanzas taken over from *Filostrato* 3.38–39, where Chaucer wishes a bad end on non-loving niggards and contemners of love, and prays that God will advance "every lovere in his trouthe" (3.1386). We are to assume that even if lovers lose their loves their life is preferable to that of misers who keep their gold. But at the end of the poem, Chaucer will warn against love altogether, or at least against the lose-able loves of this world.

As we noted in the Introduction, in *Poetics* 13 and 14 Aristotle produces two quite different rankings of tragedies, in terms of their effectiveness in engaging the sympathies of an audience. Chaucer too may well have had

---

[17]   That is, when he prepares her to see Troilus in Deiphebus's house (2.1741–50), and when, in his own house, he conjures up Troilus's supposed jealousy (3.850–65, 896).

[18]   *Boece*, book 2 pr. 4: "This is a thyng that greetly smerteth me whan it remembreth me. For in all adversites of Fortune the moost unzeely kynde of contrarious fortune is to han ben weleful" (*Riverside Chaucer*, p. 411).

[19]   In *Locksley Hall*, Tennyson is citing not Boethius but "the poet," namely, Dante, who has Francesca da Rimini say:

> Nessun maggior dolore
> Che ricordarsi del tempo felice
> Ne la miseria.   (*Inferno* 5.121–23)

different views of the best kind of tragedy, if not at the same time, at least at various times in his life, or even at various stages of the *Troilus*. Let us try to imagine, for the sake of discussion, how he might have assessed tragic plots in the context of the third book. Unlike Aristotle, he would not have had to consider plots with straightforward happy endings, such as

> Men sen alday, and reden ek in stories,
> That after sharpe shoures ben victories,   (3.1063–64)

or cases of last-minute reprieves like that exemplified in *Iphigenia Among the Taurians*, or the somewhat parallel case to which Chaucer compares Troilus's situation:

> Right as he that seth his deth yshapen
> And dyen mot, in ought that he may gesse,
> And sodeynly rescous doth hym escapen,
> And from his deth is brought in sykernesse.   (3.1240–43)

In such instances we have the converse of Pandarus's Boethian dictum: "al swich hevynesse" is "torned to gladnesse" (3.1399–1400). But for Chaucer tragedies must have unhappy endings.

Presumably the "least tragic" of all such endings would be the downfall of the vicious. Chaucer gives three examples of deserved misfortune coming upon the avaricious: he predicts or prays that they will "forgon the white and ek the rede, / And lyve in wo" (3.1384–85); he recalls the fate of Midas (who grew ass's ears); and he alludes to Crassus (who after being slain in battle had molten gold poured down his throat).

Next perhaps should be ranked the stories of those who never prosper, like Chaucer himself, who is unworthy of love, and like Pandarus, who does not succeed in love. Both of these examples are presented with humorous overtones, but Troilus suggests a more painful variety of the species:

> In his mynde he gan the tyme acorse
> That he com there, and that, that he was born,
> For now is wikke torned into worse,
> And al that labour he hath don byforn,
> He wende it lost—he thoughte he nas but lorn.   (3.1072–76)

If in fact Troilus's efforts to gain Criseyde had been aborted and his first sorrow had become his last, the story would be touching, perhaps, but not altogether gripping, and it is questionable whether Chaucer would have considered such a story to be a tragedy at all, for the adversity would not have been preceded by prosperity, except in the sense of his having been a carefree prince of Troy. However, the Modern Instances of the *Monk's Tale* really give us no more of a sense of previous prosperity than this; and we must remember that at least one of them, the *Tragedy of Bernabo*, was probably written after the *Troilus*.

The highest kind of tragedy would seem to entail, at a minimum, a good man's possession of prosperity and its subsequent loss. It goes without saying that the greater the prosperity, the greater the loss. The happiest prosperity would seem to be that which is fully deserving. As Pandarus says, "Men shal rejoissen of a gret empryse / Acheved wel" (2.1391–92), which we may read in the light of Chaucer's definition of love as virtue (3.1393*beta*).[20]

But Pandarus's statement about the pain of loss suggests that there are subspecies within this highest category of tragedy. It would be more moving to read of one who lives to realize the extent of his loss than of one who is somehow spared such a realization. And Pandarus implies that the loss of prosperity is all the more bitter for the loser if it has been caused by his own rashness or neglect. But if this is true, does it also follow that the audience is likely to have greater compassion in such a case? Was Aristotle right to think, in his thirteenth chapter, that a downfall or loss incurred through a protagonist's *hamartia* is more effective in eliciting the tragic emotions than losses incurred by other means, say by the malice or neglect of others, or by different external pressures? It may well be that such a question, posed in the abstract, is incapable of a definite answer, for too much depends on the individual circumstances of each story and on the skill with which it is told.

It is clear that Chaucer had at his disposal a number of alternatives, and it is discussable whether he could have made a more effective choice than he did. But before such a discussion could take place without talking at cross-purposes, there would have to be agreement upon what story line Chaucer actually chose. There has, in fact, been sharp disagreement about every stage of the essential plot: the nature of Troilus's prosperity and his means of achieving it, on the one hand, and the nature of his loss, its causes, and its implications on the other. Some say that Troilus's love is immoral and idolatrous, or at least misguided, and achieved by culpable deceit. Others (I count myself among them) maintain that it is a noble love, innocently sought and virtuously attained. Still others find him guilty of some moral offenses but virtuous or innocent in other respects. If his love is perceived as basically bad, our reaction to his loss of Criseyde will naturally be quite different from what it will be if we regard it positively. And our assessment of his culpability or degree of culpability or lack of culpability in loving Criseyde will affect our opinion of whether or not he is at fault in losing her.

Some readers attempt to place Troilus in Aristotle's most famous category, of a good but not perfect man who falls through some flaw, whether moral, intellectual, or social, in keeping with similar assessments of heroes like Beowulf, Roland, and Arthur.[21] If they cannot blame him for the rashness or

---

[20] The *beta* text of 3.1392–93, accepted by Root in his edition, reads:

> To techen hem that coveytise is vice,
> And love is vertu, though men holde it nyce.

The *gamma* text, accepted by Robinson, Windeatt, and Barney, is:

> To techen hem that they ben in the vice,
> And loveres nought, although they holde hem nyce.

[21] I am happy to see that justice has been done to Roland recently by Robert Francis Cook, *The Sense of The Song of Roland*; see especially pp. x–xiii, 49–50, 64–66; and see the reviews by Ross G. Arthur and Rupert T. Pickens. I argue against finding a causative flaw in the Arthur of the *Alliterative Morte Arthure* in "The Non-Tragedy of Arthur," pp. 110–14. Gaston Paris rightly

neglect that Pandarus cautioned him against, they blame him for the opposite: his lack of decisiveness and his excessive caution and concern, or for some similar failing.[22] Others find other faults, such as blindness to the nature of human love.[23] Or, since the Aristotelian *hamartia* need not be a moral or intellectual defect but only a mistaken action, we could blame Troilus, as he does himself, for deciding to go along with Criseyde's plan rather than insisting on a more realistic course of action.[24]

Part of the faultfinding that occurs in standard readings of great works has to do with an un-Aristotelian hankering after poetic justice: a moralistic assessment of works, or an assumption that the authors of the works were under such moralistic constraints. A partial remedy for this sort of monolithic view can be had in Lubomír Doležel's concept of "narrative worlds," which he derives from modal logic, as follows:

(1) The *alethic* world in which the narrated actions are subject to the restrictions of the 'classical' modalities—possibility, impossibility, and necessity.

(2) The *deontic* world in which the narrated actions are governed by the modalities of permission, prohibition, and obligation.

(3) The *axiological* world in which the narrated actions are dominated by the modalities of goodness, badness, and indifference.

(4) The *epistemic* world in which the narrated actions follow the course given by the modalities of knowledge, ignorance, and belief.[25]

In the applications that he makes of these modalities, Doležel goes on the assumption that any given individual narrative is to be analyzed on the basis of only one narrative world. However, Stanislav Segert in adapting Doležel's system to a study of the Bible assumes that works can participate in more than one world at once. Thus, he finds that the deontic and axiological models are most helpful to analyzing the Book of Jonah, while the alethic model, that is, considering the events of the book in terms of reality and unreality, has not been satisfactory.[26]

notes that even heroes like Odysseus and Tristan, who seem to us to have condemnable faults, are not condemned by the authors who first elaborated their stories. See my "Varieties of Love in Medieval Literature According to Gaston Paris," p. 309, citing Paris's "Tristan et Iseut," pp. 172–73.

[22] To take an example at random, Alan T. Gaylord, "The Lesson of the *Troilus:* Chastisement and Correction," p. 35, says that Chaucer shows Troilus choosing not to choose, actively entering into passivity, and that it is this "condition of despair" rather than the loss of Criseyde or her faithlessness that makes the work a tragedy. (Gaylord is working from his own notion of tragedy, rather than from Chaucer's: for him the central implication of tragedy seems to be "accountability" [see p. 27].) Compare Milo Kearney and Mimosa Schraer, "The Flaw in Troilus," who point to Troilus's excessive timidity in society and moral cowardice.

[23] So Willi Erzgräber, "Tragik und Komik in Chaucers *Troilus und Criseyde*," p. 146.

[24] See Ann M. Taylor, "Troilus' Rhetorical Failure (4.1440–1526)." As will be evident from my analysis below, I entirely agree with Taylor in finding Troilus weak in his efforts to dissuade Criseyde from going to the Greek camp.

[25] Lubomír Doležel, "Narrative Worlds," p. 544. "Fantasy" is characteristic of the alethic world, "test" of the deontic, "quest" of the axiological, and "mystery" of the epistemic.

[26] Stanislav Segert, "Syntax and Style in the Book of Jonah: Six Simple Approaches to Their Analysis," p. 130. I should add that in my view the alethic model could well be used to illuminate the action of Jonah, since it allows for the fantastic to be treated in realistic terms.

The "hamartial" view of Troilus would fall into the deontic world of obligation and temptation, with the concomitants of sin and guilt and punishment, to the neglect of the axiological world, the struggle for values, where even though losses are incurred one's honor can remain intact—as in the cases of Beowulf, Roland, and Arthur.

Let me state my own view about the *Troilus*, which I arrived at long before I thought of applying Chaucer's views of tragedy to the poem.[27] Just as I do not think that Troilus is presented as morally culpable in loving Criseyde, so too I do not think that Chaucer means to blame him either for losing physical posssession of her or for losing his place in her heart. This blame-free judgment is, in fact, Troilus's own assessment of himself when he apostrophizes Criseyde:

> Ne, but I hadde agilt and don amys,
> So cruel wende I nought your herte, ywis,
> To sle me thus!   (5.1684–86)

Furthermore, *pace* Aristotle and Aristotelians, I do not see how he could have made his poem a better tragedy (according to his own ideal of a good tragedy, a well-told account of a lamentable fall from prosperity) by giving Troilus a *hamartia*. If such an idea occurred to him, to implicate Troilus in the course of his misfortune by some sin, defect, blunder, or mistaken judgment, he must have rejected it, and rightly so (according to my assessment of the poem).[28]

Before we go on to examine the falling action of the *Troilus* in detail, let us review the "risen" action. In order to make us fully appreciate the magnitude of Troilus's sense of loss, I have argued, Chaucer wished to immerse us totally in his sense of possession, by making us forget for the moment that Criseyde would not live up to her present high resolve, or her own and Troilus's high expectations of her. It is easy to be ominous, and equally easy to avoid all reference to future disasters. Chaucer chose the difficult third course of facing up to possible complications and failures without actually foreshadowing the disaster that he had previously stated was to come. It is his great achievement that his picture of antecedent prosperity is authentically prosperous; not only the characters but the readers as well are caught up in the joys of the present, without thought for the sorrows of the future. One of the chief means to this end is his expansiveness in telling the story: he stretches it out to such an extent, especially in the long invented episodes in the houses of Deiphebus and Pandarus, that we forget everything but the longed-for climax of Troilus's courtship of Criseyde.

In short, we find Troilus at the beginning of the poem in great estate and prosperity. Though not exactly suffering a loss in his state, he suddenly senses in himself a lack and a need, namely, Criseyde's love. The sorrow and

---

[27] For some of the bases of my judgments, see the chapters on *Troilus* in my *Love and Marriage* (see below, p. 144 n. 106).

[28] Compare C. David Benson, " 'O Nyce World': What Chaucer Really Found in Guido delle Colonne's History of Troy," p. 313: Chaucer does not wish to account for ultimate moral responsibility, but seeks rather to point up "the helplessness and ignorance of human beings."

unhappiness that he suffers in the course of attaining his goal have nothing to do with tragedy, however defined, for there is good hope throughout that he will achieve his desires. When he does achieve them, the memory of his sorrows only increases his happiness. This characterization is confirmed by Chaucer's own summing up of the first part of his poem. He is addressing his spiritual inspirers, namely, Venus, Cupid, and the nine Muses:

> Thorugh yow have I seyd fully in my song
> Th' effect and joie of Troilus servise,
> Al be that ther was som disese among.   (3.1814–16)

So much for Troilus's first sorrow.

FUTURE CONTINGENTS

By means of a series of stanzas which in some manuscripts forms an epilogue to book 3, while in others it stands as the prologue to book 4, Chaucer destroys the sense of well-being and joy into which he has lulled his readers. He begins by stating a general rule, that happiness of this sort lasts only a short time:

> But al to litel, weylaway the whyle,
> Lasteth swich joie; ythonked be Fortune,
> That semeth trewest whan she wol bygyle,
> And kan to fooles so hire song entune
> That she hem hent and blent, traitour comune!
> And whan a wight is from hir whiel ythrowe
> Than laugheth she, and maketh hym the mowe.   (4.1–7)

As often with Chaucer, there is much that is stereotypical and even inappropriate in this reference to Fortune. His treatment of Troilus throughout the poem belies the overt suggestion of this stanza that he is to be regarded as a typical "hent and blent" fool. The real point, I take it, is simply that he is the victim of "a cruel turn of events." Troilus is not being criticized for failing to meditate constantly on worldly mutability after the fashion of Criseyde in her momentary bout of depression over Troilus's supposed jealousy.

No doubt if the Monk or the earlier Chaucer were telling this story, he would have urged such a lesson: that is, if Troilus had lowered his expectations, had kept his mind fixed on the law of worldly mutability, his disappointment would not have been nearly so great (though, of course, he would also have sacrificed a good deal of his joy), and his story would not have become a tragedy. But in the story as we have it, Troilus is not being faulted for his fall; rather, his fall is merely being explained: Fortune, not Troilus, is to blame. Blame will also attach to Criseyde, unfortunately, though Chaucer holds out some faint hope at this point that her guilt has been exaggerated by false reports.

In the second and third books, Chaucer invoked Clio and Calliope, and it has been uniformly assumed that they are the Muses of history and heroic

poetry from the Pseudo-Catonian tradition. If so, then Chaucer must have
known of Melpomene and her *tragicus boatus*; and it would have been natural
for him to have invoked her when his tragedy took its turn for the worse.
Since he does not, we must suspect that his Clio and Calliope come from
some independent source, like the Fulgentian tradition, which was repeated
by Boccaccio, where Clio governs the beginning of the poetic process, and
Calliope the end, with Melpomene controlling one of the intermediate
steps.[29] It has been suggested that Chaucer was inspired by the opening of
the *Consolation of Philosophy* in his depiction of the Muses as departing
when the story turns sad,[30] but Boethius has two sets of Muses, both of
whom specialize in sorrow: the strumpet Muses do so ineffectually or harm-
fully, whereas Philosophy's Muses are constructive. But Chaucer and Lydgate follow a tradition (unless Chaucer invented it) according to which the
Muses refuse to deal with sorrowful themes.[31] In the *Troilus*, the end of book
3 marks the departure not only of the nine Muses, but also of Venus and
Cupid: they have all served as guides for his account of Troilus's joy (3.1807–
15). In book 4 he turns instead to his original source of inspiration, the Fury
Tisiphone, but names as well her sisters Megaera and Alecto, and, for good
measure, cruel Mars. He asks for help to give a full account of Troilus's
"losse of life and love yfeere" (4.27). But this is not a just characterization of
the contents of the next two books, for they will be devoted almost entirely to
the impact that the loss of Troilus's love will make upon him before he comes
to lose his life; though perhaps it could fairly be said that his loss of Criseyde
causes him to "evere dye and nevere fulli sterve" (4.280).

Chaucer does not immediately continue with the conceit of Fortune in telling his story. When Antenor and others are captured and "the folk of Troie /
Dredden to lese a gret part of hire joie" (4.55–56), there is no suggestion that
this is a component of Fortune's malicious plot to "caste hym clene out of his
lady grace" (4.10). Rather a strange new numen, Infortune, which in Latin is
in the neuter gender (Infortunium), seems to be the operative metaphysical
force:

> For Infortune it wolde, for the nones,
> They sholden hire confusioun desire.[32]   (4.185–86)

---

[29] Fulgentius, *Mythologiae* 1.1 (pp. 25–27); Boccaccio, *Genealogia* 11.2. See above, chap. 2, p.
46, for Walsingham on the three traditions of the Muses. But whereas Pseudo-Cato associates
Calliope with heroic poems ("Carmina Calliope libris heroica mandat"), Walsingham interprets
her as Mercury, and says that the name means "optima vox" or "sonoritas" (*Archana* 1.8, p. 17).
In the *Thebaid*, Statius invokes the Muses ("deae") in general (1.4) and Clio in particular (1.41)
as well as Calliope, called queen of the grove of song (4.34–35, cf. 8.374), but they all indiscrimi-
nately inspire battle-poetry, whereas in Chaucer they do not.

[30] Phillipa Hardman, "Chaucer's Muses and His 'Art Poetical,'" pp. 491–94.

[31] For Lydgate, see the next chapter, pp. 155–56, 169.

[32] Lydgate in the *Fall of Princes*, when Adam addresses "Cousin Boccaccio," makes Infortune
feminine:

> Thou that art besi to serche over all
> Off Infortune the maner to enquere,
> Hir sodeyn chaung, turnyng as a ball,
> Off erthli pryncis from ther estat roiall.   (1.485–88)

It is not clear that Chaucer is finding a moral fault in the people of Troy for ignoring Hector's strongly worded objections to the transfer of Criseyde. He does blame their lack of discretion in choosing Antenor over Criseyde: Criseyde has done them no harm, but Antenor will betray them (4.204–10). If it were taken as an accusation of wrongdoing, it would hardly be valid. One could just as easily say the reverse. Antenor has done them no harm (and has done them a great deal of good), whereas Criseyde will betray them.[33] The real point that Chaucer wishes to make, I think, is that we cannot know what is good for us. It is our lack of predictive power that constitutes our tragic condition.

Ironically, the lesson comes just after a rather convincing reminder that the future is in fact susceptible to religious or scientific scrutiny. Calkas received word directly from Apollo that Troy would be destroyed, and he checked this result by all other available methods: "by astronomye, / By sort, and by augurye ek" (4.115–16), and he came to the Greeks, as he tells them, "to teche in this how yow was best to doone" (4.84). Apparently the inevitable future, like the Marxist rule of the proletariat, can be hurried along by the prudent choices of free will, or the well informed efforts of sympathetic "volunteers."

When Troilus hears of the Greek demand, he is of course profoundly shocked, but says and does nothing. Far from being blamed for his inaction, however, he is praised: "With mannes herte he gan his sorwes drye" (4.154). He suffers in secret, in order to prevent his love for Criseyde from becoming known (we are not to notice that he could easily have supported Hector's position under cover of fraternal loyalty). Subsequently, when he is by himself and no longer in danger of revealing his love to the world, his expressions of sorrow might seem to be both unmanly and premature, and even foolish, as in his almost absurd address to Fortune, taken over from the *Filostrato*, claiming that he has always honored her above all the gods (267–69). Such extreme outbursts should not be taken to brand Troilus as a permanent fool of Fortune. They do show that in his present state he is, like Boethius, in great need of rational consolation. It is doubtless no accident that Chaucer has Troilus characterize his condition in terms of the Boethian *locus classicus* of Fortunal tragedy:

> O Troilus, what may men now the calle
> But wrecche of wrecches, out of honour falle
> Into miserie, in which I wol bewaille
> Criseyde, allas, til that the breth me faille.   (4.270–73)

Troilus goes on, in his ravings about Fortune and her "foule envye," to suggest some alternative tragic endings, namely, the death of Priam or of his brothers—or even his own death, which he would prefer to his present "undead" condition (274–80). He intends to end his days like the blinded

---

[33] Robert M. Durling, *The Figure of the Poet in Renaissance Epic*, p. 57, says that the lines call for readers to complete the pattern for themselves, by thinking of Antenor's past loyalty and Criseyde's future betrayal.

Oedipus, and he envisages a peculiar kind of afterlife for himself: he wishes his soul to leave his corpse and remain always in Criseyde's company (295–308). In keeping with this fantasy, he makes a last will and testament, bequeathing his spirit to her (319–21).

Chaucer very likely had Oedipus's full story in mind: "how that Kyng Layus deyde / Thorugh Edippus his sone, and al that dede" (2.101–02), including the discovery that his wife was also his mother. At the beginning of book 4, he freshly reminded his readers that Criseyde too will be revealed to Troilus in a painful new guise; and now the picture of Troilus's ghost hovering about her as she forsakes him (or, at least, is "unkind" to him) should bring home to us how thoroughly incapable Troilus is of imagining the true dimensions of the tragic end in store for him.

A bit later, when speaking to Pandarus, Troilus produces two further—and contradictory—visions of his death and afterlife. On the one hand, he will lament his separation from Criseyde forever in the underworld (4.470–76). On the other hand, Death will end all his sorrows (501–18). It is to this last notion that he will most frequently return when the true nature of his loss begins to become apparent.

After Troilus imagines his death in the first of the three ways listed above, he apostrophizes lovers in the style of an auto-epitaph:

> O ye loveris, that heigh upon the whiel
> Ben set of Fortune, in good aventure,
> God leve that ye fynde ay love of stiel,
> And longe mote youre life in joie endure!
> But whan ye comen by my sepulture,
> Remembreth that youre felawe resteth there;
> For I loved ek, though ich unworthi were.   (4.323–29)

We note that he speaks in terms of Fortune's favor and God's preservative powers for other lovers, for whom a long life of joyous love is possible. It is significant that he hopes that they will always find "love of steel," for that is precisely what he will not always find in Criseyde.

As was true of his first sorrow, Troilus's lamentations at this stage are much more extreme than the known circumstances warrant; and it once again falls to Pandarus to attempt to put his plight into perspective, and to give him a measure of comfort. He does so by first playing up his sorrow and then playing it down. He says, in effect, that this is the worst tragic event to occur in the history of the world; but then he points out that it is the sort of thing that everyone can expect—for no one has a personal claim to any of Fortune's gifts (386–92). Pandarus continues to minimize Troilus's reasons for sorrow by bringing up other considerations, some of them quite outrageous. Chaucer indicates that Pandarus knows very well what he is doing: "For douteles, to don his wo to falle, / He roughte nought what unthrift that he seyde" (430–31).

Pandarus's shock-treatment seems to have a measure of success. Troilus pretends not to listen, but in fact he is stirred up enough to refute some of his friend's suppositions. One of Pandarus's gambits resembles Abelard's method of consolation in his *Historia calamitatum*, namely, to point to worse misfortunes in his own life (393–98). Troilus is able to counter this argument easily, by recalling Pandarus's Boethian characterization of remembered loss: "That hym is wors that is fro wele ythrowe, / Than he hadde erst noon of that wele yknowe (482–83). But, as we shall see, this is not the final judgment on this question in the *Troilus*.

Pandarus then changes his approach. Whereas earlier, in his "unthrifty" gambit, he had advocated taking a wait-and-see approach to chance, telling Troilus that his relationship with Criseyde was a "casuel plesaunce" that some other "cas" might make him forget (419–20), he now urges an active role. Instead of mourning over an event that has not yet occurred, he says, Troilus should take the future into his own hands and alter the expected outcome. Perhaps he will even be assisted by Fortune, who favors the brave (600–02). Pandarus will be there to help, being a friend "in every cas" (628). Troilus, however, replies that "for no cas" will he do anything without Criseyde's consent (633–37). In other words, he will be absolutely firm, and impervious to chance and Fortune, in doing only what Criseyde wants.

In the following section of book 4, Chaucer shows us Criseyde's reaction to the disastrous news: "For which disaventure / She held hireself a forlost creature" (4.755–56). Many readers have found signs of superficiality in her lamentations, which they see as predictive of her change of heart. My own assessment is that Chaucer intends her sorrow to be entirely sincere, and to have the effect of distracting us once more from what will happen in the end. I find her view of death and the afterlife no less touching than Troilus's three alternatives, as she bequeathes her spirit to mourn forever with him in Elysium, like Orpheus and Eurydice (4.785–91).[34]

Pandarus likened Troilus to a potential martyr at one point (4.623), but when he sees Criseyde, she seems already to be a martyr in the throes of death (818–19). However, she is more ready than Troilus to see sorrow at the end of every love, and to regard love as just one example of transitory human joy:

> Endeth thanne love in wo? Ye, or men lieth!
> And alle worldly blisse, as thynketh me.
> The ende of blisse ay sorwe it occupieth.   (4.834–36)

The last line is a proverb found in the Book of Proverbs 14.13. The full verse reads, "Risus dolore miscebitur, et extrema gaudii luctus occupat"; that is, "Laughter shall be mingled with sorrow, and mourning taketh hold of the end of joy." The Nuns' Priest will speak the same sentiment later: "For evere the latter ende of joye is wo" (3205), and Chaucer himself had resorted to it earlier, in his story of Constance:

> O sodeyn wo, that evere art successour
> To worldly blisse, spreynd with bitternesse!
> The ende of the joye of oure worldly labour!

---

[34] In chapter 6, I compare Criseyde's testament, formulated in this passage, with Cresseid's testament in Henryson's poem, specifically her bequest of her soul to Diana (below, p. 255).

> Wo occupieth the fyn of oure gladnesse
> Herke this conseil for thy sikernesse:
> Upon thy glade day have in thy mynde
> The unwar wo or harm that comth bihynde,
> *(Man of Law's Tale* 421–27)

where one can perhaps see its inspiration in Innocent III's *De miseria humane conditionis* and the general *contemptus mundi* tradition.[35]

In his "epitaph" Troilus wished all lovers long success in love, and, like Chaucer at the beginning of the poem, sought their sympathy as they remembered him. Criseyde instead tells everyone to look on her as an example that all happiness will come to an end:

> And whoso troweth nat that it so be,
> Lat hym upon me, woful wrecche, ysee
> That myself hate, and ay my burthe acorse,
> Felyng alwey, fro wikke I go to worse.   (4.837–40)

In saying that she goes from wicked to worse, Criseyde echoes Troilus's words when he was pretending to think that she had another lover (3.1074); and perhaps Chaucer intends her statement to foreshadow her coming "deterioration." But I think it more likely that he means us to take her words innocently, and without irony.

The action of book 4 is quite simple. The exchange of Criseyde for Antenor is agreed upon. Troilus laments it, Criseyde laments it, and, through Pandarus's mediation, they lament it together. As Chaucer first conceived the

---

[35] Innocent quotes Proverbs 14.13 in 1.21, where he also says: "Semper mundane letitie tristicia repentina succedit, et quod incipit a gaudio desinit in merore" ("Sudden sadness always follows upon worldly joy, and what begins in joy ends in sorrow"). Presumably Innocent would have gathered optimistic apophthegms in his projected *De dignitate humane nature.* I should note that since in Chaucer's view a tragedy is the written record of lamentable falls, he could have concluded to the pre-existence of innumerable cosmic tragedies, if he believed what he said in the *Man of Law's Tale*:

> Paraventure in thilke large book
> Which that men clepe the heven ywriten was
> With sterres, whan that he his birthe took,
> That he for love sholde han his deeth, allas!
> For in the sterres, clerer than is glas,
> Is writen, God woot, whoso koude it rede,
> The deeth of every man, withouten drede.
>
> In sterres, many a wynter therbiforn,
> Was writen the deeth of Ector, Achilles,
> Of Pompei, Julius, er they were born;
> The strif of Thebes; and of Ercules,
> Of Sampson, Turnus, and of Socrates
> The deeth; but mennes wittes ben so dulle
> That no wight kan wel rede it atte fulle.   (190–203)

Another conclusion that we can draw from this passage, presumably, since Turnus is specifically mentioned, is that Vergil's account of the death of Turnus at the end of the *Aeneid* constituted a tragedy.

story,[36] after Pandarus leaves Criseyde and goes to summon Troilus, he finds him alone in a temple. He overhears him begging the gods to rescue him or let him die:

> Besyking hem to sende hym other grace
> Or fro thys worlde to doon hym sone pace.   (4.951–52*alpha*)

In what was originally the next stanza, Pandarus upbraids him:

> "O myghty God," quod Pandarus, "in trone,
> I! Who say evere a wis man faren so?"   (1086–87)

Chaucer seems then to have added the stanza made up of lines 1079–85 to introduce Pandarus's outburst. The first part of the stanza gives a direct text of Troilus's prayer before Pandarus appears on the scene:

> Thanne seyde he thus: "Almyghty Jove in trone,
> That woost of al this thyng the sothfastnesse,
> Rewe on my sorwe, and do me deyen sone
> Or bryng Criseyde and me fro this distresse!"   (4.1079–82)

The rest of the stanza tells of Pandarus's arrival:

> And whil he was in al this hevynesse,
> Disputyng with hymself in this matere,
> Com Pandare in, and seyde as ye may here.   (4.1083–85)

Root suggests that Chaucer then changed the text of stanza 946–52, where the substance of Troilus's prayer was given in indirect discourse. The new version of the indirect prayer reads:

> To doon hym sone out of this world to pace;
> For wel he thoughte ther was non other grace.   (4.951–52)

But though this reading now corresponds to the order of the direct-address prayer to Jove, in that death is mentioned first rather than last, it rules out the alternative solution of rescue: now there is no "other grace." It may well be, then, that these lines were modified thus pessimistically, not to conform

[36] Root and Robinson, and most other scholars as well, agree in thinking that Troilus's meditation on free will was not in the first stage of the work. For a dissenting view, see Barry Windeatt, "The Text of the *Troilus*," pp. 6–11, who argues that the free-will passage, like the two other large-scale additions (Troilus's Boethian song in book 3 and his ascent to the heavens in book 5), were intended by Chaucer from the beginning, or at least, as he states it in his Oxford Guide to *Troilus*, there is no manuscript evidence proving "that these passages were 'later' additions to a poem previously existing and 'published' without them" (p. 26). For a convincing response to his position, see Charles A. Owen, Jr., "*Troilus and Criseyde:* The Question of Chaucer's Revisions." See the editions of Root and Windeatt for full accounts of the MSS, and Barney, *Riverside Chaucer*, p. 1161, for a summary. As above, I accept Root's designation of *alpha* for the earliest version.

to stanza 1079–85, but to introduce a massive new interpolation, lines 953–1078, on predestination and free will, which Chaucer inserted between Troilus's indirect-discourse prayer and his direct-discourse prayer.

In any case, stanza 946–52 should have been further modified to eliminate the line in which Pandarus is said to find Troilus in the temple all alone, for it gives us the impression (later contradicted) that he overhears Troilus's entire dissertation on free will.

Let us now examine Troilus's thought processes in the final version of this section of book 4.

After he prays for death because no other grace is possible (951–52), he falls into despair and prepares to die (954–55). But his despair is not the Christian theological vice. He does not despair of eschatological salvation; rather, he despairs of seeing a favorable outcome to his difficulties here on earth: God foresaw that he would lose Criseyde, and therefore he can do nothing about it (960–66).

The whole tenor of his meditation confirms that he has not lost his faith and hope in God: he is simply puzzled by the philosophical problems involved. The upshot of his thoughts is as follows. He rejects as blasphemous any suggestion of imperfection in God: to say that God has no clear knowledge of events would be "fals and foul and wikked corsednes" (994); another "fals sentence" is the idea "that thyng to come sholde cause His prescience" (1064). This objection, of disrespectfully doubting God's powers, does not apply to the alternative solution, that man does not have free will, but Troilus is reluctant to accept it. His final point is that when he knows something will happen, it must happen. This conclusion somewhat resembles the Monk's principle, that when Fortune decides to flee, she will flee. But whereas the Monk's premise is granted by authorial revelation, Troilus begs the question of his premise and the fallacy remains. For he does not in fact *know* that he must lose Criseyde; he only *fears* that it will happen. Pandarus expresses the matter well:

> What, parde, yet is nat Criseyde ago!
> Whi list the so thiself fordoon for drede?   (4.1090–91)

When we reexamine Troilus's prayer to Jove (1079–82) in the light of the tortuous reasoning that now precedes it, can we say that it has taken on a different meaning? I think not; rather, the prayer negates the entire thrust of the meditation, for in the prayer Troilus assumes that God still has freedom of disposition with regard to His creatures: He can pity Troilus and let him keep Criseyde, or He can bring him to an early death.

But Troilus's monologue does at least serve to show us his dispiritedness and abulia, and it helps to explain his willingness to rely on Criseyde's plan of action rather than his own.[37] Pandarus's reliance on Criseyde is less easy to understand. When he tells Criseyde that "Women ben wise in short avysement" (4.936), it makes as much sense as Chanticleer's interpretation of

---

[37] Cf. John Nist, "The Art of Chaucer: *Pathedy*," p. 5: Troilus rationalizes "a passive resistance to fate by means of a do-nothing philosophy."

Mulier est hominis confusio as "Womman is mannes joye and al his blis" (*Nuns' Priest* 3164–66). Nothing we have seen of Criseyde can justify this judgment: she has had to be manipulated in all of her actions, and no one should know it better than Pandarus. Are we to assume that he is relying on her inaction, as when he tells Troilus, "Myn herte seyth, 'Certeyn, she shal nat wende'" (4.1118)? Perhaps; but I believe that Pandarus's uncharacteristic abdication of responsibility (which I have made more obvious than it seems to have appeared to most readers) has a different explanation: it was necessary for the story line. Because the disastrous course of the story was predetermined in the mind of its re-creator, having decided to keep this part of his inheritance from Benoit and Boccaccio inviolate, he had to remove all obstacles to its fulfilment. He portrays Pandarus now not as a long-range plotter, but as a short-term consoler, who mingles thrift and unthrift together. He is made to urge Criseyde's wisdom on Troilus and on Criseyde herself as a way of alleviating their immediate distress, and then he is dropped from the action altogether until the treaty of exchange is carried through.

When Troilus obeys Pandarus's summons and goes to Criseyde, only to have her die in his arms (as he thinks), he at first seems both indecisive and prayerful. After lamenting her death for a long time,

> [He] pitously gan for the soule preye,
> And seyde, "O Lord, that set art in thi throne,
> Rewe ek on me, for I shal folwe hire sone."   (4.1174–76)

But it soon becomes apparent that he has decided to act for himself: to bring his bad ending in this world to a close by suicide; and his tone changes to one of irreligion, as he denounces "cruel Jove" and "Fortune adverse" (1192). I will argue in the chapter on Henryson that Chaucer is careful not to have his characters blaspheme God but only the pagan gods, and that Jove in this case is treated as one of the latter.[38] Troilus defiantly insults the deities as cowardly and says that no death will be able to separate him from his lady; but then he asks the gods to begrudge him the favor of letting his soul be together with Criseyde's in the otherworld (1204), and he calls upon Criseyde to receive his spirit (1210).

However, "as God wolde" (1212), the story does not end like Ovid's tragedy (so Chaucer would classify it) of Pyramus and Thisbe. Criseyde recovers and convinces Troilus that they must part, and must blindly trust that things will then take a prosperous turn. Her distortion of reality is caused by her anxiety to console both Troilus and herself. She is too pessimistic about alternatives that have a fair chance of success, and too optimistic about her own plan of being able to talk her way around Calkas. She is overly confident of her "seductive" powers. Perhaps her unwonted fluency at this point does hold out some hope for her ability to do as she says she will do, but Troilus is only half convinced, and gives in reluctantly. He tries to urge on her his counsel of how to provide against tragedy: "That folie is, whan man may

---

[38] See below, chap. 6, pp. 240–41. For a survey of references to the deities in *Troilus*, see Sanford B. Meech, *Design in Chaucer's Troilus*, pp. 215–26.

chese, / For accident his substaunce ay to lese" (4.1504–05); and: "It were a
gret folie / To putte that sikernesse in jupertie" (1511–12). But Criseyde has
a different hierarchy of substance and accident, or security and insecurity.
To her the important thing is that their honor is secure, and it would be
endangered, not only by a drastic action like elopement, but by any revelation of a love interest between them. She warns Troilus not to "juparten" his
name (1566), for the result would be tragic: "thus were al lost" (1574), and
"thus were I lost" (1582). She counters his bird-in-hand philosophy with
four proverbial considerations, allegedly the voice of reason arguing for passivity:

> Forthi sle with resoun al this hete!
> Men seyn, the suffrant overcomith, parde;
> Ek, whoso wol han lief, he lief moot lete;
> Thus, maketh vertu of necessite
> By pacience; and thynk that lord is he
> Of Fortune ay, that naught wole of hire recche,
> And she ne daunteth no wight but a wrecche.   (4.1583–89)

When Chaucer defends her by saying that she meant well, "And was in purpos
evere to be trewe: /Thus writen they that of hire werkes knewe" (1420–21),
he *is* being ominous. Both Troilus and Criseyde protest their trouthe, but
only Criseyde speaks of what she should suffer if she is not true—namely, an
early death and an eternity in hell (1534–47). They both worry about the bad
ends that may result from the failure of Criseyde's plan. Troilus fears that
her father will convince her of Troy's imminent destruction, or that she will
be swayed by the attractiveness of the Greek knights, unless the "virtue" or
strength of her trouthe intervenes (1478–91), and Criseyde is also concerned
about the strength of Troilus's trouthe, when she seeks assurance that while
she is gone "no plesaunce / Of oother do me fro youre remembraunce"
(1642–43). Troilus's worries do in fact come true, but not his prediction of
how he will react if she lingers among the Greeks: "I wol myselven sle if that
ye drecche" (1446).

However, in spite of our uneasiness about Criseyde's perseverance in
virtue, which is fed by Troilus's doubt about the feasibility of her plan of
action, Chaucer succeeds in soothing our fears somewhat when he comes to
the end of the fourth book, by showing Criseyde at her best; and he shows
her at her best by having her give a striking tribute to Troilus and his "moral
vertu, grounded upon trouthe" (4.1672). If she is capable of such sentiments,
surely she will somehow be found guiltless, a passive victim, in the coming
betrayal. In affirming her devotion to Troilus, which "may lengthe of yeres
nought fordo, / Ne remuable Fortune deface" (1681–82), she affirms, in
effect, that tragedy on this level is beyond Fortune's power, if only one is *willing* to oppose her. When she goes on to pray that Jupiter, who has power to
make "the sorwful to be glad" (1684), will allow them to meet before ten
nights pass, she descends to the region where bad endings are not completely
avoidable by the exercise of one's will: for physical actions are dependent on
other agencies as well.

Troilus's decision to let Criseyde go to the Greek camp will turn out, in retrospect, to be a mistake, and to have dire consequences. An author other than Chaucer, especially one familiar with post-medieval commentaries on Aristotle's *Poetics*, might well have pointed up Troilus's decision as a tragic error. But Chaucer (it seems to me) takes pains to prevent our thinking that Troilus is at fault in the matter: he had freedom not only of will but of action, but, after weighing various alternatives, all of them problematic, he reluctantly chose the one that seemed, at the moment, to promise the least of many evils.

OUTRAGEOUS FORTUNE

In real life, we cannot know what forces have combined to produce certain events. But the creator of a story can freely assign any set of causes he chooses. Chaucer introduces the catastrophe of his poem by designating Criseyde's departure and Troilus's grief and time of death as a matter of divine predestination. But he decorates the statement in "the forme of olde clerkis speche / In poetrie" (5.1854–55). Here is what he says:

> Aprochen gan the fatal destyne
> That Joves hath in disposicioun,
> And to yow, angry Parcas, sustren thre,
> Committeth, to don execucioun;
> For which Criseyde moste out of the town,
> And Troilus shal dwellen forth in pyne
> Til Lachesis his thred no lenger twyne.   (5.1–7)

Which is as much as to say, "The jig is up." Chaucer and his readers know now that there is no more hope; but our knowledge is constantly contrasted with the characters' lack of knowledge.

Troilus accompanies Criseyde to effect the exchange, like one who has already lost all his joys (5.23). We know that his loss is certain, for Chaucer calls out to him, "Troilus, now far-wel al thi joie" (27). Troilus, however, is not certain; he keeps asking himself why he does not stop it before it happens (39–40). Chaucer gives us Troilus's alleged reason for not doing "so fel a dede" as to take her away by force, namely, that she might be killed in the uproar ("rumour") that it would entail (50–56). Therefore, "ther is non other remedie in this cas" (60).

As the exchange proceeds, it turns out that, for all of his previous caution, Troilus betrays his relationship with Criseyde to the sharp-eyed Diomede. The offhandedness with which Diomede begins his attempt to win Criseyde—"At the werste it may yet short oure weye" (5.96)—could well remind us of Pandarus's words: "For syn it is but casuel plesaunce, / Som cas shal putte it out of remembraunce" (4.419–20).

Our interest in Diomede's methods of "amending" Criseyde's sorrow (5.136–40) would doubtless blunt our sympathy for Troilus's plight if we continued to observe them. But Chaucer gives us instead an immediate view of Troilus's sorrows. The bulk of the fifth book consists of an account of Troilus's agonies of suspense between the time that Criseyde leaves and the time that he finds out for sure that she has given herself to Diomede. All of Troilus's confrontations with unpleasant realities, including his initial falling in love with Criseyde in the first book, and his reactions to his perceived problems, make up an interesting case study from a psychological point of view; but this final, extended account is particularly amenable to such analysis, particularly in terms of Henry Murray's concepts of "alpha press" (the objective power for good or ill that a given situation has, as far as careful inquiry can establish it) and "beta press" (a person's own interpretation of the phenomena).[39] As applied by Clyde Kluckhohn, the alpha press gives rise to "fears" (reactions proportionate to the danger one has to face), while the beta press often produces "anxieties" (disproportionate reactions to danger or even reactions to imaginary dangers).[40]

Troilus's beta press is conveyed in about 1150 lines, and it is divided into nearly equal parts by a first-person narrative of what happens to Criseyde. In the first part of the Troilus narrative, which tells of how he whiles away the first nine days of his wait, his sorrow might seem to be excessive, as it did when the treaty of exchange was made. But in both cases his pain is increased by an incalculable and inexplicable foreboding, and this time, of course, it is also increased by the actual shock of separation. In effect, Chaucer gives us Troilus's "widowhood": he shows how he would have mourned her if she were dead, remembering her as wholly lovely and loving. This is not the tragic sorrow he will experience, but rather the sort of suffering undergone by Boethius's wonderfully virtuous wife, who is so sorrowful at being separated from him that she wants to die: "Sche lyveth loth of this lyf, and kepeth to the oonly hir goost, and is al maat and overcomen by wepynge and sorwe for desire of the."[41] In Troilus's view, Criseyde is experiencing these same emotions.

Troilus is by turns irreverent and reverent towards the gods. Immediately upon his return to Troy, we are told:

> In his throwes frenetik and madde,
> He corseth Jove, Appollo, and ek Cupide,
> He corseth Ceres, Bacus, and Cipride,
> His burthe, hymself, his fate, and ek Nature,
> And, save his lady, every creature.   (5.206–10)

But in a calmer mood he thinks once again of his death, which his sorrow must soon bring about. He leaves the details of his burial and the distribution of his goods to Pandarus, but he is specific about the pieties to be observed towards the gods. And now, not his soul but his ashes are to go to Criseyde. He seems indifferent to the fate of his soul, and simply prays to Mercury as psychopomp to take it where he pleases (5.295–322).

---

[39] Henry A. Murray, "Proposals for a Theory of Personality," pp. 41–42, 115–23.

[40] Clyde Kluckhohn, *Navaho Witchcraft*, pp. 87–88, drawing also on Karen Horney, *The Neurotic Personality of Our Time*, pp. 43–44.

[41] Chaucer, *Boece*, book 2 pr. 4 (*Riverside Chaucer*, p. 412).

But the greater part of this first phase of Troilus's lamentations seems to be a reflection of Boethius's dictum about prosperity and adversity: the greatest adversity is the recollection of lost prosperity. Pandarus reasonably advises Troilus to think of past happiness in terms of the same sort of happiness that will come again (393–96). Troilus, however, is unable to think of any pleasure apart from Criseyde, and she is gone: "I have lost the cause of al my game" (5.420). There is something decisive about this simple statement which sums up Chaucer's tragic theory, in spite of the qualification that follows (Troilus's expected joy when Criseyde returns).

Troilus does not treat his loss as merely spatial and temporary. This is clearly shown in his use of the *ubi sunt* convention:

> Wher is myn owene lady, lief and deere?
> Wher is hire white brest? Wher is it, where?
> Wher ben hire armes and hire eyen cleere,
> That yesternyght this tyme with me were? (5.218–21)

Normally the answer one expects to the "Where?" of such laments is "Nowhere," or "Gone for good,"[42] whereas in this case the answer called for by the alpha press, on the realistic and literal level of Troilus's expectations is, "A few miles away, for a few days." But in the depths of his misgiving heart she is only a memory.

In his conscious mind, Troilus's misgivings are directed towards himself: he underestimates his own endurance, and sees his imminent death as predicted by dreams and omens (316–20). Pandarus takes a skeptical view of such matters (358–85), and in this case he is right, for Troilus's auguries are not borne out. Pandarus himself is worried about the future, but in a more realistic way. He does not directly doubt Criseyde's character but he does doubt the success of her plan: he questions her ability to carry it off, because of his assessment of Calkas's character (507–08).

After the failure of the "Sarpedon cure," which succeeds only in raising Troilus's hopes that Criseyde has already returned, Chaucer shows Troilus augmenting his sense of loss in a number of ways. The festivities at Sarpedon's house are nothing but a source of sorrow because of Criseyde's absence (449–62). He constantly speaks to her, asks her how she has fared since her departure, bidding her "Welcome," perhaps in anticipation of her return (463–67). Chaucer seems to be suggesting that Troilus's sense of Criseyde's presence at these moments becomes quite vivid, for he adds that it was all a "maze" or delusion, part of Fortune's scheme to mock him (468–69).

Troilus also summons up the past by rereading Criseyde's letters, "Refiguryng hire shap, hire wommanhede, /Withinne his herte, and every word or dede /That passed was" (473–75). He does the same when revisiting all of the places connected with her and his love for her, beginning with her palace. For his apostrophe, especially in the lines, "O hous of houses whilom best ihight, /O paleys empty and disconsolat" (540–41), Chaucer may be drawing on a modified Arabic poem, *O domus egregia*, supposedly cited by Aristotle in his *Poetics*, according to Robert Holcot's *Commentary on the Book of*

---

[42] See the example cited by Averroes, below.

Wisdom, a work that Chaucer is known to have used.[43] In the course of citing examples of the transitoriness of this life, Holcot says, "Thus therefore it is clear that our life is always compared to transitory things, as in the response a certain old palace is said to have given according to the fable of a certain poet adduced by Aristotle in his *Poetry*, in these words." I translate it as we have it in Holcot, where Alemannus's rhymes have been partially lost:

> "O noble house! I am moved to tears in seeing thy solitude."
> But she trembled in pity for me at the multitude of my tears.
> I say to her, "Where, I beg of thee, are those who once dwelled
>   within thee,
> And led a happy life in the security and delightfulness of the
>   time?"
> She, however, responds: "Those temporal people, going forth
>   temporally with time,
> Dismissed me as well, and I also am to pass away at some
>   time, under time's allotment,
> For no things are stable which are fluxible, and flow with the
>   flux of this time."[44]

[43] For Chaucer's knowledge of Holcot's commentary, see Robert A. Pratt, "Some Latin Sources of the Nonnes Preest on Dreams," and, for suggested uses in the *Troilus*, see Alastair Minnis, *Chaucer and Pagan Antiquity*.

[44] Robert Holcot, *Commentary on Wisdom*, lesson 17, text as given by Smalley, *English Friars and Antiquity in the Early Fourteenth Century*, p.170:

> Sic ergo patet quod vita nostra semper rebus transitoriis comparatur, juxta responsionem quam quoddam vetus palatium desertum dicitur respondisse, unde Aristoteles in *Poetria* inducit fabulam cujusdam poete in hiis verbis:
>
> "[O] domus egregia! Compungor ad lacrimas, tuam intuens solitudinem!"
> At illa contremuit, compassa michi propter lacrimarum multitudinem.
> Cui inquio: "Ubi, queso, sunt qui quondam in te habitaverunt,
> Et jocundam vitam cum securitate et temporis amenitate duxerunt?"
> At illa, "Temporales," inquid, "exeuntes [*lege* existentes] temporaliter cum tempore [transierunt],
> Et me quoque sub sorte temporis quandoque transituram dimiserunt.
> Res nempe nulle stabiles que cum fluxu hujus temporis fluxibiles fluunt [*lege* fuerunt]."

Hec responsio palatii.

For Holcot's use of Alemannus's translation of Averroes's *Commentary on the Poetics*, which Smalley noted belatedly (pp. 379–80), see above, chap. 2, pp. 39–40 n. 4; for this passage, see the editions of William F. Boggess (pp. 54–55) and Lorenzo Minio-Paluello (p. 61), and see Boggess, "Hermannus Alemannus' Latin Anthology of Arabic Poetry," p. 666, where he edits the poem according to Alemannus's rhymed lines (I indicate the correct readings of Alemannus's text in brackets). Holcot used the abbreviated recension of Alemannus that attributed some Arabic material to Aristotle; see ARISTOTLE-AVERROES-ALEMANNUS, p. 175. The original poem as cited by Averroes is by Qais al-Magnun b. 'Amir, and it concerns not a house but a mountain and surrounding villages. Here is Butterworth's translation (pp. 106–07):

> I broke into tears when I saw Mount Tubadh, and it praised the Compassionate [God] when it saw me.
> So I said to it, "Where are those I knew so well dwelling around you in safety and blissful tranquillity?"
> And it said, "They went away and left me their villages for safekeeping. For who will remain in the face of adversity?"

Troilus carries on through a sentimental journey of "yonders," while telling Pandarus "his newe sorwe, and ek his joies olde" (558). In the prayer that he makes to Cupid in the midst of these recollections, he says that the history of his adversities, which he has relived in his mind, can easily be turned into a book:

> Thanne thoughte he thus, "O blisful lord Cupide,
> Whan I the proces have in my memorie,
> How thow me hast wereyed on every syde,
> Men myght a book make of it, lik a storie."   (5.582–85)

He does not, however, want the book to be a tragedy (if we can fairly assume that Troilus shared his creator's generic categories), for he hopes for a happy ending. It would in that case be a comedy.

Chaucer sympathetically but realistically points out that Troilus has let his imagination run away with him in thinking that his sorrow has taken greater physical toll on him than it actually has (617–27), and it may be too that Troilus's notion of Cupid's vengeance against him is another example of a subjective "fantasie," an imaginary anxiety. At any rate, nothing more is made of the idea, either by Troilus or by Chaucer.[45]

At the end of this part of the depiction of Troilus's agony, he finally moves his gaze from the yonders of the past to the yonders of the present: "Lo, yonder is myn owene lady free, /Or ellis yonder, ther tho tentes be" (669–70). His notion that the breeze is caused by Criseyde's sighs serves as a transition to the site of the Greek camp, where we will finally see what it is that Troilus will really have to sorrow about.

We are not shown Criseyde's attempt to carry out her plan of convincing Calkas to let her return; we only hear her tell herself that she has tried and failed: "My fader nyl for nothyng do me grace /To gon ayeyn, for naught I kan hym queme" (694–95). It is nothing but the plain truth that Criseyde speaks: "Now is wors than evere yet I wende" (693). For she had staked everything upon her being able to return to Troy, with the acquiescence of her father, even if only for brief visits to her kinsfolk. The only other solution that she had thought of was that the war might suddenly end peacefully (4.1345–58). She had never expressed any notion whether to herself or to Troilus, that she might have to escape by stealth. Yet she now sees this as the only alternative.

As she considers its feasibility, the first objection that strikes her is that she may be caught by the Greeks and convicted as a spy, or else that she may fall into the hands of "som wrecche" (5.701–05). But she later disregards these possibilities and thinks only of the risk to her honor—a risk that she is determined to run for the sake of her happiness with Troilus; she will be content to have happiness without honor: "Felicite clepe I my suffisance" (763).

[45] Howard Patch, "Troilus on Determinism," p. 82, states that Criseyde's infidelity is meant to be seen as punishment visited upon Troilus for his sins against the Court of Love at the beginning. But we have seen that Love's "punishment" of Troilus was immediate and beneficial. In chap 6 below, pp. 240–41, I argue that Henryson does show Cupid as fatally vengeful against Criseyde, a motif that is then dropped in favor of the idea of general mutability.

It seems plausible that Chaucer means us to agree that Criseyde should have attempted an escape, rather than simply remaining loyal to Troilus while agonizing over her separation from him. If so, why, in the last analysis (that is, in Chaucer's presentation), does she not make the attempt?

A recent assessment finds the key to her actions in the social constraints of her position as a woman in high society—not, however, the high society of ancient Troy, but of Chaucer's own time and place. David Aers maintains that, far from trying to transport his readers "away from contemporary reality to a distant and romantic Troy," as Karl Young would have it, or exemplifying preexistent and well-known ethical universals, as set forth by Morton Bloomfield, Chaucer "was *exploring* the position of woman in aristocratic society, ideology, and literary convention" of fourteenth-century England.[46] He says that "upper class woman was totally subordinate to man and to land, aristocratic marriages being primarily land transactions, and child marriage commonplace," and he quotes Eileen Power's assessment of the landowning lady under the common law: "When she married, her rights, for the duration of the marriage, slipped out of her hands. The lands of which she was tenant-in-fee at the time of her marriage, or which she might acquire later, forthwith became her husband's for the duration of the marriage."[47] Rather than marry Troilus, then, Criseyde maintained a secret relationship with him, which allowed her to be bartered to the Greeks, where she is shown to be, as before, in the midst of "the crippling social reality and ideology which constitute her circumstances" and which account for her failure to attempt a clandestine escape.[48] In other words, her alpha-press situation is sufficiently daunting without needing to be influenced by any beta-press anxieties.

Stephen Knight is hesitant to accept this view of Criseyde, which he calls "protofeminist," but his own assessment, that "Chaucer is not so much creating a female position in its own right as exploiting the fact that women did not share in feudal and patriarchal power,"[49] also needs to be treated with

[46] David Aers, "Criseyde: Woman in Medieval Society," pp. 179, 198 n. 8, citing Karl Young, "Chaucer's *Troilus and Criseyde* as Romance," and referring to Morton W. Bloomfield, "Distance and Predestination in *Troilus and Criseyde*." In the revised version of his essay, "Chaucer's Criseyde: Woman in Society, Woman in Love," pp. 118, 219, Aers omits the reference to Bloomfield.

[47] Aers, "Criseyde," pp. 180, 185, citing "The Lady," one of the popular essays of Eileen Power (1889–1940) posthumously published by M. M. Postan, p. 38; in "Chaucer's Criseyde," pp. 124–25, 220 n. 9, Aers keeps the reference but omits the quotation.

[48] Aers, "Criseyde," p. 194; cf. p. 193: "By the opening of Book Five Troilus and Criseyde have accommodated themselves to the crippling social reality against which Troilus suggested they rebel." Aers's views of the debased conditions of society in Chaucer's day are influenced, as with many Chaucerians, by the satirical pictures of William Langland and John Gower and by a "realistic" view of Chaucer's fabliaux and his other contemporary settings. For more positive assessments, especially of ecclesiastical institutions and practices, see R. N. Swanson, *Church and Society in Late Medieval England*, and Eamon Duffy, *The Stripping of the Altars: Traditional Religion in England, c. 1400–c. 1580*, and see my "Sacraments, Sacramentals, and Lay Piety in Chaucer's England."

[49] Stephen Knight, *Geoffrey Chaucer*, p. 45. Aers develops his feminist reading of Criseyde somewhat further in "Masculine Identity in the Courtly Community: The Selfloving in *Troilus and Criseyde*," where he notes that the men in the Trojan parliament "turn Criseyde into a commodity, perceiving women as mere objects in a system of exchange to be operated in what they

caution (as Knight himself seems to do). If we are to speculate about social influences in *Troilus and Criseyde* from Chaucer's own time, it would be more realistic to consider *postfeudal* aspects, as Paul Strohm does in looking at the place of oaths in the poem.[50] And though it is true that Chaucer has elevated Criseyde's status in his poem—Knight points out that he gives her a palace rather than the house she had in Boccaccio[51]—we can hardly think of her (or, for that matter, of anyone else in Chaucer's presentation of the besieged city-state of Troy) as the sort of larger landowner governed by the common-law custom of the King's Court. We only hear, vaguely, of her "possession," which Poliphete, whom Criseyde expects to be backed by his friends Antenor and Aeneas, supposedly wants to wrest from her by new advocacies (2.1416–75). This seems to be more on the level of Chaucer's own legal dealings and on the level of wealthy women like the Wife of Bath and May (if she cooperates with January's proposal of a postnuptial agreement)[52] and, in real life, Margery Kempe, for whom the independent use of wealth even while married was a reality upheld by powerful local customs. Such customs were frequently favored against the common law in the king's courts, as Mary Carruthers has noted.[53]

But all such considerations seem to be very much in the background of Chaucer's presentation, for, as even Aers recognizes, Criseyde is shown to be "aware that the relevant problems go beyond the issue of marriage and male domination to embrace the way any full and serious love for another person necessarily involves risking oneself, jeopardizing a self-possession often won with great pain and difficulty."[54] Furthermore, Troy is at war with the Greeks, and, as Knight says of book 4, "the margins of this story have suddenly swarmed across the page";[55] and Criseyde is caught up in her personal problems stemming from her father's treason, as well as with complicated notions of honor that are only shadowed forth to us and not fully explained.

take to be their own interest" (p. 132). Compare Dinshaw, *Chaucer's Sexual Politics*, who says that "trafficking in women is a fundamental activity in Troy" (p. 58). Aers, however, notes that the exchange of Criseyde is made over Hector's objections (p. 125). Hector in fact indicates that such trafficking is highly unusual: "We usen here no wommen for to selle" (5.182). In a "second-generation" feminist analysis (see Jonathan Dollimore, *Radical Tragedy*, pp. xxxiii–xxxiv), Elaine Tuttle Hansen in *Chaucer and the Fictions of Gender* takes issue with Aers's view (pp. 141–43), not on grounds of a historical social analysis, but by questioning the nature of Chaucer's sympathy for Criseyde. From the social-political point of view, she finds Troilus and Pandarus just as powerless as Criseyde against those with power over them (pp. 173–74).

[50] Paul Strohm, *Social Chaucer*, pp. 102–04, in the section, " 'Trouthe' in a Postfeudal Society."

[51] Knight, *Geoffrey Chaucer*, p. 45.

[52] Chaucer, *Merchant's Tale* 2160–75; according to Joseph Allen Hornsby, *Chaucer and the Law*, "January is promising to override his gift of dower by executing a conveyance that would vest his property in her immediately rather than upon his death" (p. 94). Presumably one of January's requirements is that May agree to be true to him after his death and promise not to remarry (see 2077–80), even though he tells her that she is free to make up the charters as she wishes (2173).

[53] Mary Carruthers, "The Wife of Bath and the Painting of Lions," p. 210; she takes up Margery Kempe on p. 219 n. 11. Criseyde, of course, would undoubtedly have been perceived by Chaucer as belonging to a higher social level than Margery.

[54] Aers, "Criseyde," p. 186; "Chaucer's Criseyde," p. 125.

[55] Knight, *Geoffrey Chaucer*, p. 55.

This is the immediate social pressure brought to bear on her as she finds herself in the Greek camp.

Therefore, Aers's conclusion about the cumulative effect of her experiences upon her: "Her total situation, with all its pressures working on an individual trained by her society to *accommodate* to an antagonistic reality rather than rebel (as Troilus recommended) now expands to include a new aristocratic lover, Diomede,"[56] seems to me less plausible than Knight's more positive view of her earlier circumstances: "Although she is oppressed by the public world and its pressures, she is not thrown into dysfunctional passivity by the privatizing impact of love, and that is because she possesses or has developed resources in the private domain"; if she is fearful, it is "because she recognizes problems; she is also a person of private status and strength." Her acquiescence to Diomede's importunities is not love but "rather it is the complex of social pressures that led medieval women to marry where they felt they must, to make a contract for want of a better option, and then to set themselves to keep its terms."[57] The end result may seem the same as in Aers's analysis, but a stronger Criseyde earlier on makes it harder to give a convincing picture of her later actions. Yet I agree that in showing her capitulation to Diomede Chaucer does achieve a "brilliantly realized understanding of how and why people make decisions that go against their inner wishes and feelings."[58] Let us analyze his achievement.

He indicates that the real reason she stayed in the Greek camp was that she changed her mind about wanting to leave:

> But God it wot, er fully monthes two,
> She was ful fer fro that entencioun.
> For bothe Troilus and Troie town
> Shal knotteles thorughout hire herte slide;
> For she wol take a purpos for t'abide.   (5.766–70)

In so saying, he does not explain her motivation. But later he singles out three factors, none of them specifically related to the dangers of an escape attempt, that were the basis of her decision to remain with the Greeks: namely, (1) the impression that Diomede's words and great estate made on her; (2) her fear that Troy would be destroyed; and (3) her lack of friends (1023–29).

Earlier, Criseyde blamed her present situation, of being separated from Troilus, on her lack of prudence in not taking the course that Troilus advised:

> Prudence, allas, oon of thyne eyen thre
> Me lakked alwey, er that I come here.
> On tyme ypassed wel remembred me,
> And present tyme ek koud ich wel ise;
> But future tyme, er I was in the snare,
> Koude I nat sen; that causeth now my care.   (5.744–49)

---

[56] Aers, "Criseyde," p. 194; "Chaucer's Criseyde," p. 135.
[57] Knight, *Geoffrey Chaucer*, pp. 47, 60.
[58] Ibid., p. 61.

She is right about her inability to assess the future; and whether or not she was capable before this time of understanding the implications of past and present, she is not equal to it now; and it is this inadequacy that causes her further downfall.

Like Troilus, she calls up the image and words of her beloved (715–21), and also like him she is moved by the physical reminders of happiness in Troy (729–33). But her long-range and necessarily dimmer view of the buildings of Troy is symbolic of the diffused focus of her insight, surrounded as she is by dangers and the temptations of Diomede, as opposed to the acuteness of Troilus's inner vision. When she wonders how Troilus is coping with the separation, she casts some doubt upon his perseverance in love: " 'O Troilus, what dostow now?" she seyde. / 'Lord! wheyther thow yet thenke upon Criseyde?' " (734–35). One might say, of course, that Troilus is just as lacking in insight as Criseyde: she is wrong in so readily thinking of weakness in him, and he is wrong in not considering the likelihood of weakness in her. But Troilus did warn her of the possibility that she might be swayed by Greek gallantry, "but if routhe / Remorde yow, or vertu of youre trouthe" (4.1490–91). However, Troilus's strength of insight lies primarily in his true appreciation of meanings and values, a nobility of mind that by its very nature entails a belief and hope for similar nobility in Criseyde. It would be unworthy of him to think otherwise without good reason.[59]

When Jill Mann says that "the real tragedy of *Troilus and Criseyde* is not simply that Troilus is separated from Criseyde, it is that she ceases to exist as the Criseyde he has known and loved,"[60] she is speaking of the grounds for *our* lamentation; but her statement also reveals the differences in the personal tragedies of Troilus and Criseyde, that is, the grounds for their lamentation: the adversity of remembering lost prosperity. Because of what happens beween her and Diomede, we must doubtless conclude that she no longer fully appreciates Troilus and the love that he and she shared, and that therefore her memory of it is not as intense as Troilus's. But it is tragic nonetheless, especially when combined with other motives for grief. For even if it is true that Diomede "refte hire of the grete of al hire peyne" (5.1036), he did not remove from her her sense of loss and the guilt of betrayal; she has lost not only Troilus but her honor as well:

> Allas, for now is clene ago
> My name of trouthe in love for everemo!
> For I have falsed oon the gentileste
> That evere was, and oon the worthieste![61]   (5.1054–57)

The honor that she was so afraid of injuring in her relationship with Troilus was primarily her external reputation, since she did not believe herself to be

---

[59] I do not mean to say that Troilus is always reasonable in his ideas of and demands on Criseyde, in expecting her, for instance, to escape, helpless and unaided, from the Greek camp. On this point see Aers, "Masculine Identity," summarized in "The Self Mourning: Reflections on *Pearl*," 54–55.

[60] Mann, *Geoffrey Chaucer*, pp. 30–31.

[61] These expressions are straight superlatives: "the greatest" and "the worthiest," not, "among the greatest and worthiest." See Barney's note on 3.781–82, *Riverside Chaucer*, p. 1040.

doing anything shameful in loving Troilus (unlike Boccaccio's Criseida, who admits that Troiolo is to have full pleasure of her without becoming her husband).[62] She might have lost the "name of trouthe" by exposing her moral love for Troilus to the view of a public that would judge it immoral, but her resulting ill-fame would have been groundless. She would still have had the reality of trouthe, by remaining true to Troilus and true to herself. She could still hope to content herself with felicity. But by changing her devotion from Troilus to Diomede, she sacrifices not only public esteem but her self-respect as well, and forgoes all hope of true felicity.

One cannot say that Criseyde's ending in *Troilus and Criseyde*, merely because she has gone over to Diomede and lives on, is a happy one, as has sometimes been implied.[63] Anyone who can sympathize with Chaucer's final words on her: "For she so sory was for hire untrouthe, /Iwis, I wolde excuse hire yet for routhe" (1093–99), must agree that Criseyde's story, if told by itself, would be an effective tragedy, in Chaucerian terms. It would fulfill Harry Bailly's requirement of being well reported and moving. We will see later what can be said of Robert Henryson's attempt to take Criseyde's tragedy "further than the story will devise."

Criseyde predicts that nothing good will be reported of her (1058–60), which is belied by Chaucer's sympathetic treatment, and also, as we shall see, by Henryson's presentation. But she is justified in saying that her guilt will be exaggerated and that people will make her out to be worse than she is: we need only remember Pistol's "lazar kite of Cressid's kind,"[64] which is a distortion of Henryson's account. Chaucer shows her as thinking primarily of what other women, and the authors of books, will say; but we will see him describing even Troilus as at least tempted to think of her in unfairly vicious terms.

Chaucer's main concern is the tragedy of Troilus, and he makes Criseyde's loss less grave, in part by limiting her capacity to understand, to suffer, and to sympathize. When she partially rationalizes her betrayal of Troilus with her promise of a pale *amor amicitie*, she adds: "And, trewely, I wolde sory be /For to seen yow in adversitee." (1082–83). She means, obviously, some adversity or trouble other than that which he is in by her betrayal of him— not realizing or admitting that he could have no greater adversity.

It is often thought that Chaucer intended to give an honest summation of Criseyde's character in the portrait that he presents of her in this section of the poem, between the portraits of Diomede and Troilus. But in all three portraits the terms are mainly eulogistic. Even the report of some men that Diomede was "large" of tongue (5.804) could be taken *in bonum*.[65] In the three

---

[62] Boccaccio, *Filostrato* 2.45.

[63] See, for example, Alfred David, "Chaucerian Comedy and Criseyde," p. 92: "Unlike the tragedy of Troilus, the comic action has no ending, for Chaucer does not tell us what became of Criseyde." See also Boitani, "Eros and Thanatos," p. 283.

[64] Shakespeare, *Henry V* 2.1.76. "Lazar kite" means "leprous whore."

[65] The description is based on Boccaccio, *Filostrato* 6.33.1–5:

> Egli era grande e bel della persona,
> Giovane, fresco, e piacevole assai,
> E forte e fier, sì come si ragiona,

stanzas devoted to Criseyde, only her joined eyebrows are noted as a defect, and that merely a defect in her physical beauty. As for her character, the list of her attributes ends thus:

> Charitable, estatlich, lusty, and fre,
> Ne nevere mo ne lakked hire pite,
> Tendre-herted, slydynge of corage.   (5.823–25)

Most readers have taken the last phrase to indicate not a strength but a weakness, even a tragic flaw, which would explain how she came to let Troilus and Troy "slide" through her heart (769); and they take it to correspond to Benoit's expression, "Mais sis corages le chanjot."[66] But in the context of Chaucer's lines, coming as the culmination of a series of positive qualities, without any adversative particle, the expression looks very much as if it is meant to be an amplification of Criseyde's pitying and tenderhearted nature, meaning something like, "easily moved."[67] If so, we have in this strangely placed portrait not an *ad hoc* explanation of why Criseyde fails as she does, but simply a timeless encomium of her as a generous and tenderhearted beauty. Similarly, the portrait of Troilus that follows would not be meant to contrast Troilus's strength of character with Criseyde's weakness, but merely to praise his physical prowess. The expression, "trewe as stiel in ech condicioun" (5.831) seems to be not a moral assessment, but rather an amplification of the previous line, "Yong, fressh, strong, and hardy as lyoun."

> E parlante quant' altro Greco mai,
> E ad amor la natura avea prona.

R. K. Gordon translates thus: "He was tall and fair of person, young, fresh, and very pleasing, and mighty and proud, it is said, and as ready of speech as ever any Greek was; and by nature he was inclined to love" (p. 106). The translation of Robert P. apRoberts and Anna Bruni Seldis is similar, except for a less favorable rendering of line 4: "and as smooth-tongued as ever any other Greek" (p. 335). Barney interprets "large" as "lavish of speech" and Windeatt as "free of tongue." The *Middle English Dictionary* takes a more dubious view (perhaps partially based on the editors' dislike of Diomede?): this passage serves as the earliest entry in category 12 under "large, *adj.*," in which "large of tonge" or "large of langage" means "unrestrained or untruthful in use of language." Chaucer uses the word neutrally in *Legend of Good Women* 2515: Phyllis's letter was "ryght long and therto large." In *Parliament of Fowls* 556 it becomes unfavorable (in a humorous sense) by being linked with "golee" ("mouthful").

[66] *Roman de Troie* 5286, cited by Barney, p. 1053.

[67] Chaucer uses "sliding" in a positive or at least neutral way in *Boece*, book 5 m. 1 (*Riverside Chaucer*, p. 458): "the flowinge ordre of the slydinge watir." John Lydgate in his *Troy Book* gives a version of Criseyde's portrait (attributing it entirely to Guido of Le Colonne) in which he introduces postpositive adversative language that makes even tenderheartedness a defect. The portrait ends thus:

> Also sche was, for al hir semlynes,
> Ful symple and meke and ful of sobirnes,
> The best norisshed eke that myghte be,
> Goodly of speche, fulfilde of pite,
> Facundious, and therto right tretable,
> And, as seith Guydo, in love variable—
> Of tendre herte and unstedfastnes
> He hir accuseth, and newfongilnes.   (2.4755–62)

If this explanation is correct, one might argue that the portraits of Criseyde and Troilus should have been put at the beginning of the story, when the characters were first introduced. Only the portrait of Diomede is properly placed. Perhaps what happened is that when Chaucer came upon the description of Diomedes in Joseph of Exeter's *Iliad of Dares*, he also found those of Troilus and Briseis, and decided to give similar portraits of all three characters at this juncture: better late than never. They are, in fact, impressive where they stand.

But even though the portraits seem to have been written in abstraction from the vicissitudes of the story, they cannot help but be affected by what has happened and what is in the course of happening. Diomede's largeness of speech, Troilus's steely trouthe, and Criseyde's tenderheartedness take on specific connotations and implications in accordance with the action. To focus on Criseyde, it is, according to Robert apRoberts, precisely the virtues constituting her womanly perfection, including tenderness of heart, as described in the first four books, that make it impossible to attain the kind of heroic virtue and rare strength of character necessary to remain faithful in the adverse circumstances of book 5.[68]

The second phase of Chaucer's description of Troilus's agonized wait for Criseyde takes up where the first left off, on the last day of the agreed-upon time of return. Our attitude towards his plight has now changed, since we not only know for sure that all is lost, but we have witnessed it, whereas Troilus goes on as before: but not for long.

It is clear that once Troilus begins to suspect Criseyde, his sense of adversity deepens. In view of this development, which seems altogether natural, should we not question the truth of Boethius's statement that the worst adversity is the memory of lost prosperity? It is, of course, not meant to be true in the large context of Boethius's work. In absolute terms, the worst adversity, whether or not it is perceived as such, is to lose sight of God and turn to evil. But here we are dealing not with objective but with subjective adversity: specifically the grief of mind of one who has not yet received the consolation of philosophy. For such a person, it is unquestionably painful to lose prosperity. But, in some cases, at least, it must be even more painful to proceed to the realization of having been deceived in the very midst of prosperity.

Like the protagonist of *Oedipus rex*, Troilus experiences a growing recognition, rather than a sudden recognition, of a terrible truth. We, the audience, know the truth, while Troilus wonders about it, hopes it is not so, seeks confirmation of yea or nay, and resists in the face of mounting evidence until all resistance is impossible.

When Troilus seeks expert interpretation of his dream of the boar from his sister Cassandra, he furiously rejects her confirmation of his suspicions, and counters it by likening Criseyde to Alcestis. He recounts the history of Alcestis thus:

> Whan hire housbonde was in jupertye
> To dye hymself, but if she wolde dye,

---

[68]   Robert P. apRoberts, "Criseyde's Infidelity and the Moral of the *Troilus*."

She ches for hym to dye and gon to helle,
And starf anon, as us the bokes telle.   (5.1530–33)

By omitting the happy ending, Troilus converts the story into the kind of tragedy that he earlier saw himself as inspiring (while hoping for a transformation into a comedy): "Men myght a book make of it, lik a storie" (585)—that is, of a husband grieving over the loss of his faithful wife. He cannot yet believe that he will provide the subject matter for a crueler tragedy, which is unfeelingly summed up by Cassandra:

Thy lady, wherso she be, ywis,
This Diomede hire herte hath, and she his.
Wep if thow wolt, or lef! For, out of doute,
This Diomede is inne, and thow art oute.   (5.1516–19)

Some readers think that Troilus brought his tragedy upon himself for trusting Criseyde as he did: that is, they see his trust as a fault, even a moral fault. My own perception is that, as Chaucer presents him, he would have been wrong not to trust her. He did the best that he was capable of, and the best as he saw it demanded full confidence in Criseyde. He was himself incapable of defection, and he was right to expect the same of Criseyde. He was disappointed in his expectations, and therefore mistaken, but he was not at fault. This is not to say that we have to agree with his course of conduct. Just as some lover in Chaucer's audience might say, "so nold I nat love purchace" (2.33), so another could justifiably think that there would be a better way to protect his love. But it is Troilus's story, not ours. Troilus himself has provided an answer to those critics who think that there is, or was, some theoretical objection to his trust in Criseyde.[69] His example of Alcestis shows that it is not unreasonable to look for heroic virtue in another person, even in a woman! This is not, of course, to deny that in practice, as opposed to theory, Criseyde's actual circumstances could be seen to be more problematic than the clear choice that Alcestis perceived.

When Troilus finally realizes the truth, through discovery of the brooch, Chaucer's account of his reaction to this revelation, toward which the whole poem has been moving, is surprisingly brief, in comparison with the exhaustive detailing of the time of agonized uncertainty. There is a parallel, perhaps, in the *Book of the Duchess*. Chaucer spends a long time consoling the Man in Black for his indeterminate sorrow, but when its true nature is revealed to him, he can only say: "Is that youre los? Be God, hyt ys routhe!" (1310). Troilus tells all to Pandarus, but Chaucer is succinct in reporting it (1668–71). Troilus seems to think now that much of his suffering was needless; he chides Criseyde for not telling him of her change of heart and for leading him on with false hopes (1678–80). But Criseyde doubtless intended to soften the

[69] For example, T. P. Dunning, "God and Man in *Troilus and Criseyde*," who says that Troilus had a fundamental error in his understanding of human love, in "overcharging it beyond the limits of human nature" (p. 174); he holds that only God could match Troilus's constancy (p. 181). Dunning's remarks are cited with approval by Alfred David, *The Strumpet Muse: Art and Morals in Chaucer's Poetry*, p. 32.

blow, and perhaps succeeded in doing so. Troilus finds her giving of his brooch
to Diomede particularly painful to think of, and assumes at first that she
must have acted "for despit." But he immediately adds another reason: "and
ek for that ye mente / Al outrely to shewen youre entente" (1693–94)—
which, of course, is in direct opposition to his idea that she was deliberately
"holding him in hand" (1680).

In so blaming Criseyde, Troilus is not speaking the truth;[70] nor is he right in
thinking that she has cast him clean out of her mind (5.1695–96). She is not
spiteful, or heartless; she still loves him in her way, and sorrows over what
has happened between them, especially what she has brought about through
her own fault. But though Troilus in his disappointment does not articulate
an accurate judgment of Criseyde, his feelings seem to be closer to the truth.
He does not, like Pandarus, hate Criseyde for what she has done. In the last
words that we hear from him he addresses her as "swete may" (1720), thus
acknowledging that she must still be much as she was in the past. It is not
only because of the strength of his trouthe that he cannot find it in his heart
to "unlove" her a quarter of a day (1696–98), but also because he still values
her for what she is. He puts the chief blame upon Diomede, and seeks to
punish his vicious seduction of Criseyde as an act of virtue, and he prays for
divine aid:

> "Now God," quod he, "me sende yet the grace
> That I may meten with this Diomede!
> And trewely, if I have myght and space,
> Yet shal I make, I hope, his sydes blede."   (5.1702–05)

TERMINAL MISERY

Chaucer is at great pains towards the end of his poem to clarify the context
and meaning of Troilus's misfortune. He points up the narrow context of personal loss through the conceit of Fortune: Fortune "thenketh for to jape"
both Pandarus and Troilus as they await Criseyde's return on the tenth day
(5.1134). Later we hear, "Gret was the sorwe and pleynte of Troilus, / But
forth hire cours Fortune ay gan to holde" (1744–45). Furthermore, "Fortune
it naught ne woulde" that Diomede or Troilus should die at the other's hand
(1763–64). There is also the wider context of the fall of empires; for what do
tragedies lament if not Fortune's random and unexpected overthrow of
happy kingdoms? An example of such a tragedy, or series of tragedies, was
provided, in Chaucer's opinion, in Statius's *Thebaid*. The substance of the
epic is recalled by Cassandra, as she recounts to Troilus "a fewe of olde stories" of "how that Fortune overthrowe / Hath lordes olde" (1458–60). Much
of what she tells is a paraphrase of the twelve Latin hexameters summarizing
the twelve books of the *Thebaid*, which are given in most of the manuscripts

[70] See Richard H. Osberg, "Between the Motion and the Act: Intentions and Ends in Chaucer's
Troilus," p. 263: "Troilus's painful realization demonstrates that at last he has pierced through
complexity and obscurity to identify a single concrete fact—Criseyde's 'untrouthe'—although
even here the intention Troilus imputes to Criseyde is wide of the mark."

of the *Troilus*.[71] This material contains hardly any "prosperity for a time," but has a plentiful supply of irreversible wretchedness ending with the burning of Thebes (1510).

After Troilus's encounter with Cassandra, Chaucer says that "he drieth forth his aventure" (1540), while at the same time Fortune prepares another subject for large-scale tragedy, namely, the destruction of Troy:

> Fortune, which that permutacioun
> Of thynges hath, as it is hire comitted
> Thorugh purveyaunce and disposicioun
> Of heighe Jove, as regnes shal be flitted
> Fro folk in folk, or whan they shal be smytted,
> Gan pulle awey the fetheres brighte of Troie
> Fro day to day, til they ben bare of joie.   (5.1541–47)

It can hardly be said in this case that Fortune's overthrow of Troy was brought about by a single *ictus indiscretus*. But the deadliest blow of all, the sad fate of Hector, was clearly an "unwar strook":

> For as he drough a kyng by th'aventaille,
> Unwar of this, Achilles thorugh the maille
> And thorugh the body gan hym for to ryve.   (5.1558–60)

In Guido's account, it is clearly Hector who was unaware of what was happening: "non advertente Hectore."[72] But in Chaucer it is ambiguous and therefore open to both the active and passive meaning of the Latin *indiscretus*: Achilles may not have realized that his victim was Hector, and Hector was clearly taken by surprise.

Hector's death is unmistakably the sort of misfortune that could provoke a *tragediarum clamor*, and Troilus's sorrow is especially intense (1562–64). Earlier, we recall, when Troilus feared the departure of Criseyde, he asked Fortune why she did not visit him with a lesser disaster, such as the death of his brothers (4.274–77). Now she has done both, and will do more.

One of the lessons that we, the audience, are to learn from Troilus's private tragedy (the loss of Criseyde), and perhaps also from his public tragedy (the loss of Hector) is resignation:

> Swich is this world, whoso it kan byholde:
> In ech estat is litel hertes reste.
> God leve us for to take it for the beste!   (5.1748–50)

Chaucer spoke in nearly the same terms earlier:

> But Troilus, thow maist now, est or west,
> Pipe in an ivy lef, if that the lest!

---

[71] F. P. Magoun, Jr., "Chaucer's Summary of Statius's *Thebaid* II–XII," shows that Chaucer also used the twelve-line Latin arguments for the individual books of Statius's poem, and perhaps also the poem itself.

[72] Cited by Root, p. 557.

> Thus goth the world. God shilde us fro meschaunce,
> And every wight that meneth trouthe avaunce!   (5.1432–35)

On the face of it, I suppose, these lines ask God to protect us from a misfortune like Troilus's; but they are also capable of conveying a hope that God will reward the virtuous (those who mean trouthe) in spite of, or even because of, the misfortunes they endure. To take in good part Criseyde's disingenuous sentiment, "Th' entente is al" (5.1630), if God rewards even sinners who repent, why should He not reward those who remain true? We saw that Pandarus once told Troilus, in an "applied" context, "Thow shalt be saved by thi feyth in trouthe" (2.1503), and on another occasion he pointed out to him that if he died a martyr he would go to heaven (4.623). It can be argued that something of this sort was, if not Chaucer's first view of Troilus's fate, at least his final judgment.

If we accept the hypothesis that Chaucer did not at first think of giving Troilus an ascent to the heavens, as is suggested by the omission of lines 1807–27 in some of the manuscripts,[73] the flow of thought at the end of the poem would be as follows:

(1) I will not detail Troilus's military feats, since his love is my main subject.   (1765–71)
(2) Criseyde should be a warning against all false lovers, men as well as women.   (1772–85)
(3) I hope this tragedy is properly understood.   (1786–99)
(4) But to return to Troilus's deeds of war against the Greeks, he killed thousands, until, alas, he too was slain by Achilles.   (1800–06)
(5) He ended this way for love, an end typical of the brittleness of the false world we live in.   (1828–34)
(6) The only way to cope with the world satisfactorily is to ignore it entirely and love Christ alone, for He will never betray us.   (1835–48)
(7) In contrast, you can see in the course of this work the troubles brought on by trust in false gods and by the wretched desires of the world, which I have set forth in the style of the ancient poets.   (1849–55)
(8) I ask Gower and Strode to accept, and if necessary to correct, this book, and I beseech God to protect us and make us worthy of His mercy.[74]   (1856–69)

---

[73] See Root, p. lxxii. Windeatt, "Text of the *Troilus*," pp. 5–6, argues that Chaucer always intended to insert these three stanzas, which are based on Arcita's soul journey in the *Teseida*, but wrote them out on a separate sheet, to be inserted between his rendering of stanzas 27 and 28 of book 8 of the *Filostrato*, corresponding to *Troilus* 5.1800–06 and 1828–34. But even so, the idea of inserting the *Teseida* passage need not have come to him immediately, but could have occurred to him sometime later, though still in the original "compositional phase" (to use Windeatt's expression on p. 20, when speaking of the proems to books 2, 3, and 4). I will defend below the likelihood that Chaucer intended to keep his renderings of *Filostrato* 8.27–28 a unit, and that the *Teseida* material was mistakenly inserted one stanza too early.

[74] William Kamowski, "A Suggestion for Emending the Epilogue of *Troilus and Criseyde*," proposes, on the basis of sense, that the stanzas represented by sentence 2 in my summary should go before sentence 6, and the stanzas summarized in sentence 3 should go before sentence 8.

It may be that the reader-response that Chaucer sought from Gower and Strode at the end of his poem had a substantial effect, and that at their suggestion he made alterations or additions to the poem. I have earlier noted the possibility that Chaucer had a collaborator in his Boethian research, with Strode being the most likely candidate. If so (or even if not), it would not be pushing excessively against the limits of fantasy to think that the philosophical dedicatee of the poem had something to do with Chaucer's decision to make the large Boethian additions in books 3 and 4.[75] A similar speculation is in order concerning the epilogue itself. It had to occur to him at some time, whether by his own inspiration or at the prompting of a friend, that something of the same sentiments set out in the epilogue (in sentences 6–8 of the above summary) could be seen in Boccaccio's account of Arcita's death in the *Teseida*. Chaucer may in fact have already incorporated the account into his *Palamon and Emily*, where Gower could have seen it. Boccaccio expressed his sentiments not from the viewpoint of Christian revelation, but from the incomplete yet valid view of natural theology. Arcita ended unhappily for love, though, we might hasten to add, not as unhappily as Troilus. But in a way his loss was greater, for Emilia was more worthy of his affections than Criseyde was (in the end) of Troilus's. Once Arcita died, the "tragedy" was over, for him (though not for those he left behind, or those who were to hear of his death). He died, as Troilus might have done, naming her whom he loved more than anyone else in the world: "Finito Arcita colei nominando, / La qual nel mondo più che altro amava." But then, as a disembodied spirit, he forgets her completely, in his admiration of the beauties of the heavens. When he looks down on the earth he has just left, he finds that it cannot compare with heaven. He looks at his dead body and sees those who mourn him, but does not single out Emilia. He condemns the vanity of the whole human race for blindly seeking after the false beauty of the world while ignoring heaven. He then goes to the place appointed to him by Mercury.[76]

If Chaucer ever intended to follow Boccaccio in sending Troiolo to the never-never land "where Love dwells,"[77] he decided against it; but his account of Arcita's soul-journey is equally unreal, from the viewpoint of Christian truth, since it involves the intervention of a nonexistent pagan deity, Mercury.

---

[75] See above, chap. 2, pp. 54–55. Windeatt, Oxford Guide to *Troilus*, p. 28, argues for a connection between Strode and Troilus's soliloquy on predestination, which, he thinks, must have been a part of the poem before Chaucer ever considered it to be finished: "Indeed, without this soliloquy, which so affects the overall philosophical tone of the whole poem, there would have been rather less aptness in Chaucer's dedicating the poem to 'philosophical' Strode, a dedication present in all extant manuscripts."

[76] Boccaccio, *Teseida* 11.1–3; all three stanzas are conveniently given by Root, p. 560, and even more conveniently by Windeatt on p. 558 of his edition, parallel to Chaucer's adaptation.

[77] At least, this is one way of interpreting *Filostrato* 8.33:

> Ed orazione
> Per lui fate ad Amor pietosamente,
> Che 'l posi in pace in quella regione
> Dov' el dimora.

That is, in the translation of apRoberts and Seldis, "And piously make a prayer for him to Love, that he may repose in peace in that region where he dwells." The "he" of "he dwells" can refer either to Love or to Troiolo.

Still, even though he carried over the existential role of one of the discredited pagan gods, he did make an important modification or clarification in Arcita's sentiments. Whereas Arcita explicitly mentions only the physical splendors of the heavens, Troilus is aware of "the pleyn felicite / That is in hevene above" (5.1818–19); and if the line, "Sholden al oure herte on heven caste" (1825) is part of his reflection, as seems likely, or even if it is Chaucer's as narrator, it would indicate that Troilus himself is eligible to enjoy the celestial happiness. This would be in keeping with his blissful ascent (1808) and his laughter at the futility and senselessness of those who are weeping for his death (1821–22). Troilus is now beyond tragedy, and we have hope that he has endured his afflictions successfully, by being able to enjoy the felicity with Christ, who now sits "in hevene above" (1844).

Such an ending would be beyond Troilus's greatest expectations about the aftermath of life on earth. He has had various notions of survival after death, in which Criseyde was to remain in the center of his consciousness; but now he thinks of death in a way that is similar to occasional earlier thoughts, as surcease of sorrow, the only remedy (1210, 1270), which alone can restore his rest (1673). If he does not lose total consciousness of Criseyde, she figures insignificantly as one of the transitory objects of the "blynde lust" of all men (1824).

The question must be raised of whether Troilus deserves eternal salvation (that is, of course, whether Chaucer presents him as deserving of salvation), granted that he is forgiven his ignorance of matters that could be known only to a Christian. Has he not been taken up in wrong pursuits? The answer is yes and no. The activity denounced by Troilus in his astral meditation, and specifically that which Chaucer warns his young Christian auditors against, is not primarily what is sinful and detrimental to salvation, but rather what is unnecessary to salvation—activity, namely, that is invariably transitory, disappointing, and needlessly painful. Salvation depends on virtue, or on a virtuous recovery from vice, and on a proper orientation to the divine order, and it was available even to pagans, as Dante shows by admitting Troilus's Trojan colleague Rifeo (Chaucer's Rupheo) to the sphere of Jupiter in Paradise. His heavenly vision is quite similar to Troilus's:

> Chi crederebbe giù nel mondo errante
> Che Rifeo Trojano in questo tondo
> Fosse la quinta de le luci sante?
> Ora conosce assai de quel che 'l mondo
> Veder non può de la divina grazia,
> Ben che sua vista non discerna il fondo.[78]

---

[78] Dante, *Paradiso* 20.67–72. See lines 118–29 for a description of Rifeo's life and how he was saved. Boccaccio doubtless had this canto in mind when he mentions him in the midst of other Trojan warriors like Sarpedon and gives the epithet Trojan only to him (*Filostrato* 4.3). Chaucer follows suit in *Troilus* 4.51–53:

> Maugre Polydamas or Monesteo,
> Santippe, Sarpedoun, Polynestore,
> Polite, or ek the Trojan daun Rupheo.

For ideas of the salvation of pagans during the Middle Ages, see Louis Capéran, *Le problème du salut des infidèles*, esp. vol. 1, chap. 6: "La théologie du moyen âge" (pp. 170–218); Thomas

(Who would believe, down in the erring world,
    that Ripheus the Trojan in this circle
    was the fifth of the holy lights?
Now he knows much of that which the world
    cannot see concerning the divine grace,
    even though his sight does not discern the depths.)

On the question of the intertextuality of Dante's *Comedy* with the *Troilus*, I agree with Richard Neuse against those readers (among whom he includes himself in a former incarnation) who see the recurrent Dantean echoes "as ironic reminders of another, sublime world of values by comparison to which Chaucer's Trojan world falls pitifully short." What links the two works, he says, "is that in both, erotic love possesses a powerful religious, even theological dimension."[79] The differences between them, he holds, is that the one is a comedy and the other a tragedy. He finds that the final visions of Dante and Troilus "might well serve as symbolic epitomes, not of opposed metaphysical systems, and certainly not of Christianity and paganism, but of a comic and a tragic hero's final perspectives, the one with his heaven-conquering love, the other with his greatly diminished sense of what love avails 'in this wrecched world adoun.' "[80] I would only add a reminder that—in my analysis, at least—Dante's idiosyncratic notion of comedy and tragedy did not involve joy and sadness or beginnings and ends, and he would not have thought of his auto-protagonist as a "comic hero" in the way that a plot-based understanding of the genre (which Chaucer undoubtedly had) might suggest.[81]

G. Hahn, *God's Friends: Virtuous Heathen in Later Medieval Thought and English Literature* (he deals with Chaucer's *Troilus* on pp. 396–417); Minnis, *Chaucer and Pagan Antiquity*, pp. 47–59 (the section on "Pagan Forerunners and 'Friends of God' "); Janet Coleman, *Piers Plowman and the "Moderni,"* pp. 108–46 (chap. 4, "the Righteous Heathen and Exceptional Salvations"); and Cindy L. Vitto, *The Virtuous Pagan in Middle English Literature*.

[79] Richard Neuse, "*Troilus and Criseyde*: Another Dantean Reading," p. 200. He draws especially upon the analyses of McAlpine, *Genre of Troilus*, pp. 152ff., and Winthrop Wetherbee, *Chaucer and the Poets: An Essay on Troilus and Criseyde*, pp. 145, 146, 172, 178, for establishing that Dante's relationship with Beatrice served as a model for the love between Troilus and Criseyde (p. 205); but both McAlpine and Wetherbee are among the ironizers he opposes (pp. 199–200).

[80] Ibid., p. 210.

[81] On the question of intertextuality, see A. C. Spearing, "*Troilus and Criseyde*: The Illusion of Allusion." He questions "the assumption that when Chaucer alludes to a source he expects or hopes for a reader who will be able to call to mind the whole of that source and to bring it to bear on the context in which the allusion occurs" (p. 265). In my view, Chaucer himself had not mastered the *Comedy*, and it would have been next to impossible to have found a reader of the *Troilus* who was acquainted with any part of it. But even in the case of works that were familiar to an audience, we must keep in mind what Jill Mann says: "Nothing is more characteristic of the Middle Ages than the constant refashioning of old stories, and this refashioning depends precisely on the reader's willingness to suppress the details of the older versions and accept the new one on its own terms as a valid account" (*Geoffrey Chaucer*, p. 37). Gerard O'Daly, *The Poetry of Boethius*, pp. 195–201, 230–31, distinguishes between simple verbal reminiscences, on the one hand, and, on the other, allusions that are meant to refer to the content of the original and constitute a comment on it; he is specifically disagreeing with Seth Lerer, *Boethius and Dialogue: Literary Method in the Consolation of Philosophy*, pp. 153–65, that the latter kind of allusions can be found in Boethius's Orpheus meter (book 3 m.12)—allusions, that is, calling up the content of Seneca's *Hercules furens* (see Lerer's response in his review of O'Daly, pp. 543–44).

On the basis of the above-stated criteria for salvation, Troilus seems to qualify rather well, given his circumstances. Neuse shows that all three major characters in *Troilus and Criseyde* are given a "very considerable number of oaths, interjections, asseverations, and asides of a plainly Christian character," the effect of which, he thinks, is that "the reader is seduced into accepting perhaps not just the compatibility but even the interchangeability of pagan and Christian."[82] I would not go quite so far, since, as we have seen, the pagan gods can be treated both reverently and irreverently by turns. But I agree that sometimes the equation is made, especially in the case of Troilus, and at the end he is respectful not only of God but also of the pagan deities: he recognizes that "the goddes shewen bothe joie and tene / In slep" (1714–15), as "God it woot" (1713).[83] He prays for the grace of being able to punish Diomede's crime, though he wonders why God himself does not punish him instantly:

> "O God," quod he, "that oughtest taken heede
> To fortheren trouthe, and wronges to punyce,
> Whi nyltow don a vengeaunce of this vice?"　(5.1706–08)

But he is not doubting the goodness and omnipotence of the divine nature, any more than he did in his reflections on predestination.

I suggest that when Chaucer set about to account for Troilus's final destiny, something went awry with his modifications both of the *Filostrato* and the *Teseida*. One problem is that the three stanzas from the *Teseida* interrupt two stanzas from the *Filostrato* that clearly belong together. The insistent anaphora of "swich fin" originally referred to Troilus's death at the hands of Achilles, and the line "Swich fyn hath his estat real above" (1830) was meant to contrast his miserable death with his elevated status while he was alive. But once the *Teseida* stanzas are thrust between the *Filostrato* stanzas, the "swich fin" must refer to Troilus's better situation after death, when he is looking on "the pleyn felicite / That is in hevene above," which transforms his "real estat above" into mere vanity.

This problem would have been avoided if the *Teseida* stanzas had been inserted after rather than before the "Swich fin" stanza. The sequence would remain as it is in Boccaccio, where Troiolo's death is contrasted with his glorious life; and then, with the adaptation of the *Teseida* passage, his former glorious life "above" is transformed into an insignificant "below" by the vision of higher things. I think it likely that this was in fact Chaucer's intention, and that the three stanzas were mistakenly placed by a scribe one stanza too early. We can easily see how it could happen by considering the Huntington Library manuscript of the *Troilus*, where the three stanzas are copied on a separate inset leaf,[84] and remembering Chaucer's complaint about the mistakes that his scribe Adam made in copying the *Troilus*.[85]

---

[82] Neuse, "*Troilus*: Another," pp. 201–02.

[83] Earlier Troilus thinks "that Joves, of His purveyaunce, / Hym shewed hadde in slep the signifiaunce / Of hire untrouthe" (5.1446–48).

[84] See Barney's note, p. 1177, referring to MS Ph (= Phillips 8252, now Huntington 114).

[85] The likelihood that the *Teseida* stanzas were misplaced in the *Troilus* was first suggested to me by Catherine Corman. S. S. Hussey, "The Difficult Fifth Book of *Troilus and Criseyde*,"

In any case, no matter how the stanzas were meant to be arranged, the result is less satisfactory than it might have been if Chaucer had made a thoroughgoing revision of the passages, or if he had struck out on his own path and praised Troilus for winning a celestial reward by nobly struggling with adversity.

In a later work, the *Legend of Good Women*, Chaucer explains his purpose in the *Troilus* as follows:

> God woot, yt was myn entente
> To forthren trouthe in love and yt cheryce,
> And to ben war fro falsnesse and fro vice
> By swich ensample; this was my menynge.   (F 471–74)

Chaucer could have held Troilus up as an example to others, in much the spirit recommended in *Boece*:

> Goth now thanne, ye stronge men, ther as the heye wey of the greet ensaumple ledith you. O nyce men! why nake ye your bakkes?
> As who seith, "O ye slowe and delicat men! Whi flee ye adversites, and ne fyghte nat ayeins hem by vertu, to wynnen the mede of the hevene?")
> For the erthe overcomen yeveth the sterres.
> (This is to seyn, that whan that erthly lust is overcomyn, a man is makid worthy to the hevene.)[86]

---

p. 727, following unnamed others, argues that the interpolation "would go better" a stanza later, but he blames Chaucer himself for the faulty placement. Kamowski, "A Suggestion," p. 418 n. 13, misreads Hussey, as rejecting any need for change. Kamowski's own reason for rejecting such a shift would seem to be that the final lines of the interpolation, "And forth he wente, shortly for to telle, / Ther as Mercurye sorted hym to dwelle" (1826–27), do not lead in logically to what he wants to be the next lines, "Bysechyng every lady bright of hewe," and so on (1772–85). In place of the present lead-in, "But for that I to writen first bigan / Of his love, I have seyde as I kan" (1768–69), interrupted by a parenthetical aside: "His worthi dedes, whoso list hem heere, / Rede Dares, he kan telle hem all ifeere" (1770–71), Kamowski's rearrangement has the end of the "Swich fin" stanza: "And thus bigan his lovyng of Criseyde, / As I have told, and in this wise he deyde" (1833–34). However, the parenthetical "As I have told" (1834) is not as convincing a referent for "Bysechyng" (1772) as is the main clause, "I have seyde as I kan" (1769). If one does not follow Kamowski's switches, the insertion of the three *Teseida* stanzas after the "Swich fin" stanza introduces another problem: the reference to an existential Mercury is juxtaposed to Chaucer's address to the "yonge, fresshe folkes", in which he urges love of Christ, and then goes on to despise the pagan gods as worthless (and, presumably, nonexistent). But I fall back on my original position: Chaucer's introduction of the *Teseida* passage is awkwardly adapted. I should note here for the record the suggestion, which I find to be unlikely, of Thomas J. Garbáty, "*Troilus* 5.1786–92 and 5.1807–27: An Example of Poetic Process," that the addition of the adapted *Teseida* stanzas was Chaucer's realization of his hope of being able to "make in some comedy," that is, to match the tragedy of Troilus with a perspective like that of Dante's *Comedy* (Garbáty implies that Chaucer would have been familiar with the *Epistle to Cangrande* and taken it to be by Dante). A similar view of "making in some comedy" is taken by Martin Stevens, "The Winds of Fortune in the *Troilus*," p. 303. Wetherbee, *Chaucer and the Poets*, p. 225, understands the wish to "make in" some comedy as a hope that the *Troilus* will wind up as a comedy, or, as John Fleming interprets Wetherbee in his review, p. 264, as a desire to add more from Dante's *Comedy* before the author or narrator dies.
[86] Chaucer, *Boece*, book 4 m. 7 (*Riverside Chaucer*, p. 457). David Lawton, "Irony and

One might allege that Troilus has not been especially brave in standing up to his troubles, given the excesses of grief to which they drive him. His grief, however, is not to be taken as indicating a weakness of character, but rather as showing the intensity of his trials and the strength of his virtue in withstanding them: he cannot, and may not, withdraw or break his trouthe to Criseyde. He considers it a sign of the cursed time in which he was born that he still loves her "best of any creature," in spite of the woe that she causes him to endure (5.1699–1701); but is he not, by this unswerving dedication, somehow similar to Christ, who "right for love" died upon a cross to redeem our undeserving souls? It is Criseyde, rather, who, though capable of "suffering" both natural and celestial love (1.978–79), "naked her back" to adversity. But Chaucer did not undertake to write a theological or philosophical *summa*. He was not in the mood for a measured and reasonable assessment of the uses and abuses of adversity; no doubt he would have considered such a presentation unsuitable for the end of a tragedy.[87]

Louise Fradenburg says that "loss articulates not only particular works written by Chaucer, but also Chaucer's generic choices."[88] This would seem to be verified above all by his virtually single-handed creation of the genre of tragedy, for, as we have seen, in his understanding of it, loss—permanent loss—is at the very center of its essence. She goes on to say, "At times Chaucer's poetry, as well as his critical tradition, is shaped by the inability to confront worldly loss," but at other times it "refuses to re-figure loss as transcendence."[89] I maintain that in spite of the fact that he decided to reveal Troilus's transcendent destiny, Chaucer did not thereby eliminate in his readers the sense of Troilus's loss that they have experienced and lamented.

He emphasizes the theme, "Such is this world," but brings it a step lower than it was earlier, when his reaction was to "take it for the beste" (1750). His advice now is detachment; this is the upshot of the stitched-in stanzas from the *Teseida*, and the bent of all the stanzas that follow.

The Monk introduced his tragedies with the following exhortation: "Lat no man truste on blynd Prosperitee; /Be war by thise ensamples trewe and olde" (1997–98). In light of some of his examples that followed, one could justify taking this warning, as we have done earlier, to mean that if a prosperous man is not blindly trusting in his continued good fortune, he can at times stave off disaster. But some of the other examples, as well as the immediately preceding lines about the impossibility of reversing Fortune when she decides to flee, suggest another meaning: we should be so distrustful of worldly prosperity that we avoid it altogether. This is the final message of the *Troilus*, though not the only or the most important message of the poem.

To sum up. Chaucer does not call the *Troilus* a tragedy until the end. We cannot be certain that he intended to make it a tragedy when he first started

---

Sympathy in *Troilus and Criseyde*: A Reconsideration," p. 111, suggests that this passage actually influenced Chaucer in his adaptation of the *Teseida* passage.

[87] Cf. Kaske's remarks cited above, chap. 2, p. 78, on Chaucer's not being obliged to give a full Boethian picture in the *Monk's Tale*.

[88] Louise O. Fradenburg, "'Voice Memorial': Loss and Reparation in Chaucer's Poetry," p. 177.

[89] Ibid.

to work on it, but we can emphatically affirm that the work fits the conceptions of tragedy of the *Boece* and the *Monk's Tale*, and that it can be seen as further developing those ideas. Perhaps he was inspired by additional reading on tragedy as well. For instance, he may have been encouraged by Ovid's *Tristia* to choose a love story for development in the grave form of tragedy, and to flavor it with humor and even a touch or two of ribaldry.

The outstanding characteristic of the *Troilus* in terms of Chaucer's definition of tragedy is that the "prosperite for a tyme" takes such a long time to set forth that the readers are induced to enter into it so fully as to forget about the coming adversity. It is treated as a true and lasting prosperity, and it becomes so for us as well as for Troilus. Even the preliminary sorrows are made pleasurable by way of anticipated prosperity. The humor and merriment of this part of the poem seems to encourage and sustain our sense of the serene enjoyment of happiness. Then comes the "unwar strook" of Criseyde's transfer to the Greek camp. The rest of the poem is filled with dread at the reverberations of this blow, which turn out to be worse that Troilus ever imagined; and when he does imagine them, he cannot accept them until he has no remaining alternative. The final shattering of his joys is made to coincide with the larger tragic movement of the destruction of Troy, which Chaucer conveys by the image of Fortune plucking out the feathers of a brightly colored bird. But the whole movement of the last two books would perhaps best be illustrated by the well worn figure of Fortune and her wheel, executing a downward turn. She would not be seen in this case to give the wheel a fast spin, but rather to move it with excruciating slowness. The poem ends with the one-sided but wholly appropriate and understandable desire to avoid any similar wretchedness at all costs.

TROILUS IN RECEIVERSHIP

I have been most concerned in this chapter with a "quantitative" or objective description of the way in which Chaucer's *Troilus* conforms to, and expands upon, his ideas of tragedy—although, in spite of my efforts to remain a Werckmeisterian Marxist, as defined in the Introduction, and to be faithful to the noncritical spirit of our era, I have undoubtedly made some qualitative judgments along the way, for which I apologize. But the judgments of others as to what constitutes a good tragedy, and whether or to what extent *Troilus and Criseyde* measures up, are still within critical bounds, because they can be studied under the rubric of reader reception.

The selective introduction of Aristotelian criteria of excellence in tragedy has been a source of untold confusion in modern discussions of tragedy. For Aristotle, the "raw material" to be classified, that is, the mass of plays or stories already categorized as tragedies, was distinguished by "seriousness," and included a large number of cases with happy endings. In the Middle Ages, according to several authorities, the unhappy ending was one of the main generic distinctions of tragedy. This idea has become so ingrained in us that we tend to assume that it was also Aristotle's idea: that is, we assume that Aristotle was working from a medieval definition of tragedy, and we tend to edit out or ignore his recognition of tragedies with happy endings: especially, as already noted, his discussion in the fourteenth chapter of the *Poetics* where he says that a tragedy like Euripides's *Iphigenia in Tauris* best achieves the desired tragic effects.

It is Chaucer rather than Aristotle who sets forth the acceptable limits of our modern idea of tragedy, and it is Chaucer who can be said to have fixed these limits for the modern world. For Chaucer was not simply handing on standard medieval doctrine. There was no standard medieval doctrine on the point; or, if there was, it was not what Chaucer came up with. Ideas of tragedy were comparatively rare in the Middle Ages, as we have seen, and they came in great variety. Some authors, like Dante, considered tragedy mainly a matter of style, poetic form, and static content, having nothing to do with disastrous events. It is true, however, that many, or most, definitions of tragedy included an unhappy ending; but the ending usually referred to deserved retribution visited upon the wicked. It was Chaucer's good fortune that he received from his Boethius glossator an unrestricted definition of tragedy, which left every sort of misfortune eligible for inclusion. Chaucer's definition corresponds to the modern everyday idea of tragedy, the range of which can be tested by considering the applications of the expression, "What a tragedy!" We will find, I think, that we use the word for irreversible disasters and misfortunes that come in all forms and for all sorts of reasons, and against all hope and expectation. This global emphasis, considered a debasement of the word by neo-Aristotelian purists, who have mistakenly taken one statement of the best kind of tragedy as the *sine qua non* of all tragedy, is essential to our untainted ideas of what can qualify as real or true tragedy. And it is more common for our sense of the tragic to be evoked by the sight of suffering innocence than of suffering guilt. In fact, the greater the guilt, and the more heinous the evil, the less likely we are to endow its overthrow with the name of tragedy.

We find this global range of tragedy not only in our present-day usage, but in Shakespeare's time as well. There is between Chaucer and Shakespeare a direct line of transmission: in *The Fall of Princes*, Lydgate turned Boccaccio's exempla of falls into Chaucerian tragedies, and Lydgate was not only passed on in print to the Elizabethan era, but his tragedies were supplemented in *A Mirror for Magistrates*, one of the most popular and influential works of its time. Acceptance of tragedy in Chaucer's sense can be seen from a review not only of how Shakespeare's characters use the term, but also from the uses to be found in Sidney's *Arcadia*—even though when Sidney characterizes tragedy in the *Apology for Poetry,* he restricts it, like other academic theorists of the time (George Puttenham, Thomas Lodge, and Sidney's disciple John Harington), to the crimes and punishments of tyrants.[90] This latter view coincides

---

[90] See my "Chaucer and Shakespeare on Tragedy," pp. 198–200. Fulke Greville's views are more complex; see Dollimore, *Radical Tragedy,* pp. 121–22. Greville characterizes the tragedies of his contemporaries as aiming "to point out God's revenging aspect upon every particular sin," while his own tragedies (*Mustapha* and *Alaham*) were more like mirrors for magistrates, for he wished "to trace out the highways of ambitious governors and to show in the practice of life that the more audacity, advantage, and good success such sovereignties have the more they

with what Isidore in book 18 of his *Etymologies* says about the wickedness of kings as the subject matter of tragedy, but it represents a didactic ideal of poetic justice that Aristotle found to be lacking in the desired tragic effects.[91]

In contrast, then, to the narrow moralizing tragedy of the theorists, the authors and playwrights of sixteenth-century England adopted the open-ended view of tragedy that Chaucer had introduced to the modern world. He gave a series of various kinds of short tragic stories in the *Monk's Tale*, which Harry Bailly found to be undistinguished, not well told—a judgment acquiesced in by many subsequent readers—and an elaborately wrought example of a tragedy of undeserved, or largely undeserved, misfortune in *Troilus and Criseyde*. Presumably Harry Bailly would have found the *Troilus* to be well told, which is the view of most canon-makers and arbiters of taste down to the present day.

Aristotle hit upon the evocation of certain emotions (pity, fear, and suchlike) as the proper goal of tragedy, and he proceeded to judge the artistic merits of individual tragedies by their effectiveness in achieving this goal. Perhaps we can derive a similar criterion, or criteria, of excellence for Chaucerian tragedy by taking the effective imparting of the general lessons of caution and resignation (as set forth in the *Monk's Tale*) as one goal, and the effective creation of sympathy, or motivation for "bewailing" the outcome, as another.[92] *Troilus*, I think, stands up well to such a standard. The poem brings home vividly the untrustworthiness of prosperity and the unpredictability and irreversability of certain events. Do not all readers share the sense of worldly futility that Chaucer evokes at the end, and feel a profound sense of sorrow at the final turn of events? Doubtless most do, but not all. Such judgments must always remain to a certain extent subjective.

The same is true of all qualitative definitions of tragedy, especially those that generate seemingly objective rules of structure and content based on philosophical and aesthetic principles. J. V. Cunningham points out that the formulators of such definitions are taking a Platonic approach: that is, they presuppose that there exists an Idea or Essence of Tragedy, and that the more a given work participates in the Idea, the more it is deserving of the name of tragedy.[93] Sometimes, as Lubomír Doležel notes, such evaluative

---

hasten to their own desolation and ruin." There may be sin involved in the ambition and audacity, but it seems to be more the actual high position that brings on disaster. By contrast, the purpose of ancient tragedy was "to amplify the disastrous miseries of man's life, where order, laws, doctrine, and authority are unable to protect innocency from the exorbitant wickedness of power, and so out of that melancholy vision, stir up horror or murmur against divine providence" (*Life*, chap. 18, p. 138; text modernized). In other words, Seneca's tragedies portrayed only the unpunished wickedness of tyrants, which their victims blamed on God.

[91] See the citation from *Poetics* 13 above, p. 85 n. 194.

[92] Osberg, "Between the Motion," sees a "serious and single-minded purpose" expressed at the beginning of *Troilus*: namely, to elicit sympathy for the lovers; and he finds that this is a purpose well achieved (pp. 264, 266).

[93] J. V. Cunningham, "Tragedy as Essence." Cunningham characterizes his own approach, which is similar to mine in this study, in the following involuted way: "I should prefer to define such a notion as tragedy in terms of those principles of order that enter into the intention of a given work or given body of works insofar as the explicit recognition by the author of those principles as the principles of what he calls tragedy and their intended recognition by the reader is guaranteed by historical evidence" (p. 129).

standards are only implicit in supposedly objective or descriptive poetics and constitute a "hidden axiology," that is, a judgmental subtext, or underlying aesthetic or ideological program.[94]

There have been surprisingly few overt attempts to evaluate *Troilus and Criseyde* as a tragedy in the way in which Shakespearean plays are evaluated, no doubt largely because dramatic form is usually considered a prerequisite to genuine tragedy. But I suspect that the work is often evaluated covertly on similar but unstated principles, like those, for instance, derived from A. C. Bradley.[95] Let us look at two above-board assessments, those of Willard Farnham and John Bayley, and see whether their arguments or similar ones are detectable in less forthright evaluations.

Farnham's history of the development of pre-Shakespearean tragedy has been of immense influence, not only for his description of various forms of tragedy from the fourteenth to the sixteenth centuries, but also for his evolutionary ideas of tragic concepts. His invention of the concept of *"de casibus* tragedy," which he fathered on Boccaccio, as we saw in the first chapter above, has been virtually unchallenged to the present day. His whole enterprise, he says, is "guided by a conception that tragic expression is a special artistic and critical approach to the mystery of man's suffering on earth." He regards this mystery itself as "the tragic fact." Its artistic embodiment need not be dramatic in the sense of being designed for the stage, though it has in fact been so in its highest incarnations: "Tragedy has always taken the form of drama when it has been able to reach its fullest expression and its eminently rightful manner."[96] But tragedy in any worthy meaning of the word, he maintains, *must* be dramatic in the sense that it provides scope for active struggle; the struggle must be concerned with the hardships of this world, but it cannot proceed to the point of *contemptus mundi:* "When tragedy becomes pessimistic about the worth and meaning of man's activity in this world,

---

[94] Doležel, *Occidental Poetics*, p. 29, speaking of Aristotle on tragedy: "Aristotle's theory is not an a priori construct; it is based on a thorough knowledge of extant Greek tragedies. But the explicit process of theory formation is preceded by a silent intuitive axiological operation; by means of this invisible aesthetic filter a few tragic works are selected into a privileged set, the corpus on which (and for which) the theory will be constructed. Poetics of the ideal structure is a theory of the poetician's favorite artworks. Tragedy is 'imitation of an action' because Aristotle's favorite tragedies are structured on the dominance of the plot. Tragedy fulfills the function of catharsis because this is the effect produced by the works Aristotle judges to be the best representatives of the genre. Aesthetic intuition shapes the theory of the tragedy by building preferential restrictions into the structural model. Aristotle's criticism is based on poetics, but the ultimate foundation [of] *both poetics and criticism* is intuitive axiology. In the marriage of poetics and criticism, criticism acquires the status of a justified axiology, but poetics, becoming a hidden axiology, loses its descriptive innocence and turns into the normative mode."

[95] See Dollimore, *Radical Tragedy*, pp. 53–56, referring to A. C. Bradley, *Shakespearean Tragedy* (1905). He notes that "Bradley's metaphysic of tragedy has remained dominant," even though his method of character analysis has been widely rejected (p. 53). Bradley's tragic universe, Dollimore says, "blends mystical intuition with an etiolated version of the Hegelian dialectic"; the ultimate force is on the side of good and antagonistic to evil (p. 54). He traces similar notions in Richard B. Sewall, "The Tragic Form" (1954), Dorothea Krook, *Elements of Tragedy* (1969), and G. K. Hunter, "Seneca and English Tragedy" (1974). In the introduction to his second edition, pp. xvi–xvii, Dollimore finds the Bradleian concept of tragedy as well in Reinhold Niebuhr, *Beyond Tragedy* (1938) and George Steiner, *The Death of Tragedy* (1961).

[96] Farnham, *Medieval Heritage*, pp. xi–xii.

there is quite obviously a limit beyond which it cannot go and still be tragedy, if we agree that tragedy should have dramatic quality even though it may depart from the form of stage presentation. The pessimistic tragic poet reaches that limit when he represents life as never justifying hope, yet ironically producing the momentary will to live and some consequent struggle. Deeper pessimism can only produce apathy which nullifies all struggle and consequently all dramatic quality."[97]

Chaucer was at a disadvantage, he holds, because his age "was just beginning to give recognition in philosophy as well as in literary practice to the conception that a tragic event is the product both of fate for which the individual is not responsible and of characteristic deed for which he is."[98] But there was "another and more capital reason" for the failure of the *Troilus* to reach "the stature of the greatest tragedies in the Greek or Christian European traditions," namely: "Chaucer finds his fable in a love story told with all the myopic attention to the details of tender individualized emotion that romance demands." He says that Chaucer also took over from Boccaccio's *Filostrato* much that is "trivial in tragic import."[99]

Farnham adds the objection that it takes "an effort in our concentration" to avoid considering Troilus a mere lovesick boy.[100] If one were to counter with the observation that the same is true of Romeo, he would doubtless deny *Romeo and Juliet* entrance to the ranks of undoubted tragedies.[101] John Lawlor, who analyzes both *Troilus and Criseyde* and *Romeo and Juliet* as tragedies, would seem to agree that Troilus is lacking in tragedy, at least a certain kind of tragedy. He says, "Troilus's unheroic lament is very different from tragic grandeur; but it is not the less penetrating on that account."[102] Winthrop Wetherbee finds Troilus similarly lacking: when he becomes angry with Cassandra, "for the first time, it seems, he is prepared to *act* in response to what he sees as his fate, to embrace his destiny like a tragic hero. But the potential significance of this moment of renewal and seeming reorientation is never realized."[103] He finds the Monk's protagonists similarly defective:

---

[97] Ibid., pp. 8–9.

[98] Ibid., p. 157. Farnham's contention that *A Mirror for Magistrates*, being later in time than Chaucer and Lydgate, shows an increase of responsibility in protagonists for their falls (and therefore, we should say, a corresponding increase of poetic justice), is contested by William Perry, "Tragic Retribution in the 1559 *Mirror for Magistrates*."

[99] Ibid., pp. 158–59.

[100] Ibid., p. 159.

[101] Later in his study he distinguishes *Romeo and Juliet* from Shakespeare's "later and greater tragedies" (pp. 397–98).

[102] John Lawlor, *The Tragic Sense in Shakespeare*, p. 84.

[103] Wetherbee, *Chaucer and the Poets*, p. 220, cited by Haas, "'Kissing the Steppes,'" p. 304, who comments: "On the basis of a modern understanding of tragedy—or perhaps rather *cliché*—anger is praised in the hero and energetic activity is demanded of him." These expectations, she says, tend to work against women as tragic protagonists. See also Mann, *Geoffrey Chaucer*, pp. 110–11: "When one compares the complexity and sensitivity with which Chaucer works out his vision of a relationship freed of male coercion and female hypocrisy, with the irritable and reductive complaints about Troilus's inertia and weakness so familiar on the lips of Chaucer critics and students, one can measure the hold that the conventional notion of sexual roles still has over modern culture." Hansen, *Chaucer and the Fictions of Gender*, finds Troilus "tragically feminized" (p. 176), but she concludes, unlike Mann, that the feminization of Troy and the leading male Trojans "by no means brings with it any particular understanding of

"With astonishing regularity the Monk's versions of the lives of his tragic heroes attenuate their tragic force and rob them of the moral and historical complexity inherent in their biblical and classical sources."[104]

Richard Neuse, who takes a more consciously Chaucerian perspective of tragedy, finds the parallel between *Troilus* and *Romeo* a useful one; he sees a similar "precipitate" in the two tragedies, namely, the war between the Greeks and Trojans in the one and the family feud in Verona in the other, but a different tragic "idea":

> In the case of the *Troilus* that idea has less to do, directly, with the lovers as individual characters than as representatives of what I am inclined to call simply *another way* of love, life, religion. For all their exaltation and all their suffering, neither Troilus nor Criseyde has the stature of Romeo and Juliet, say, who at a crucial moment take matters in their own hands and assert a heroic will as well as a personal grandeur that makes them anything but passive victims of their elders' bloody folly. Troilus and Criseyde, to the contrary, without incurring any blame for it, conform their wills to the political and military imperatives of the world around them.[105]

Farnham believes that there is a feature in Chaucer's treatment of love that is not shared by Shakespeare. All through Chaucer's poem, he says, "we feel the influence of that courtly love code which is inherited from the *Filostrato* and which excludes itself from any ethical consideration except the loyalty of lover to beloved."[106] Similarly, John Bayley, writing almost a generation later (in 1960), fits *Troilus* into the category of courtly-love stories. Like

women or effective concern for their well-being," since "they struggle in different ways to be more manly" (pp. 178–79).

[104] Wetherbee, "The Context of the *Monk's Tale*," p. 167.

[105] Neuse, "*Troilus*: Another Dantean Reading," p. 208. Neuse notes that he is at pains to guard against "the impulse to locate the 'cause' of the love tragedy in some pseudo-Aristotelian character flaw of either protagonist or in their kind of love" (p. 208).

[106] Farnham, *Medieval Heritage*, p. 159. The idea that there was a pervasive code in the Middle Ages that ignored ethical considerations or excluded marriage from love is now generally discounted. But one still sees appeals to a code of courtly love, defined in different ways, or left undefined. For my own views of how Chaucer transformed the admittedly illicit union of Troiolo and Criseida in the *Filostrato* into a virtuous love in the *Troilus*, see my *Love and Marriage*, chap. 2, "Criseida and Criseyde" (pp. 49–67), chap. 9, "Filocolo and Troilus" (pp. 217–42), and chap. 12, "The Mystical Code of Married Love" (pp. 286–332); see also "Shades of Incest and Cuckoldry: Pandarus and John of Gaunt," pp. 122–25, clarifying my position. I argue that Chaucer took advantage of the uncertainty surrounding medieval marriage (the marital bond was effected only by the internal intentions of the partners) and was able to treat the pair as neither definitely unmarried nor as definitely married. See Patricia Brückmann, "*Troilus and Criseyde* 3.1226–1232: A Clandestine Topos," who sees in Chaucer's image of the tree encircled by the woodbine a parallel to the ambiguous nature of secret marriage. I should note that readers who do not condemn the love of Troilus and Criseyde as idolatrous passion, after the lead of D. W. Robertson, consider it as vaguely moral even though they rule out all question of marriage; see, for instance, Minnis, *Chaucer and Pagan Antiquity*, pp. 101–02. But Hansen, *Chaucer and the Fictions of Gender*, p. 168, assumes that their relationship is unlawful, and, presumably, immoral (she speaks of "Pandarus's and Troilus's deliberate obfuscation of an intention that knows itself to be illicit").

Farnham, he looks back at Chaucer from Shakespeare and finds the *Troilus*
wanting as a tragedy; and, also like him, he draws upon a universal essence
of tragedy, but he is much less certain about its properties. As with all
courtly-love stories, he says, *Troilus* "is quite lacking in the qualities which
we usually associate with tragedy. It is notoriously difficult to say just what
these are, and probably there is no one characteristic of the poem—its
humor, its helpless and unheroic protagonists, its homely detail, protracted
catastrophe, or abruptly Christian palinode—which couldn't be found in
some indisputably tragic work."[107] He implies that the combination of the
traits he has named drastically reduces the work's tragic potential. But
almost the same set of characteristics, in the judgment of another critic, is
what transformed the romance of the *Filostrato* into a tragedy. Donald
Howard, speaking of Chaucer's various adaptations, says: "He made Boccaccio's tale more emotional, more exciting, more complex, more often
funny, more poignant, and in the end more philosophical and more religious.
In doing all this he gave it tragic proportions."[108] To another reader, S. S.
Hussey, the protracted catastrophe is precisely what makes the *Troilus* trans-
cend medieval tragedy. He assumes that Chaucer's definition of tragedy in
the *Boece* was "the normal medieval concept of tragedy," and that Chaucer
proceeded to refine it as the *Troilus* progressed. *Troilus* conforms to the
simple definition, but Chaucer "came to see that, although the inevitable
turns of Fortune's wheel sends the unfortunate tumbling down, he could
show the descent in some detail. Troilus's *gradual* loss of hope, and his slow
realization that Criseyde has transferred her love to Diomede, while they do
not depart from the medieval tradition, are closer to our modern idea of tragedy and may be one of the marks of modernity we fancy we discern in the
poem." Chaucer's expansion of the last part of the work resulted in "the
increased complexity and depth of his tragic vision."[109]

C. S. Lewis, writing in the same year as Farnham (1936), notes that Troilus's suffering is the kind that we have all experienced, whereas the sufferings
of Lear and Oedipus are not. In sparing us no detail of "the prolonged and
sickening process to despair," Chaucer makes the experience "so painful that
perhaps no one without reluctance reads it twice. In our cowardice we are
tempted to call it sentimental. We turn, for relief, to the titanic passions and
heroic deaths of tragedy, because they are sublime and remote, and hence
endurable."[110] Lewis may be agreeing with Aristotle that a story like Troilus's
is too painful for tragedy, or he may simply be saying that those works that
are recognized as tragedies do not produce such moving effects in us.[111]
Others who agree that the *Troilus* is not too diffuse and is sufficiently moving
for tragedy are Walter Clyde Curry, writing before Lewis's time (1930), and

---

[107] John Bayley, *The Characters of Love: A Study in the Literature of Personality*, p. 67, in the
chapter "Love and the Code: *Troilus and Criseyde*," pp. 51–123.

[108] Donald R. Howard, Introduction to *Troilus*, p. xvii.

[109] Hussey, "Difficult Fifth Book," pp. 728–29.

[110] C. S. Lewis, *The Allegory of Love*, pp. 196–97.

[111] Lewis concludes that *Troilus*, "despite this terrible conclusion, is not a depressing poem" (p.
196); rather, "despite the tragic and comic elements," it is primarily "a great poem in praise of
love" (p. 197).

Willi Erzgräber, writing later (1964).[112] Curry considers *Troilus* to have the sublimity and dependence on Fate of Greek tragedy and the fatality of character of Shakespearean tragedy. However, this judgment holds true of the poem only up to the epilogue; the epilogue itself he considers to be a sorry performance, contradicting what goes before.[113]

Bayley goes on to state more definite flaws: "It is its artificiality which makes the poem so fundamentally untragic, and it is also its absence of discovery."[114] He notices that Pandarus resembles the fool in a great tragedy like *King Lear*; but he asserts that the *Troilus* is not a tragedy because it has "no evil, sublime, or majestic character"; all the participants are "more than human in their hopes and fears, their cowardice and amiability."[115] But it is noteworthy that Bayley himself, seemingly without realizing it, twice admits the tragic stature of the work. When news of Criseyde's exchange with Antenor comes, he says, "It is the tragedy of the lovers that they are bound to the Code at this moment."[116] And in summing up, he says: "Like Shakespeare, Chaucer shows us the resources of human freedom so naturally that we take them for granted. Both give us the impervious as well as the tragic man, the Wife of Bath and Parolles as well as Troilus and Othello, resilience and unmeaning as well as shape and destiny. And their awareness of separate people goes deeper into abstractions like love and grief and the 'truth' about men and women."[117]

The Wife of Bath's imperviousness is seen, Bayley says, in her reaction to the memory of joys past, in contrast to Troilus's grief-stricken prostration:

> But, Lord Crist! whan that it remembreth me
> Upon my yowthe, and on my jolitee,
> It tickleth me aboute myn herte roote.
> Unto this day it dooth myn herte boote
> That I have had my world as in my tyme.   (469–73)

In other words, the Wife of Bath can be seen as adhering more closely to the Wordsworthian formula of emotion recollected in tranquillity, whereas Troilus exemplifies its converse.

The Wife of Bath, of course, did not fall from high estate or great prosperity or lose a love as strong and deep as Troilus's. However, she is not entirely

---

[112] Walter Clyde Curry, "Destiny in Chaucer's *Troilus*," pp. 63–66, cited approvingly by Ertzgräber, "Tragik und Komik," p. 146.

[113] Curry, "Destiny", pp. 66–69.

[114] Bayley, *Characters*, p. 67. Bayley seems to be using discovery in a different way from Aristotle, for whom it is not a question of the audience's sudden recognition of some detail with catastrophic implications; Sophocles's auditors knew what was coming even better than Chaucer's. Rather, the recognition is on the part of the characters themselves. It is their unawareness of the surprise in store for them that constitutes the dramatic irony of tragedy. Troilus's discovery of the events which lead to Criseyde's separation from him and his discovery of her flawed character would seem to result in the sort of agonized reactions that occur in the most moving of Greek *anagnoriseis*.

[115] Ibid., pp. 85–86.

[116] Ibid., p. 82.

[117] Ibid., p. 123.

impervious, for it cannot be said that her present state is wholly tranquil; she goes on to say:

> But age, allas! that al wole envenyme,
> Hath me biraft my beautee and my pith.
> Lat go, farewel! The devel go therwith!
> The flour is goon; ther is namoore to telle;
> The bren, as I best kan, now moste I selle
> But yet to be right myrie wol I fonde.   (474–79)

Her cheery bluster has something in it akin to the bloody-but-unbowed posture of many tragic heroes, and she undoubtedly participates in the mystery of human suffering.

The Wife of Bath has been seen by some of Chaucer's readers as a tragic figure, but by their own definition of tragedy rather than Chaucer's.[118] Nevertheless, it may well be that Chaucer's general conception of tragedy should be accepted and modified so that the Wife of Bath would fit it. We need simply put aside that excess baggage, Fortune, and interpret the Monk's "high degree" in a more democratic sense, so that even the death of a salesman could be an eligible subject. What remains essential is the fall from prosperity to adversity. The requirement of adversity in tragedy need not exclude a protagonist who retains or even achieves some measure of personal integrity, even if it might be considered a triumph over his defeat. Of the protagonists of the *Monk's Tale*, Samson perhaps best illustrates this notion.[119] But in Chaucerian tragedy, which we have inherited, unlike Greek tragedy, the defeat must endure. In the tragedy of Troilus, Chaucer shows us a man who suffers defeat and disappointment; and even though he can be seen to be rewarded after death for his integrity, his suffering remains with the readers to the end of the poem.

This partial survey of assessments of how well, or ill, reported Chaucer's *Troilus* is as a tragedy will serve to illustrate, I hope, how varied the critical "receptors" of readers can be, especially when perceptions are filtered through individual experiences and assessments of Chaucer's literary descendant William Shakespeare. It also confirms, I venture to say, Bayley's conclusion that "every critical formula for supreme tragedy contains the possibility of abuse."[120]

To return to Chaucer's understanding of tragedy: it was based mainly on a simple criterion of content (movement from prosperity to adversity) and not on form, and so it admitted both verse and prose. He would, and did, consider

---

[118] See especially F. M. Salter, "The Tragic Figure of the Wyf of Bath," and the writers cited by him on p. 2.

[119] Bloomfield draws a picture of such a protagonist in "*The Man of Law's Tale*: A Tragedy of Victimization and a Christian Comedy," p. 388. As I noted in the Introduction, Bloomfield in this article is not using "tragedy" in its Chaucerian sense.

[120] Bayley, *Characters*, p. 137. He is opposing the ideas of T. S. Eliot and others on tragedy, which would jeopardize Othello's tragic stature. When Eliot insists on the impersonal in tragedy, Bayley asks: "Why should a tragedy of personality automatically be slighter than an impersonal one?"

Boccaccio's prose *casus virorum illustrium* to be a series of tragedies. However, he did not consider all narratives with such a movement towards adversity to be tragedies, but only those that had the added purposes of
lamentation and appropriate moralizing about the failure to avoid avoidable
disasters and the unavoidability of other disasters.

There is no reason to believe that Boccaccio considered his *Filostrato* to be
a tragedy, any more than the narratives of the *De casibus*. Chaucer undoubtedly did, but he must also have concluded that the method of narration
needed improvement in order to arrive at a more moving "scenario" for
lamentation and sad meditation. The result of turning Troiolo into Troilus
was that a rather distant figure who was meant to serve as a victim of woman's
unfaithfulness became Fortune's fool, whom many readers, judging him
from their own perpectives, consider to be a tragic hero on the level of Shakespeare's Romeo, but less rash and more reflective, who is given ample scope
for bewailing his sad misfortunes.

4

Lydgate on tragedy

Chaucer's Monk, or Daun Piers, as the Host finally decides to call him, says that he has a hundred tragedies in his cell. Forty years later, a real-life monk, Daun John by name, found himself possessed of well over three times that number, all written in French prose, which he was enjoined to transform into English verse. John of Lydgate, member of the Benedictine abbey of Bury St. Edmunds, who received this commission from Humphrey, Duke of Gloucester, admired Chaucer as his superior and master. He had some poetic strengths of his own, including even a taste for satire and a sense of humor that sometimes produced results mildly comparable to Chaucer's drolleries. But, in addition to fostering a general tone of geniality, he was careful to project a sense of being a sincere and devout religious. These features are brought out best perhaps, when he portrays himself as joining Chaucer's pilgrims on their return trip from Canterbury in the prologue to the *Siege of Thebes*.

Lydgate professes to be an admirer of the tragedies told by Chaucer's Monk, and he shows no evidence of considering them to be any other than straightforward well-executed stories with admirable morals. He says in the *Fall of Princes*, "The Monk off stories newe and olde /Pitous tragedies be the weie tolde" (1.349–50). He does not allude to the humorous setting of the tragedies, nor to the fact that they were told by a monk who was by no means a shining example of his profession. Lydgate was too loyal a son of the Church to wish very often to repeat satire or invective against it, especially against his beloved Order of St. Benedict, though he undoubtedly recognized the existence of faults among priests and religious. In his *Temple of Glass*, he speaks of nuns who entered religion at a young age without proper counsel:

> That conseiles[1] in hir tender youthe
> And in childhode, as it is ofte couthe,
> Yrendred were into religioun
> Or thei hade yeris of discresioun,
> That al her life cannot but complein,
> In wide copis perfeccion to feine,
> Ful covertli to curen al hir smert
> And shew the contrarie outward of her hert.

[1] That is, "counsel-less."

> Thus saugh I wepen many a faire maide,
> That on hir freendis al the wite thei leide.   (199–208)

Lydgate himself had entered the monastery at the age of fifteen, and he would surely have known not only of such religious as these, who managed, at least in public, to put a good face upon their lack of vocation, but also of those who were not able or willing to conceal their ineptitude for the life of the vows.

Lydgate's sense of humor, and sense of human weakness, were such as to permit him to take a joke upon himself and his order, especially from a man like Chaucer, who presents himself as kindhearted rather than sharply satirical or scornful in his first-person accounts. He does not seem to have harbored any resentment over the master-poet's gentle gibes against the infringers of monastic discipline in the persons of Daun Piers and Daun John. Like them, Lydgate was something of an outrider, in that he was largely dispensed from the communal duties of his profession because of his talents. But he seems to have taken care to show how such outriding should be done, and he succeeded in avoiding all scandal.[2]

When he presents himself as one of the Canterbury pilgrims, he does mention one of the unsavory ecclesiastics, namely the Friar—though he mistakenly thinks that the Friar was angered by the Pardoner, to whom he gives the physical characteristics of the Summoner and Simkin the Miller (lines 32–35). But he does not allude to the Monk (nor to Chaucer himself, for that matter), and he gives the impression that he is the only monk present; and, though he has the Host make fun of him, it is not for his worldliness but for his poverty and simple piety.

Lydgate's faulty recollection of the characters of the *General Prologue* suggests a different reason for his failure to refer to the satirical setting of the *Monk's Tale*: he may not have remembered it. He may even have had at hand only the Monk's Tale itself, without its front- and back-matter (that is, the Prologue, with the Host's introduction, and the Knight's and Host's interruptions at the end).[3] But in whatever form he had it, and even though he praises the Monk's tragedies, he does not seem to have bothered to reread most of them, for he does not ordinarily draw upon them when he deals with the same subjects in the *Fall of Princes*.[4]

The clearest indication of Lydgate's neglect of the *Monk's Tale* comes in his account of Hugolino:

---

[2] See David Knowles's assessment of Lydgate as a monk in *The Religious Orders in England*, 2:273–75.

[3] Huntington Library MS 144, though it is very late (c. 1480–1500), may illustrate the sort of compilation that Lydgate might have used. It contains some of Lydgate's own works as well as two of the tales of Canterbury praised by him, *Melibeus* and the *Monk's Tale*; but they are not identified as by Chaucer, and the frame material is missing—including therefore Harry Bailly's interruption of *Sir Thopas* and the Knight's interruption of the *Monk's Tale*, as well as the Monk's Prologue, which comes after the *Melibeus*. The *Melibeus* is titled *Proverbis*, and the *Monk's Tale*, as was mentioned in chap. 2, has for a running title the name of Lydgate's work, *The Falle of Princis* (p. 67 above, n. 131).

[4] He does refer to Chaucer's account of Zenobia (*Fall* 8.670–79); and he may have been misled by *Monk's Tale* 2697 into calling Caesar's assassin Brutus Cassius (6.2877), as is noted by Derek Pearsall, *John Lydgate*, p. 253 n. 32.

To Jhon Bochas appeered Hugolyn,
Callid whilom the noble Erl of Pise,
Til the Pisanys gan ageyn hym rise;
Most vengably, cruel, and unkynde,
Slouh hym in prisoun; no mor of hym I fynde,
Sauff his childre, of hatreede and envie,
Wer moorderid eek, in a deep prisoun.[5]   (9.2051–57)

This passage also shows that Lydgate neglected Dante's "report verray celestial" (he does not call it a comedy) sung among the Lombards, whose three books tell of heaven, purgatory and hell (4.137–40). The reason for his neglect of Dante was, presumably, not faulty memory but faulty knowledge; for, as was demonstrated long ago by Emil Koeppel, Lydgate could not read Italian.[6] However, it is possible that Lydgate could have read the *Comedy* in the Latin translation and commentary of John Serravalle, the Franciscan Dantist who visited England around 1398 and who was commissioned to make his translation by two English bishops at the Council of Constance (1414–17).[7] Duke Humphrey possessed a copy of it, as well as a copy of the original Italian.[8]

THE DRAMATIC TRAGEDY OF OLD TROY

We can see in the works of John Lydgate a culmination of many of the traditions that we have been studying. He takes over the medieval emphasis upon the disastrous end as providing the "specific difference" or defining characteristic of tragedy. Like Averroes and Chaucer, he insists upon the importance of the didactic purpose of tragedy, and he inherits from Chaucer the idea of calling narrative accounts of misfortunes tragedies. But like Boccaccio, and unlike Chaucer, he was aware that the ancient world had a different form of tragedy, which had an acted dimension.

Boccaccio wrote his series of *casus* for the purpose of instructing princes, and Lydgate had the same goal in setting down his tragedies, which were expanded from Premierfait's expansion of Boccaccio's work. But Lydgate also wrote at the command of princes and addressed his works directly to them. *Troy Book* was commissioned by Prince Henry, the future King Henry V, and the *Fall of Princes* was undertaken, after Henry's death, for his brother

[5] Henry Bergen, Lydgate's editor, says, "It looks very much as if Lydgate had another source of information about Ugolino in mind, as he says that he was slain in prison" (4:375). But perhaps Lydgate came to this conclusion himself from Laurence de Premierfait's words: the Pisans constrained him and his children to die "cruellement et par mesaise."

[6] Emil Koeppel, *Laurents de Premierfait und John Lydgates Bearbeitungen von Boccaccios De casibus virorum illustrium*, pp. 76–83. Laurence de Premierfait could not read Italian either; he translated the *Decameron* into French by employing a friar who first translated it into Latin (Hortis, *Studi*, p. 633). Herman Alemannus worked in a similar way in his translations from the Arabic, using assistants who were familiar with the tongue.

[7] IDEAS AND FORMS, pp. 207–08. Serravalle was among those who considered Dante's poem to consist of three comedies, as is evident from his commentary.

[8] W.F. Schirmer, *Der englishe Frühhumanismus*, pp. 10–11, 49.

Humphrey, Duke of Gloucester, who had by that time become his principal patron.

The concept of ancient drama as consisting of the author's recitation accompanied by a dumbshow, which was first set forth by Isidore of Seville, had at least some precedent in the practices of the Roman stage and auditorium.[9] But in the Middle Ages (including Isidore's time, of course) it was thought by almost everyone who gave any thought to the subject—John of Salisbury was a notable exception—that this was the exclusive form of production. We have seen Boccaccio talk about it for comedy, and the idea receives its greatest elaboration for both tragedy and comedy in Lydgate's *Troy Book*, which was begun in 1412 and finished in 1420. He ascribes the origin of the "rite of tragedies," which was held in April and May, to King Priam (2.917–25). "Lusty fresche comedies" as well as the "dites" of tragedy originated there at that time (842–44).[10] After defining the difference between comedy and tragedy, he concentrates on tragedy and explains how such works were performed:

> Whan thei wer rad or songyn, as I fynde,
> In the theatre ther was a smal auter
> Amyddes set, that was half circuler,
> Whiche into the est of custom was directe,
> Upon the whiche a pulpet was erecte,
> And therin stod an awncien poete
> For to reherse by rethorikes swete
> The noble dedis that were historial
> Of kynges, princes, for a memorial.   (2.862–70)

Further details of the contents of the tragedies follow (we shall deal with them below). Then he says:

> Al this was tolde and rad of the poete,
> And whil that he in the pulpit stood,
> With dedly face al devoide of blood,
> Singinge his dites, with Muses al to-rent,
> Amydde the theatre schrowdid in a tent
> Ther cam out men gastful of her cheris,
> Disfigurid her facis with viseris,
> Pleying by signes in the peples sight,
> That the poete songon hath on hight;
> So that there was no maner discordaunce
> Atwen his dites and her contenaunce.
> For lik as he alofte dide expresse

[9] IDEAS AND FORMS, pp. 16–23 ("Ways of Performing Tragedy"); 36–50 ("Isidore of Seville").

[10] Lydgate's main source, Guido of Le Colonne (quoted by Lydgate's editor, Henry Bergen, 4:121), says only that tragedy and comedy are said to have originated in Troy; but he adds that Sicily is held by some to be the birthplace of comedy. The Sicilian origin of comedy was reported by Isidore, *Etymologiae* 14.6.33 (above, p. 41 n. 15). See Cloetta, *Komödie und Tragödie*, pp. 45–46.

> Wordes of joye or of hevynes,
> Meving and cher, bynethe of him pleying
> From point to point was alwey answering,
> Now trist, now glad, now hevy, and now light,
> And face chaunged with a sodeyn sight,
> So craftily thei koude hem transfigure,
> Conformyng hem to the chaunteplure,
> Now to synge and sodeinly to wepe,
> So wel they koude her observaunces kepe.   (2.896–16)

What were Lydgate's sources for this conception of ancient drama? He was aware, at least by the time of the *Fall of Princes*, that Seneca composed traged-ies in Roman times (*Fall* 1.253–54). He uses them as an example of one style of oratorical declamation:

> An hevy mateer requereth an hevy cheer;
> To a glad mateer longeth weel gladnesse;
> Men in pronouncyng mut folwe the mateer.
> Old oratours kan bern herof witnesse:
> A furious compleynt uttrid in distresse,
> This was the maner, as poetis do descryve,
> In his tragedies whan Senec was alyve.   (*Fall* 6.3347–53)

These tragedies, characterized as "sad" (probably meaning "grave" as much as "sorrowful"), were preserved for posterity by the medium of writing (4.59–63). In fact, Duke Humphrey possessed a copy, which he gave to Oxford University in 1439.[11]

The only previous awareness of the contents of Seneca's tragedies that we have seen in England is in Trevet's commentary and Walsingham's summa-ries, but there is no indication that Lydgate knew either work. He could have learned that Seneca wrote "tragedies" from Higden's *Polychronicon*.[12] He seems to know at least the titles of some of the plays, but the three times in the *Fall of Princes* that he cites the tragedies as sources, he does so *in globo*. In his tragedy of Jocasta and Oedipus, he says: "And Senek writ eek in his tragedies" (1.3580). In summing up his own and Thyestes's cruel deeds, Atreus says:

> Senech rehersith hem in especiall
> In his tragedies, and ther he doth devyde
> Our compleyntis, our malice, and our pride,
> Our fatal eende in sorwe and myscheeff fyned,
> Whan Antropos our lyvys threed hath twyned.
> (1.4203–07)

In the story of Medea, he says:

> And fynali, as writ Ovidius,
> And moral Senec concludith in substaunce,

---

[11] *Epistolae academicae Oxon.*, 1:179, 182.
[12] See above, p. 40.

> In his tragedies makyng remembraunce,
> How Medea, lik as poetis seyn,
> Onto Jason restored was ageyn.   (1.2383–87)

Seneca in fact says nothing of the kind about Medea, as Koeppel points out (the same is true of Ovid in the *Metamorphoses* and *Heroides*), nor does the *Thyestes* proceed to the deaths of Atreus and Thyestes; and in none of the places cited does Lydgate add anything to what is to be found in his major text, Laurence de Premierfait's translation of the *De casibus*.[13]

It may be then that Lydgate had only heard of the tragedies, say, from Vincent of Beauvais's excerpts or from the citations of Seneca in Boccaccio's *Genealogia*; Lydgate uses the latter work in his *Siege of Thebes*,[14] composed between the *Troy Book* and the *Fall of Princes*. Both Vincent and Boccaccio quote from the *Oedipus, Thyestes*, and *Medea*, and in fact Lydgate seems to refer specifically to the *Oedipus* in the *Siege*:

> But ye may reden in a tragedye
> Of Moral Senyk fully his endynge,
> His dool, his meschief, and his compleynyng,
> How with sorow and unweldy age
> This Edippus fille into dotage,
> Lost his wit and his worldly delit,
> And how his sones had hym in despit,
> And of disdeyn tok of hym no kepe.   (994–1001)

Needless to say, this is not what happens in Seneca's play.

Perhaps Lydgate had only seen and not studied Humphrey's copy of Seneca. If so, he may not have realized that the tragedies were a purely dramatic form of composition, consisting only of dialogue. Or he may have noticed the dialogue form (since he speaks of Seneca's "dividing" the complaints of Atreus and Thyestes), without digesting the contents of the plays. But when he mentions Seneca's "tragedies of gret moralite" (1.254) after speaking of Chaucer's fresh comedies and piteous tragedies, he gives no sign of knowing that they are different in kind from Chaucer's narratives.

I think we must conclude, then, that Lydgate knew no more about Seneca's plays than about Cicero's "many fressh dite" (1.256), to which he refers after speaking of Seneca's tragedies. I cannot see that Lydgate (or Chaucer, for that matter) ever used "dite" to mean anything not in verse,[15] and therefore his implicit claim to know about Cicero's metrical compositions must be discounted.

---

[13] Koeppel, *Laurents de Premierfait*, p. 63. Koeppel also notes that Lydgate refers to Statius concerning Oedipus's killing of the Sphinx (1.3477), whereas in fact Statius says nothing about the matter. For Premierfait's source, see below, p. 184 n. 14.

[14] He cites Boccaccio's work by name in *Siege* 3538ff. In lines 199–227, he draws upon *Genealogia* 5.30, in which Seneca's *Hercules furens* is cited (Lydgate's editors give Boccaccio's text in the notes, 2:101).

[15] The definitions and examples for "dite" in Bergen's glossaries to *Troy Book* and *Fall of Princes* should be read in conjunction with the entry in the *MED*.

As for the "dites" of the ancient Trojan tragedians, Lydgate gives the impression that the poet intoned a straight narrative, which was accompanied, when appropriate, by the gestures of mummers who wore masks and changed them to match the mood of the moment. Could Lydgate have thought of a modern tragedy, say Chaucer's *Troilus*, as being performed in this way? That is, while Chaucer narrated the events, with actors playing the roles of Troilus, Criseyde, Pandarus, and the other characters coming into view and matching their movements to both the purely descriptive passages as well as to the direct discourse given to them? We must answer, as far as the *Troilus* is concerned, that Lydgate not only gives no sign of such an idea of Chaucer's poem, but also never indicates that he considers it to be a tragedy at all.

It is hardly likely that Lydgate could have missed seeing that Chaucer called his *Book of Troilus* a tragedy, for he draws on it several times in the *Troy Book*. When he tells of Criseyde going to the Greek camp, he is clearly echoing the end of Chaucer's work:

> Lo here the fyn of false felicite!
> Lo here the end of worldly brotilnes!
> Of fleshy lust, lo here th' unstabilnes!
> Lo here the double variacioun
> Of worldly blisse and transmutacioun:
> This day in myrthe and in wo to-morwe!
> For ay the fyn, allas, of joie is sorwe.   (*Troy* 3.4224–30)

I think it likely, then, that he deliberately refrains from calling the *Troilus* a tragedy when writing the *Troy Book,* reserving the term for the ancient dramatic form he described in book 2. Later on, when writing his own narrative tragedies after the model of Chaucer's *Monk's Tale*, he seems to have restricted the form to short and pithy biographies, which would exclude a large work like the *Troilus*.

He speaks of the old form of tragedies again in the *Troy Book* when he comes to lament the death of Hector. He wonders how to proceed; he cannot call upon the Muses, who sing only in harmonious sweetness. He, like Chaucer, has obviously never heard of Melpomene as the Muse of Tragedy, for he goes on to say:

> It syt hem nought for to help in wo,
> Nor with maters that be with mournynge shent,
> As tragedies,[16] al to-tore and rent,
> In compleynynge pitously in rage
> In the theatre, with a ded visage.   (3.5437–42)

Even though the ancient tragedians did, as we have seen, move from "rethorikes swete" to "Muses al to-rent," Lydgate may have felt that it was not

---

[16] It is not clear from Lydgate's elliptical grammar whether he means tragedies or tragedians. A few years after his time of writing, as we saw above, p. 43, John Capgrave translated the Latin word *tragedi*, that is, "tragic poets," as "tragedies." See Richard Axton, "Chaucer and 'Tragedy,'" pp. 34, 36.

appropriate for the Muses to appear thus. The "lacerated Muses" (*lacere Camene*) who are driving Boethius into a deep depression at the beginning of the *Consolation,* are, as we know, denounced by Lady Philosophy as "theater whores." There is no suggestion here that Lydgate himself is writing a tragedy in telling of Hector's fall or of the lamentation that followed it, or when he comes to tell of Troilus's death. In the latter context he says that no one could describe the woe that followed, not even Boethius, famous for his ability to complain to Philosophy about Fortune (4.3008–11). Statius likewise fails to come up to what is required in writing of sorrow and adversity (3014–17). He concludes his account of Troilus's death by saying that Priam had a rich tomb made for Troilus and Menon where they were solemnly buried. The "festis funeral / And other ritys ceremonyal" then followed, too long to detail (3090–97). We will see that elsewhere he says that tragedies are part of funeral celebrations, but at that point he has a different idea of tragedy in mind.[17]

There are several striking aspects about Lydgate's description of Trojan drama: the small half-circular, "oriented" altar with a pulpit on top of it; the tent from which the pantomime actors emerged; and the disfigured visors or masks which the actors wore. An altar was in fact essential to early Greek drama, the actors did wear masks, and for the earliest plays of Aeschylus the changing room was probably a tent or booth (which is the original meaning of *skēnē*).[18] Lydgate might have seen Boccaccio's brief characterization of the production of comedy in the *Genealogia* ("They composed their pernicious pieces and recited them in the scenes while mimes made their appearance," 14.19), but it would not have been of much help.

Huguccio of Bologna's *Magne derivationes* or one of its descendants could have supplied him with the idea of masked persons emerging from the scene or shelter to match their movements to the words of a reciter,[19] and Lydgate might easily have rendered *scena* as "tent," as did Geoffrey Anglicus in his *Promptorium parvulorum* some years later (1440),[20] especially if it were explained by Huguccio's term, *umbraculum.* The Ordinary Gloss to Acts 18.3, in explaining St. Paul's *scenofactoria ars* or tent-making, says, "Scenes are called tabernacles because they provide shade" ("Scene tabernacula dicuntur quia obumbrant"), and it gives Bede's explanation of exiles and pilgrims building tents (*tentoria*) to use on their journey, and of scenes as shade-structures made by people of old out of blankets, tree-fronds, or shrubbery ("Scene vel scenomata obumbracula que sagis vel arborum frondibus vel virgultis veteres componebant").[21]

As for the altar, apart from the references to the stage altars in the plays of Plautus and Seneca, which do not seem relevant to Lydgate's context, I know of no likely source from which such a detail or description could legitimately

[17]   See below, p. 170.

[18]   See Bieber, *History of the Greek and Roman Theater,* pp. 55–59.

[19]   Huguccio, *Magne derivationes* s.v. *scenos*; fol. 164vb; text in IDEAS AND FORMS, p. 107 n. 201.

[20]   *Promptuarium parvulorum,* pp. 211 (s.v. "hale, or tente") and 827 (s.v. *scena*); see Marshall, "*Theatre* in the Middle Ages," p. 380.

[21]   *Biblia latina cum glossa ordinaria* (1481), 4:493; *Biblia sacra cum glossa ordinaria* (1617), 6:1179–80.

have been drawn. Donatus's *Commentary on Terence* also refers to the stage altars,[22] but with similar irrelevance, and there is little chance that Lydgate could have known the work; for even on the Continent it had not yet been fully rescued from the obscurity into which it had early fallen.[23]

Perhaps then we should think of an "illegitimate" source for Lydgate's description, say, a miswriting or misreading of Higden's report from Trevet that the theater was a semicircular *area:* "Est autem theatrum . . . area quedam semicircularis." Higden's account also has a little house called a scene, and poets reciting their poems in or on a pulpit, while mimes imitated the described action with bodily movements.[24] The Trevet-Higden account is based on Isidore, of course, and it is possible that Isidore's own description of the theater, "Theatrum est quo scena includitur, semicirculi figuram habens" (18.42.1), was interpreted to mean that the *scena* rather than the *theatrum* had a semicircular shape. The *scena,* it was clear, had a pulpit: "Scena *autem* erat locus infra theatrum in modum domus, instructa cum pulpito" (18.43), which the comic and tragic poets ascended; and while they sang their verses others made gestures: "Ibi enim poete comedi et tragedi ad certamen conscendebant, hisque canentibus alii gestus edebant" (18.44). In the chapter on the amphitheater, he says, "Theatrum vero ex medio amphitheatro est, semicirculi figuram habens" (18.52.2); and then he goes on to describe the equestrian *ludus,* in which two *equites* or knights came forth, "unus *a parte orientis alter* ab occidentis" (18.53). In order to find here a semicircular altar in the midst of the theater facing east, one would, of course, have to mistake *alter* for *altar* (and perhaps even *autem* in 18.43 for *altar*) and not be able to understand the rest of the context; but it is possible that these phrases were abstracted from Isidore's context in such a way that they would give rise to Lydgate's understanding.

An example of how Isidore's explanations could be distorted is provided by the Dominican chronicler Galvano Flamma (1283–1344), in his various accounts of the ancient theater of Milan. According to Flamma, the theater was a very tall semicircular edifice with external stairways on which people stood and looked through windows at the performance within. In the middle of the theater was a round pulpit of marble on which *ystoriones* sang certain beautiful histories, or virtuous acts, or histories of wars. After these historions finished their singing, mimes came forth and played lyres and cithers and glided around with graceful bodily movement.[25] In another of Flamma's accounts, the pulpit is simply *altum* rather than *rotundum ex marmore,* and he likens the histories of the theatrical historions to "what is nowadays sung of Roland in the marketplace," that is, *in foro*; and after telling of the mimes,

---

[22] Donatus, *Commentum Terenti* 1.3, 2.1, 8.3. The term used is *ara* rather than *altar* or *altare*.

[23] See M. D. Reeve and R. H. Rouse, "New Light on the Transmission of Donatus's *Commentum Terentii*," who do, however, show that there was slightly more knowledge of Donatus than previously thought. To their findings could be added the evidence of Donatian influence on Papias; see above, pp. 47–49.

[24] See above, p. 41 n. 14.

[25] Galvano Flamma, *Chronicon extravagans de antiquitatibus Mediolani,* p. 466. Dino Bigonnogiari, "Were There Theaters in the Twelfth and Thirteenth Centuries?" p. 211, has a faulty citation of the text. The passage is also given by Pio Rajna, "Il teatro di Milano e i canti intorno ad Orlando e Ulivieri," p. 16.

he sums up: "Thus the people were delighted by melody and instructed by history."[26] As for Milan's ancient amphitheater, Flamma sees it as the site, not of Isidore's straightforward equestrian games, but of lawless trials by combat.[27] The building was round, with two *porte* or gates, one on the east and the other on the west: "una versus oriens altera versus occidens." The first part of this phrase, *una versus oriens altera*, could have been misinterpreted as an oriented altar in a corrupt text or by an ignorant reader. The same is true of Flamma's statement of how the dualists were positioned: "*Alter per portam orientis*, alter per portam occidentis."

When Lydgate speaks of the poet with Muses in tatters, he may be thinking, as Henry Bergen suggests, of a pantomime chorus constantly "on stage" and reacting to the poet's words. But more probably he is simply referring to the poet's mournful style during the catastrophic portions of his poem, when, after the fashion of the chantepleure (the "sing-weep" mode), he moves from joy to sadness.[28] As for the actors whom Lydgate definitely specifies, one might think at first that they went through their dumbshow only at the point of disaster. But since Lydgate goes on to say that they portrayed joy as well as sorrow, he clearly means the acting to occur during the whole play; and when the actions dealt with the triumphs of the heroes, the masks would doubtless not be "ghastly vizards" but expressive of more appropriate emotions, only later to be "changed with a sudden sight."

Glynne Wickham believes that Lydgate's account may "portray quite accurately" the mummings and disguisings of his own day. We can admit that there are, at least at times, some correspondences between the account and Lydgate's own plays. In one, held for the eight-year-old Henry VI at Windsor Castle during the Christmas festivities of 1429, a dumbshow of King Clovis and Queen Clotilda follows a spoken exposition. In another, a disguising played at London before "the great estates of this land" a couple of years earlier, the silent figures of Fortune and the four Cardinal Virtues appear one by one as they are described by the speaker; but apparently no action takes place between the characters. At the end, the four Virtues stand ready to sing a song at the audience's request, while Fortune is dismissed to play somewhere else.[29] These productions, however, seem a far cry from the sort of simultaneous interaction that Lydgate envisages in the ancient Trojan performances, and there is no sign that his mummers or disguisers used masks—though we know that masks had been used in English entertainments as early as the time of Edward III.[30]

---

[26] Flamma, *Chronica major*, passage edited by Rajna, "il teatro," p. 17, and also in Rajna's "Il titolo del poema dantesco," p. 11. Cf. the short account from Flamma's earliest chronicle, the *Galvagnana*, given in the latter article, pp. 11–12 n. 6.

[27] Flamma, *Chronicon extravagans*, pp. 467–68.

[28] Troilus may be referring to the chantepleure, a form that Chaucer defines in the *Anelida and Arcite*, in his letter to Criseyde, 5.1375: "My song, in pleynte of myn adversitee."

[29] See Glynne Wickham, *Early English Stages*, 1:193–95. The text of the *Mumming of Clovis and Clotilda* is in Lydgate's *Minor Poems*, 2:691–94; see also Walter F. Schirmer, *John Lydgate: A Study in the Culture of the Fifteenth Century*, pp. 106–07. The *Disguising of Fortune* is in *Minor Poems*, 2:682–91; see Schirmer, pp. 104–05; Wickham, pp. 192, 196.

[30] See Wickham, p. 188: forty-two players' masks were supplied for the king's Christmas entertainment in 1347, and ninety-one for the 1348 plays.

Much closer to Lydgate's account is the splendid new way of illustrating Terence's comedies that appeared in France at the beginning of the fifteenth century. It is first found in the frontispiece of Latin Manuscript 7907A of the Bibliothèque Nationale in Paris, which was executed in Paris in 1406–07 and presented to John Duke of Berry on January 1, 1408. The illustration was the work of an artist whom Millard Meiss has named the Josephus Master. Meiss believes that he was inspired by the Carolingian illustrators of the comedies, but, in view of considerations noted by Claudia Villa, such influence must be deemed unlikely.[31] One important difference is that whereas the Carolingian tradition shows Calliopius reading the plays in one illustration, and the masked players in others, the Josephus Master combined the motifs (masked players, unmasked recitor) in a single picture of extraordinary liveliness. His illustration was imitated by the Luçon Master around 1412 in the frontispiece of the *Terence des ducs* (Arsenal Latin Manuscript 664).[32]

Except for the masks worn by the actors (whom the Josephus Master calls *gesticulatores* and the Luçon Master *joculatores*), these pictures of ancient comedy resemble the description given by Boccaccio in his *Commentary on Dante's Comedy*. For the actors share the scene (a curtained booth) with the poet's reciter, Calliopius, and use it as a changing room.[33] In contrast, Lydgate has the poet himself stand in a pulpit while the actors are shrouded in a tent.

The accessus of the commentary contained in the two illustrated manuscripts (given in full in the Arsenal text, but abbreviated in Paris 7907A) does not speak of masks but rather of "persons" who come out of the scene, which is an *umbraculum* with a curtain; the persons are said to speak, imitating the voice of the reciter.[34] No indication is given of the position of the reciter, Calliopius. A Terence manuscript of the middle of the fifteenth century, Paris B.N. lat. 7907, identifies the author of the commentary as Laurentius, and Villa suggests that it is Laurence of Premierfait, who will show himself well acquainted with Terence's *Eunuch* in his translation of Cicero's *De amicitia*.[35] But, as we will see below, Premierfait when dealing with Nero's tragedies explains *scena* in both of his translations of *De casibus* as the *place commune*, probably meaning "public square," where the tragedies and comedies of the

---

[31] Claudia Villa, *La "Lectura Terentii,"* 1:245–47: no proof has been brought forth that any such Carolingian manuscript was present, let alone studied, in a French library of the early fifteenth century; the text of the plays and of Laurentius's commentary (see below) reflects rather the vulgate fifteenth-century version.

[32] Millard Meiss et al., *French Painting in the Time of Jean de Berry*, part 2, *The Limbourgs and Their Contemporaries*, 1:41–52. When Meiss observes (pp. 50, 52) that there are no masks on the figures in the illustrations of the individual plays, I think he is wrong in assuming that the illustrators intended to depict scenes as staged; rather, they seem to have treated the plays like ordinary narratives, and illustrated them accordingly. I should also note that Meiss is misled by Allardyce Nicoll's erroneous citation of Isidore, and that he himself overreads Raoul de Praelles to say that the actors used the scene as a changing room and employed masks (IDEAS AND FORMS, pp. 43 n. 26, 166 n. 241).

[33] A similar arrangement is to be found in a fifteenth-century Italian manuscript account of Terence, written in barbarous Latin. See Remigio Sabbadini, "Biografi e commentatori di Terenzio," p. 304 (nos. 10–12); for Sabbadini's dating of the manuscript, see p. 324 n. 3. See also Antonio Stäuble, *La commedia umanistica del Quattrocento*, p. 189 n. 1 for an emended text of the passage.

[34] Laurentius, *Accessus Terentii*, ed. Jenö Abel. I cite the pertinent text below.

[35] Villa, *La "Lectura Terentii,"* 1:241–46.

ancient poets were recited, whereas Laurentius understands *scena* as a curtained structure, as noted, and also as a subdivision of an act.[36] He defines comedy as "a metrical description of private things and inferior persons in a humble style."[37] Every comedy ends in joy and applause, though it can (but need not, we note) take its beginning from any kind of mental perturbation.[38] His reasoning on this point is not such as to make it obvious that he would consider tragedies to have an opposite development.[39]

No doubt any similarities between Lydgate's understanding of ancient drama and the practices of his own day in England are largely coincidental. However, if there was a causal connection, it was most likely in the direction suggested by E. K. Chambers. For unlike Wickham, who seems to think that the *Troy Book* description was modeled upon English medieval drama, Chambers thinks that Lydgate's peculiar method of "interpreting" dumbshows may very well have been based upon his conception of the methods of the classical stage.[40]

[36] Laurentius, *Accessus Terentii*, p. 43: "Scena est portio actus multarum aut solius personarum solitariam vel alternam ostendens prolocutionem cum gestibus, et licet scena vere dicatur umbraculum habens cortinam protensam a quo emittuntur persone que locuntur vocem recitatoris imitantes, scenam tamen hic recte accipio pro mutatione personarum respectu scene precedentis; plerumque scena solius persone proloquium habet, sed in prospectu aliam contingit proximam adesse" ("A scene is a part of an act showing the solitary speech of one person or the alternating speech of many persons, with actions; and although scene properly refers to the shaded structure with a hanging curtain from which the persons are sent forth to speak in imitation of the recitor's voice, nevertheless I rightly take scene in this context to refer to the changing of persons from the preceding scene; often a scene has the speech of only one person, but with the prospect of being joined by another nearby person").

[37] Ibid., p. 42: "Comedia . . . est metrica rerum descriptio privatarum et inferiorum personarum humili stilo procedens." Every comedy consists of three parts: argument, prologue, and narration, the narration being the extended description of the matter divided into acts and scenes ("narratio est extensa materie descriptio per actus et scenas rite distributa," p. 43).

[38] Ibid., p. 43: "Sumit equidem finem omnis comedia in gaudio et plausu, quamvis illam liceat a quacunque animi passione exordiri."

[39] He is answering the question, "Why does every comedy end in joy and applause, even though it might begin otherwise?" ("Quare in plausu atque gaudio omnis comedia finem sumat, licet exordium ceperit aliunde?" p. 42). He goes on to distinguish between old and new comedy: in the new, vices are attacked, but in the old, funny and ridiculous situations are presented for the entertainment of the people, and it was right for the last act of this kind of comedy to bring to peace and concord everything that was in discord and tumult in the first four acts ("Nam cum genus comicorum sit duplex, vetus scilicet et novum—quo indistincte queque singulorum vitia carpuntur; vetus autem quo res jocose ac ridiculares confinguntur ad ingerendam animis letitiam et populi aures permulcendas—rite oportuit finalem actum comedie in quo ad pacem et concordiam reducuntur quecunque in primis quatuor actibus sub discordia fuerunt et tumultu," p. 43). He never mentions tragedy in his discussion, but he does contrast the meter of comedy with that of heroic verse (p. 45); and in explaining why Terence does not invoke a god or a Muse, he says that it sufficed Lucan in writing about illustrious men to invoke the reigning Caesar, Nero, and therefore it should have been sufficient for Terence to ask the favor of the various citizens and officials of Rome; in contrast, it suits Vergil, Ovid, Statius, and others like them to invoke gods and Muses, since they deal with the things of the "machines" of both worlds in grandiloquent style (pp. 44–45). But he would have known something about the style and content of tragedy if he was familiar with the *Ars poetica*, as seems likely from his knowledgeable quotation, in the above discussion, of Horace's advice on avoiding gods: "Nec deus intersit nisi dignus vindice nodus / Acciderit" ("Nor let a god intervene unless there occurs a knot worthy of such a liberator," lines 191–92; the received text has *Inciderit* for *Acciderit*).

[40] E. K. Chambers, *The Mediæval Stage*, 2:161 n. 1.

Lydgate's distinction between comedy and tragedy in the *Troy Book* emphasizes both class difference and plot movement:

> And to declare, schortly in sentence,
> Of bothe two the final difference:
> A comedie hath in his gynnyng,
> At prime face, a maner compleynyng,
> And afterward endeth in gladnes;
> And it the dedis only doth expres
> Of swiche as ben in povert plounged lowe;
> But tragidie, who so list to knowe,
> It begynneth in prosperite
> And endeth ever in adversite;
> and it also doth the conquest trete
> Of riche kynges and of lordys grete,
> Of myghty men and olde conquerouris
> Which by fraude of Fortunys schowris
> Ben overcast and whelmed from her glorie.   (2.845–59)

He further details the contents of tragedies as follows:

> The noble dedis that wer historial
> Of knyges, princes, for a memorial,
> And of thes olde, worthi emperours,
> The grete emprises eke of conquerours,
> And how they gat in Martis highe honour
> The laurer grene for fyn of her labour,
> The palme of knyghthod disservid by old date,
> Of Parchas made hem passyn into fate.   (2.869–76)

The intervention of the third Parca, Atropos, in the downfall of the tragic heroes is then taken up briefly, but thereafter it is rather the wickedness of human enemies and of Fortune that is blamed for the catastrophes, which are told with appropriate emotion and style by the poet:

> And after that, with chere and face pale,
> With stile enclyned gan to turne his tale
> And for to synge, after all her loos,[41]
> Ful mortally the stroke of Antropos,
> And telle also, for al her worthihede,
> The sodeyn brekyng of her lives threde;
> How pitously thei made her mortal ende
> Thorugh fals Fortune, that al the world wil schende,
> And how the fyn of al her worthines
> Endid in sorwe and in highe tristesse,
> By compassyng of fraude or fals tresoun,

---

[41] That is, "their praise."

> By sodeyn mordre or vengaunce of poysoun,
> Or conspiringe of fretyng fals Envye,
> How unwarly that they dide dye;
> And how her renoun and her highe fame
> Was of hatrede sodeynly made lame;
> And how her honour drowe unto decline;
> And the meschef of her unhappy fyne;
> And how Fortune was to hem unswete—
> Al this was tolde and rad of the poete.   (2.877–96)

The most striking thing about this long description of tragic themes is that the heroes are uniformly heroic. They are not soldiers of fortune who have merely lucked on to their successes, nor have they achieved their high standing through skulduggery; but rather they are men worthy of the praise they have received; and their downfalls have been caused by no folly or mistake on their part, but solely by ill fortune and the ill will of others.

Lydgate therefore resembles Chaucer in not conforming to the primary Lactantian or patristic characteristic of tragedy, a focus on criminal activity. In fact Lydgate's account might even be taken to exclude sinful protagonists from the genre altogether, since they do not figure at all in his extended survey of motifs.

What of the fifteen or sixteen other possible characteristics of tragedy we considered in our discussion of Chaucer?[42] Lydgate shares with Chaucer the specification of persons of high rank (2), sorrowful ending (4) from happy beginning (11a), emphasis on unexpected or undeserved misfortunes (14), and lamentation (5). The tragedies were in verse (7), and were publicly recited (9). The idea of tragedies in prose would hardly have entered his mind at this point, especially in the context of the *Troy Book*, where he is thinking only of the practices of ancient times (6). Another criterion that Lydgate shares with Chaucer, which we could add to our original list, is that the protagonists are historical persons.[43] Lydgate goes beyond Chaucer in specifying the accompanying actions of pantomime actors (10). I will take up later the question of whether he used tragedy figuratively (12, 13).

Lydgate resembles Chaucer in showing no knowledge of dramatic form, that is, restricting the text to the speeches of characters (8); he doubtless considered the tragedies to be narrative accounts (15), which could, of course, include dialogue, like the unacted narrative tragedies he would consider later as belonging to a still-current genre (16). It has been claimed that Lydgate's reference to sweet rhetorics, enclined style, and shredded Muses supposes a criterion of high style (3).[44] But these expressions imply only that the style was appropriate to the mood and content of the moment, not that it was different in kind from the style of comedy. His meaning can be clarified from his remark on the Muses and tragedy cited above: the sweet rhetorics and the inspiration of the harmonious Muses are appropriate to the first

---

[42] See above, pp. 49–50.

[43] Noted by Cunningham, *Woe or Wonder*, p. 42, along with a number of other characteristics, especially the emphasis on sudden and violent death.

[44] So Cunningham, *Woe or Wonder*, p. 42, citing lines 868, 878, and 899.

part of tragedy (and, we might add, to the last part of comedy), where one describes happiness and prosperity. But the style must "incline" (that is, turn)[45] from joy to sorrow when adversity comes, and then the Muses must flee in a disheveled rout. We shall find a similar notion still operative in the *Fall of Princes*.

Lydgate must have used some specific account of comedy and tragedy for his account in the *Troy Book*. Perhaps it was simply a gloss in his copy of Guido's *History of the Destruction of Troy*. Whatever it was, it clearly had an idiosyncratic listing of characteristics. As an example of the sort of thing he might have been drawing upon, let us look at an accessus to the pseudo-Plautine comedy *Querolus* in a fifteenth-century Italian manuscript. In it the material of book 8 of Isidore's *Etymologies* is "updated" in a way that is reminiscent of the Paduan protohumanists. After an etymological discussion of comedy, the author points out that comedy has certain features in common with tragedy: namely (1) they are in iambic verse; (2) they are entirely in dialogue (that is, attributed to persons); and (3) they attack vices.[46] The two genres differ as follows: (1) comedy narrates private matters, tragedy public; (2) comedy narrates lifelike fictions, tragedy the histories of kings; (3) comedy narrates humbly, tragedy grandly; (4) comedy does everything with persons, tragedy represents some things only in words; and (5) comedy begins in sadness and ends in joy, whereas tragedy ends glad beginnings with a mournful outcome.[47] There are, furthermore, two kinds of comedy, old and new. The old, such as that of Plautus, Accius, and Terence, is jocular, whereas the new, which is also called satiric, is that of Flaccus, Persius, and Juvenal, where the vices of each man are openly criticized. In this new form, the effect and the intention of the writer is comic, but not the manner of speaking. The same is true of tragedy, in which Seneca may be taken to exemplify the old, Vergil the new.[48]

The author probably means that in the newer forms the text is not restricted to the dialogue of characters; but the movements of events from sadness to joy or vice versa are also notably lacking. When he says that in the original form of comedy and tragedy, tragedy sometimes does not assign everything to persons, he may be thinking of the choruses in Seneca's plays, if he is actually thinking of the differences between the comedies of Plautus and Terence

---

[45] For the meaning of "encline" in this context, see Bergen's glossary to *Troy Book,* 4:313–14, and the *MED* s.v., no. 2a and 2b. Compare *Troy Book* 2.4962–63: "Nowe after hym, to Eccuba the quene, / Lik the story, my style y mote encline." Here "style" means *stylus*, that is, "pen."

[46] *Accessus ad Querolum*, Florence, Bibl. Ambros. MS Ambros. H. 14 inf., fol. 48, ed Remigio Sabbadini, p. 329: "Hec cum tragedia communia quedam habet, videlicet quod iambico metro constat, quod tota personis attribuitur, quod vitia generaliter notat."

[47] Ibid.: "In hoc autem inter se differunt, quod hec privatas, tragedia vero res publicas narrat; hec argumenta fabularum ad veritatis imaginem ficta, illa regum historias; hec humiliter, illa granditer; hec omnia personis agit, illa quedam verbis tantum representat; hec a tristibus inchoans in gaudio desinit, illa leta principia mesto claudit exitu."

[48] Ibid.: "Sunt preterea duo genera comedie, vetus et novum. Vetus joculare, ut Plauti, Accii, atque Terentii; novum, quod et satiricum, ut Flacci, Persii, Juvenalis, ubi vitia cujusque manifeste carpuntur. In hoc autem novo licet sit effectus comicus simul et scribentis intentio, non tamen modus loquendi. Idemque per omnia dicendum est in tragedia, in qua exemplum veteris sit Seneca, novi Virgilius." Sabbadini thinks that the author thought of Plautus and Accius as one person, Plautus Accius. Plautus's name was in fact T. Maccius Plautus.

on the one hand and the tragedies of Seneca on the other.[49] At any rate, he is aware of the dialogic nature of some ancient drama, unlike Lydgate, but he does not share Lydgate's knowledge of the acting out of drama. His statement on comedy and tragedy seems not to have been fully integrated with his first-hand knowledge of *Querolus*, especially in the matter of the metrical form (unless of course he thought that the rhythmic prose of *Querolus* was iambic verse!). Similarly, Lydgate seems not to have retained a full measure of what he had learned about ancient tragedy and comedy when he considered them as "working genres," rather than as obsolete forms. At least he never again refers to their mimetic aspect. Perhaps this is a reason to doubt any link at all between his *Troy Book* account of pantomimed tragedy and his own mummings. But we need not assume that there was no carry-over at all from his ideas of tragedy and comedy. One of the playlets discussed above, the *Disguising of Fortune (A Mumming at London)*,[50] may throw some light on the matter.

In the first section of the work, the speaker/commentator gives four examples of men affected by Fortune. Two of them, Alexander and Caesar, are straightforward heroes that fit the descriptions of the *Troy Book*: that is, they are first triumphant and then they fall, and no fault on their part is mentioned. But the other two, Gyges and Croesus, are said to have had faults. Gyges came to his worthiness from base estate by means of a (magic?) ring and by "fals mourdre" (99), and, for all we know, he stayed there, for no fall is spoken of. He is offered as an example of Fortune's irrational whimsicality. As for Croesus, he was "surquydous in his pryde" (103); and he was brought down in his pride (118). But the accent is still on the "fals lady" who has cast down "the worthynesse of conquerroures" (119–22); and though we are told that we can oppose her malice, pomp, surquedy, and pride (130–31) by means of the cardinal virtues, no responsibility is directly placed upon the worthy conquerors for causing their own downfall. Even Croesus is not said to have brought about his ruin by the sort of negligence or overconfidence that could have been remedied by prudence; the point is simply that he did not believe it could happen.[51] The speaker then notes that further examples of such falls can be found elsewhere:

> Reede of poetes the comedyes,
> And in dyvers tragedyes
> Yee shal by lamentacyons
> Fynden theyre destruccyouns,
> A thousande moo than I can telle.   (123–27)

Comedies and tragedies are referred to here as if they were genres different from the present one—and, interestingly, comedies as well as tragedies are

---

[49] This is Sabbadini's suggestion, p. 329 n. 1.

[50] Lydgate, *Minor Poems*, 2:682–91.

[51] In his poem *Of the Sudden Fall of Certain Princes of France and England Now Late in Our Days* (*Minor Poems*, 2:660–61), which was probably written before the *Fall of Princes* (Schirmer, *John Lydgate*, p. 226), some of the princes, including Edward II and Richard II, were at fault, others were not. Fortune often has a hand in their falls, but there is no reference to the notion of tragedy.

said to contain falls. We can conclude that while Lydgate does not exclude the feature of miming from comedies and tragedies, the fact that he does not mention such a feature in a mumming of his own when speaking of comedies and tragedies could well indicate that it was no longer a prominent part of his idea of the forms.

Another point to be considered is that in the *Disguising of Fortune* Lydgate is drawing on a source quite different from whatever source he had for the *Troy Book* description: namely, Fortune's monologue in Boethius's *Consolation of Philosophy*. He is therefore doubtless now thinking primarily of Fortune's random attack upon the prosperous. But it is probable that he read the Boethian passage with the aid of a commentary that not only added the tragic end to Croesus (in Boethius, Fortune adduces him as an example of a fortunate outcome) but also contributed the unusual name of "Leryopee" for Croesus's daughter (line 115 of the mumming) and the further details that in his dream Juno[52] set Croesus in the air while Jupiter gave him water for his hands and Phoebus held the towel for him (108–11); it no doubt also contained the interpretation of the two jars on the threshold of Jupiter's house as two tuns in Fortune's cellar (83).[53]

The same source may have inspired Lydgate's statement that disaster stories can be found in comedies as well as tragedies. This would hardly fit his *Troy Book* description of "lusty fresh comedies," which, though they have a kind of complaining at the beginning, end in gladness. But he might have been able to associate destruction with comedy if he had read something like William of Conches's gloss to Boethius; for Conches implies that comedy contains the same kind of adversity as tragedy, only in a different part of the story. We can verify that Lydgate was capable of finding tragic themes in a work that he would doubtless have classified as comedy rather than tragedy (if required to make the choice): namely, Chaucer's *Knight's Tale*. At the end of his poem *A Thoroughfare of Woe*,[54] he says:

> O ye maysters that cast shal yowre looke
> Upon this dyte made in wordis playne,
> Remembre sothly that I the refreyd tooke
> Of hym that was in makyng soverayne,
> My mayster Chaucier, chief poete of Bretayne,
> Which in his tragedyes made ful yore agoo,
> Declared triewly and list nat for to feyne,
> How this world is a thurghfare ful of woo.   (184–91)

---

[52] The text reads "Iuvo," but surely Juno is meant. There is a sidenote at this point referring to Ecclesiasticus 26, which deals with good and bad women.

[53] John Walton in his verse translation of the *Consolation*, which he composed in 1410, speaks of the tuns as being laid "withyn the threshfold" of Jupiter's cellar (rather than house): p. 72, stanza 183. Just above (stanzas 182–83), he translates Fortune's question about tragedy thus:

> Wiche crieth all tragedenus verse
> But pleyneth al on myne instabilite?
> They wepen that so sodenly I smyte
> And welthful rewmes ofte overthrowe.

[54] Lydgate, *Minor Poems*, 2:822–28.

He has mistakenly remembered the line spoken by Egeus in the *Knight's Tale*, "This world nys but a thurghfare ful of wo" (2847), as coming from the *Monk's Tale*.[55]

CONTEMPORARY NARRATIVE TRAGEDIES

Even after he was commissioned to write the *Fall of Princes* in 1431, Lydgate does not seem to have reviewed the *Monk's Tale* with any care (as we noted earlier); but he was clearly following Chaucer's lead in applying the term tragedy to Boccaccio's falls of famous men, even though the accounts were in prose—for one can conclude from Lydgate's Prologue that he assumed Boccaccio's Latin text to be in prose, like the French text of Laurence de Premierfait. Even when he says at the end that "this noble poete of Florence and Itaile" wished to pause in his great work (9.3059–60), he need not be taken to mean that the *De casibus* itself was written in verse. The same is true when he says that though Bochas "floured in poetrie," his prejudiced writing against the English in the *De casibus* "gaf no mortal wounde" (9.3169–70), or when he says that both Petrarch and Bochas wrote tragedies and were poets (9.3421–27).[56] In all of these cases, he could simply mean that these poets also wrote prose. But we are given pause when he characterizes his source for the *Fall of Princes* thus:

> The profunde processe was so poetical,
> Enttirmedlyd with chaunges of fortune
> And straunge materys that were hystoryal,
> Towchyng estatys that hadde a sodeyn fal;
> The Frenssh unkouth compendyously compyled,
> To which language my tounge was nat affyled.
>
> (9.3325–30)

It may well be that Lydgate, like other authors of his time, did not restrict the meaning of poetry to metrical compositions.[57]

Lydgate had to enlarge his conception of the content of tragedy to include all of the various kinds of protagonists and all of the themes that he found in Boccaccio's work, as interpreted and expanded by Premierfait. In the *Disguising of Fortune* he spoke of tragedies as telling of the falls of a thousand men. Now in his own cell he had in a single work the stories of a third of a thousand falls. We shall see how he deals with some of them, and their accompanying morals, in the following chapter. Here we shall look at some of his explicit mentions or discussions of tragedy.

When he begins to describe Chaucer's works in the *Fall of Princes*, he seems at first to include all of them in the two categories of comedy and tragedy:

---

[55] Pearsall, *John Lydgate*, p. 212.
[56] I quote the text on the next page.
[57] See the *OED* s.v. "poesy" and "poetry." The *MED* is much less clear on this point.

> My maistir Chaucer, with his fresh comedies,
> Is ded, allas, cheeff poete off Breteyne,
> That whilom made ful pitous tragedies.   (*Fall* 1.246–48)

When he goes on to say, "The fall of pryncis he dede also compleyne" (249), he could be taken as distinguishing the Monk's stories from tragedies, but we soon learn that this is not the case; for Chaucer recounted "how the Monk off stories newe and olde / Pitous tragedies by the weie tolde" (349–50). It appears, then, that the line about the fall of princes should be taken in apposition with the previous line, as an explanation of what his tragedies consisted of:

> That whilom made ful pitous tragedies:

[That is,]

> The fall of pryncis he dede also compleyne.

We see something similar, with clearer meaning, at the end of the *Fall of Princes*:

> Ryght so my mayster hadde nevir pere—
> I mene Chauceer—in stooryes that he tolde;
> And he also wrot tragedyes olde,
> The fal of pryncers gan pitously compleyne,
> As Petrark did, and also John Bochas,
> Laureat Frounceys, poetys bothe tweyne,
> Toold how pryncers for ther greet trespace
> Wer ovirthrowe, rehersyng al the caas
> As Chauceer dide in the Monkys Tale.   (9.3419–27)

If "piteousness" is to be regarded as the main criterion of tragedy, then the *Book of the Duchess* would qualify, for it includes "the pitous story off Ceix and Alcione, / And the deth eek of Blaunche the Duchesse" (*Fall* 1.304–05). So would *Anelida and Arcite*, which is also a complaint: "Off Anneleyda and of fals Arcite / He made a compleynt, doolful and pitous" (320–21). But the complaint is also a lyric form: "Compleyntis, baladis, roundelis, virelaies" (353). Lydgate probably learned of the "chantepleur" from the *Anelida*, where Chaucer uses the word in English for the first time and defines it: "I fare as doth the song of chauntepleure, / For now I pleyne and now I pleye," except that he reverses the required sequence of moods.[58] We recall that Lydgate in the *Troy Book* spoke of the tragic mummers as conforming themselves to the chantepleure. Perhaps he regarded the chantepleure as the lyric counterpart to the narrative form of tragedy. He refers to it three times in the *Fall of Princes*: the tragedy of Cadmus is like the chantepleure (1.2159), and so is

---

[58] Chaucer, *Anelida and Arcite* 320–21. See my *Chaucer and the Cult of St. Valentine*, p. 95, for a possible source for Chaucer, namely, the Genoese poet Lanfranco Cigala.

the whole work (9.3623), because of the movement from joy to sorrow. But Fortune resembles the chantepleure not only because she goes from joy to sorrow, but also because at other times she moves from sorrow to joy (6.8–9).

At one point in the *Fall of Princes* Lydgate will come close to saying that Chaucer's *Legend of Cleopatra* is a tragedy: he declines to tell the tragedy of Antony and Cleopatra because Chaucer tells of them in the *Legend of Cupid* (6.3620–26).[59] Earlier he refers to the *Legend of Martyrs of Cupid of Women That Were Called Good* for the "story" of the fifty daughters of Danaus (actually Chaucer tells of only one, Hypermnestra, in a legend that is unfinished), and for the "martirdam" and "passioun" of Procne and Philomela (1.1781–85, 1797).

However, the overall impression that Lydgate gives in his description of Chaucer's works in book 1 of the *Fall of Princes* is that he consciously considered only the stories of the *Monk's Tale* to be tragedies.

When he goes on to mention the tragedies of Seneca, the ditties of Cicero, Petrarch's *Book of Two Fortunes*, and John Bochas's *Fall of Princes*, he is not necessarily to be taken as saying that all of these works were tragedies, but rather that all of these writers, like Chaucer, "gret worshipe dede unto ther nacioun" (1.273). But he does seem to know Petrarch's *De remediis utriusque Fortune* at first hand, though he may have seen one of Duke Humphrey's three copies.[60] He rightly characterizes the first book as "a dialoge twen Gladnesse and Resoun" (264), and the second as a dialogue between Reason and Worldly Heaviness. But perhaps he is only guessing at the contents when he says it rehearses "many fressh stories" (262); for though Petrarch alludes to innumerable cases of good and bad outcomes, his examples can hardly be characterized as fresh, in the sense of brilliantly executed; for most of them are only a phrase or a sentence long. We saw that at the end of the *Fall of Princes* Lydgate clearly associates Petrarch with the writing of tragedies. It may be then that he did think of the *De remediis* as containing tragedies. But he may have been thinking instead, or as well, of Chaucer's mistaken reference to Petrarch's history of Zenobia in the *Monk's Tale*. Lydgate seems also to have thought that Petrarch wrote an *Of Famous Women*, which contained the story of Griselda (*Fall* 4.125–26), though when he wrote the *Siege of Thebes* he knew that the *De mulieribus claris* was by Boccaccio:

> Lok on the book that John Bochas made
> Whilom of wommen with rethorikes glade,
> And direct be ful sovereyn style
> To fayre Jane, the Queen of Cecile.   (3201–04)

The first work of Chaucer's that Lydgate singles out for special mention in the Prologue to the *Fall of Princes* is *Troilus and Criseyde*, which he thinks is a translation that Chaucer made in his youth of a book called *Trophe* in the Lombard—that is, Italian—tongue (1.283–87). As in the *Troy Book*, he does not refer to it as a tragedy and in fact does not even speak of it in terms appro-

---

[59] Noted by Renate Haas, "'Kissing the steppes of Uirgile,'" p. 298 n. 1.
[60] See F. N. M. Diekstra, *A Dialogue Between Reason and Adversity: A Late Middle English Version of Petrarch's De remediis*, p. 26.

priate to tragedy. Rather he characterizes it as a work that brings great pleasure to lovers (1.288–89).

I have noted above that Lydgate followed Chaucer's example in applying the term tragedy to the stories that he derives from Bochas (I will use "Bochas" to mean Boccaccio as Lydgate found him in Premierfait's French text or as Lydgate presents him in the *Fall of Princes*).[61] But he does so matter-of-factly, with no hesitation and no explanation, and with no definition of tragedy. He simply refers to "the tragedies which that I shal write" (1.466). In so doing, however, he says that he will "sette apart all rethoriques sueete" (455), which, as we recall, is the phrase he applied to ancient tragedy in the *Troy Book*. The reason he states as follows:

> Dites of murnyng and of compleynynge
> Nat appertene onto Calliope,
> Nor to the Muses, that on Parnaso synge,
> Which be remembrid in noumbre thries thre;
> And onto materes off adversite,
> With ther sugred aureat licour
> They be nat willi for to doon favour.   (1.456–62)

He is at least consistent with his idea of the Muses in the *Troy Book*, even though he does not find any place at all for them in tragedy. His words also confirm the point that he does not know of a requirement of elevated style in tragedy.

Lydgate frequently gives the name of tragedy to the stories he finds in Bochas or to his own versified versions, particularly in the envoys that he adds to his source's materials. But it is only when he is half way through his vast work that he pauses in one of the envoys, namely that following the story of Jugurtha, to define the genre:

> This may be weel callid a tragedie,
> By discripsioun takyng auctorite;
> For tragedie, as poetes spesephie,
> Gynneth with joie, eendith with adversite;
> From hih estat men cast in low degre.   (5.3118–22)

This explanation of tragedy does not differ essentially from that given in the *Troy Book*; the movement of the plot is the same. But the substance of Jugurtha's tragedy is much different from those told by the Trojan tragedians. For Jugurtha was a good knight only at the beginning. When he returned to his homeland, after founding the city of Numantia in Spain,

> He chaunged knihthod into cruelte;
> With covetise so bleendid was the siht
> Of Jugurtha, that was first a good kniht.   (5.3129–31)

---

[61] It is quite clear that *Bochas* is simply Lydgate's way of spelling the French *Boccace*. *Boccace* would presumably have been pronounced bo-KASS by Frenchmen and BOK-ass by Englishmen; *Bochas* would also be pronounced BOK-ass.

His ending was bad not only in a material but in a moral sense as well: "His gynnyng good: a cursid eende had he" (3143); and he was brought down by his own viciousness.

Jugurtha's moral deterioration set in while his material prosperity was on the rise. It was the cause of the prosperity and also the cause of his downfall, by a natural process of cause and effect. He got to high place by murder, and murder called for vengeance: that is, his people rebelled. Jugurtha arranged a stay of execution for himself by bribing a corrupt Roman praetor, Actilius, but his uncorrupt successor Gaius Marius defeated him for good. Fortune is given no role in his overthrow, except an indirect one by her favor to Marius: "And Fortune, which helpeth hardi man, / Gaff hym gret favour bi her influence" (3071–72).

At the end of the *Fall of Princes*, when justifying the stark style of his verses, Lydgate alleges a social function for tragedy different from that of the spring festivals of Troy:

> Off this translacyoun considred the matere,
> The processe is in party lamentable;
> Wooful clausys of custom they requere,
> No rethoriques nor florysshynges delyctable:
> Lettrys of compleynt requere colour sable,
> And tragedyes in especial
> Be rad and songe at feestys funeral.   (9.3443–49)

He does not seem to be speaking of the antique Senecan tragedy, "A furious compleynt uttrid in distresse" (6.3351), but rather sad poems of disaster, suitable for occasions when a somber mood should prevail. One of Shakespeare's falling princes puts it well:

> For God's sake, let us sit upon the ground
> And tell sad stories of the death of kings.
> (*Richard II* 3.3.155–56)

Lydgate says something similar in his poem *Misericordias Domini in eternum cantabo*,[62] when contrasting secular poetry with religious:

> At funeral feestys men synge tragedies
> With wooful ditees of lamentacioun;
> In thorpys smale be songe comedies
> With many unkouth transmutacioun;
> Ech man folwyng oppynyoun,
> Somme in rejoisshyng, somme in compleynyng;
> But for moost sovereyn consolacioun,
> Eternally Thy mercies I shal syng.   (63–72)

[62] Lydgate, *Minor Poems*, 1:71–77.

Walter Schirmer thinks that this poem was composed in Lydgate's first period as a poet, before the death of Chaucer.[63] If so, he must have gone from a purely narrative or lyric idea of tragedy as a living form to an understanding of tragedy as an obsolete theatrical form, and then returned to, or added, something like his original idea. But the notion of lamentation remains consistent throughout.

Lydgate also remained faithful, at least in practice, to the Chaucerian vision of tragedy as primarily concerned with Fortune's victims rather than with criminals who met with deserved disaster, though like Chaucer he included the villainous as well as the virtuous as tragic protagonists. But he may have been influenced by a darker view of tragedy as the *Fall of Princes* progressed.

He did have an opportunity in the first book of the *Fall* to pass on the Lactantian idea of tragedy as restricted to the villainies of villains, but he decisively rejected it. I am referring to Laurence de Premierfait's handling of Boccaccio's remark about the "infinite tragedies of credulity." In his first translation of the *De casibus*, which he dedicated to Louis duke of Bourbon in 1400,[64] his rendition of the passage is fairly straightforward: "The tragedies of poets cry out at every crossroad" how credulousness has brought about terrible disasters.[65] But in his second, expanded version, composed for John Duke of Berry and completed in 1409, he inserted a characterization of tragedy derived from book 18 of Isidore's *Etymologies*. Now he says, "The words of tragic poets, writers of the foul and fearful deeds of kings, cry out at every crossroad" the devastation caused by credulity.[66] On seeing this statement, Lydgate perhaps detected a view of tragedy limiting it to stories of high-ranking men who by their sins brought about their own downfall. But whether he did or not, or whether or not he objected to such a characterization

---

[63] Schirmer, *John Lydgate*, pp. 23, 178.

[64] Bergen, *Fall*, 1:xiii and 4:125–29. I use the edition of Premierfait's first version printed at Bruges by Colard Mansion in 1476: *De la ruyne des nobles hommes et femmes*, and, as noted below, compare it with the Huss and Schabeler edition of Lyons of 1483; see Bergen, *Fall*, 4:127–29. For Premierfait's career, see Carla Bozzolo, *Manuscrits des traductions françaises d'oeuvres de Boccace*, xv siècle, pp. 3–29; idem, "Le 'Dossier Laurent de Premierfait'"; Colette Jeudy, "L'abrigé de la *Thébaïde* de Laurent de Premierfait"; R. C. Famiglietti, "Laurent de Premierfait: The Career of a Humanist in Early-Fifteenth-Century Paris"; and Claudia Villa, *La "Lectura Terentii"*, chap. 8: "Laurencius" (pp. 237–59). His name was Laurens Guillot, and he came from Premierfait, a small town in the diocese of Troyes (Famiglietti, p. 28).

[65] Premierfait, *De la ruyne* 1.11: "Les tragedies des poetes crient par chascun carrefour que les parolles emmielleez et les ammonnestemens de ceulx qui ont deux langues jetteez a ceulx qui tost croient ont amene destruction et brulement de citez, desrobemens de pays, bestournemens de royaumes, et les destruisemens de ceulx qui folement croient. . . ."

[66] Laurence de Premierfait, *Des cas des nobles hommes et femmes* 1.11.9, ed. Patricia May Gathercole, p. 157: "Les paroles des poetes tragiques, escrivains les ortz et puans faitz des roys, crient par chascun quarrefour que les parolles mielles et les enhortemens de ceulx qui ont deux langues ont esté cause de destructions et de arsins de citez, de roberies de pays et de bestournemens de royaumes et de destruction a ceulx qui tost et follement croient les paroles et les admonnestemens de ceulx qui ont deux langues." Gathercole's edition extends only to the end of book 1. For the other books I will cite the edition of Nicholas Couteau, Paris 1538 (Bergen, *Fall*, 4:132), which, unfortunately, is often quite faulty. The passage just cited begins thus: "Les parolles des poetes *m*agicques, escrip*t*ians," etc. (fol. 11v).

of tragedy, he took the onus from the consciences of the kings and placed it on their elevated status:

> But poetes that write tragedies,
> Ther compleynyng is al off hih estatis,
> Rehersyng ever ther pitous juparties,
> Ther sodeyn chaungis and ther woful fatis,
> Ther dyvysiouns and ther mortal debatis,
> And ay conclude ther dites, who can reede:
> "Hiest estatis stonde ay most in dreede."　(1.4796–802)

When Premierfait first came upon Boccaccio's next reference to tragedy, in book 2 of the *De casibus*, in his remark about the mean birth of Euripides and Demosthenes, he identified Euripides as a "tragedian," and translated *tragediarum clamores ingentes* as "the great cries and tragedies."[67] But the second time around he characterized Euripides as a "most noble tragedian" who, if he had to depend on the spirit and wisdom of his parents, "would not have written so subtly in verse the cries and doleful complaints that he made against the wicked and horrible deeds of the kings and great lords of the world."[68] Once again, then, Premierfait has given a dark picture of the genre of tragedy, which was probably inspired by Isidore's explanation of theatrical tragedians. But whereas the Boccaccian context of the "tragedies of credulity" would make one think that Premierfait had a plot-criterion in mind (the fall of evil princes), his characterization of Euripides's tragedies makes us doubt this assumption. He may have thought of tragedies as nothing more than versified denunciations of evil princes. Isidore's statement, in fact, need imply nothing more: "Tragedians are those who sang in verse before the onlooking people the old deeds and doleful crimes of wicked kings."[69] But Premierfait may also have been influenced by the contemporary French usage of Mézières and Deschamps of taking tragedy to mean lament or complaint, or Christine de Pisan's idea that it presented the bad deeds of princes.[70]

This time Lydgate accepts Premierfait's account. He says that Euripides was

> Callid in his tyme a gret tragician,
> Because he wrot many tragedies,
> And wolde off trouthe spare no maner man,
> But hem rebuken in his poetries,

---

[67] Premierfait, *De la ruyne* 2.17: "Ne aussi Euripides tragedien ne Demostenes rethoricien des quelz pour la vilte du lignage le pere de lun et la mere de lautre ne furent pas cogneus, cest a dire que on ne sceust leurs noms, iceulz Euripides et Demostenes ne amenerent pas du ventre des femmelletes les grans cris et tragedies et les doulceurs emmillees deloquence."

[68] Premierfait, *Des cas* 2.17 (fol. 39): "Se les hommes eussent les courages et la sapience de par ceulx qui les engendrent, le poete Euripedes, qui fut tresnoble tragedien, n'eust pas si subtillement escript en vers les criz et les griefs complains qu'il fist contre les maulvaises et horribles oeuvres des roys et des grans seigneurs du monde." He then enlarges upon Boccaccio's obvious moral, and adds the irrelevant story of how Euripides died, and finally goes on to speak of Demosthenes.

[69] Isidore, *Etymologiae* 18.45.

[70] IDEAS AND FORMS, pp. 176–85.

Touchyng the vices off flesshli fantasies,
Compleyne in pryncis ther deedis most horible,
And ech thyng punshe that was to God odible. (2.3067–73)

Perhaps he followed Premierfait's characterization of tragedy because it is not put forth as a universal norm but only as applying to the works of one author. But we will see in the next chapter that at the beginning of book 2 Lydgate was working from a more retributive conception of tragedy; it comes close to the terms used by Boccaccio in his Preface to the *De casibus*, where he seems to limit his case-histories to protagonists overthrown by the judgment of God, as a lesson to evil-living princes.

As for Boccaccio's third reference to tragedy, his account of the tragedies composed by Nero, I originally thought that Premierfait must have been puzzled by the passage when he made his first translation, for the 1483 edition, instead of saying that the emperor "feigned the tragedies of heroes" and danced them like a mime, says that he "feigned in playing or counterfeiting the fool while the Roman people looked on, and jumped about like a buffoon in the scene, that is, the public square, where the follies and fallacies of the poets were recited."[71] However, the puzzlement must have been on the part of an editor, for the 1476 edition gives what is clearly Premierfait's authentic version: Nero "feigned the tragedies of great lords" and leaped about in the scene, "where the tragedies and the comedies of the poets were recited."[72] In his revised version he says:

> Nero frequently made and composed poems and tragedies of the deeds of the great lords of the world; and in playing these tragedies of the great lords, while the people of Rome looked on, Nero would leap about after the fashion of tumblers in the public square or in the theater—that is, the public place where in former times at Rome the tragedies or the comedies of the ancient poets were recited.[73]

He may have come to this understanding of the passage by reading Isidore on the theater. Perhaps he realized now that the word *saltare* meant some kind of acting (Isidore: "saltabant histriones et mimi"; "ubi saltator agere posset"),[74] but he may not have realized that it referred to the mimetic "dancing" or ballet of pantomimists. It is true that in his first version he translated *quam docte psalleret* as "combien il chantoit sagement et dansoit," whereas

[71] Premierfait, *De la ruyne* 7.4 (1483): "Et il le plussouvent faingnant en faisant ou contrefaisant le fol voyant le peuple rommain saulta en guyse de bateleur en la scene, cest a dire en la place commune ou len racontoit les folies et les fallaces faittes par les poetes." See above, p. 14.

[72] Premierfait, *De la ruyne* 7.4 (1476): "Et il le plussouvent faingnant tragedies de gran seigneurs voyant le peuple rommain saulta en guyse de bateleur en la scene, cest a dire en la place commune ou len racontoit les tragedies et les comedies faittes par les poetes."

[73] Premierfait, *Des cas* 7.4 (fol. 158v): "Neron aussi moult souvent fist et composa dictez et tragedies des faictz des grans seigneurs du monde, et en jouant ces tragedies des faictz des grans seigneurs, Neron, voyant le peuple de Romme, sailloit comme les basteleurs saillent en la place commune ou dedans le theatre, c'est a dire, a la place commune ou l'en recomptoit jadis a Romme les tragedies ou les comedies des poetes anciens."

[74] Isidore, *Etymologiae* 18.43–44.

he left the dancing out in the second: "comme chantoit habillement." But this need not mean that he now understood that dancing was associated with "acting the mime." However, we will see below that he probably included grimacing in the function of the mime or *bateleur*. We note that Premierfait this time avoids referring to the criminal content of tragedy; he is content to take his lead from Boccaccio's "heroes" rather than Isidore's "scelerate kings."

How, we may ask, would Lydgate have understood Premierfait's second rendering? If he remembered what he wrote in the *Troy Book* about the production of ancient drama, he might have taken Bochas to mean that, rather than recite his own tragedies to the accompaniment of mummers, Nero himself served as one of the mummers. But whatever his specific interpretation of the passage was, he decided not to render it at length, but instead to summarize the larger report of Nero's activities, of which the composing of tragedies formed a part. This report, in Bochas, included the emperor's singing out in the open, in the common place, and his competing on the harp with jongleurs of Greece and Egypt; he also showed his skill in singing and in charioteering, and he exercised himself in all of the games among the ribalds and impure and infamous people of Rome. Then comes the account of his tragedies, and next the statement that the emperor won victories at home and abroad among the whores and ribalds for singing, harping, tumbling, charioteering, and grimacing ("en chantant, en harpant, en saillant, en chariant, en grimassant"). And sometimes, he concludes, Nero would go in disguise at night to taverns and bordellos.[75] Lydgate sums all of this up as follows:

> Of Grece and Egipt with dyvers jogulours[76]
> And among vileyns hymsilfe disporting,
> Lefte the presence of olde senatours
> And among ribaudis he wold harp and synge,
> Made comedies dishonestli sownyng,
> At the bordel dide hymself avaunce
> With comoun women openli to daunce.   (7.684–90)

His most striking departure from the text is to make Nero the composer of shameless comedies. He seems to have dismissed the idea that Nero could have composed tragedies of great lords. Perhaps it was because of the high regard in which Lydgate held tragedy, or perhaps he felt that comedy fitted the situation better than tragedy. It is not clear whether Lydgate dropped the notion of the theater altogether, or whether he identified the theater in this context with "brothel" (a meaning that Isidore reports). Nor is it clear whether Nero's dancing corresponds to Premierfait's *saillant*, and, if so, whether Lydgate recognized a reference to dramatic acting. If he did, he must have wished to picture Nero as putting on farcical plays in a whorehouse.

---

[75] Premierfait, *Des cas* 7.4 (fol 158v). The last phrase that I cite reads, "en cavernes et bordeaulx," where *cavernes* is a mistake for *tavernes*.

[76] See Bergen, 4:412–413 on the various readings and proper form of this word. Premierfait's text, which in the printed editions reads "les iongleurs de grece et degypte," should no doubt also read "iogleurs" for "iougleurs," since the intrusive *n* (which came from a misreading of *u*) had probably not yet been established in his day.

He could have found confirmation of Nero's avocations in Higden's *Polychronicon,* where the emperor is said to have sung in the theater and, as we saw earlier, to have sung the *Iliad* with tragic bellowing when Rome was burning.[77] In the *Legenda aurea,* which Lydgate cites elsewhere in the *Fall of Princes,* Nero is reported to have sung the *Helyed* in a "turgid" rather than a tragic costume; but we do hear that he surpassed all citharists and tragedians (*tragedi*).[78]

If Bochas's account of Nero as tragedian triggered Lydgate's memory of his own account of dramatic tragedy and comedy in the *Troy Book,* it would have come too late to affect his ideas of tragedy in most of the *Fall of Princes* or to have an effect on his own tragedy of Nero or on the tragedies that follow. But apart from the acted dimension of tragedy, the *Troy Book* account can be easily harmonized with his references to tragedy elsewhere in his works, and can be harmonized with Chaucer's understanding of tragedy as well. A synoptic characterization might run as follows. Tragedy deals primarily with the sudden fall of great men, and it gives rise to lamentation. If the men are innocent of wrongdoing, then Fortune or some human enemy gets the blame. If the men are sinful and deserve to fall, then they are blamed, but there is still room for lamentation. The only potentially unharmonious element in Lydgate's ideas of tragedy is the occasional implication that the tragic subjects or protagonists are always responsible for their fall. We will take up this matter in the second section of the next chapter.

---

[77] Higden, *Polychronicon* 4.9 (4:392–94); see p. 41 above.
[78] James of Varazze, *Legenda aurea,* chap. 89 (St. Peter, for the feastday of June 29), p. 377; IDEAS AND FORMS, p. 167.

5

Lydgate's fallen princes

Chaucer accepted Boccaccio's *De casibus* as containing a series of tragedies, but rather than translating it, or a part of it, he chose to imitate it with
a small series of versified tragedies of his own choosing. He thereby avoided
a direct confrontation between Boccaccio's emphatic morals and his own
concept of tragedy. But we do find this sort of confrontation in Lydgate's
Fall of Princes, with the added factor of Premierfait's interpretations and
additions.

As we can surmise from Premierfait's two noble patrons, Boccaccio's
"mirror for magistrates" found favor with at least some men of high rank.
We may assume that the translator's efforts were well received, if not well
read. It was Premierfait's second version that came to the attention of Humphrey of Gloucester, who commissioned Lydgate to render its prose accounts
into English verse, a labor that occupied him on and off for eight years
(around 1431 to 1439).

In his Second Prologue (the *Prologue du translateur*) of his second version,
Premierfait gives as the purpose of the work the manifestation of the miserable condition, and the turning and changeable estate, of the things of Fortune, the recognition of which is to make men and women hold such things in
less repute and to despise them the more, while esteeming the divine and heavenly things that possess true security and lasting joy. In setting forth the
sweet and bitter fortunes of illustrious men and women of all ages, he says,
this book is of singular value and a noble example of virtue.[1] In admitting
that there are sweet as well as bitter fortunes, Premierfait recognizes that pessimism about worldly affairs is not warranted in every case. But it is called
for as a rule; for he goes on to say that Fortune casts down almost everyone
whom she exalts to the top of her wheel.

[1] Premierfait, *Des cas* Prologue 2.6–7, that is, sections 6–7 of the Second Prologue as given in
Gathercole, pp. 89–90. Gathercole's text has been confusedly printed: the textual variants of Prologue 1 (Premierfait's Dedicatory epistle to the Duke of Berry) appear as if they were a headnote
to Prologue 2 (the Prologue of the Translator), and the variants to Prologue 2 look like the headnote to Prologue 3 (Boccaccio's Preface). The Prologue of the Translator is also given in Bergen's
edition of the *Fall of Princes*, 1:lii–liv, taken from the first printed edition, that of John du Pré
(Paris 1483–84). Couteau's 1538 edition carries this Prologue as modified by Anthony Verard in
his edition of Paris 1494, in which he dedicates the work to Charles VIII (see Hortis, *Studi*, p.
827). The Dedication to the Duke of Berry (Prologue 1) and Boccaccio's Preface (Prologue 3) do
not appear at all in the 1538 edition.

Premierfait knows well enough the content of Boccaccio's Preface; for he gives it as his Third Prologue, reproducing the literal translation that he had made of it for his 1400 version. But whereas Boccaccio's main stress is upon the sinful princes of his own day and the lessons that they can learn from seeing similarly placed princes suffering falls through the judgment of God, he stresses in his Second Prologue only the corollary of worldly inconstancy. This theme is of course brought into great prominence on many pages of the *De casibus*, and perhaps Premierfait wanted to give it "equal time" with ideas of sin and punishment in the prefatory discussions.

BOCHAS IN ENGLISH: THE FIRST PHASE

Lydgate tells us that it was the lesson of inconstancy that epitomized the whole work for Duke Humphrey:

> The noble book off this John Bochas
> Was, accordyng in his opynyoun,
> Off gret noblesse and reputacioun
> And onto pryncis gretli necessarie
> To yive exaumple how this world doth varie.
> (*Fall* 1.423–27)

And he commanded Lydgate to translate it, "to shewe th'untrust off al worldli thyng" (429).

Humphrey would have done better to take more to heart the lesson of providential punishment—a theme that Lydgate does not fail to stress, as we shall see. But, as Bergen says, Humphrey probably read Lydgate's gravely offered moral and political wisdom with the same serious and wholly detached interest with which the Duke of Berry must have received Premierfait's philosophy, for the two dukes appear to have been "equally egoistic, avaricious, untrustworthy, intriguing, and dissolute."[2]

Premierfait's most direct advice to the Duke of Berry comes in his long Dedication or First Prologue, which however is omitted in most of the manuscripts of his work.[3] In it he sets Fortune into the general providential order of things. She is the "efficient cause" of the falls dealt with in this work (sect. 5). Everyone became subject to her because of original sin (7–8), and she acts as the chamberlain of God for the punishment of sins (10). Adam and Eve orgulously broke the divine law laid upon them; and, as a consequence, by the justice of God, all men participate in the mockery of Fortune as she plays at lifting them up and casting them down (13). Fortune seems to act in a confused manner, but the reasons for her actions are known to God (10). Sometimes, however, the reasons are evident, as Premierfait shows by citing

---

[2] Bergen, 1:xvi. See below, pp. 211–15; for Duke Humphrey.
[3] Gathercole, p. 39. She edits it on pp. 75–87, and Bergen on 1:liv–lxv. I cite it according to Gathercole's sections.

"Alan the poet": for though it seems that wicked and unjust men are lifted to the highest estates of the world, Fortune brings them up in this way only in order to throw them down with more grief and to crush them according to the weight of their iniquities (16–17).[4] He draws on Seneca (not his tragedies) to show that the wise man is not subject to Fortune, because he values only his virtues, which she cannot take from him (22–26). For lack of this wisdom, Adam and Eve and all their descendants became subject to Fortune (27), and Premierfait laments at great length the troubles and sins in all three estates of his own day (27–65).[5]

Premierfait's Dedication (Prologue 1) must not have been in the copy of his work that Duke Humphrey gave to Lydgate, since Lydgate would surely have used it if he had seen it. He does refer to Premierfait's Second Prologue, and creatively adds to what he says about the creative adaptation of other authors' works (1.1–42, 85–98). He also passes on in his own way the French author's emphasis on Fortune: he says that Laurence's purpose in recounting the fall of nobles was:

> Therin to shewe Fortunys variaunce,
> That othre myhte as in a merour see
> In worldly worshepe may be no surete.   (1.54–56)

Laurence supposedly wished men to read of the adventures of princes,

> And have a maner contemplacioun
> That thynges all, wher Fortune may atteyne,
> Be transitory of condicioun;
> For she off kynde is hasti and sodeyne,
> Contrarious hir cours for to restreyne;
> Off wilfulnesse she is so variable,
> When men most truste, than is she most chaungable.
>   (106–12)

After attributing these chestnuts about Fortune to Laurence, Lydgate goes on to give Laurence's actual conclusion to Bochas himself:

> And for hir chaung and for hir doubilnesse,
> This Bochas biddeth that men sholde enclyne
> Sette ther hertis, void off unstabilnesse,
> Upon thynges which that been devyne,

---

[4] He is no doubt drawing on Alan of Lille's *Planctus Nature*, as Gathercole surmises (p. 24).

[5] He draws on Boccaccio's Dedicatory Epistle to Mainardo Cavalcanti in sections 35ff. (see the original in Bergen, 1:xlix–l). The letter was written in 1373 and was not only attached to the revised *De casibus* of 1373–1374, but was also sometimes affixed to the first version of the *De casibus* (1356–1360; 1370) and also issued independently (see above, chap. 1). Premierfait probably used a copy of the early *De casibus* with the attached epistle to Cavalcanti. In his first translation (that done in 1400), he included a rendering of the entire letter (Bergen, 1:xiii–xiv). Gathercole, p. 11, mistakenly states that Boccaccio wrote the letter in 1363 or 1364 as a dedication to the first version of the *De casibus*, and on p. 23 she says that Premierfait cites it from the volume of Boccaccio's epistles, whereas in fact he speaks only of "a familiar epistle written by John Boccaccio."

Whereas joie perpetueli doth shyne
Withoute eclipsyng in that hevenli see,
Void off all cloudis off mutabilite.   (113–19)

Bochas, he says, dealt especially with those princes who were unable to know themselves, and were suddenly cast down by Fortune (68–70), in order to provide a mirror of how the world will fail and how Fortune has jurisdiction over princes, in spite of their high renown (159–61).

The following stanzas represent Lydgate's version of Boccaccio's Preface, but he gives a greater stress to Fortune than to God's action:

> The whiche thyng, in ful sobre wise,
> He considred in his inward entent,
> In his resoun gan to advertise,
> Seyng off princis the blynd entendement,
> With worldli worshep how that they be blent,
> As thei sholde ever ther estatis keepe,
> And as Fortune were i-leid to sleepe;
>   As thei hadde off Fortune the maistry,
> Here enchauntid with ther pociouns
> Bi sum craft off newe sorcery,
> Or bi power off incantaciouns,
> To make stable ther domynaciouns
> With iren cheynys for to laste longe,
> Lokkid to rokkis off adamantis stronge;
>   Supposynge in ther surquedie
> Ther estatis sholde be durable;
> But Fortune kan frowardli denye,
> Pleynli preve that thei be chaungable,
> And to pryncis, for thei be nat stable,
> Fortune ful offte, for al their gret estat
> Unwarli chaungith and seith to hem chekmat.
>   For lordis summe in ther magnificence
> Off roial power sette off God riht nouht;
> Thei nat considre His long pacience,
> Nor advertise His power in ther thouht;
> But in ther hertis, yiff it were weel souht,
> How He is meek and pacient to abide,
> Thei wold off resoun ther pompe leyn aside.
>   But for ther tarieng and ther necligence,
> That they to Hym wil nat resorte ageyn,
> Yit off His mercy and benyvolence,
> Withoute vengance, rigour, or disdeyn,
> As a meek Fadir, in all His werkis pleyn,
> Assaieth His yerde off castigacioun,
> So for to brynge hem to correccioun.
>   Summe He can ful fadirly chastise,
> Where he loveth, by punshyng off siknesse,

> And off His mercy in many another wise
> B'adversite off sum worldli distresse;
> And He nat askith, for His kyndenesse,
> Off hih nor low, whoso can adverte,
> Noon othir tresor but a mannys herte.   (1.162–203)

We see that he does not speak of the judgment of God on the princes of the past, but only Fortune's unforseen reversals. God's action is limited to paternal discipline and correction.

Earlier, Lydgate stated that Bochas dealt with all estates, of high and low degree (128), and he goes on now to attribute to him a purpose that Boccaccio did not express in his Preface (though in his revised Preface he noted that the bad example of the nobles corrupted the ignorant multitude): namely, to call the lower people from their error by the examples of fallen princes (204–10). And he ends with a promise of simple poetic justice: God will reward the good and punish the wicked, no matter how highly or lowly placed:

> Who hym repentith, the Lord will hym avaunce
> And hym accepte, in hih and louh estate,
> The meek preserve, punyshe the obstynat.   (222–24)

This unrealistic assessment of God's activity in this world does, finally, correspond to Boccaccio's stress upon exemplary divine judgments. But then, with no other transition than a humble reference to his own naked style, Lydgate turns realistic, saying that he will set eloquence aside,

> And in this book bewepen and compleyne
> Th'assaut off Fortune, froward and sodeyne,
> How she on pryncis hath kid her variaunce
> And off her malice the dedli mortal chaunce.   (1.235–38)

This sudden intervention of the theme of Fortune, which, abstracted from its rectified providential context, carries all before its onslaught, is a good indication of what is to come in the rest of Lydgate's enormous poem. Deserved falls knock about with undeserved falls, and we hear of the wickedness sometimes of the faller, at other times of the feller, whether man or Fortune—and there are good fellers as well as bad. Lydgate mingles in his own morals with those of Boccaccio and Premierfait, especially in the envoys at the end of major sections, which Duke Humphrey asked him to compose, at least for book 2. As I pointed out above, it is in these addenda that he most frequently refers to the stories as tragedies.

A note on Lydgate's sources. He refers to Boccaccio only as the author of the *De casibus* (in Premierfait's French rendition). Premierfait also made a translation of the *Decameron*, of which Humphrey possessed a copy,[6] but

---

[6] Hortis, *Studi*, p. 646 n. 5. See above, p. 151 n.6.

Lydgate shows no signs of knowing about it. Premierfait used Boccaccio's *Genealogia* extensively for his expanded translation of the *De casibus*,[7] and Lydgate too uses the *Genealogia* independently in the *Fall of Princes*, though without giving its title. At one point where he is drawing on it, he cites as his source "John Bochas the poete excellent" (1.2137),[8] which of course would not reveal that he is using anything but his usual source, Premierfait's translation of *De casibus*. He did cite the *Genealogia* by name and author earlier on in the *Siege of Thebes*, where he also cited the *De mulieribus* as by Boccaccio, as we have seen.[9] He does not seem to have known anything about Boccaccio's metrical compositions. As noted above, he knew that Chaucer's source for the *Troilus* was an Italian book, but he did not realize that it was a narrative poem by Boccaccio.

When Premierfait translated the *De casibus*, he retained, as a rule, Boccaccio's remarks in the first person: for instance, the first book begins, "As I was considering and thinking over in various ways the tearful miseries of our predecessors," and so on (1.1). Lydgate, however, consistently speaks of Bochas in the third person: "Whan John Bochas considered hadde and souht / The woful fall off myhti conquerours ..." (1.470–71). Adam's appeal to Boccaccio, which begins in the original without salutation, is given a more personal touch by Premierfait: Adam addresses him as "Beau nepveu Jehan Boccace" (1.2). Lydgate takes the meaning of "nepveu" to be "nephew" rather than "grandson," and translates, "Cosyn Bochas" (1.484).

The fall of Adam and Eve has great potential as a tragedy, according to almost any definition of the term, and the story has often been touchingly told, beginning with its first appearance in Genesis.[10] One can think of *Genesis B* and *Paradise Lost*, and the analogous story of C. S. Lewis's *Perelandra*. But there is little that is moving or "well-reported" about the Boccaccio-Premierfait-Lydgate version. It is hardly more than a prosaic statement of great loss after great benefit. Some readers might find a certain charm in the descriptions of the world in the state of innocence; but there is no attempt to understand the way in which the first parents were brought to commit their misdeed.

Lydgate explains the fall simply. The first man and woman possessed all kinds of delights, but experienced evil when Adam fell into "dotage" and held strife with God through the "exciting" of his wife, breaking His command through wilful negligence (1.556–61). He expands upon their motives only by further name-calling, accusing them of presumption and disobedience (570), vainglory, false ambition, and covetousness (674–76). They banished themselves from that blisful life "Whan Adam gaff credence to a snake / And wrechedli gan trustyn on his wiff" (632–33).

When he deals with Bochas's discourse against disobedience, he is unable to

---

[7] Koeppel, *Laurents*, pp. 23–24.

[8] See Ibid., pp. 59–60.

[9] See pp. 154, 168 above.

[10] There is no reference to this striking story elsewhere in the Old Testament, and this is one of the reasons that lead me to conclude that the "second creation account" of Genesis 2–3 was a late addition, say around 400 B.C. See my "Devil at Large," p. 521.

resist bringing in the conceit of false Fortune and her wheel, but eventually he returns to Boccaccio's context of divine punishment:

> Which exaumpil ouhte inouh suffise,
> In al this worlde thouh there were no mo,
> T'exemplefie to folkis that be wise,
> How this world is a thoruhfare ful off woo,
> Lich fals Fortune, which turnyth to and fro
> To make folkis, whan thei most cleerli shyne,
> In ther estatis onwarli to declyne.
>
> For thouh that thei her hedis leffte aloffte
> Hih as Phebus shyneth in his speer,
> Thynke themsilffe, as it fallith offte,
> Ther renoun rechith above the sterris cleer,
> And how ther fame surmountith every speer,
> Ther trust corrupt hath a sodeyn fall,
> For to declare how they be mortall.
>
> O worldli folk, advertisith off entent,
> What vengaunce and what punycioun
> God shal taken in His jugement
> For your trespas and your transgressioun,
> Which breke His preceptis agayn al resoun!
> Ye han forgoten how with His precious blood
> You for to save He starff upon the rood.
>   (1.792–812)

And, of course, unlike Boccaccio, he terms the fall of man a tragedy:

> And off meek herte lat us oursilff dispose,
> Bi this tragedie to have knowlechyng
> Off our myscheeff how roote and eek gynnyng
>   Was the vice off inobedience,
> Surquedie and fals disobeissaunce.
>   (1.943–47)

We have seen earlier that Lydgate attributed the figure of the world as a thoroughfare full of woe, which he uses in the passage cited above (line 795), to "Chaucer's tragedies," that is, the *Monk's Tale*. The poem in which he makes this mistake, which has been given the name *A Thoroughfare of Woe*, contains a number of historical illustrations, beginning with Adam and Eve and ending with the earl of Salisbury, whose death Talbot in *1 Henry VI* calls "a woeful tragedy."[11] But it is not clear whether Lydgate himself, even in the *Fall of Princes,* went so far as to consider, or at least to call, tragic events tragedies. That is, we cannot tell whether he is limiting the notion of tragedy to the written account of a great man's fall or whether he means to include the

---

[11] Shakespeare, *1 Henry VI* 1.4.77; see my "Chaucer and Shakespeare," p. 199.

fall itself, thus applying the term in the metaphorical sense avoided by Boccaccio and Chaucer (Boccaccio's conceit of such events being incorporated into tragedies and shouted out at the crossroads is clearly not the same sort of thing). Lydgate knew and used parts of the *Policraticus* of John of Salisbury,[12] who did apply the notions both of tragedy and comedy to world events.[13] But the chances are that he did not read this section, just as he must have overlooked John's accurate notion of how Roman comedy was acted. So far in this later era, that is, Chaucer's time and beyond, we have found only Lydgate's fellow Benedictine Thomas Walsingham who employed a figurative idea of tragedy.

The envoy to Lydgate's first tragedy ends, after the fashion of envoys, with a direct address to princes. He claims that the lesson he enjoins follows from the tragedy:

> Wherefore, ye Pryncis, avisili doth see,
> As this tragedie in maner berth witnesse,
> Whereas wantith in any comounte
> Subjeccioun, for lakkyng off meeknesse,
> And with povert pride hath an interesse,
> Ther folwith afftir, thoruh froward insolence,
> Among the peeple fals inobedience.
>   And, noble Pryncis, which han the sovereynte
> To governe the peeple in rihtwisnesse,
> Lik as ye cherisshe hem in pes and unyte
> Or frowardli destroie hem or oppresse,
> So ageynward ther corages thei will dresse
> Lowli t'obeie to your magnificence
> Or disobeie by inobedience.
>
>   (1.988–1001)

The message here is not entirely clear. In the first stanza he seems to be saying that if the princes' subjects mix pride with their poverty, they will become rebellious. This may in fact be his meaning, if we grant that the second stanza introduces an entirely new lesson. If it does not, then the first stanza must refer, as Bergen's marginal summary states, to the lack of meekness and the pride and insolence of princes, to which their subjects will respond in kind. If so, the moral is hardly appropriate to the story as Lydgate has told it, for he has not mentioned the subsequent rebelliousness of the creatures that had been subjected to Adam, or the lack of subjection in his own bodily members, or the vicious turn taken by his son Cain. But at least the lesson as he gives it (according to Bergen's interpretation) would provide princes with a practical reason and method for avoiding the vice that brought the first parents to ruin.

Further on in the first book, Lydgate adds an envoy to Bochas's story of Nimrod: his tragedy has the straightforward lesson that he fell because of his pride (1.1380–400). Another envoy comes after a rapid survey ending with

[12] Bergen, 4:175.
[13] IDEAS AND FORMS, pp. 78–81.

the story of Philomela and Procne. This tragedy (that is, the whole of the previous history, from Adam down to Tereus) shows various disasters and teaches that Fortune is deceitful and everything is insecure (1814–41). The envoy at the end of the life of the admirable Cadmus gives a similar lesson. The tragedy is like the chantepleure, which begins in joy and ends in wretchedness: "Al worldi blisse is meynt with bittirnesse" (2161).

He then comes to the story of Aeetes, Medea's father, which he introduces by saying that Bochas continued to compile the generations "of many noble, famous off estate— / I meene, off such as were infortunat" (2176–77). In so saying, he admits in effect that Boccaccio was being very selective, in omitting the stories of those who were fortunate. But the story of Aeetes and Medea is so expanded by Premierfait that it eventually falls into the excluded category: Medea was finally reconciled with Jason by some unknown means, and some writers say that by Jason's help Aeetes was restored to his kingdom.[14] Lydgate, we recall, assumed that Seneca in his tragedies was one of these writers (1.2384–87). His conclusion is that worldly affairs are always mixtures of sorrow and joy (2402–07). And the same thing, he says, is illustrated in the next story: "Record of Mynos, the noble worthi kyng" (2408). Now while it is true that sorrow is meddled with gladness in the life of Minos, the sequence in which the two conditions occur is crucially unlike that of Aeetes: it is in accord with the recipe proper to a work that purports to recount tragedies of the fall of princes. That is to say, after various triumphs, Minos comes to a bad end and stays there.

In the previous story, Lydgate is perhaps being true to history as he sees it when he follows Premierfait in restoring Aeetes, Medea, and Jason to happiness; but he is definitely not being true to form. However, though he mentions Seneca's alleged treatment of Medea's reconciliation in his tragedies, he himself does not call her story a tragedy. He withholds this designation until he sums up the fall of Sisera and the defeat of the Midianites, in the envoy that follows their histories (1.3126).

The stories of Sisera and the Midianites can be regarded as double-plotted tragedies on the order of the *Odyssey*, as defined by Aristotle,[15] since they end with the downfall of the wrong side and the victory of the right: Deborah triumphs over Sisera, and Gideon over the Midianites. After introducing Sisera as one of the complainers who appeared to Bochas—he was a proud duke whom Fortune began to menace (1.2888–90)—Lydgate expands upon Bochas by turning to the Bible. This tyrant was a mortal enemy of the Jews, and he took great delight in killing them, sparing neither man nor child; but he was sent to be their scourge by God Himself, to punish them for their sins (2901–09). When the punishment has the desired effect of reforming them, God sends Deborah to their rescue, and soon it is all up for Sisera. Sisera, of course, made a bad mistake to confide in the blandishments of Fortune, for she does not long suffer tyrants to endure in their "fals usurped tirannye" to which she has summoned them "under a colour off fals collusioun" (2987–

---

[14]   Premierfait, *Des cas* 1.7.7, probably drawing on Boccaccio *De mulieribus* 16.9 (p. 86).

[15]   Aristotle, *Poetics* 13: "The second-best pattern (which some hold to be the best) is the kind which involves a double structure (like the *Odyssey*) and contrasting outcomes for good and bad characters"; IDEAS AND FORMS, p. 3. See above, p. 89.

93). The general lesson follows: lordship, no matter how mighty and famous, will not endure unless it is virtuous (2998–3000).

In another context, like that of Premierfait's Dedication where Fortune is named as God's chamberlain, we could expect Fortune, as well as the female champions Deborah and Jael, to be congratulated for their role in the divinely directed discomfiture of Sisera. But Lydgate has only harsh words for Fortune. It is not simply a matter of his continuing to regard her from Sisera's point of view—it was, after all, his complaint to Bochas that initiated the story. He pictures her thus because he casts her in the role of a tempter to evil, like the devil, and gives her actively immoral qualities. But in spite of these features, we are not meant to think of her as a real being who shares in Sisera's guilt. She is rather a symbol of the inconstancy of worldly things. The fault is all Sisera's: he falls not only because of his crimes against the people of God, but also because of his pride, that is, his misplaced trust in his power and achievements (3015–17).

The story of Gideon's triumph over the Midianites ends with a celebration of divine power and mercy:

> Thus can the Lord off His magnyficence
> The meeke exalte and the proude oppresse,
> Lich as He fyndeth in hertis difference,
> So off His power He can His domys dresse,
> Merci ay meynt with His rihtwisnesse,
> His jugementis with long delay differrid;
> And or He punshe, pite is ay preferrid.   (1.3095–101)

This theme of divine forbearance is take up again in the short story of Jabin, immediately after the envoy: the Lord "forbar His hand with ful long suffraunce" (3138). However, the sentiment is contradicted in short order; God's sufference does not last long at all: "God wil nat suffre ther power longe laste" (3150). But at any rate we have here and in the previous accounts another variation on the formula for worldly success that ended the envoy on Adam and Eve. In its simplest terms it can be expressed thus: "Be good." It is not a cure-all for the evils of the world, but Lydgate's records show that it has at least a partial effectiveness in preventing disaster.

In the envoy itself, he takes occasion to address female as well as male rulers, perhaps because of the example of Princess Deborah:

> O Pryncis, Pryncessis, most sovereyn and enteer,
> In this tragedie conceyveth by redyng,
> How that estatis by ful unwar chaungyng,
> Whilom ful worthi, ther lyves dede fyne,
> Whan fro ther noblesse thei wer maad to declyne.
> (1.3125–29)

The next notable tragedy is that of a woman, Queen Jocasta, of whom Bochas was inspired to make a lamentation of "unkouth sorwe" that assailed her, to weep and bewail her lifelong troubles with a tragedy (3174–78). But the tragedy will also describe the fortune of Oedipus, who was likewise unfortunate all his life (3470–72). In this case, then, Lydgate explicitly accords with Seneca in naming the accounts of this royal couple tragedies (3580).

After unknowingly killing his father and disposing of the serpent-Sphinx,[16] Oedipus married his mother Jocasta, again unknowingly. The gods and Nature took offense at this deed, Lydgate says, but he thinks that the fault must have been precipitated by some sort of astrological cause (3483–3500). Jocasta's suspicion of the truth grows without suspense into certainty, and she and Oedipus mourn together (3608–30). The story ends as in Boccaccio: in keeping with Oedipus's prayer, his unnatural sons Eteocles and Polynices destroy themselves, and Jocasta commits suicide.

Lydgate then engages in a typical *Memento mori*, a meditation upon death removed from any thought of the afterlife, like the dust-to-dust curse pronounced upon Adam and Eve. A variation of this curse was recited by the priest when he placed the ashes on the foreheads of the people on Ash Wednesday: "Memento, homo, quia cinis es, et in cinerem reverteris."[17] But in Genesis it is preceded by the promise of a Savior who will crush the head of the Serpent. In the Lenten ritual, the admonition was accompanied by the Sign of the Cross, and in the prayer that preceded the ceremony, God's promises to the penitent were recalled. There is nothing of the sort in Lydgate's outburst: Death devours all, both joy and sorrow, both rich and poor, striking with an "unwar strook" (3792)—the phrase by which Chaucer twice translated Fortune's *ictus indiscretus* in Boethius. We might expect Lydgate to go on in this vein and speak of the body as food for worms, as Hamlet does in his graveyard meditation,[18] or (to take an earlier example) as the resurrected Lazarus does in the Townley *Play of Lazarus*: after thanking Jesus for reviving him he ignores Him and addresses a sermon to the audience on the decay of the grave.[19] Instead, Lydgate conforms to his context and presents death as no more than a quietus from the slings and arrows of outrageous Fortune, with no hint of the moral objections against suicide:

> Bet is to deie than lyve in wrechidnesse,
> But is to deie than ever endure peyne,
> Bet is an eende than dedli hevynesse,
> Bet is to deie than ever in wo compleyne.[20]   (1.3795–98)

[16] Lydgate follows Premierfait 1.8.10 in identifying the Sphinx as a serpent. For other references to her serpentine qualities, see my "Metamorphoses of the Eden Serpent," pp. 313–16. According to Lydgate, Fortune sometimes appears as a woman-headed serpent, that is, as a mermaid (6.64–65, 479). See the same article, pp. 311–12, on serpentine mermaids and Sirens.

[17] *Manuale ad usum percelebris ecclesie Sarisburiensis*, p. 12. Genesis 3.19 reads: "Quia pulvis es, et in pulverem reverteris" ("For dust thou art, and into dust thou shalt return"), which was the wording of the formula in the Roman rite.

[18] The nature of Hamlet's discourse as a *Memento mori* was pointed out by the late Alfred Harbage in a course that I attended at Harvard in 1961. He also explained various notions of tragedy that the Elizabethans had inherited from the Middle Ages. His remarkably original insights into these matters were an important inspiration for the present study.

[19] *The Towneley Plays* no. 31, 1:424–31. The sermon is in lines 103–236.

[20] Cf. the speech that Chaucer gives to Troilus beginning, "O Deth, that endere art of sorwes alle" (*Troilus* 4.501). See my *Love and Marriage*, pp. 59–60 for more examples of failure to indict

In the envoy, he includes in the foregoing tragedy everything that occurred since the last envoy, namely, the pride and false presumption of King Jabin, the great adversity of Queen Jocasta, the inclination to all vices of King Oedipus, and the division between the two brothers, Eteocles and Polynices, which inspires the refrain: "Kyngdamys devyded may no while endure" (3816–22). It might seem unfair of Lydgate to characterize Oedipus as he does, after giving no indication of any conscious guilt on his part; but he is no doubt assigning his *hamartia* once again to the stars, and is speaking of "th'ynclynacioun / Off sum fals froward constellacioun" (3490–91). His chief moral continues the theme of the refrain:

> Pryncis, Pryncessis, which han the sovereynte
> Over the peeple and domynacioun,
> Yiff ye list lyve longe in felicite,
> Cherisshith your subjectis, doth noon extorsioun,
> And advertisith, off wisdam and resoun,
> As this tragedie doth to you discure,
> Kyngdamys devyded may no while endure.   (1.3837–43)

Jocasta especially must be exempted from this indictment of misrule; her adversity was due to Fortune alone (3775). She was faultless even in the condemnation of the infant Oedipus to death. This was Laius's doing, which she lamented (3218–27). And, as we have seen, Lydgate commends her decision to kill herself.

After the tragedy of Thyestes and Atreus, where, as in the stories of Medea and Oedipus, Lydgate refers to the tragedies of Seneca, he takes up the tragedy of Theseus. He carries over Boccaccio's blame of women and credulity (the "tragedies of credulity") and Fortune—Fortune being called "this blynde goddesse in hir consistorie" (1.4537)—but he has Theseus take upon himself the blame for the death of Hippolytus and Phaedra's suicide. He was being punished, he decides, especially for his malicious treatment of Ariadne (4462–66).

Lydgate's antifeminism is mingled with sly humor, unlike Boccaccio's (in fact, Boccaccio has little place for any kind of humor in his work, and the same is true of Premierfait).[21] For instance, he says here that Bochas in his invective at this point was not talking of English women:

> He meneth off women that be born in Crete,
> Nothyng off hem that duelle in this contre:
> For women heer, al doubilnesse they lete,
> And have no tech off mutabilite;
> They love no chaungis nor no duplicite;

the self-slain. Other instances in Lydgate can be seen in the stories of Lucretia and Dido, treated below; see also the suicides of Antony and Cleopatra, likewise dealt with below. But he condemns Hannibal for poisoning himself (5.2152–58).

[21] On the subject of antifeminism in the *Fall of Princes*, see also Hortis, *Studi*, pp. 652–54, and Pearsall, *John Lydgate*, pp. 236–39.

> For ther husbondis, in causis smal or grete,
> Whatever they seyn, thei can nat countirplete.
> (1.4726–32)

In the story of Hercules, which Premierfait added to Boccaccio's series, Lydgate's attacks against women are straightforward and lacking in whimsy. When referring to Hercules's shameful submission to Iole, he "excuses" women because it is their nature to corrupt, and their influence is overwhelming (1.5153–59). In other words, women are excused because they are inherently evil, and their male victims are excused because female enticements to evil are irresistible. Unlike Chaucer, whose tragedy of Hercules he does not mention, he condemns Dejanira for the hero's death without granting her the benefit of good intentions (5447–53, 5503–09).

He returns to the humorous treatment of women in the story of Orpheus, which Premierfait expands from Boccaccio's one-sentence account by drawing on Ovid's *Metamorphoses*, Boethius's *Consolation*, and Boccaccio's *Genealogy*. Premierfait "naturalizes" the story from the realm of the nether gods to an explicitly human framework: Eurydice is abducted (he does not say by whom), and permitted to return to Orpheus only on condition that he not look back—"an easy enough law, if the love of man for woman could obey any law."[22] This corresponds to Boethius's remark, which Arcite repeats in the *Knight's Tale* (line 1164): "Who shal yeve a lovere any lawe?" Lydgate draws directly on the *Metamorphoses* and the *Genealogy* and specifically returns the action to hell. He repeats the Boethian sentiment: "Ther may no lawe lovers weel constreyne, /So inportable is ther dedli peyne" (5802–03). But he goes on to remark that if some husbands could lose their wives by a sudden glance, they would bear their loss patiently and even thank God for delivering them from prison (5804–10). Orpheus, though, loves Eurydice and feels he must die when he loses her. But in spite of his good experience with marriage, he refuses to marry another and thereby go back to "prison," since one hell is dreadful, and two are even more perilous (5835).

The joke is out of place, of course, and in the envoy Lydgate comes to a more sober conclusion: the tragedy shows how Orpheus endures joy mingled with sorrow; when he married in his youth, he felt the great felicity of wedlock until Fortune intervened and destroyed his worldly bliss (5881–86). As usual in medieval retellings of the story, Lydgate omits Ovid's eschatological happy ending, when after his death Orpheus joyfully embraces Eurydice in the fields of the just.[23] Lydgate goes so far, it seems, as to say that he was deprived of all postmortal consolation. True, his harp was stellified, but Fortune denied him burial (5850–52).

Lydgate goes along with the antifeminism of the story of Samson (1.6347–510), but shortens the Boccaccio-Premierfait chapter *In mulieres* and sets

---

[22]   Premierfait, *Des cas* 1.12.59.
[23]   Ovid, *Metamorphoses* 11.61–66. See *Love and Marriage*, pp. 91–92. See also John Block Friedman, *Orpheus in the Middle Ages*, who however in his account of Lydgate (p. 237 n. 41) does not note the playfulness of Lydgate's treatment. For Criseyde's transformation of the otherworldly reunion of Orpheus and Eurydice from a happy encounter to one of perpetual mourning, see above, p. 111, and below, p. 255.

into greater prominence Bochas's admission that he meant to attack only bad women. Good women, he says, should lightly pass by and shake their sleeves (6704). He elaborates upon the point in a ballade (6707–34).

For the history of Troy, he refers to his *Troy Book*, commissioned by Henry V, of whom he takes occasion to give a brief panegyric. But he misses the opportunity to call his account of the king's glorious life and sudden death a tragedy, even though he says that "this lond may seyn he deied al to soone" (1.5978). Perhaps we are to take this as a sign that he did not think of real-life events as tragedies until they were reduced to literature. But he could have provided the literature himself, like Chaucer with his "Modern Instances."

Like Boccaccio, Lydgate spends some time in praise of Poverty, who is free from the assaults of Fortune (6126ff.), but nevertheless he considers Priam quite miserable for falling into this allegedly happy condition:

> This tragedie pitous and lamentable
> And dolerous to writen and expresse,
> That worthi Priam, of kynges most notable,
> Was falle in povert from his gret richesse,
> Fro kyngli honour into wrechidnesse.   (1.6308–12)

The cause of the fall, in this case, was the "false adultery" of Paris and Helen (6314).

THE CRIMINOUS TRAGEDIES OF BOOK 2

At the beginning of his second book, Lydgate's presentation of Bochas's doubts is reminiscent of the Knight's objection to the earlier series of tragedies told by a monk: namely, that more than enough tragedies have been told to make the teller's point. (It is, of course, quite possible that Chaucer himself was drawing on Boccaccio's prologue to book 2 in giving the Knight his lines.) Lydgate, instead of answering such an objection, anticipates it by the rhetorical ploy of *anteoccupatio* or *procatalēpsis*, which refers, literally, to "the capture of the enemy's territory beforehand"—that is, by raising and refuting an objection before the opposition has a chance to introduce it. He begins thus:

> To summe folk, par cas, it wolde seem,
> Touchyng the chaunges and mutabilites
> By me rehersid, that thei myhte deeme,
> Off Fortunes straunge adversites
> To pryncis shewed, doun pullid from ther sees,
> The tragedies auhte inouh suffise
> In compleynyng, which ye had herd devise;
>   The stori pitous, the processe lamentable,
> Void off joie, al gladnesse, and plesaunce,
> A thyng to grevous and to inportable,

> Whereas no merthe is medlid with grevaunce,
> Al upon compleynt standith th'alliaunce,
> Most whan Fortune, who that hir cours weel knewe,
> Chaungith old joie into sorwes newe.   (2.1–14)

And he goes on to express the Boethian doctrine of past joys increasing present sorrow:

> For onto hym that never wiste off wo,
> Remembraunce off his old gladnesse,
> Whan his weelfare and plesaunce is ago,
> And never aforn knew off non hevynesse,
> Such unwar chaung, such unkouth wrechidnesse
> Causith in pryncis, thoruh newe dedli trouble,
> Afftir ther fallyng, ther sorwes to be double.   (15–21)

But Lydgate's excuse for proceeding is not that given by Boccaccio at this point, that is, the continuing need to demonstrate the mutability of the world (this too was the Monk's chief lesson, and Theseus also relied heavily on it in the *Knight's Tale*). Rather, Lydgate stresses a lesson corresponding to the thrust of Boccaccio's Preface: the purpose of these stories is to keep men from vice, and thereby to prevent sudden falls:

> Olde exaumples off pryncis that have fall,
> Ther remembraunce off newe brouht to mynde,
> May been a merour to estatis all,
> How thei in vertu shal remedies fynde
> T'eschewe vices, off such as wer maad blynde,
> Fro sodeyn fallyng hemsilven to preserve,
> Longe to contune and thank off God disserve.   (22–28)

For, as he finally makes explicit, all the business about Fortune is nothing more than a poetic fiction. She is not at all to blame for the fall of princes:

> It is nat she that pryncis gaff the fall,
> But vicious lyvyng, pleynli to endite:
> Thouh God above ful offte hem doth respite,
> Long abidith, and doth His grace sende
> To this entent, they sholde ther liff amende.   (45–49)

The main message, therefore, is to turn vice into virtue, before the sword of vengeance carves and bites (94). This purpose was clearly seen by Duke Humphrey, who called on Lydgate one day when he was embarking on the first tragedy of the second book, that of King Saul, and gave this charge to the poet:

> That I sholde in everi tragedie,
> Afftir the processe made mencioun,
> At the eende sette a remedie,

With a lenvoie conveied by resoun,
And afftir that, with humble affeccioun,
To noble pryncis lowle it direct,
By othres fallyng thei myht themsilff correcte.
(2.148–54)

In other words, Humphrey wished Lydgate's adaptation of Premierfait's translation to take the form of first presenting a historical disaster and then giving advice on how his readers can prevent similar disasters from occurring to them. The form called for is like that of some treatments of the deadly sins, for instance, Chaucer's *Parson's Tale*, where the vices are first analyzed and then remedies are detailed.

Duke Humphrey's schema presupposes a quite different idea of tragedy from that which Lydgate has hitherto been drawing upon. For he implies that "in everi tragedie" the princely faller caused his own fall, and could have prevented his fall by right conduct.

It is true that Lydgate himself presented such a picture in book 1 when he gave the substance of Boccaccio's Preface, but he partially neutralized it by ending with the theme of bewailing Fortune's malice, and he did not associate it directly with tragedy as such. He also demonstrated in his concrete examples of tragedy in book 1, and his explicit statements about tragedy, that while tragedy might be inclusive of such a moralistic pattern, it was not restricted to it or completely adaptable to it.

We should therefore take seriously the idea that Humphrey himself provoked this limitation on the concept of tragedy: namely, that all of the falls of tragedy are caused by the fallers' wrongdoing. It may even be the case that Humphrey wished to bring Lydgate's work into conformity with Boccaccio's prefatory remarks, which stress that the falls are to warn readers of the judgments of God, and that he read the Preface in the original Latin. We know that the duke possessed a copy of the *De casibus*, for he gave it to Oxford University in 1443. This in fact is the only evidence that the original form of Boccaccio's work was in England at this time.[24]

Duke Humphrey's paradigm does work well enough for the tragedy of Saul, but it involves Lydgate in false generalizations. When telling how David overcame Saul's tyranny by "prudent meekness," he says that this sort of thing always works (2.400–06). In the envoy he tells princes that if they wish to keep their high position, they should be just and follow God's commands (526–32). In his expansion of Bochas's commendation of obedience, he discourses on the preservative qualities of religious piety:

For who that serveth the Lord of lordis all,
And hath the peeple in his subjeccioun,
God will keepe hym that he shal nat fall,
Longe preserve his domynacioun.   (2.575–78)

In saying such things, Lydgate is badly misleading any princely reader who takes him seriously, because these sentiments are belied by life itself and by

[24] Edwards, "The Influence of Lydgate's *Fall of Princes*," p. 428.

many of his own examples. For there are all sorts of reasons (some of them known only to God) why princes who live lives of virtue do not always remain long in prosperity.

In fact, Duke Humphrey's next suggestion, that Lydgate incorporate into his work a rendering of Coluccio Salutati's *Declamation of Lucretia,*[25] involves just such a case. Only at the end are we told that Lucretia's virtuous disaster was the cause of the villain's fall: "And bi occasioun off this pitous deede, / Tarquyn exilid, and hooli his kenreede" (1336–37), a point repeated in the next envoy (1429–35). The story itself involves a long discussion of Lucretia's desire to kill herself, but her husband and father in their attempt to dissuade her do not resort to the argument that it would be an offense against God; and she herself, as she sends forth her pure and immortal soul, expects a wholly favorable verdict from the infernal judges (1310–16).

Lydgate modestly says that he did not wish to treat of Lucretia's story because he could not hope to surpass Chaucer's account in the *Legend of Good Women* (974–1001). He decided to go ahead, however, not only because Humphrey wished it, but also, apparently, because her story is so appropriate: "It were pity hir story for to hide" (1003). He even gives her history again in book 3 (932–1148), which is where it occurs in Bochas. In both instances, he tells her story very well, and perhaps even Chaucer would have found them to be better reported than his own legend of Lucrece.

The tale of Dido, which Lydgate takes up in book 2, is similar to that of Lucretia. He follows Boccaccio's version of the story, according to which her affair with Aeneas is unhistorical. Lydgate here attributes the Aenean legend to Ovid (2151), though he clearly knows Vergil's version (he cites it in 4.67–70). Later on in the *Fall* he accepts her "false betrayal" by Aeneas as historical (5.2621–23). In the Boccaccian story, Dido commits suicide not because of being abandoned by a lover, but because of being forced to marry, after the death of her first husband, an unwelcome suitor.[26] In the first of his two envoys, Lydgate holds her up as an exemplar to widows, and praises her suicide (2.2171–98); in the second he says with mock severity that her action was folly and urges modern widows to be fickle and newfangled (2199–233). He is, of course, imitating *L'envoy de Chaucer* at the end of the *Clerk's Tale*, in which the Clerk tells archwives not to imitate Griselda.

We find, then, that in the cases of Lucretia and Dido, Lydgate does not suggest a remedy in his envoys, or instruct princes how to avoid falls that are caused by lack of self-correction. On the contrary, he holds up their conduct as exemplary. What then has become of Duke Humphrey's directive? Lydgate carried it out dutifully enough for King Saul, as we have seen, and he did so also for the next story, that of King Rehoboam: in the envoy princes are warned to heed good counsellors, and so avoid destruction (778–805). The moral discourse that follows (806–917) is in keeping with the theme. But then he tells the story of the admirable Mucius Scaevola, who sought to deliver Rome from siege by killing the enemy leader King Porsenna. When he mistakenly killed the wrong man, he punished himself by burning off his hand.

---

[25] Schirmer, *John Lydgate,* p. 215; Bergen, *Fall,* 4:172 n. 1.
[26] See above, p. 38.

No envoy follows, but rather a rapid and awkward transition to the story of Lucretia. Scaevola's example, he says, shows the sort of thing men have done for the common good: as Brutus did, when he drove Tarquin from Rome for what he did to Lucretia (967–73). After telling of Lucretia's death and its aftermath, Lydgate proceeds immediately, without an envoy, to tell the story of Appius's lust for Virginia and his subsequent downfall (he does not allude to Chaucer's version of the incident in the *Physician's Tale*, which Harry Bailly liked but most subsequent auditors and readers have not). Then follow brief accounts (one stanza each) of how Philip of Macedon and Hasdrubal of Carthage were killed by poor men they had oppressed (1345–428).

Only now does Lydgate insert an envoy, in which he says that "this trage-die" tells of the falls of Tarquin, Appius, Philip, and Hasdrubal because of the outrages committed against the poor, and princes are advised to act other-wise (1429–63). Fortune returns, after a long absence, in the stanza on King Philip, where she takes a very moral stance: the greatest cause of his fall was when Fortune assailed his pride because, once again, of crimes against the poor (1447–49).

Lydgate does therefore manage to carry out Duke Humphrey's injunction, by ignoring Mucius Scaevola and by considering Tarquin rather than Lucre-tia as the protagonist of Lucretia's story, and by assimilating her to the out-raged poor. In fact, Lucretia was of the same rank as her oppressor, who was her husband's cousin; and Lydgate does not give a contrary impression when he tells the story. Neither this account nor the next, in book 3, seems promis-ing material for a Marxist analysis of fifteenth-century English social pres-sures, whether on the upper or lower classes.

Lydgate continues by saying that six kings then appeared to Bochas, namely Jeroboam, Zerah, Adab, Zimri, Ahab with his wife Jezebel, and, finally, not a king but a queen, Athalia. He concludes with a summary envoy that begins by saying that these tragedies declare the deceptions of Fortune's false mutabilities to estates and degrees; but he continues more to Hum-phrey's point by saying that they show how princes refused to rise from their sins, even though they "hadde off God warnyng," and so "onwarli" lost their possessions (1863–69). These are sentiments that would not contradict Chau-cer's ideas of tragedy, or Lydgate's earlier views, so long as one did not exclude the possibility of no-fault tragedies.

Next comes the story of Dido: "Now must I putte my reude stile in pres, / To Queen Dido make my passage" (1898–99). It is here that, for the first time in the second book, he fails to carry out Duke Humphrey's plan. True enough, in the second envoy, as we have seen, he sarcastically advises widows how to avoid Dido's fate (2199–233), but this is hardly what his patron had in mind. He reverts to the duke's pattern in his treatment of Sardanapalus (2234–548) and in telling of Amaziah, Uzziah, and Zedekiah (2549–779, 2794–940). An intervening king, Hoshea, falls not by his own fault but by Fortune's envy; another, Senacherib, King of Assyria, besieges Jerusalem in his surquedy and is defeated by God's angel; both receive short shrift (2780–93), and neither is mentioned in the cumulative envoy (2941–61).

The long account of King Astyages follows, where Lydgate carries over Premierfait's dour characterization of Euripides's tragedies (2.3067–73), which we saw in the last chapter. King Astyages tried to prevent the ascent to power of his grandson Cyrus, which was divinely ordained. Cyrus overcame all obstacles and triumphed. He did not take vengeance against Astyages, but generously arranged for him to live in honorable retirement. It is not much of a tragedy, and Lydgate does not call it one. In his envoy, he does not explain to princes how to avoid a like fate, but rather tells them it cannot be avoided (3326–46).

Next he tells the story of Candaules, King of Lydia, who trusted his friend Gyges too much and foolishly showed him the naked beauty of his queen. Gyges thereupon killed Candaules and took over both queen and kingdom. Lydgate adds to Bochas the idea that the wife connived with Gyges, and adds this also:

> But whosoever was therwith loth or fayn,
> Giges was afftir crownyd kyng off Lide,
> Whan that his lord was by tresoun slayn.
> Off hym the surplus Bochas set aside.   (2.3424–27)

By leaving Gyges triumphant, as he did in his *Disguising of Fortune*, he supplies us with an example of knavery winning out over foolishness.

The story of Midas follows (3428–93). As with the account of Candaules, no moral is addressed to princes. There is such a moral after the next story, that of Balthazar. He is contrasted with his father Nabuchodonosor, who repented his sins and was restored to his possessions (3543–46).

Lydgate clearly did not draw upon the tragedies of the *Monk's Tale* for his treatment of Nabuchodonosor and Balthasar, but followed Bochas instead. The same is true of the next story, the history of Croesus, where he neglects as well his own account in the *Disguising of Fortune*. According to Bochas, Croesus is neither foolishly nor sinfully proud but rather wholly admirable. He has a dream that is prophetic not of his own but of his son's death, which occurs only because of Fortune's mischief-making (3610–12). But whereas Boccaccio and Premierfait simply note Croesus's sorrow and move on to the next part of the story,[27] Lydgate says first that Croesus eventually got over his grief, for joy gradually follows great sorrow "thoruh Fortunys variaunce" (3646). Then he says that Bochas wrote no more of his sorrow over his son because it was irremediable, and proceeded to tell the manner of Croesus's own fall (3648–54). Croesus is captured by Cyrus, who by now has become evil. When he gives order for Croesus to be beheaded, he is unmoved by one miracle, but another, arranged by God and Fortune (3717), convinces him to spare the king's life. This is the outcome that Fortune herself considered fortunate in Boethius's *Consolation* before she went on to speak of unfortunate falls and the clamor of tragedies. In the present case Croesus's fall consists in this, that though Cyrus allows him to return to Lydia, he is no longer to be king.

The story of Croesus, who did not fall through his own fault, inspires no message for princes. It is not until we hear about Cyrus, how God and Fortune

---

[27] Boccaccio, *De casibus* A 2 (p. 67); B 2.20.8 (p. 180); Premierfait, *Des cas* 2.20 (fol. 42v).

made him suddenly descend from his royal stage (748–49) that we get that sort of raw material. He was defeated by a woman, Queen Tomyris, with a divine *ictus indiscretus*: for where vengeance dominates in worldly princes, "with onwar strok God can hem weel chastise" (3906). In the envoy, princes are warned to take note (3942–62).

Book 2 ends with the story of the founding of Rome. Lydgate is pleasantly satirical in relating the conception of Romulus and Remus by the vestal virgin Rhea, who by "natural miracle" began to increase in holiness (4005–07). He has more to say on the subject of pagan virtue and the lack of it after he gives the history of these vicious brothers: Remus was ignominiously killed with a pickax, and Romulus suddenly disappeared amidst thunder in a cloud. Lydgate refutes the idea that Romulus was deified after death. Rather, all tyrants must endure the pains of hell. But rulers who maintain right and trouthe, redressing wrongs and sustaining the poor, will reign in heaven above the stars (4208–28). Pagan sinners, then, like Christian sinners, are punished after death. But Lydgate also seems to accord to virtuous pagans the possibility of eternal salvation, a doctrine that had a not inconsiderable following in medieval England.[28] He returns to the idea in his final envoy, a noble appeal addressed to Rome herself. She is asked where her great men have gone, and is reminded how both the good and the wicked have fallen. She is invited to turn her affection from the false gods to love of Christ:

> O Rome, Rome, al old abusioun
> Off cerimonies falsli disusyng,
> Ley hem aside, and in conclusioun,
> Cri God merci, thi trespacis repentyng!
> Truste He wil not refuse thyn axyng,
> The to receyve to laboure in His vyne,
> Eterneli to save the fro ruyne.   (2.4579–85)

There is no sign that he is allegorizing present-day Rome, nor does he seem to be alluding to the Christian conversion of ancient Rome. Rather he seems to be holding out to the people of Antiquity a share in Christ's redemption, at least to the individuals who served God well according to their own lights.

Lydgate's concluding envoy in book 2 is preceded by the story of Metius Suffetius, a man of low birth whom Fortune made king of the Albans (2.4270). The Romans seem to have been particularly irked by his mean birth and high status, and they determined to make him descend with a sudden fall. God and Fortune join to overthrow his pomp (4271–84). Hostilius defeats him and he agrees to become an ally of the Romans, but he is secretly disloyal, and finally Hostilius orders him pulled apart by two chariots. Lydgate gives Bochas's meditation against dissimulation, and then anticipates from Bochas's book 3 the fate of Hostilius himself. After all of his triumphs, Fortune made him become slothful in sacrificing to Jupiter, and for this reason he was suddenly consumed by lightning (4446–52). Lydgate seems to

---

[28] See the studies cited above, pp. 134–35 n. 78, especially Hahn, *God's Friends*.

accept the reality of this action by a pagan god, perhaps by tacitly translating it into the sort of understanding perspective discussed above: meaning that sincere dedication and upright devotion to pagan gods would be accepted by God as directed towards Him. Lydgate uses this event as a springboard to introduce his envoy: one can see Fortune's "double purveiaunce" in the way that the greatest of Roman champions suddenly came to misfortune. And in order to memorialize how their great conquests were turned from joy to woe, he addresses this envoy to these unfortunate champions (4453–59). At the very end of the long envoy, he finally speaks to his princely readers:

> O noble pryncis, off hih discrecioun
> Seeth in this world ther is non abidyng,
> Peiseth conscience atwen will and resoun
> Whil ye have leiser, off herte ymagynyng,
> Ye ber nat hennes but your disservyng:
> Lat this conceit ay in your thouhtis myne,
> B'exaumple off Rome how al goth to ruyne.   (2.4586–92)

In this final address to princes, then, Lydgate tells them to be virtuous, as before; but virtue now will not prevent tragic falls. It turns out that nothing can prevent falls. Virtue is its own reward, or rather the only means to receive reward after the prosperity of this life, and this life itself, is over.

Apart from the eschatological perspective of the end of book 2, however, Lydgate has been fairly successful in carrying out Humphrey of Gloucester's suggestion to concentrate on tragedies of vice, given the presence of some intractable material in the corresponding section of Bochas. But because his presupposition that tragedy deals only with flawed victims was not explicitly stated, the examples presented and lessons drawn are not noticeably out of keeping with the more catholic concept of tragedy that admits innocent as well as guilty victims to the ranks of tragedy, and in fact some such cases, for instance, those of Dido and Croesus, are included side by side with villanous protagonists. In effect, then, Lydgate followed Humphrey's suggestion *when appropriate*. Not all tragedies have guilty protagonists, but a lot of them do, and when they do he points out the faults and tells others how they can avoid similar fates. We see how his characterization of Euripidean tragedy (2.3067–73)[29] can fit into this grand pattern as well: whenever the tragedian sees vice, he condemns it, whether it appears in the tragic protagonist or in an antagonist of the protagonist (for instance Tarquin, whether regarded as protagonist or antagonist), or in an accomplice or evil genius (for instance, Jezebel). But sometimes no one is guilty, and unless one lashes out against the straw woman Fortune, one can only lament. The doctrine of exclusively criminous tragedy, therefore, which intruded itself at the beginning of book 2 of the *Fall of Princes*, has been absorbed and subordinated to a more universal view, and the same will be true when it comes to the fore again, that is, whenever, Bochas remembers that he is supposed to be telling only of illustrious men whose falls are meant to illustrate the punitive action of God.

---

[29] Quoted in the last chapter, pp. 172–73.

FALLINGS OFF AND BEGINNINGS ANEW

Chaucer's Monk first proposed that he tell the *Life of St. Edward*, "or ellis, first, tragedies wol I telle, / Of whiche I have an hundred in my celle" (*Monk's Prologue* 1971–72). He thereby gave the impression that he intended to carry on with his *vita sancti* after telling the hundred tragedies, or at least an appropriate number of them.

Just so, the Monk of Bury, after telling the seventy or so tragedies of the first two books of the *Fall of Princes*, turned aside to write his large-scale *Lives of Saints Edmund and Fremund*. He had wearied of his task of translating Bochas, not only because of the immensity of the undertaking, but also, it seems, because of the overabundance of Gloucester's advice and the paucity of his material support.[30] But, as he says in the Prologue to book 3, his patron's generosity rescued him in his need, and he was encouraged to make a fresh start (3.71–91).

Bochas began his third book, Lydgate says, with a story told him by his teacher Andalus the Black, recounting a debate between Fortune and Glad Poverty. It ended with the debaters coming to blows, or rather engaging in a wrestling match. Poverty momentarily lost some of her gladness as she manifested her pride (in the virtuous sense of the term, of course), as well as showing, it would seem, a touch of righteous wrath. She was physically in top condition, unlike her flabby adversary, as she "ageyn Fortune proudli gan hir dresse, / And with an ougli, sterne, cruel face / Gan in armys hir proudli to embrace" (544–46). The result of the bout was that Fortune for once had the tables turned on her, and she suffered a bad fall. Poverty's victory is described and explicated:

> Maugre Fortune, in the hair aloffte
> Constreyned she was to Wilful Poverte,
> That to the erthe hir fal was ful onsoffte:
> For off Povert the bony sharpe kne,
> Sclendre and long and leene upon to see,
> Hitte Fortune with so gret a myht
> Agayne the herte, she myht nat stond upriht:
> To signefie that Povert with gladnesse,
> Which is content with smal possessioun
> And geveth no fors off tresour nor richesse,
> Hath over Fortune the dominacioun,
> And kepith hir ever under subjeccioun,
> Wher worldli folk, with ther riche apparaile,
> Lyve ever in dreed Fortune wolde faile.   (3.568–81)

Yet, just before this, in his own Prologue to this book, Lydgate told of an encounter that he himself had with Poverty, when she had none of that alacrity of spirit nor cheer of mind that she was wont to have, as characterized by

---

[30] See Schirmer, *John Lydgate*, pp. 215–16.

Andalus, nor was she so trimly athletic: "Povert approchid, in stal crokid age" (3.65). It turns out that she is really not the same person, for Lydgate identifies her later as False Indigence (77), whose threats ceased when Duke Humphrey finally came to his assistance. Still, she goes by the name of Poverty, and Lydgate seems completely oblivious of the incongruity of his taking such a tone with her, he being a monk vowed to her service. A little care would have enabled him to set forth the difference between "small possession" and "indigence" without such incongruity; but, as is so often the case in medieval discourse, the access between his conceptual pigeonholes was temporarily blocked. Averroes-Alemannus warned against the indiscriminate introduction of personifications into tragedy, on pain of arousing the listeners to ridicule.[31] Lydgate has violated this principle, and must rest in peace, content with receiving his just deserts.

Lydgate does not relate any of this material explicitly to tragedy, but he has already established the principle that all of his accounts of falls are to be regarded as tragedies; therefore, anything that is connected with the causes and conditions of falls can be taken to refer to tragedy. Thus, when Andalus the Black holds that the fall of princes "cam off themsilff and off Fortune nouht" (3.175), we might conclude that he would not admit of innocent protagonists in tragedy, were it not for an implicit qualification: "Ther owne desert is cheef occasioun /Off the onhap, whoso takith heede" (183–184). That is, *most of the time* princes deserve their falls and cause their falls; but not always.

I could, therefore, continue to give a blow-by-blow analysis of the disasters that occur in the next seven books of the *Fall of Princes*, whether or not tragedy is mentioned specifically. But since many of the stories add little to the ideas and themes that we have already seen, I shall be brief.

The first falls of book 3 are those of Italian princes. Instead of passing on Bochas's dictum that a fisherman finds fire hotter than a carpenter,[32] Lydgate elaborates the Boethian sentiment of the pain of remembered prosperity, and connects it with the previous discourse on poverty, for it is more severe in those who have had no previous reason to complain about Fortune 715–28). The first prince treated is the same Hostilius whose fall ended book 2. Now we are told that he had received from Fortune all that he desired, until he fell ill. He recovered somewhat after making a pious pilgrimage to various temples. Then he defeated the Albans: there is no reference to their leader, Metius Suffetius, whose story was told at length earlier; we only hear that Hostilius subjected them to Rome "be ful gret cruelte" (760)—but his action is not perceived as a fault. Lydgate then retells the story of Hostilius's sacrifice to Jupiter and his death by lightning. But this time rather than siding with the gods against Hostilius, Lydgate says that he acted not with sloth but with great reverence, and he places the onus upon the gods: they became indignant

---

[31] Averroes-Alemannus, *Middle Commentary on Aristotle's Poetics*, on chap. 9: "Non ergo oportet ut innitatur talibus in tragedia. Nam iste modus commotionis imaginative non est in quo conveniant quelibet nature. Immo derident ipsum et subsanant seu vilipendunt plures hominum" (ed. Boggess, p. 31; Minio-Paluello, p. 52 has *utitur* for *innitatur*). See Kelly, ARISTOTLE-AVERROES-ALEMANNUS, p. 167 n. 19.

[32] See Bergen, *Fall*, 4:186.

because Hostilius made some technical error in his offering. Lydgate ends by observing that his false gods were of no help to him, and he warns princes not to magnify earthly things and create false gods (740–91).[33]

Hostilius's successor, Ancus Martius, is another devout pagan dedicated to the common weal, who is murdered with the connivance of his evil wife and a foreign usurper named Licinio. Thus Ancus fell from the wheel of Fortune (834) and Licinio became king. But then God decreed that he too should have a fall (859). In the envoy the word tragedy is used for the first time in book 3:

> This tragedie by cleer inspeccioun
> Openli declareth in substaunce
> How slauhtre of princis causith subversioun
> Off rewmys, cites put out off ordynaunce,
> Off mortal werre long contynuaunce.   (890–94)

That is, the moral applies only to Licinio, not to Ancus or Hostilius.

Next, Lydgate tells the story of Lucretia at great length, following Bochas, and gives a rendering of Bochas's long tirade against lustfulness in princes. He recounts, for instance, how God took great vengeance upon Samson (1187), and he ends with the story of what happened to Holofernes because of his "fervent dronken lecherie" (1555). Then he adds an envoy in which he calls the whole discourse against lecherous princes a tragedy:

> This tragedie yeveth us a gret warnyng,
> Be cleer exaumples of manyfold resoun,
> How many a prince for their myslevyng
> And many a riche, roial, myhti toun,
> Many a cite, and many a regioun
> Have been eversid, ful notable and famous,
> For synne off pryncis that wer lecherous.   (3.1569–75)

But as he goes on he puts a good deal of the blame on women, and ends with its being entirely their fault (1632–38). I should note that in Chaucer's *Tragedy of Samson* and *Tragedy of Holofernes* all mention of lechery is studiously avoided as a cause of the protagonists' downfall, though women are held responsible in both cases: Samson's wives are blamed, and Judith is praised, for their destruction of a good man and a bad man, respectively.

Lydgate's next envoy comes after the stories of Coriolanus and Meltiades, and faults are now assigned not to the princes but to their people. In "this tragedie," he says, one can see the inconstancy of every community, depending

---

[33] Premierfait, *Des cas* 3.2 (fol. 48v), makes no slur against the gods. Boccaccio's account of Hostilius is very brief. He says that the figure of Hostilius who appeared before him uttered unspeakable execrations against Jupiter and the other gods for destroying him in his prime. Boccaccio found this funny and would have continued to listen to him, laughing, if Tarquin had not distracted him (text in Bergen, 4:186). Premierfait says only that he would have listened to the king's complaints longer ("Je eusse escoute les complainctes au roy Tulius plus longuement"), without indicating that he was blaspheming the gods or that Boccaccio was laughing.

on the whims of Fortune (2164–67). Like Chaucer in the *Monk's Tale*, he warns against trust in prosperity (2199–205). According to the envoy to the story of Xerxes, his tragedy is to remind us of Fortune's unsavory nature, and also of the fact that God will not allow a ravenous prince to last for long (2605–32).

Lydgate retells another story found in book 2, that of Appius and Virginia. "This little tragedy," he says, shows the mischief that unjust judges can cause (3.3088–90). Then a good prince, Alciabiades, follows. Though in the body of his story we are told that he was blinded by Fortune (3573) and discomfited by lack of foresight (3596), the moral of the tragedy is entirely sympathetic to him (3683–717).

Good, or guiltless, princes continue to be mixed with evil ones in the rest of book 3, and yet in the proem to book 4 he sums up Bochas's intention as follows:

> To remembre by many story old
> Th'estat of pryncis, in chaieres hih sittyng,
> And for vices ther unwar fallyng,
> Yivyng exaumple, as I afferme dar,
> Of fals Fortune how thei shal be war.   (157–61)

And he sums up the first part of the work thus:

> His firste thre bookis, by ful cleer merours,
> Fulli accomplisshed, as Bochas undirtook,
> The cause of fallyng of many conquerours,
> Only for trouthe and vertue thei forsook.   (162–65)

Furthermore, Bochas intends to continue to write with the same purpose "ageyn th'outrage of pryncis that wer proude, / Which wer brouht lowe for ther frowardnesse" (171–72).

Lydgate does not leave much room in these statements for faultless princes, especially since he goes on to give examples only of wicked princes: Priam (who upheld false adultery), Astyages, Cyrus, Tarquin, and Artaxerxes. He omits Bochas's first example of Croesus, who was beloved by all.[34] Nevertheless, Lydgate could be read as saying that only a good many of the tragedies of Bochas are of the fall of vicious princes, while some are of virtuous or heroic leaders. At any rate, we have the testimony of the text that there are such tragedies. An instance in book 4 is the tragedy of Callisthenes, whom Alexander dismembered because of his trouthe (1422–28). On the other hand, Alexander himself provides an example of a fall through vice, as does his mother Olympias. In Alexander's story, Lydgate once again goes counter to Chaucer, who in his *Tragedy of Alexander* only mentions a couple of vices as blemishes on Alexander's character, which in no way were connected with his assassination. In the case of Olympias, Lydgate refuses to follow Bochas

---

[34] Premierfait, *Des cas* 4, prologue (fol. 74): "le trebuschement de Cresus roy des Lidoys qui de ses hommes liges et aussi des estranges fut moult ayme. Et si perdit son royaulme et fut contrainct de vivre comme ung autre prive homme." See Bergen 4:205.

in praising the courage with which she died, but he does call for ruth and mercy from "alle ye that shal this tragedie see," to see a princess thrown down so unwarily by Fortune from her imperial see—the chief occasion of her fall being that she took pleasure in three things: vicious lust, murder, and vengeance (2570–76). Not much of a reason for pity.

In the tragedy of Agathocles, a knave of ignoble stock who rose to a position of power, Lydgate sets forth his notions of the virtuous proclivities of noble blood, which are not shared by those of lower estate. The most contrarious mischief to be found on earth, he says, occurs when a wretch, churlish of nature, is lifted by the violence of Fortune to the status of princes (4.2656–60). He argues, in other words, for innate strengths and flaws of character. This tragedy, he says, shows how man and beast is flavored by his roots (2927–33). Gentle blood is always inclined to mercy and pity, whereas villains who gain power are, of custom, vengeful and cruel, following their villainous lineage (2955–61). This is not to say that bluebloods cannot be vicious in their government; but their royal blood requires them to avoid such conduct (2967–68), and presumably makes it easier for them to do so.

In his fifth book, Boccaccio tells the story of Marcus Atilius Regulus, a man illustrious in every good sense of the word, in order to shame other illustrious men who are more sluggish than he, and in order to glorify outstanding youths of whatever origin they might be. He thereby shows that he does not share Lydgate's bloodbound prejudices.[35] But Premierfait changes the object of his praise, and addresses it instead to "noble youths of all countries,"[36] while Lydgate leaves out the rationale altogether. That is, he designs the story neither as a cause of embarrassment nor as a source of self-congratulation for any particular group of men, but presents it solely as a "hagiographic" tragedy for the edification of anyone who can give it his attention:

> This tragedie, who that can take heede,
> Is entermedlid with wo and gladnesse:
> Joie for the worshep and synguler manhede
> That was in Mark bi excellent noblesse;
> To reede his fall it is gret hevynesse,
> Which ches to deie, wheras he stoode fre,
> Only for proffit of the comounte.   (5.806–12)

This is a tragedy calling for unadulterated lamentation, in Chaucerian terms, since the subject is a wholly virtuous man who gave no reason to rejoice at his downfall. But Lydgate goes one step further and calls for joy over his outstanding character. Bochas proceeds to a discourse against those who show

---

[35] Boccaccio, *De casibus* A 5 (p. 121); B 5.2.8 (p. 386). When Boccaccio says later that nobility cannot be inherited (A 6 [p. 146]; B 6.3.1 [p. 488]), Lydgate repeats the sentiment, but the example he gives shows only that a man *without* nobility cannot pass it on to his children: "Off wikked weede come non holsum flours" (6.1307). But, of course, the children can still be virtuous, like Euripides: "Yit was this poete, for al his villynage, / Most vertuous founden at assaies" (2.3064–65).

[36] Premierfait, *Des cas* 5.2, fol. 101v.

themselves lacking in Regulus's patriotic qualities, but Lydgate lets well enough alone and omits it.

The next envoy is for the tragedy of the vicious Antiochus,[37] where there is neither woe nor gladness, but only condemnation (5.1590–621). The envoy to the tragedy of the three noble Scipios expresses only somberness at the transitoriness of power (1846–885). In the envoy to Hannibal's tragedy, Lydgate feels pity and horror that such a renowned prince should murder himself by drinking poison (2157–58). The tragedy of Alexander Balas "naturally complains" about the vice of unkindness (2509–10). Finally, there is the tragedy of Jugurtha, where, as we have seen, tragedy is defined as beginning in joy and ending in adversity. Jugurtha is too far gone in vice to excite pity at the end, when we remember "off this moordrer the hatful tyrannye" (3141).

Boccaccio begins his sixth book with an account of how Fortune appeared to him. She tells him that he is laboring in vain in his efforts to teach men to know themselves. She herself has tried to educate them in her laws, but without success. Boccaccio, however, responds that her ruinations do not serve as a warning to men but simply leave them thunderstruck; soft words are no less profitable than lashes, to those who can be corrected ("Corrigibilibus non minus prosunt lenia verba quam verbera"). He then praises her power and humbly begs her to favor his work and make his name illustrious. Fortune smiles at his guile (or, perhaps more precisely, at a manifestation, rare in his later years, of his old sense of humor). She recalls to him how often he has written against her and insulted her; and now he tries to deceive her with flattery and lies as if she were an inexperienced little girl. She well knows what store he sets by her powers. However, she suddenly says, never mind what his intentions are; he has succeeded in making her change her mind. She will support his work, and his name will be glorified. As proof of her favor, since she sees that he is having trouble deciding which of the miserable wretches standing before him he should write about, she will assist him. She proceeds to pick out some of them and to describe their careers. After running through some possible examples, she leads up five men for his especial attention: Gaius Marius, Mithradates, Hyrodes (Orodes, king of the Parthians), Pompey, and Cicero. After she disappears, Boccaccio decides to take her advice.[38]

Lydgate takes up this scene with great gusto. He describes Fortune at length before she speaks, and when she does he has her add many details about herself. For instance, her house is called the House of Fame (6.109), and she describes it in accord with Chaucer's poem. Bochas too (in Lydgate's version) discourses at large upon her, mainly in Boethian fashion (239–427).

Of the five men presented by Fortune, Cicero would deserve no attention if Boccaccio had kept to his expressed intention of dedicating his work to falls aimed at frightening sinful princes. But since he has also given much space to the sub-subject of Fortune, the merits of telling Cicero's story can be defended. However, when he comes down to describing the great man's murder, Boccaccio wonders why God did not immediately strike down his

---

[37] Antiochus III Magnus, father of Antiochus IV Epiphanes, the subject of Chaucer's tragedy.
[38] Boccaccio, *De casibus* A 6 (pp. 141–44); B 6.1 (pp. 466–78); Premierfait: see Bergen, 4:246–50.

assassin (thus exemplifying, of course, his prefatory paradigm of the divine overthrow of the wicked, and vindicating the naive notion that poetic justice operates in our world). He is at a loss to know the reason for God's failure to act. But whatever it was, he says that Cicero's misfortune not only instructs us not to confide in any mundane state of eminence; but it also convicts the Roman *plebs* of impiety. Covered with great shame, they were moved to compassion at the sight of the terrible deed done to their own champion.[39]

Lydgate omits all of these reflections. At one point, after listing Cicero's works as given in Vincent of Beauvais's *Speculum historiale*, he says that the orator, "mid his worshepes, stood alwey in dreede / Of Fortune" (6.3176–77). By this, however, he does not seem to mean that he was always aware of Fortune's mutability, but only that he was in constant danger of misfortune.

A tangent in defense of rhetoric follows the account of Cicero, and it is here that Lydgate adds to Premierfait the example of Senecan tragedy as an example of oratorical gravity: a furious complaint uttered in distress (6.3347–53).

Boccaccio did not treat of the fall of Julius Caesar, but Premierfait inserted him and his story between Pompey and Cicero, and attributed his downfall to Fortune.[40] Lydgate follows him, by saying, after the tragedy of Pompey, that it would be vain to write a new tragedy of Caesar (6.2556–57), but he will at least fill out the story. However, he adds an envoy that in effect considers it a new tragedy, for he says that in reviewing all of the tragedies in this book, none strikes him as more woeful than the fall of Caesar (2871–74), and he goes on in the envoy to stress the lessons of instability. Neither in the envoy nor in the previous 300 lines is there to be found any obvious use of the themes that Chaucer introduced into his *Tragedy of Caesar*, but, as was pointed out above, Lydgate resembles Chaucer in misnaming the murderer Brutus Cassius.

When Lydgate comes to the "piteous death and hateful fall of the great Antony and Cleopatra," he says that he will set aside the tragedy of these two, because Chaucer, chief poet of Britain, remembered them together in his book, the *Legend of Cupid*, seeing that their hearts could not part: they suffered as one, and they were buried in one sepulture (6.3620–26). But he does go on to give Bochas's account of how Cleopatra corrupted and destroyed Antony. In the end, however, he returns to Chaucer's mood of pity. Antony's suicide is almost made to look like an accident: "With a sharp suerd his daungeer to dyverte / Hymsilff he roof unwarli to the herte" (3660–61), and Cleopatra's death at her own hands is excused by madness: she "slouh eek hirsilfe, love so did hir rave" (3667).

The short seventh book begins with the victims of Octavian (Caesar Augustus) approaching Bochas to have their stories told. Neither Boccaccio nor his translators seem to have noticed that Octavian has entered and departed from this cast of casualties still in full possession of his powers.

The account of Nero comes in this book, and we recall that Lydgate transformed him from a tragedian to a comedian. But it is surprising that he also refrains from mentioning the tragedies of the man who was Nero's master in

---

[39] Ibid., A 6 (p. 160); B 6.12.19–20 (pp. 542–44); Premierfait: see Bergen, 4:246–50.
[40] Premierfait, *Des cas* 6.11, fol. 142.

all moral virtue, namely, moral Seneca, who exerted all his efforts to restrain him from all vices (7.618–20), even though he goes on to say that Seneca "dide excelle gretli in poetrye" (643). At the end of the *Fall of Princes* too Lydgate mentions "moral Senek, moost sad of his sentence," but here he is referring to his "moralytees" rather than to his poetry or tragedies (9.3391–92). In the envoy that Lydgate attaches to the history of Nero (7.775–795), he does not call the account a tragedy, but then he does not use the term at all in book 7, whether in the envoy to the story of Herod (246–77) or in the envoy to Bochas's chapter on temperance (1314–34), or in the story of the Jews at the end of the book.

He omits Bochas's long invective against the Jews, which follows upon the historical account, and only refers to it in a single stanza at the beginning of book 8. He then continues with Bochas's Prologue to that book. Bochas begins to debate with himself, warning himself against the desire for glory, and alleging the futility of his labors. Lydgate gives him a personified interlocutor, Lady Sloth (8.49). Petrarch then visits him, and rouses him out of his depression.

Lydgate too admits to weariness—he is over sixty years old now, the freshness of youth is past, and the colors of rhetoric that assisted him in his translation are faded away; his soul is dry, for in the village of Lydgate, where he was born, Bacchus's liquor flowed so sparingly as not to have given his spirit sufficient moisture. But, true to his duty, he follows Bochas in these last two books (190–203). To the seventy tragedies in the 12,000 lines of books 1–2, he has added another 150 in books 3–7 (17,000 lines), and before he finishes he will have versified yet another 110 (7,000 lines).

One of the signs of Lydgate's failing inspiration is the lack of envoys at this stage. Zenobia, for instance, rates only a few lines of reflection at the end of her story:

> A wynde contrarye of Fortune hath so blowe
> That she, alas, hath pitousli made fall
> Hir that in prowesse passed women all.　(8.740–42)

He has taken a hint from Bochas's bitter exhortation at this point to those who do not remember their human condition: let them go ahead and climb on high; they will either be frightened at the wind of Fortune, who breathes upon high things, or will lapse into a slumber and by a great knock of Fortune fall to death, which no man can avoid.[41]

Zenobia's is the only tragedy treated by Chaucer to which Lydgate specifically refers in the *Fall of Princes*. He does so as an excuse for his own summary presentation:

---

[41] Premierfait, *Des cas* 8.6, fol. 176v: "Allez loing, dicy, vous hommes qui navez point en memoire lestat ne la condition de vie humain, se vous montez aux haultes seigneuries du monde, il convient ou que vous doubtez le vent de Fortune qui souffle les haultes choses, ou se vous estes endormis il convient que parle trop grant hurtiz de Fortune vous cheez en la mort, qui est trescertaine que nulz hommes ne leschappe." Cf. Boccaccio, *De casibus* A 8 (p. 193; Bergen, 4:303); B 8.6.16 (p. 682), who says that it will take only the slightest blow of Fortune to send the drowsy to a most certain death ("sopiti impulsu minimo in mortem certissimam corruatis").

But for Chauceer dide hym so weel aquite
In his tragedies hir pitous fall t'entrete,
I will passe over, rehersyng but the grete.
   In his book of *Cauntirbury Talis*
This sovereyn poete of Brutis Albioun,
Thoruh pilgrymys told be hillis and bi valis,
Wher of Zenobia is maad mencioun,
Of hir noblesse and of hir hih renoun,
In a tragedie compendiousli told all,
Hir marcial prowesse and hir pitous fall.   (8.670–79)

In Boccaccio's series on the fallen Roman emperors, *Nunnulli infelices Cesares et Augusti*, the victorious Constantine makes no appearance except as a victor and as the father of his less happy sons.[42] Premierfait expands Constantine's role only slightly,[43] but Lydgate gives a very long account, which he draws from the life of Pope St. Sylvester in the *Legenda aurea*. He says that he will stint a while of the matter at hand, turning away from Constantius, and follow his own "strange opinion," by making a digression to his father, since Bochas makes only a short mention of him, in spite of the abundant records of his notable deeds (1170–76). Perhaps Lydgate calls his decision strange because the success story of Constantine is a non-tragedy and out of place in Bochas's collection? His motive for introducing it is clear enough; he wants to sing the praises of his native country, which fostered so notably sovereign a prince (1450–53).

He mentions Constantine's death in the next stanza, but only as a culmination of his brilliant career: the sun was not seen for a month, and a great comet drew towards the palace in Nicomedia where he died (1457–63). He could have given a kind of tragic twist to his death if he had wished to do so, by presenting the rule of Julian the Apostate as the disastrous aftermath of his passing. But, as it is, he simply notes the two rules as chronologically related: after the death of the martial Constantine comes his cousin Julian, who was cursed in his beginning and had a cursed end (1464–68)

The history of Theodosius is similar to the account of Constantine: Lydgate adds to Premierfait's notice by drawing again on the *Legenda aurea*, using this time the life of St. Ambrose. The emperor's story ends in effect like a "divine comedy": where virtue reigns, virtue abounds, and because this prince was obedient to all virtue, he now has his guerdon above with Christ Jesus (2105–07). This time there is no apology for digressing, and no disastrous upshot to the great man's death to use as a segue to tragedy.

Boccaccio lets slip the opportunity to describe the workings of Fortune upon Boethius, when that revered figure came to stand before him, with the excuse that the celebrated fable of the Britons stood in the way: that is, King Arthur, who came groaning into Boccaccio's presence.[44] Premierfait manages to say that Boethius's story should teach us to fear Fortune's attack, since

---

[42] Ibid., A 8 (p. 196); B 8.10 (pp. 694–96).
[43] Premierfait, *Des cas* 8.10, fols. 179v–180.
[44] Boccaccio, *De casibus* A 8 (p. 204); B 8.18.5–7 (p. 726).

she could cast down so holy and learned a man as he.[45] Lydgate, however, though he devotes five stanzas to Boethius's life and martyrdom (8.2626–60), says not a word about Fortune or about Philosophy's remedies, but only refers to his "dyvers bookis of philosophie."

Boccaccio considers King Arthur to have been a historical figure, in spite of the lack of trustworthy sources on him, for the opinion of the whole world is seen to testify to his greatness. He tells of Arthur's successful efforts to extend the boundaries of his kingdom and to add to the glory of his name, with no whisper of blame for his enterprises or for his fall, which Modred brought about by taking the opportunity that he believed Fortune gave him. Boccaccio reaches contradictory conclusions: he first says that Arthur's fame survived with great glory; but at the end he says that his fame was reduced to obscurity and infamy.[46]

Lydgate treats Arthur in the conventional terms of Fortune. Arthur had the best chance of any prince to control Fortune's favor (2661–67); but when Fortune smiles she is often to be most feared (2861–63), and there is no certainty in her (3088–89). However, Arthur's fame is guaranteed by the constellation named after him, and by his being the first Christian of the the nine Worthies (3102–08). Lydgate ends with an envoy, the only one in book 8. He seems to call the envoy itself a tragedy: "This tragedie of Arthour heer folwyng /Bit princis all bewar of fals tresoun" (3130–31). If so, it would approximate the French usage of taking tragedy to mean a complaint or a lamentation. But to judge by his practice elsewhere in the work, where the envoy is the conclusion of the tragedy, "folwyng" should probably be interpreted to mean "continuing" or "concluding."

We are told in the envoy that, in spite of Arthur's great merits, "the disposicioun /Of Fate and Fortune, most furious and wood, /Caused his destruccioun be unkynde blood" (3148–50). Lydgate calls Modred simply Arthur's cousin (3000, 3071), thereby rejecting the view of Bochas that he was Arthur's own son by a concubine.[47] Both Bochas and Lydgate are silent on any role of Arthur's queen in his destruction.

In order somewhat to redress his tendency to favor the males of the species as subjects for his work, Boccaccio closes his eighth book with an account of the wicked Queen Rosamund of Lombardy. He ends with a warning to matrons to take note of their own *mobilis voluntas*.[48] Lydgate omits this lesson, and says he finds but little fruit in this chapter, except the fact that "moordre affor God requereth ay vengaunce" (3357).

Mindful of the shame aroused in him by Petrarch, Boccaccio gamely carries on to the ninth and last book,[49] which begins in the seventh century and passes rapidly into more modern times. He includes a couple of further female villains, Queen Brunhilde (d. 613) and Pope Joan, who supposedly

[45] Premierfait, *Des cas* 8.18, fol. 190.

[46] Boccaccio, *De casibus* A 8 (pp. 204–06; Bergen, 4:327–28); B 8.19 (pp. 728–34); cf. Premierfait, *Des cas* 8.19, fols. 190–91v (Bergen 329–34). For more details, see my "Non-Tragedy of Arthur," pp. 106–07.

[47] Bergen, 4:327 (Boccaccio); 332 (Premierfait).

[48] Boccaccio, *De casibus* A 8 (pp. 207–09); B 8.22–23 (pp. 740–46).

[49] Ibid., A 9 (p. 209); B 9.1.1 (p. 748).

held the Roman see after Leo V (d. 903). Brunhilde pushed her way past Mahomet, thereby preventing him from telling his story, but it is told anyway by Premierfait and Lydgate. The tragedy of Brunhilde rates an envoy from Lydgate (9.477–504), followed by a rendition of Bochas's excuse for telling the tale: though it is not based on reliable sources, her insistence was so great that he complied with her request to set it down in solemn style (524–27). Lydgate finds the story of Pope Joan, who adopted her male disguise in England, so distasteful that he soon passes on (1010–12).

English history comes more prominently to the fore as Boccaccio moves into the eleventh century, in the story of Robert Curthose, Duke of Normandy, and his attempt to take the rule of England from his younger brother, Henry I. But though Lydgate amplifies Premierfait's account,[50] he omits the point that Henry is said to have been a monk who told the clergy, nobility, and people of England that his brother had accepted the kingship of Jerusalem and intended never to return across the sea—which Premierfait sarcastically labels a "holy lie." Lydgate simply says, "God wot the cas stood al in other wise" (9.1254).

In the tragedy of Andronicus I Comnenus (d. 1185), Lydgate says in an envoy that Bochas exclaims against all vicious princes (9.1478–80). But, as usual, some of the princes whose stories follow are simply victims of Fortune. For instance, Tancred, King of Sicily, is warred against by the "ungoodli excitacioun" of his enemies and finally dies of pestilence "thoruh Fortunys transmutacioun" (1604–17). Another "pure victim" is Hugolino (9.2051–57); we saw in the last chapter that Lydgate neglected to use Chaucer's tragedy on him to elaborate Boccaccio's brief account.

Just before his notice of Hugolino (d. 1289), Boccaccio tells the story of the glorious Charles of Anjou (d. 1285), who comes before him not with the mournful appearance of the other fallen princes, but with courageous countenance and lofty bearing, as if spurning underfoot, by reason of his great spirit, the ruinations visited upon him by opposing Fortune. Yet at the end of his account Boccaccio shows him a broken-spirited man overwhelmed by Fortune. No fault on Charles's part is mentioned to account for his downfall. Boccaccio simply says that after many successes, he seemed to have made Fortune stable, but then everything turned around, by the action of an unfavorable constellation. First, his only son and heir died, some say by poison. The next reverses were caused by the treachery of Fortune ("fabricante Fortuna dolos"): Charles became unpopular to the Sicilians because of the avarice and lechery of his retinue. He acted in such a way that the noble and astute John of Procida took offense at the violated chastity of his wife and organized a revolution, and this disaster led to others, until Fortune left him an old man with only a small portion of the three kingdoms he once ruled.[51]

Premierfait follows Boccaccio closely, for the most part, but he translates the *elatus* of Charles's first appearance before Boccaccio as "orgeilleux et haultain," and includes him in the avarice and lechery of his court: "tant pour l'avarice comme pour la luxure de luy et de ses gens." However, he

---

[50] Premierfait, *Des cas* 9.10 (fol. 205).
[51] Boccaccio, *De casibus* A 9 (pp. 225–227); B 9.18.6; 9.19.1–25 (pp. 812–20).

removes Boccaccio's implication (perhaps unintended) that Charles himself was involved in the affair of John of Procida's wife; he says, it happened that the wife's chastity was corrupted by a Frenchman of King Charles's *hostel*.[52]

Lydgate for his part eliminates any notion of pride from Charles's appearance before Bochas: he shows himself with "good cheere" and "fressh on ech parti," as he defies Fortune (9.1856–69). In the following story, he gives him no hint of overconfidence. It is Fortune who is the agent of his son's death: she "caste a fals mene" for Charles's destruction (1978); and perhaps her action is to be seen also in subsequent events: he was "disclaundrid" of avarice, the great vice of tyrants, and "diffamed" as well of false adultery, "which was susteened thoruh his meyntenaunce / Withynne that londe by a kniht of Fraunce" (1982–88). This account is ambiguous, since "disclaundrid" and "diffamed" can mean either "wrongly accused" or "rightly accused," and "meyntenaunce" could mean "wrongful support" or simply "retinue."[53] In other words, the lines could be read to mean that the charge of avarice was a slander, and that only one of his retainers was guilty of adultery. In any event, "John Prosithe" was determined "that Kyng Charlis sholde ber the blame" (1998). Lydgate sums up by saying that Charles fell to mischief "be th'occasioun of fals avoutrie" (2014). In the envoy, where he points the lesson of "this tragedie," he compares Charles's career to a beautiful day that becomes darkened with clouds. Charles was right wise, right manly, right virtuous of living, and called the flower of chivalry until maintenance of adultery came into his court to hurt his name, grieve his life, and put him in jeopardy of death (2027–31). Lydgate comes closer to accusing Charles, but then seems to deflect the charge to his household: virtuous life magnifies princes, the contrary hinders them; where cursed lechery is used, the household may not prosper (2034–38). In the final stanza of the envoy, he addresses all princes in terms of personal virtue and vice (2041–48). In the last analysis, the nature of Charles's tragedy remains ambiguous.

Boccaccio enters the fourteenth century with an extensive history of James, Master of the Temple, and the extermination of the Knights Templar under Philip the Fair of France. Lydgate treats the story in a very uninspired way, seeming to admit their guilt (9.2126–37), and Henry Bergen wonders at his "indifference to this terrible tragedy"; he decides that Lydgate's attitude "is sufficiently explained by his profession and station in life"[54] —which does not seem like much of an explanation. This story is followed by an account of three virtuous "philosophers" commended for their patience, including, once again, Mutius Scaevola, who burned his own hand off as a punishment. Whereas in Bochas these examples are used to praise the fortitude of the heroic Templars, Lydgate composes a panegyric to patience in the form of a long envoy (2371–433). Presumably all the examples of heroic endurance here noted should be considered tragedies, but Lydgate does not make a point of saying so.

---

[52] Premierfait, *Des cas* 9.18–19, fols. 209v, 210v.
[53] Cf. *Fall of Princes* 3.3151: "Lordshipe that tyme avoided meyntenaunce," preceded by the line: "Poore folk lyved by labour off ther hond." See *MED* s.v. "maintenaunce," 1b.
[54] Bergen, *Fall*, 4:376, 380.

A similar kind of heroism in the face of injustice is noted in the story of Dante's exile, which Bochas offers to tell (2534–35). Lydgate characterizes the revered figure as "Daunte of Florence, the laureat poete, / With his ditees and rethoriques sueete" (2514–15), once again using the phrase of stylistic commendation which he attributed to the Trojan tragedians and which he denies to his own tragedies. He does say, however, that Bochas rehearses the story of Philippa of Catania "by ful sovereyn stile" (2823). Surprisingly, Lydgate omits Boccaccio's "structural" excuse for ending his work with the history of a lowborn woman.[55] But perhaps it does not have so striking a correspondence to Lydgate's idea of tragedy when seen only in Premierfait's rendition:

> I think in my heart to take up Philippa not without reason, that is, to the end that the present book might be similar in each of its parts, for this present book speaks only and entirely of good and bad fortunes; and as it begins by treating of joyful things, that is to say, the happiness of Adam and his wife Eve, so it ends in sorrowful things, that is, the account of the miseries of Philippa and her husband Raymund. It therefore seems to me that as the beginning of this book has been given over to Adam, the most noble of men, so it should give its end to the ignoble woman Philippa.[56]

Lydgate only says that "Bochas was loth to spende gret lengage / On hir historie, long theron t'abide" (2814–15). But he gives her an envoy, which begins:

> This tragedie afforn rehersed heer
> Tellith the damages of presumpcioun,
> B'experience declaryng the maneer
> Whan beggers rise to domynacioun,
> Is non so dreedful execucioun
> Of cruelte, yif it be weel souht,
> Than of such oon that cam up of nouht.   (9.3022–28)

The final history in Boccaccio's *De casibus* is in fact not that of Philippa of Catania, who died in 1346, but rather that of the capture of King John the Good of France in 1356, which he tells rather briefly. One would expect Premierfait to enlarge upon it, since his patron, the Duke of Berry, was John's son, but he adds little of his own. However, he does note that the execrable deeds committed by the sluggish, ineffectual, and worthless English soldiers were directed by the Prince of Wales—whose name he takes to have been Yvain.[57]

---

[55] See chap. 1 above, p. 23.

[56] Premierfait, *Des cas* 9.25, fol. 217v: "Je pense en mon cueur recevoir Phelipote non sans cause, cestasavoir, affin que ce present livre soit pareil in aucunes siennes pars, car cestuy present livre seulement et in general parle des bonnes et malles fortunes. Et si commence traicter des choses joyeuses, cestassavoir de la bienheurete de Adam et de sa femme Eve, et si fine en choses douloureuses, cestassavoir au compte des miseres de Phelipote et de son mary Raymond. Il ma doncques semble ainsi comme le commencement de ce livre a este donne et prins par Adam le tresnoble des hommes, ainsi doit estre mise la fin en Phelipote femme ignoble."

[57] Boccaccio gets the name of the prince correctly. Bergen, *Fall*, 4:396, gives both the Latin and the French texts of the account of King John's capture.

Lydgate restores to the prince his proper name of Edward, and gives a highly favorable account of him. He chastises Bochas for warring against the famous chivalry of Englishmen with his pen and ink. Such partiality, he says, ill becomes a chronicler (9.3162–89). Surprisingly he does not surmise that the slurs against the English were the work of Premierfait rather than Boccaccio, though he did come to such a conclusion earlier, in the history of Charles of Anjou:

> Thes woordis be nat take out of myn auctour;
> Entitled heer for a remembraunce
> Bi oon Laurence, which was a translatour
> Of this processe, to comende Fraunce:
> To preise that lond set al his plesaunce.   (9.1884–88)

It so happens that in this earlier case he was wrong: Laurence was simply repeating Boccaccio.

Lydgate admits that King John deserves praise for not fleeing when he lost the day; but the victory was on the side of truth (9.3190–96). He sums up this final tragedy in an envoy, of which this is the first stanza:

> Off Bochas book the laste tragedie
> Compendiousli put in remembrance
> How Prince Edward with his chevalrie
> Fauht at Peiteres with King John of France,
> And thoruh his mihti marcial puissaunce
> Grounded his quarel upon his fadres riht,
> Took hym prisoneer ful lik a manli kniht.   (9.3204–10)

As the refrain in the following stanzas makes clear, it is Prince Edward who is being commended as a manly knight, not King John. The victory was a heavenly sign sent by God (3219–23). The tragic aspect of the story, King John's defeat, which apparently had been lamented earlier in a Latin prose work entitled *Tragedia super captione regis Francie Johannis*,[58] is here completely obliterated in the triumph of right. The antagonist has changed places with the protagonist, but Lydgate does not notice that the tragedy no longer rates as a tragedy.

THE LONG GOODBYE

Lydgate begins the 400–line conclusion to his great compilation of cautionary tales with a chapter on the way in which Fortune has treated all worldly people, including "religious with al ther brode crownis" (9.3265), and shows "how sodenli she made hem to descende" (3270). But she makes people rise as well as fall, whether they are virtuous or wilful, industrious or

---

[58] IDEAS AND FORMS, p. 184.

idle: "oon goth upward, another doth descende" (3278). From the point of view of Fortune, therefore, one's merit is irrelevant. We could do here with Boccaccio/Bochas's final instruction: if you fall, make sure that it is Fortune's fault, not your own.

When he sums up the work in the first envoy to Duke Humphrey, Lydgate says that it contains nine books of Fortune's transmutations, telling of those who fell from exalted estate; and some of them, he says, fell all the way to hell (3457–63). They fell thus for their sins, and those who neglect religion can expect a similar fall, and that without delay:

> For whoo is rekkelees to serve our Lord Jesu,
> Fortunys wheel shal soone hym ovirthrowe,
> Though Famys trompet of gold alowde blowe
> His victoryes, his marcial renouns,
> Rad and remembryd in dyvers regiouns;   (3466–70)

whereas if you trust in God, "He shal nat faylle / To be your socour in pees and in bataylle" (3476–77).

These are, of course, false generalizations; nothing can guarantee worldly failure or worldly success of this sort. Lydgate is on no stronger ground when he says that lack of religious trust and devotion caused all of the mischiefs recorded by Bochas (3478–84). But he is accurate enough when he adds that the work treats of those who trusted in Fortune (3499–500), though of course it is not limited to them exclusively. He implies that Adam is the first example of such misplaced trust (3503–07); later, however, he says that it was precisely Adam's fall that set Fortune turning like a ball (3520–26).

A second envoy to Gloucester appears in some manuscripts, in which Lydgate seems to get his doctrine right at first: Humphrey is to remember that he comes of a royal line, and that virtue appertains to dignity. If he acts accordingly, "Maugre Fortunys mutabilite, /Ye shal to-godward encresyn and ascende" (9.3547–48). But he goes on to imply that all of the falls recorded in his work were punitive, and that virtue is an unfailing panacea:

> Fal of othir thorugh vicious lyvyng,
> Somme dysgradyd unto ful lowh degre,
> Off Providence lat ther chastysyng,
> For lak of grace, to you a merour be.
> Wher vertu regnyth, ther is felycite
> In suych as lyst ther froward lyff t'amende;
> Whoo lovith that Lord which hath the sovereynte
> Shal ay be grace encresyn and ascende.   (3557–64)

Still, one can admit that some vicious princes seem to have suffered a providential catastrophe; and if one restricts the felicity gained by virtue to one's internal state, the moral stands.

In the next stanza, his footing is sure: no glory can last, for Age and her cousin Infirmity will claim their due, and Death will send no warning of his coming; but Humphrey can prepare himself by daily increasing in virtue

(3565–72). He then goes on to place the duke's fate into an entirely different context: he will receive reward or punishment according to his deserts. But Lydgate is speaking now not of divine but of human sanctions, and the rewards and punishments are the good or bad reports that men will make of him: "Beth war afforn, folk have ther tounges fre. /Lyk your dyscert shal rede your legende" (3577–78). If he is virtuous, men will not only speak well of him, but will also pray for his ascent to the Heavenly See; and he himself will be taking the best means to effect this happy end (3579–88).

Lydgate's naive confidence in the fairness of posthumous fame should have been set straight from his study of Chaucer's *House of Fame*. As for Gloucester, his life has received rather mixed reviews since his passing, though in his own era and in the following century the report seems to have been more frequently than not a favorable one: he is often referred to in Homeric style as "the good Duke Humphrey." His fall began in earnest a couple of years after Lydgate finished his grand work, when his wife was put on trial for witchcraft in 1441.[59] One can only hope that, however deserving he was of his misfortunes, he found strength and comfort from the vast collection of the falls of princes that he had commissioned.

At the end of his book, in the manner of Chaucer at the close of his tragedy of *Troilus and Criseyde*, Lydgate addresses the work itself: "Go, litil Book" (9.3589). The verse form that he uses, however, is not the rhyme royal of the *Troilus* and of the bulk of the *Fall of Princes*, but rather the eight-line stanza of the *Monk's Tale*, which he also employs in the concluding chapter on Fortune and the second envoy to Gloucester. He sums up his work thus:

> In a short clause thy content rehersing,
> As oon up clymbeth to gret prosperite,
> So another, by expert knowleching,
> Fro richesse is brouht to poverte.
> Alas, o Book, what shal I seyne of the?
> Thi tragedies thoruh al the world to sende,
> Go foorth, I pray; excuse thisilf and me.
> Who loveth most vertu hiest shal ascende.   (3613–20)

The second line is intended, perhaps, to take note of some of the triumphs without defeat recorded in his work; but he makes it clear that the accent is on defeat, which can only be counteracted by virtue:

> Blak be thi weede of compleynt and moornyng,
> Callid *Fall of Princis from Ther Felicite,*
> Lik chaunteplure, now singyng now weeping,
> Wo afftir merthe, next joie adversite,
> So entermedlid ther is no seurete,
> Like as this book doth preise and reprehende—

---

[59] For a full account of this trial, which resulted in Eleanor Cobham's conviction and the annulment of her marriage to Gloucester, see my "English Kings and the Fear of Sorcery," pp. 219–29; see also Ralph A. Griffiths, "The Trial of Eleanor Cobham: An Episode in the Fall of Duke Humphrey of Gloucester."

Now on the wheel, now set in louh degre;
Who wil encrese, by vertu must ascende.   (3621–28)

The above account of the *Fall of Princes*, long as it is, can give no idea of the tedium inherent in its thousand pages of mostly mediocre verse dealing with the fates of largely uninteresting characters—for even the potentially interesting characters are usually made uninteresting (if I may be pardoned a personal evaluation). Lydgate, of course, must not be made to bear all the blame for the form and length of the work: a heavy burden of responsibility lies upon Boccaccio and Premierfait, and upon those who applauded and encouraged the project, from Petrarch to Humphrey of Gloucester. In the opinion of most Chaucerians, who agree with the Knight and the Host, Chaucer was wise to shorten his series of tragedies as he did; but unlike Lydgate he was under no pressure from a patron, and was free to conclude that the world could be served in better ways than to remain in the cloister continually poring over a book like the *De casibus*.

Yet many people clearly did find Lydgate's efforts to be of service, and the authors of *A Mirror for Magistrates* considered it eminently worth their while to supplement it with further examples, including "two notable tragedies, the one of Humphrey Duke of Gloucester, the other of the Duchess Eleanor, his wife." However, the author of these tragedies, George Ferrers, does not seem to be aware of the irony of setting forth the misfortunes of the man who was responsible for having Bochas's work turned into English; for when he praises the duke's services to letters and learning, he does not mention this project.[60] As we have seen in chapter 1 above, William Baldwin and his fellow authors do not seem to have been thoroughly familiar with Lydgate's *Fall of Princes*. Baldwin states that he brought along "the book of Bochas, translated by Dan Lydgate," to the initial consultation of the *Mirror*'s authors, "for the better observation of his order," that is, for the way in which the tragedies were presented. But even though they may not have studied the work long or deeply, what they did read they "liked well."[61]

Modern readers too may find many of Lydgate's tales and sentiments pleasing, or at least instructive, if they can overlook his faults of style, sloppy grammar, and awkward ellipses—though some passages are entirely commendable on all scores. When one takes his material into consideration, one might well conclude that he did not make a bad job of it. Attilio Hortis much preferred the English poet's simple verses, in spite of their occasional excesses, to the sophisticated Latin prose of the original and to its florid French elaboration; and Emil Koeppel endorsed his opinion.[62]

But the work has a stronger claim upon our attention than as a book of

---

[60] Baldwin *et al.*, *A Mirror for Magistrates*, pp. 431, 444.

[61] Ibid., p. 69: Baldwin to the Reader. Though they approved of the book's method of presentation, Baldwin says, since both Bochas and Lydgate were dead, they decided that Baldwin himself should take Bochas's place and have "the wretched princes complain unto me."

[62] Hortis, *Studi*, p. 649: "Non temo di dire che i versi del Lydgate si leggono con più diletto che non il testo latino del Boccaccio o la traducione francese del Premierfait." Koeppel, *Laurents*, p. 111: "Ich kan diesem Urteil des italienischen Gelehrten nur beipflichten."

occasionally good poetry or as an *ars vivendi et moriendi*. It is a compendium of traditional medieval thought and expression. It also has some important original ideas, or, if not completely original, at least ideas not expressed or put together in quite this way before Lydgate's time of writing, or in his place of writing.

One thing that Lydgate does not do is to verify the evolutionary pattern that Willard Farnham sees in the Boccaccio-Chaucer-Lydgate series on the falls of great men; that is, a greater attribution of human responsibility for the falls in Chaucer and a still greater assignment in Lydgate.[63] Though Boccaccio does in fact lay great stress on undeserved misfortunes throughout the *De casibus*, his primary intention is to show wicked magnates, by the catastrophes that have befallen their predecessors, that if they do not reform their lives they will experience a similar fate; clearly a matter of human responsibility. Chaucer, on the contrary, is chiefly interested in the unexpectedness of the falls; and though some of the Monk's tragedies are caused by sin, most of them are not. Human responsibility is emphasized in the stanzaic prologue and conclusion of the *Monk's Tale*, but it is not so much sin as foolishness or irresponsibility that is at fault: more specifically, misplaced trust in the good things of this world.

Lydgate combines the two approaches in his Prologue, not through any originality on his part, but simply from following the lead of Laurence de Premierfait, who stresses Fortune in his Second Prologue and sin in his Third (the latter being merely a translation of Boccaccio's Preface). And, as we have just seen, Lydgate gives the two themes equal stress in his conclusion. But since neither Boccaccio nor Premierfait considered the stories of falls to be tragedies,[64] it can be said, as far as tragic theory is concerned, that Lydgate puts greater stress on human responsibility than did his predecessor Chaucer, but mainly by taking the theme over from Boccaccio.

Lydgate also differs from Chaucer in knowing about ancient tragedy as a theatrical form, that is, as poetry meant to be accompanied by acting in a theatrical setting. But unlike Boccaccio and like Chaucer, he accepts the notion that purely narrative works can properly be called tragedies, and he gives no clear indication in the *Fall of Princes* of his earlier understanding, set forth in the *Troy Book*, of the actability of tragedy.

Finally, we must not forget that, even though the *Fall of Princes* was sometimes more admired than read, it was in large measure through its pronouncements and examples that the everyday understanding of tragedy was fixed for the age of Shakespeare.[65] Shakespeare has Gloucester imagine himself to

---

[63] See above, chap. 1 p. 36 n. 120. Larry Scanlon's recent effort to revive Farnham's case for Lydgate's importance for "Renaissance tragedy" (*Narrative, Authority, and Power*, pp. 344–50) can be applauded. However, he criticizes Farnham for his "relatively vague and reductive notions of transmission and influence," and he suggests that we see Lydgate's interest in "the tragic" as promoting exemplary lay authority (p. 344). But this would be to substitute vagueness for Farnham's specific characterizations of tragedy. Scanlon accepts a modern (undefined) idea of tragedy, and, moreover, he fails to show how Lydgate's presentations differ from Premierfait's and how they constitute "the birth of tragedy out of the spirit of the exemplum" (p. 322).

[64] Premierfait, like Boccaccio, knew about ancient comedy and no doubt about tragedy as well, and probably limited his use of the terms to those no-longer-practiced forms.

[65] See above, pp. 140–41.

be the protagonist-victim of a tragic drama, along with many others. He tells Henry VI:

> I know their complot is to have my life;
> And if my death might make this island happy,
> And prove the period of their tyranny,
> I would expend it with all willingness.
> But mine is made the prologue to their play;
> For thousands more, that yet suspect no peril,
> Will not conclude their plotted tragedy.
> *(2 Henry VI* 3.1.147–53)

After he is assassinated, Warwick in accusing the perpetrators calls his death a tragedy:

> Who finds the heifer dead and bleeding fresh,
> And sees fast by a butcher with an axe,
> But will suspect 'twas he that made the slaughter?
> Who finds the partridge in the puttock's nest
> But may imagine how the bird was dead,
> Although the kite soar with unbloodied beak?
> Even so suspicious is this tragedy.[66] (3.2.189–94)

Warwick hopes to "do some service to Duke Humphrey's ghost" (3.2.231) by killing Suffolk. But in having Warwick speak thus of Gloucester, Shakespeare has joined with the authors of *A Mirror for Magistrates* in doing a more appropriate, if not truthful, service to his memory than they could have imagined, in having him embody the new "working genre" of tragedy that Gloucester's protégé John Lydgate took from Chaucer and popularized for the future. A realistic account of Gloucester's life would have provided a good Boccaccian exemplum of an illustrious man who brought about his own fall through his misdeeds. Instead, his memory had been transformed to a subject for the most lamentable kind of Chaucerian tragedy: a thoroughly good and innocent man undone by the forces of evil.

---

[66] In the following lines Queen Margaret interprets Warwick as saying that Suffolk is the butcher and Cardinal Beaufort the kite (puttock).

6

Henryson's tragedy of Cresseid

Robert Henryson shares with Chaucer and Lydgate the distinction of having written the only extant tragedies in the English language, and nearly the only ones in any vernacular language, during the Middle Ages. Like Lydgate, Henryson was following the example of Chaucer in using the word tragedy to designate a narrative poem. But whereas Lydgate did not explicitly associate Chaucer's *Troilus and Criseyde* with tragedy, Henryson's *Testament of Cresseid* was directly inspired by the *Book of Troilus*, and was designed as a supplement to it. Henryson professes to be drawing on some other book as well, one that details Cresseid's "fatal destiny." But since he proceeds to recount the story himself as if there were no such book, it is no doubt to be taken as fictitious. He may, however, have known of another account of Cresseid's end, which alleged that she became sexually promiscuous; but far from following it, I will argue, he rejected it.

If, however, Henryson was original in giving the tragic ending that he does to Cresseid, it is still possible that he was anticipated by other Scottish poets in the writing of tragedies, that is, works called tragedies. William Dunbar in his *Lament for the Makaris*, or *Timor Mortis conturbat me*,[1] speaks of Death's removal of two otherwise unknown poets who wrote ballads and tragedies:

> That scorpion fell has done infek
> Maister Johne Clerk and James Afflek
> Fra balat making and trigide.   (57–59)

Dunbar's *Lament*, published in 1508, serves as the *terminus ante quem* for the date of Henryson's own death. He is mentioned as dead in the poem just before Stobo and Schaw, whom Death took "last of all." Now we know that Stobo (John Reid) was still alive but ill in May of 1505, and was dead two months later.[2] Since Clerk and Afflek come near the beginning of Dunbar's roughly chronological list of Scottish poets, they can no doubt be vaguely located in the earlier part of the fifteenth century, while Henryson, as is generally agreed, must have flourished in the latter part of the century. But we have no way of knowing whether Clerk and Afflek themselves used the word

---

[1] *The Poems of William Dunbar*, ed. James Kinsley, pp. 178–81. I am grateful to Philippa Bright of the University of Sydney for bringing this passage to my attention.

[2] Ibid., p. 356.

tragedy, and, if so, what they meant by it, or whether Henryson was influenced by them. It is possible that these poets did not themselves use the term but that Dunbar himself applied it to their works, drawing on Henryson's example, or on the example of Chaucer or Lydgate, both of whom he mentions in the *Lament*.

In our study of Chaucer and Lydgate, we have been able to devote a whole chapter to each author's notions of tragedy. With Henryson we have much less to go on, and therefore we shall consider questions of his understanding of tragedy only in the first part of the first section of this chapter, and then go on to analyze the structure and other features of the *Testament of Cresseid*. One might allege that, since little can be known of what Henryson meant by tragedy, little can be said about the *Testament* as a tragedy. My answer is that since the *Testament* is a tragedy, once this fact is recognized and emphasized, anything that is said about it is relevant to it as a tragedy. As just noted, the subject matter of this study, "Chaucerian tragedy," is quite limited: besides the two series of small tragedies in the *Monk's Tale* and in the *Fall of Princes*, there are only two large-scale tragedies, *The Book of Troilus* and *The Testament of Cresseid*, and both deserve ample consideration.

A SINGULAR TRAGEDY

Since Chaucer's *Troilus* is Henryson's primary source for his *Testament*, we must consider it as the chief candidate among the possible influences on his understanding of tragedy. However, the *Troilus* gives no explicit theoretical explanation of the term, but only the example of the story of Troilus's life.

Chaucer, we know, called the *Troilus* a tragedy only at the end, whereas Henryson chose to identify his poem as such at the very beginning:

> Ane doolie sessoun to ane cairfull dyte
> Suld correspond and be equivalent:
> Richt sa it wes quhen I began to wryte
> This tragedie.[3]   (1–4)

Whereas Lydgate at the close of the *Fall of Princes* calls for clothing appropriate to tragedy ("Black be thy weed of complaint and mourning"), in Henryson's case the weather appropriated to tragedy seems actually to have encouraged or inspired him to write a tragedy. We can, of course, see the lines as a variation of the theme set forth by Chaucer at the beginning of the *Troilus*:

> For wel sit it, the sothe for to seyne,
> A woful wight to han a drery feere,
> And to a sorwful tale, a sory chere,   (1.12–14)

---

[3] Robert Henryson, *The Testament of Cresseid*, ed. Denton Fox (see the Bibliography for his three editions: Fox A, 1968; Fox B, 1981; Fox C, 1987). Two recent studies dealing with all of Henryson's poems are Douglas Gray, *Robert Henryson*, and Robert L. Kindrick, *Robert Henryson*.

with Henryson drawing the conclusion that by "sorrowful tale" Chaucer was thinking primarily of a tragedy.

But there are no further references to tragedy or "tragic weather" in the *Testament*, and at the end of his poem Henryson instead calls it a "ballet schort" (line 610), a phrase that should perhaps be interpreted as the same sort of self-depreciating gesture as Chaucer's "litel myn tragedye." However, since Henryson's announcement in this final stanza that the work is intended for the instruction of women seems to be at variance with the opening "set-up" of the poem, we must consider the possibility that it is an afterthought, and that he is no longer thinking in terms of tragedy.[4]

Henryson missed the opportunity, it would appear, of calling his work *The Tragedy of Cresseid*. All of the surviving evidence would seem to indicate that he called the poem after Cresseid's last will and testament, given near the end. Even though the testament takes up only fourteen and a half lines out of a total of 616, it is admittedly climactic.[5]

We know that references to tragedy were not common in the Middle Ages, and Henryson himself does not use the term elsewhere, even in contexts where it might naturally have suggested itself—for instance, in the fable of the *Two Mice,* when he says, "Yit efter joy oftymes cummis cair, /And troubill efter grit prosperitie" (290–91), and:

> As fitchis myngit ar with nobill seid,
> Swa intermellit is adversitie
> With eirdlie joy, swa that na state is frie,
> Without trubill or sum vexatioun:
> And namelie they quhilk clymmis up maist hie,
> And not content with small possessioun;   (367–72)

and: "Grit aboundance and blind prosperitie /Oftymes makis ane evill conclusioun" (377–78); or in the *Orpheus and Eurydice*, when he says:

> Warldly men sumtyme ar castin he
> Upon the quhele, in gret prosperitee,
> And wyth a quhirl, onwarly, or thai wait,
> Ar thrauin doun to pure and law estait.   (485–88)

Henryson names and explains the nine Muses in his *Orpheus*; and, whereas we could only conjecture from circumstantial evidence that Chaucer and Lydgate did not follow the Pseudo-Catonian tradition of assigning specific

---

[4] Fox A, p. 130 (= B, p. 383), takes "ballet" as "a deprecatory term," whereas H. Harvey Wood in his edition, p. 258, says that Henryson probably means to indicate that the whole poem is written in ballade-royal verse. We should note on this point that the first recorded designation of rhyme royal as ballade royal is by Caxton in 1483. It may also be significant that Dunbar associated "balat making" and tragedy in speaking of the poets Clerk and Afflek; he may even be saying that they wrote tragedies in ballade form. But just as Dunbar may have been inspired by Henryson's example to apply the word tragedy to the earlier poets, so too he may have first encountered the conjunction of tragedy and ballade in Henryson's poem.

[5] Fox assigns even fewer lines to the actual testament. See below.

genres of activities to specific Muses, with Henryson it is certain. Melpomene is about as far from being the Muse of Tragedy as one could imagine: "The secund maide namyt Melpomene, / As hony suete in modulacion" (38–39). It has been stated that Henryson's chief source for his treatment of the Muses was from a thirteenth-century addendum to the *Grecismus* of Eberhard of Béthune, a section entitled *De nominibus Musarum et gentilium*, where the Muses are listed with mainly Fulgentian characteristics, though not in Fulgentius's order. But if Henryson saw this work at first hand, he must also have been exposed to the Pseudo-Catonian tradition as well, for both are given. In the first listing, we have: "Dulce canens tibi Melpomene sit Musa secunda"; and in the second: "Tragicumque secunda / Melpomene carmen invenit."[6]

We should note here, since we have referred to Lydgate, that there is no sign of Henryson's acquaintance with the *Fall of Princes* anywhere in the *Testament*. It has been suggested that the *Fables* draws upon the *Fall* at one or two places, but the parallels are not decisive.[7] It has also been suggested that Henryson was influenced by Seneca's tragedies in writing the *Testament*, but no evidence is forthcoming, and I find the idea unlikely.[8]

It may well be that Henryson's chief acquaintance with the term tragedy came from the *Troilus*. It is of course also possible and perhaps probable that he knew of Chaucer's treatment of the subject in the *Monk's Tale*. Moreover, the fact that he classifies tragedy under the category of "careful dite" may indicate that he knew Chaucer's *Boece*, for there, we recall, in translating his glossator's modification of Trevet's gloss, Chaucer calls tragedy a dite of a prosperity for a time that ends in wretchedness. But then dite seems to have been the standard English rendition of the Latin *carmen*. We have already noted in chapter 2 that Henryson's poem does not fulfill this definition exactly, for it omits the prosperous beginning and goes straight to the wretchedness. The same is true of Chaucer's *Tragedy of Hugelino*, however, and Henryson had the further justification of presenting his work as a coda to Chaucer's *Troilus*, where the prosperity is set forth in great detail. The *Testament* also has explicit "flashbacks" to happier times, as we shall see.

Henryson could have seen Nicholas Trevet's complete gloss on tragedy, to judge from his use of Trevet's Boethian commentary in *Orpheus and Eurydice*, where he refers to him by name: "Maister Trewit, Doctour Nicholas, /

---

[6] *De nominibus Musarum*, ed. F. J. E Raby, *A History of Secular Latin Poetry*, 2:85. Béthune flourished at the end of the twelfth century, and the first eight chapters, from which *De nominibus* is taken, were probably added after his death (which occurred before 1212); the work existed in its expanded form by 1280 (Raby, p. 84). For Henryson's presentation of the Muses, see Fox B, pp. 393–94, who draws especially on Dorene Allen Wright, "Henryson's *Orpheus and Eurydice* and the Tradition of the Muses." In contrast to Henryson, Gavin Douglas in *The Palace of Honor* does draw on the tradition of Pseudo-Cato (or Pseudo-Vergil, since by his time the verses on the Muses were commonly attributed to Vergil). The fourth Muse is recorded thus: "The ferd endityth oft with chekis wet / Sare Tragedyis, Melphomyne the gent" (860–61). See the edition of Priscilla J. Bawcutt, pp. 58, 189.

[7] Fox B, pp. xx, 191–92, 194.

[8] I am referring to Gray, *Robert Henryson*, pp. 165–66, who does not quite say that Henryson was influenced by Seneca, but only that "a medieval tragedy" in some of its aspects "may well remind us of a Senecan play." He says that John Norton-Smith, *Geoffrey Chaucer*, chap. 6, has successfully demonstrated this in the case of Chaucer's *Troilus*. But, as I have noted above (chap. 2, p. 57 n. 82), I find Norton-Smith's reasoning unconvincing.

Quhilk in his tyme a noble theolog was" (421–22).[9] As we have seen, Trevet begins by citing book 18 of Isidore's *Etymologies*, which includes the Lactantian characterization of tragedy as treating the deeds and crimes of wicked kings, and then he modifies William of Conches's definition of tragedy: rather than a writing, he calls it a poem, *carmen*, which deals with great iniquities and which begins in prosperity and ends in adversity.[10] But it is doubtful that Henryson considered tragedy to be limited to accounts of the falls of wicked protagonists, given the example of Chaucer's tragedy of Troilus and Henryson's assessment of Troilus's character in the *Testament*. However, his presentation of Cresseid demonstrates that wrongdoing in highly placed persons could easily be a component of a tragic tale.

Less problematic is Fortune's characterization of tragedy in the text of the *Consolation* itself. At least, there can be no doubt that the *Testament of Cresseid* contains lamentations over Fortune's unexpected overthrow of happy states or conditions, if not of happy reigns.

There may have been further Boethian influence on Henryson's notion of tragedy. In the course of Cresseid's formal Complaint in the lazar-house, she addresses the fair ladies of Troy and Greece thus: "Nocht is your famous laud and hie honour /Bot wind inflat in uther mennis eiris" (462–63). Denton Fox suggests that Henryson is drawing here on a faulty rendering of Boethius's citation of lines from Euripides's *Andromache*, which appears in some medieval texts of the *Consolation*, namely: "O gloria, gloria, in milibus hominum nihil aliud facta nisi auribus inflatio magna."[11] If so, and if Henryson read these words in their context in the *Consolation*, he would have seen that they were appropriate for inclusion in a tragedy, for Boethius refers to Euripides not by name but as a *tragicus*.

Even though we can come to no clearer understanding of Henryson's generic notions of tragedy, we can at least analyze more closely the construction and constitutive elements of the one example he gives of the form. Apart from Chaucer's and Lydgate's repetitious series, each of the other tragedies of the Middle Ages, which amount to hardly more than a handful, is a *tragedia sui generis*, and that goes for both the *Troilus* and the *Testament of Cresseid* as well. It has been an important part of my nominalistic or taxonomic survey of ideas of tragedy from classical antiquity onwards to distill peculiar notions of tragedy from such suigeneric forms.

[9] Fox B, pp. 384–91, edits Trevet's entire commentary on Boethius's poem on Orpheus, *Consolatio*, book 3 m. 12.

[10] See above, p. 51.

[11] Pointed out by Fox A, p. 121 (cf. B, p. 374), referring to *Consolatio*, book 3 pr. 6. According to Skeat and Robinson in their notes to Chaucer's translation of this prose in his *Boece*, this is the form of the Latin gloss that appears in the Croucher Manuscript, but in fact only one *gloria* appears there, on fol. 78, accurately transcribed by Silk in his edition, p. 275. The same is true of another manuscript of Trevet, Vat. lat. 562, quoted by Silk on p. 40, and true also of the eight MSS he uses in his edition of Trevet, p. 349. But Chaucer's copy-text clearly had another *gloria*, because he translates as follows: "O glorie, glorie, thow n'art nothyng elles to thousandes of folk but a greet swellere of eres" (*Boece, Riverside Chaucer*, pp. 426–27). The expanded version of William of Conches's commentary, in London, Brit. Lib. Royal MS 15 B.3, fol. 73v, does have a double *gloria*, and so does the commentary of William of Aragon in the second half of the Croucher Manuscript, fol. 54.

I know of only one sustained effort to consider Henryson's poem as a tragedy, that of Steven McKenna, who attempts to come to an understanding of Henryson's notion of tragedy in general from his treatment of Cresseid in particular. If this is too sanguine a prospect, we shall at least be able to conclude that what we find in the *Testament* is what Henryson means by tragedy *in this particular case*. I shall refer to McKenna's conclusions as we proceed, but let me note here his observation that all commentators who treat the poem as a tragedy implicitly follow the "received opinion" that tragedy consists of a pyramidal rising and falling action; he accepts it as well, as conforming to "the general medieval association of a tragic fall being linked to the cyclical motion of Fortune's wheel." But in the case of Henryson's tragedy, he assumes that, given its status as an addendum to the *Troilus*, the catastrophe has already occurred in Chaucer's poem at the point where Criseyde rejected Troilus, and that the whole of Henryson's poem is simply the aftermath of the catastrophe, consisting of a continued fall and a subsequent rising action, a recovery of sorts, at the end.[12]

I should point out that the criticism and observations that other critics make of the poem, even it they do not explicitly consider it as a tragedy, are potentially applicable to our study, since the poem is in fact a tragedy: it is not only a Henrysonian tragedy, but a Chaucerian tragedy as well, since Henryson was at least partially inspired by Chaucer's great example of tragedy, the *Troilus*, if not his definitions or the miniature examples in the *Monk's Tale*.

Most readers of the *Testament* in the last two generations have accepted the usual evaluative criteria of the New Criticism, such as unity and coherence of theme, rich but controlled ambiguity, and so on. But I suggest that these criteria have often not been rigorously applied to the poem and that it has been judged to be a more, or less, artistic performance than it should be (on the basis of these criteria) because of extraneous circumstances. The main circumstance, of course, is that it is a sequel to the *Troilus*, and it can draw on the emotional capital that Chaucer produced in his telling of the story.[13] Usually this circumstance has worked in favor of the *Testament*, but sometimes it has been a cause of disappointment, because Henryson had "a hard act to follow" and promised more than he could fulfill. Some critics, while granting that his poem is undoubtedly moving, especially at the end, have found it to be defective as a whole—to contain many nice touches and touching moments but even more ineptitudes. One way of excusing such perceived

[12] Steven R. McKenna, "Henryson's 'Tragedie' of Cresseid," pp. 27–28. David J. Parkinson, "Henryson's Scottish Tragedy," does not analyze the *Testament* as a tragedy, but only agrees with Douglas Gray (see n. 8 above) that it may be "a medieval tragedy in the Senecan mode" (p. 355); but Edwin D. Craun, "Blaspheming Her 'Awin God': Cresseid's 'Lamentatioun' in Henryson's *Testament*," gives an interesting analysis of Henryson's work as a series of tragedies of lamentation or complaint from Cresseid's point of view: from a tragedy of divine betrayal it moves to a tragedy of fortune—following McAlpine's postulation of a standard medieval form—and then, finally, to a tragedy of character (p. 27).

[13] Other examples of such "capital transferral" can perhaps be seen in Walt Whitman's two elegies on the death of Lincoln, *O Captain My Captain* and *When Lilacs Last in the Dooryard Bloomed*, which draw on the deep and widespread mourning still felt for the martyred president. Presumably Greek tragedies that dealt with familiar stories would also often be able to rely on already established emotions in the audience.

defects, or even of converting them to strengths, has been to resort to the device of blaming them on a naive narrator distinct from the author, while judging the author himself to be in full artistic control throughout. Such ironic readings have often assumed an unbelievable level of sophistication in the poem, and predictable reactions against such overreadings have been forthcoming.[14] It is clear enough, of course, that Henryson at the beginning takes on the role of a has-been lover, no doubt inspired by Chaucer's role-playing as a would-be or "never-ran" devotee of love. But Henryson's role-playing is not carried through the rest of the *Testament*, and a similar lack of continuity can be seen elsewhere in the poem. Such inconsistencies in the compositions of Chaucer and other medieval authors have often been pointed out by scholars who have given explanations that are more historically plausible than the naive-persona theory. For instance, Robert Jordan analyzes the narrator's interruptions in the *Troilus* not as the reflections of a consistent character but rather the voicing of the author's concerns with language and fiction. These interventions serve to destabilize the plot, directing attention from story to story-telling.[15] Derek Brewer, in speaking of "Gothic Chaucer," argues that medieval notions of unity were not the same as ours, and points out that Pandarus's advice to Troilus to avoid stylistic inconsistencies ("Ne jompre ek no discordant thyng yfeere," 2.1037) did not extend to changes of style and subject matter within a work.[16]

I would like to propose an analysis of my own for the specific kind of directional changes to be found in the *Testament*; I place it under the rubric of "disjunctivism"; or perhaps a formula like *conjunctura disjuncta* would be more descriptive (or, as applied to a French author like Chrétien de Troyes, *conjointure disjointe*).[17] Another formula would be *copula interrupta*, appropriate

---

[14] For instance, J. A. W. Bennett, "Henryson's *Testament*: A Flawed Masterpiece," rejects Fox's explanation that Henryson deliberately takes on the character of "a stupid and passionately involved narrator" (see Fox A, pp. 54–56), and imputes, in effect, the stupidity to Henryson himself (p. 10). But Bennett, in my opinion, is overly zealous in finding fault with the poem; Peter Godman, "Henryson's Masterpiece," makes a good defense against some of his objections. Fox B, pp. xciii–xciv, has a more moderate characterization of the narrator than in his earlier edition. A plausible analysis of Henryson's character as narrator can be found in Gray, *Robert Henryson*, pp. 169–70; see also Thomas W. Craik, "The Substance and Structure of *The Testament of Cresseid*: A Hypothesis," pp. 25–26.

[15] Robert M. Jordan, "Metafiction and Chaucer's *Troilus*." For another convincing alternative to the consistent persona, see Martin Stevens, "The Performing Self in Twelfth-Century Culture," who deals with intermittent authorial role-playing, in which the narrator's assumed roles vary according to *ad hoc* needs. Henrietta Twycross-Martin, "Moral Pattern in *The Testament of Cresseid*," who notes an oscillation between "straight" and "obtuse" narration in both Chaucer (in *Troilus*) and Henryson, considers the narrator more of a point-of-view tool than a character inviting psychological interpretation (pp. 32–35). Alicia K. Nitecki, " 'Fenȝeit of the New': Authority in *The Testament of Cresseid*," points out a differerent kind of oscillation, namely, between an omniscient narrator and first-person observations of the characters—and among the characters she includes not only Cresseid and Troilus but also the narrator (pp. 120–21).

[16] Derek Brewer, "Gothic Chaucer," p. 5; he refers to the similar discussion of Norman Eliason, *The Language of Chaucer's Poetry*, who in turn (on p. 144) refers to Robert Jordan's analysis of gaps and lack of transitions in Chaucer as "jagged edges" or "unsewn seams"; see *Chaucer and the Shape of Creation*, p. 117.

[17] I am making an analogy with the *effet conjoncteur-disjoncteur* (describing the "cut-out" mechanisms of self-closing circuit breakers) of electromechanical theory; for a practical applica-

because the chief example by which I wish to establish this feature of literary composition deals with conjunction in the narrower sense of sexual coitus.

I refer to the episode in which Nicholas and Alison in the *Miller's Tale* come together in the master bedroom, once the carpenter is disposed of:

> Ther was the revel and the melodye;
> And thus lith Alison and Nicholas,
> In bisynesse of myrthe and of solas,
> Til that the belle of Laudes gan to rynge,
> And freres in the chauncel gonne synge.   (3652–56)

The time indicated would be just before daybreak or even later.[18] But as the tale proceeds it becomes quite clear that the coitus thus described did not last so long but was interrupted shortly after the first cockcrow, when "derk was the nyght as pich, or as the cole" (3731), well before dawn.[19]

After Absalom's first interruption, there is a resumption of sexual coitus, which is interrupted by a call of nature ("this Nicholas was risen for to pisse," 3798) before Absalom's second visitation; but neither event constitutes an interruption in the narrative juncture. However, such an interruption does apparently occur at the end of the tale: after Nicholas receives his third-degree burn and calls out for water, he and Alison seem to have taken up their coital posts in bed once again, because after the carpenter comes tumbling down to land on the floor, perhaps near or even in the bed-chamber itself,[20] the two lovers get up again: "Up stirte hire Alison and Nicholay" (3824). The same kind of speedy recovery (which I analyze as narrative disjunction) sometimes occurs in more serious pieces, as when Arcite and Palamon in the *Knight's Tale* first fight so long and fiercely that they are ankle-deep in blood, and immediately thereafter they clearly have little or nothing wrong with them.

tion, see Maurice Bailleul, *Notions de matériel roulant des chemins de fer* (Paris 1951), p. 119: "L'equipement comporte un organe appelé *conjoncteur-disjoncteur* dont le rôle est double. D'abord, il connecte automatiquement la batterie aux bornes de la dynamo lorsque la vitesse du train est suffisamment élevée (20 à 25 kmh), de façon à permettre la charge de cette batterie. Ensuite, il isole la dite batterie de la dynamo lorsque la vitesse du véhicule diminue et devient inférieure à la limite précitée." For Chrétien's use of the term *conjointure*, see Douglas Kelly, "The Source and Meaning of *Conjointure* in Chrétien's *Erec* 14. See below for my discussion of disjunctive conjunctions in Chrétien's *Lancelot*.

[18] Skeat cites Daniel Rock, *The Church of Our Fathers*, 3:2:6, who says that the Nocturns of Matins "should begin at such a time as to be ended just as morning's twilight broke, so that the next of her services, the *lauds*, or *matutinae laudes*, might come on immediately after." The bells would have been a summons for the laity to attend Lauds and the following Mass.

[19] See my *Chaucer and the Cult of Saint Valentine*, pp. 103–04, where I note that Vincent of Beauvais, in *Speculum naturale* 15.75–76, 78, has two different locations for the first cockcrow, namely, midnight and the period immediately after the middle of the night (*intempestum*); in this latter context, *gallicinium* is named after the *gallus* as *prenuncius lucis*. *Matutinum* follows, meaning the time between the departure of darkness and the coming of dawn.

[20] He fell "to the celle / Upon the floor" (3822–23), with "celle" or its variant "selle" usually taken to mean "sill" in the sense of "floor" or "flooring"—an unprecedented meaning (though "on sille" can mean "in hall"). If "celle" is meant, it is possible, given the fluid nature of the carpenter's house, that it refers to the "bower," perhaps with an ironic reference to the personal quarters of a religious (cf. Monk's Prologue 1972).

Chaucer is filled with such narrative and thematic circuit-breaks. To stay with the first two Canterbury tales, we can cite the grove first destroyed by Theseus in constructing his colosseum and then used as the site of Arcite's exequies, and also the broken-down door to Nicholas's chamber, which is later found to be in good working order, as well as other mutated constructions in the carpenter's house.[21] A more complex example is that of John Carpenter, who is said to be jealous four times but is quite clearly portrayed throughout as not jealous. Corresponding conversely to Nicholas and Alison's continued and then discontinued sexual congress is Chaucer's announcement in the *Book of the Duchess* that he fared the worse all the morrow for having read the story of Ceyx and Alcyone (99), though the sweet dream that it inspired (276) clearly made him fare the better.[22] We have just seen another example at the end of the last chapter, in recounting how Charles of Anjou comes before Boccaccio to have his story told, undaunted by Fortune, and yet at the end of his story he is very much daunted.

This sort of medieval narrative phenomenon can be compared to and contrasted with "intermittance," in the sense that Carolyn Dinshaw develops from Roland Barthes. Whereas Barthes is speaking of browsing, "the reader's choosing and skipping parts of a complete narrative" ("the intermittence of skin flashing between two articles of clothing," and so on), she extends it to "the reader's experience of the author's leaving something out." She is referring to the way in which Chaucer's narrator works in the *Troilus*: "He skips over details, makes choices, and paces his reading, taking pleasure in the encounter with the very surface of the text."[23] The notion could be taken further to include thematic intermittence, that is, the reader's perception of the periodic flashing of motifs in the midst of other material, with the assumption that there is a continuous body of meaning, or "rhizomatic network," subsisting beneath the entire text. Modern readers are inclined to assume such subsistence even when there is no real intermittence, no body joined to the flash of flesh, but only a single thematic display, or at most, a resumption of a previously introduced theme with no intervening existence or suspended animation, In other words, sometimes there is an intermittence that is truly intermittent, as in some of the examples I have just noted, and in many of the contradictory morals we have observed in Boccaccio and Lydgate.

[21] I have analyzed these discontinuities in "Chaucer's Arts and Our Arts" from the viewpoint of what might be called, using the language of formal logic, Chaucer's "gaze of second intention," that is, his preference for constructing visual descriptions, or descriptions of visual art, from previous literary descriptions rather than from actual observable instances in the external world. For a related view see Margaret Bridges, "The Picture in the Text: Ecphrasis as Self-Reflectivity in Chaucer's *Parliament of Fowles, Book of the Duchess*, and *House of Fame*," and for a counterview see Linda Tarte Holley, *Chaucer's Measuring Eye* (Houston 1990).

[22] In *Chaucer and St. Valentine*, p. 110, I suggest a similar disjunction at the beginning of book 2 of the *Troilus*: Pandarus is awakened by the swallow on May 3 before it was day, is sent back to bed by a love-pang, and is awakened again after daylight, and suffers periodically during the day; but he is subsequently portrayed not as suffering from his own love-sickness but as setting about with great gusto to alleviate Troilus's condition.

[23] Dinshaw, *Chaucer's Sexual Poetics*, pp. 41 and 211 n. 19 (citing Roland Barthes, *The Pleasure of the Text*, p. 10).

The challenge to readers of medieval literature is to judge just when there is subsistence and when there is not. Sometimes it is clear that there is not, as with the grove in the *Knight's Tale*, but at other times it is arguable. For instance, is the Wife of Bath, who is presented as a manufacturer of cloth in the *General Prologue*, still to be thought of as such in her own prologue, where her account of herself would seem to preclude it? Or does Chaucer mean for his readers to think of the Prioress, who counterfeits cheer of court in the *General Prologue*, as maintaining the same characteristic in her tale, even though he provides no further amusing flashes or glimpses of this sort of personality?[24] Our answers should be informed by the recognition that complete narrative disjunctions may be intentional and based on common esthetic principles, and not necessarily cases of authorial bungling or Homeric nodding.

To return to the context of Chaucerian tragedy: one can easily admit, I think, a low-level subsistence, or virtual persistence, of theme in the Host's mention of the Monk's bridle bells as having kept him sufficiently alert during the recitation of the tragedies to prevent his suffering a fall of his own. The readers are meant to remember Chaucer's description of the Monk in the *General Prologue*, but they are not, presumably, meant to have been hearing the bells jingling during all of the tales through the Monk's, nor are they meant to hear them after the Host turns to the Nuns' Priest for the next tale. But in the case of Chaucer's major tragedy, *Troilus and Criseyde*, there is an instance of total interruption at the very beginning, that is, his promise to tell us how Criseyde forsook Troilus "er she deyde" (1.56). It may well have been Chaucer's failure to deal with her betrayal in the context of her death that inspired Henryson to do it himself. Even if he considered "tragedy in general," like Chaucer, to consist of an account of movement from prosperity to adversity, in this case the prosperity phase could be omitted, since he was simply supplying an alternative or expanded ending to Chaucer's tragedy.

The first narrative disjunction that we are to consider in the *Testament* has already been alluded to, and it concerns his alternative ending to the *Troilus*. Henryson provides an elaborate prologue to the story that should demand, according to most postmedieval canons of literature, a continuation and conclusion in the same terms. He picks up a book that already contains the account of Cresseid's death, but we hear no more of the book as his poem proceeds. The result might seem awkward, once we think about it, but it has not often been noticed, and the same is true of other instances of lack of frame closure. If it is not the case with Shakespeare's *Taming of the Shrew*, where Christopher Sly is kept on the stage without being disposed of, Dante's *Comedy* is a different matter. Few readers, I think, have objected to being left up in the air at the end of the *Paradiso*. The same is true of a work that Henryson knew, namely, the *Consolation of Philosophy*. Towards the end of book 5, Boethius drops out as a participant in the dialogue, and Philosophy concludes

---

[24] I answer the question concerning the Prioress in the negative in "Medieval Relations, Marital and Other," pp. 142–45; so does Florence Ridley, *Riverside Chaucer*, p. 913. I hope to explore these matters further elsewhere, especially in connection with Chaucer's presentation of the Pardoner's varying characteristics, especially his strong voice (three times) and his weak, eunuch-like voice (one time).

by addressing a plural audience, presumably mankind in general; and there is no return to Boethius's prison cell, and no concluding reflection on his part as narrator.

More noticeable instances of an open-ended or unfinished framework can be seen in two of Henryson's minor poems. In the *Abbey Walk*, he starts by reading an inscription in an abbey, and then records it; the inscription forms not only the body but also the end of the poem. Similarly, in the *Praise of Age*, he recounts his overhearing of a monologue, and then simply records it, without a concluding narrative statement. In the *Testament* it is clear that Henryson's main inspiration was Chaucer's example in *Troilus* of pretending to follow a primary written source for his story. In the very first stanza of his poem, Chaucer manages to produce the contradictory situation of recounting his story orally to a group of listeners and at the same time actually writing it out in the throes of composition. This peculiarity, which we are forced to accept and overlook at the very outset, turns out to be an advantage, for Chaucer is able throughout the poem to address himself to auditors or to readers at will, and we are thereby prepared for the multiple apostrophes at the end. In contrast, Henryson's final address to women has had no preparation, on the level of overall narrative structure. But narrative structure is not the only consideration for judging the effectiveness of a work, and Henryson's conclusion, I will argue, has a greater sense of finality to it than many seemingly well-closed narratives.[25]

Henryson seems also to have been partially inspired by the opening of one or more of Chaucer's dream visions: all four of them in fact deal with books and the authority of books. But he eschews any such elaboration of the theme, and he deals with the alleged book only in the following lines:

> To brek my sleip, ane uther quair I tuik,
> In quhilk I fand the fatall destenie
> Of fair Cresseid, that endit wretchitlie.
>   Quha wait gif all that Chauceir wrait was trew?
> Nor I wait nocht gif this narratioun
> Be authoreist, or fenyeit of the new
> Be sum poeit, throw his inventioun
> Maid to report the lamentatioun
> And wofull end of this lustie Creisseid,
> And quhat distres scho thoillit, and quhat deid.[26]   (61–70)

Rather than continuing to make allusions throughout the rest of the poem to the content of this book (as he did earlier to Chaucer's book: "and thair I fand," etc., line 43), either accepting its statements as plausible or questioning

---

[25] For various aspects of finality in medieval poems, see Margaret Bridges, "The Sense of an Ending: The Case of the Dream-Vision." She notes ambiguous elements in the apparently decisive closure features of *Pearl*, finds functions of closure in the very fragmentariness of Chaucer's *House of Fame*, and sees a "comic deflation of the dream-framework and its structural conventions" in Langland's *Piers Plowman*, which undermines the narrator's waking up as a signal of closure.

[26] The last line means, "And what distress she suffered, and what death."

them as unlikely, or comparing them to what Chaucer has said, he proceeds to tell the story as if he were starting the poem from the beginning. Instead of alluding to one source, he shifts to Chaucer's alternative device of referring to a multiplicity of authorities, some of whom report that Cresseid became promiscuous. In Chaucer's work, the one device is complementary to the other, for in addition to Lollius he mentions some of the other writers who have treated the subject. Henryson could have reconciled the two devices in various way, for instance, by noting that his main authority drew upon several sources, some of them contradictory; but he did not feel the need to do so.

PUBLIC PROMISCUITY VS. SECRET SHAME

Henryson's disjunctive manner of establishing the basis of his story involves him immediately in an apparently disjunctive presentation of the facts of Cresseid's life after leaving Diomeid, which, as he tells the story, constitutes the beginning of her tragic adversity. He first seems to say that she became promiscuous, and then that she did not. Let us look at the stanza in which this allegation is first introduced:

> Quhen Diomeid had all his appetyte,
> And mair, fulfillit of this fair ladie,
> Upon ane uther he set his haill delyte,
> And send to her ane lybell of repudie
> And hir excludit fra his companie.
> Than desolait scho walkit up and doun,
> And, sum men sayis, into the court commoun.   (71–77)

Fox punctuates the last words, "into the court, commoun," taking it to mean that Cresseid reportedly frequented the royal court and became promiscuous.[27] But though one could doubtless think of a royal court in Henryson's "urbanized" version of the Greek camp, it is unlikely that this is his meaning here. Rather, he must intend to designate a "common court" or courtyard (or, to use an earlier term, "court place") in contrast either to a formal royal court or to a private court of the sort that would be the milieu of King Diomeid when besieging Troy.[28] At any rate, it is clear from the next stanza that the report of "some men" does deal with Cresseid's promiscuity, for Henryson seems to lament the "fact" of her widely exercised licentiousness, thus:

> O fair Creisseid, the flour and A *per se*
> Of Troy and Grece, how was thow fortunait
> To change in filth all thy feminitie,

---

[27] For his explanation, see Fox B, p. 345.
[28] Compare the fifteenth-century meaning of court as "a retinue, company, or troop," attested in the *Dictionary of the Older Scottish Tongue*.

> And be with fleschelie lust sa maculait,
> And go amang the Grekis air and lait,
> Sa giglotlike takand thy foull plesance!
> I have pietie thow suld fall sic mischance!   (78–84)

Henryson seems to have been inspired, at least in part, by Chaucer's technique of blaming others for damaging statements made about Criseyde, and readers have invariably assumed that Henryson, like Chaucer, is affirming the injurious reports.[29] But there are important reasons for thinking that Henryson did not mean to verify the report of her debased activities.

In Chaucer's case, we know that his refusals to confirm the reports he mentions are simply signs of his touching reluctance to admit what has or will become abundantly evident about Criseyde's transferral of love or at least fidelity to Diomede. But in Henryson's work, the contents of the reports are nowhere else verified and are so extreme as to invite disbelief; and Henryson stresses their slanderous nature:

> Yit nevertheles, quhat ever men deme or say
> In scornefull langage of thy brukkilnes,
> I sall excuse als far furth as I may
> Thy womanheid, thy wisdome, and fairnes,
> The quhilk Fortoun hes put to sic distres
> As hir pleisit (and nathing throw the gilt
> Of the), throw wickit langage to be spilt.   (85–91)

Another reason for thinking that Henryson is not concurring with the charge of Cresseid's wantonness is his subsequent emphasis on her shame at being rejected by Diomeid and her insistence on secrecy. The lines following those just cited read:

> This fair lady, in this wyse destitute
> Of all comfort and consolatioun,
> Richt privelie, but fellowschip, on fute,[30]
> Disagysit,[31] passit far out of the toun,
> Ane myle or twa, unto ane mansioun

---

[29] See, for example, A. C. Spearing, *Criticism and Medieval Poetry*, chap. 7: "Conciseness and *The Testament of Cresseid*," pp. 157–92, esp. 182–83. See also Fox A, pp. 27–28, Fox B, p. lxxxiv, and John MacQueen, *Robert Henryson*, p. 72, who interpret Cresseid's leprosy (but not that of her fellow-lepers) as a venereal disease—a view opposed (rightly, to my mind) by Spearing, pp. 186–87. I should note that there is nothing in the report of "some men" or in Henryson's reaction to it to suggest that Cresseid became a prostitute in the technical sense of selling her favors; she is rather accused of some form of nymphomania, of taking foul pleasure like a wanton woman. A similar point is made by Lee W. Patterson, "Christian and Pagan in *The Testament of Cresseid*," p. 699 n. 7, but he sees the charge (which he accepts as verified) to be that she has become promiscuous: that is, sluttish and "commoun" in a hopeless search for a new protector (p. 698). For a report that Henryson may have read a *Spectaculum Amoris*, see n. 40 below.

[30] This is the reading of the 1593 Charteris edition, whereas Thynne in the 1532 edition has "without fellowship or refute." Fox favors "refute" (in the sense of "refuge").

[31] So Charteris; Thynne has "Disshevelde."

> Beildit full gay, quhair [was] hir father Calchas,
> Quhilk than amang the Greikis dwelland was.   (92–98)

Whether we follow the reading of "disguised" or "disheveled" in the text, it is clear that Cresseid went "right privily" to her father's home.

Her secretiveness is further in evidence a bit later: she does not go to the temple to pray, as supposedly was her custom (on ordinary days?),[32] when it is filled with worshippers on a feastday, but goes instead to "ane secreit ora-ture" (line 120). The reason is that she does not want to give the people "ony deming / Of hir expuls fra Diomeid the king" (118–19). This is the cause of her shame, as she tells her father: "Fra Diomeid had gottin his desyre, / He wox werie and wald of me no moir" (101–02). She makes no mention of gen-eral wantonness among the Greeks, which would surely have revealed the dis-grace of her having been repudiated by Diomeid.

Later, she has another reason for secrecy, namely, the deformity caused by her leprosy. She tells Calchas that she does not want to be known, and asks him to take her secretly to the hospital at the end of town (380–82). He accedes to her request:

> Than in ane mantill and ane baver hat,
> With cop and clapper, wonder prively,
> He opnit ane secreit yet and out thair at
> Convoyit hir, that na man suld espy,
> Unto ane village half ane myle thairby.   (386–90)

Some of the lepers, we are told, know her well, but they apparently keep their knowledge from others who, it seems, would have known her except that her very leprosy served as a disguise. But these others assume that she is of noble kin from her demeanor, specifically her "high regret" and "still mourning" (393–98).

It is noteworthy that Cresseid's identity is not further compromised by Cal-chas, whether he or Cresseid is the one wearing the beaver hat.[33] Cresseid asked Calchas to send her "sum meit for cheritie" for her to live upon (383–84), and Henryson says that after he delivered her to the hospital, he "daylie sent hir part of his almous" (392).

[32] Henryson speaks of the temple "to quhilk Cresseid with baill aneuch in breist / Usit to pas, hir prayeris for to say" (110–11). But in light of the prayer she prays in the secret oratory, it seems unlikely that Cresseid was in the habit of praying nonblasphemous prayers. What we prob-ably have here is an example of Henryson's backing up and retelling the story from a contradic-tory point of view. We will see more examples later.

[33] J. A. W. Bennett's suggestion, favored by Fox A and still admitted as a possibility in Fox B, that Calchas wears the hat (and perhaps carries the cup and clapper for Cresseid?) does not seem to have much merit, in view of the awkward syntax it entails. If it is objected that an expensive and respectable hat would not be a suitable disguise, one could respond that, whether it is worn by her or her companion, it in fact does nothing to give away her identity as a member of the upper class. The same is true of Troilus's ring, which she is later portrayed as wearing—it is taken from her finger only when she dies (592). In view of the other contradictory elements we have seen in the poem, "unsuitability" is hardly an argument against the truth or authenticity of a particular reading.

But the rest of the poem proceeds as if these words had never been spoken. There is no further sign of any ministrations on Calchas's part. Cresseid does not have adequate food or clothing, and she is forced to beg with the other lepers. Furthermore, the suggestion contained in the word "daylie" in line 392, that a good deal of time passes before Cresseid's death in the lazar-house, is undercut by Henryson's presentation of her Complaint on the first night of her stay, and by his statement immediately afterwards that Troilus appeared on the scene "that samin tyme" (484).

To return to the notion of Cresseid's sexual promiscuity: we must come to one of two conclusions, either of which would doubtless convict Henryson of clumsiness in modern eyes rather than compliment him for producing an intriguing ambiguity. On the one hand, he may have meant to introduce the report only to deny it as a slander and to judge the slander as a species of misfortune. On the other hand, he may have intended to affirm the report in spite of denying her guilt. But if the latter supposition were correct, we would find him continuing to tell her story as if the report of promiscuousness were not true: for now there is no interval between the time she leaves Diomeid and when she goes to her father; the shame of her rejection does not become common knowledge; and there is no further mention of her giglotlike behavior among the Greeks. That Henryson was capable of the reversal and recasting of his narrative demanded by this second alternative is evident from his treatment of Cresseid in the lazar-house, which we have just seen: first, she is there a long time, succored by her father, and next she is pictured as deprived of all help and dying within a short time after arrival.

Contradictory time schemes can readily be found in other authors. For instance, Shakespeare has Richard II confiscate John of Gaunt's lands immediately after Bolingbroke goes into exile, and yet by the end of the confiscation scene Bolingbroke has already heard of it on the Continent and is now on his way back to claim his heritage. Similarly, in *Othello*, events move at a headlong pace on Cyprus, yet there is time for travel to Venice and back in the meantime. A "two-clock system" (or at least the impression of such) is to be had in Chaucer's *Troilus*. The progress of the love story seems both hurried and deliberate,[34] as does Criseyde's falling away from Troilus.[35] Chaucer also provides a good example of retelling the same events from different points of view in book 1 of the *Troilus*, where he first recounts Troilus's falling in love from a symbolic or mythological point of view (the action of Cupid), and then backs up and tells it from a realistic and psychological perspective.[36]

But Henryson's seemingly contradictory presentation of Cresseid's actions and character has more serious implications for the interpretation of his tragedy. We are, I repeat, faced with two alternatives with regard to her promiscuity: Henryson mentions it only to discredit it, or he affirms it only to ignore

[34] See Joseph A. Longo, "The Double Time Scheme in Book II of Chaucer's *Troilus and Criseyde*."
[35] E. Talbot Donaldson, *Chaucer's Poetry*, p. 978.
[36] See Jordan, *Chaucer and the Shape of Creation*, pp. 76–79. MacQueen, *Robert Henryson*, p. 81, suggests a double-time interpretation for the *Testament* which I find unlikely: he says that on the realistic level Cresseid gets her disease gradually, whereas on the allegorical level of the dream she gets it suddenly.

it thereafter. But before I examine the hermeneutic implications of each possibility, let me take up an objection that might be made to both, namely, that there is in fact further reference to her promiscuity later in the poem, in Cupid's reply to her bitter accusation against him and Venus. Cresseid cites an explicit promise on the part of these gods that she should be "the flour of luif in Troy" (128). It is not altogether clear that Cresseid is blaming them for not fulfilling this promise, or that Cupid understands her to say so when he asserts that the promise was fulfilled: "The quhilk throw me was sum tyme flour of lufe" (279). But Cresseid apparently interpreted the promise to mean that she would never lose her beauty:

> Ye causit me alwayis understand and trow
> The seid of lufe was sawin in my face,
> And ay grew[37] grene throw your supplie and grace.
>
> (136–38)

She attributes her present condition, of being excluded from both Diomeid and Troilus as an odious outcast, to the fact that her beauty has faded, the seed has been killed by frost, "And I fra luifferis left, and all forlane" (140). Cupid, however, says that "hir greit infelicitie" (281) was caused by "hir leving unclene and lecherous" (285).

Now if Cupid is to be taken as referring to a promiscuous phase that Cresseid entered into after she was rejected by Diomeid, it would make more sense to call her promiscuity an effect rather than a cause of her infelicity. It is possible, I suppose, that Henryson did wish to make Cupid indulge in a mindless inversion of the sequence of cause and effect. But it seems more probable that he intended Cupid to blame her present condition, of exclusion from Troilus and Diomeid, on uncleanness and lechery that she indulged in before Diomeid rejected her. This interpretation would certainly make the most sense in light of the last part of the poem, where Cresseid finally acknowledges that her chief failing lay in her abandonment of Troilus for Diomeid. If this is all that Cupid means, then his way of characterizing her behavior is harsh, more so than Saturn's, who speaks of "thyne insolence, thy play, and wantones" (319), and certainly more harsh than Henryson's assessment: she "was sa sweit, gentill, and amorous" (326). But it corresponds to Cresseid's own words when she comes to admit blame in herself, with her refrain, "O fals Cresseid and trew knicht Troylus!" (546). "Thy lufe, thy lawtie, and thy gentilnes," she says, "I countit small in my prosperitie, / Sa elevait[38] I was in wantones" (547–49). She specifically contrasts Troilus's sexual purity with her basic impurity:

> For lufe of me thow keipt continence,
> Honest and chaist in conversatioun;

---

[37] I interpret "grew" as "would grow," although, as E. Duncan Aswell, "The Role of Fortune in *The Testament of Cresseid*," p. 474, points out, it could mean simply "grew" in the indicative mode, in which case the line would mean that the seed of love did always grow green in the past (say, when she was still in Troy).

[38] So Charteris; Fox prefers the 1663 reading of "efflated" (cf. Thynne: "effated").

> Of all wemen protectour and defence
> Thou was, and helpit their opinioun;
> My mynd in fleschelie foull affectioun
> Was inclynit to lustis lecherous.
> Fy, fals Cresseid! O trew knicht Troylus!   (554–60)

She ends by saying that she trusted in another (namely, Diomeid), who had the same sort of infidelity as she.[39]

I conclude then that Cupid was not referring to a period of promiscuous activity after leaving Diomeid,[40] and that there is no other indication of any such licentious activity on her part in the last five-sixths of the poem. If then Henryson intended the report of "some men" in line 77 to be true, his lament in the following stanza is to be taken as inspired by the certainty of Cresseid's degradation, and he is left to wonder how it could have happened; in the stanza after that, he determines to defend her as best he can, and awkwardly denies the report in Chaucerian fashion, and never returns to the subject again.

But if we accept the alternative interpretation (which I favor) and say that Henryson meant to introduce the report of Cresseid's licentiousness so that he could expose it as a slander, his lament must be taken as hypothetical: "I have pity that you should meet with such a mischance—*if it were true that you did*"; and the next lines must be read as a denial of the hypothesis: she had no such guilt, but rather her misfortune consisted in being "spilt" through wicked language. When therefore he goes on in the following stanza to speak of her as "in this wyse destitute" (92), he must be taken to refer only to her dismissal from Diomeid.

This is the way Henryson's poem was interpreted in *The Last Epistle of Creseyd to Troyalus*, attributed to William Fowler (1560–1612), secretary to Queen Anne.[41] Fowler is able to draw on *Troilus and Criseyde* as well as the

---

[39]   I take lines 568–72, "Becaus I knaw the greit unstabilnes, /Brukkill as glas, into my self, I say— /Traisting in uther als greit unfaithfulnes, /Als unconstant, and als untrew of fay— / "'Thocht sum be trew, I wait right few are thay,'" to mean, "Because I know the great unstableness, brittle as glass, in myself, and having trusted in a similarly great unfaithfulness in another, who was just as unconstant and untrue of faith, I say, 'Though some be true, I know that they are very few.'"

[40]   See the similar arguments and conclusion of Mairi Ann Cullen, "Cresseid Excused: A Rereading of Henryson's *Testament of Cresseid*." She notes specifically that there was no time for Cresseid to become "common" (p. 152), as does Malcolm Pittock, "The Complexity of Henryson's *The Testament of Cresseid*," p. 207. Cullen, p. 141, suggests that the report of Cresseid's commonness, which Henryson rejects, is to be thought of as contained in the "quair" that he is reading. She accepts that he may actually have read such a report of Cresseid in the Latin original of the *Spektakle of Luf*; this work, written by G. Myll in 1492, says that Cresseid forsook Troilus for Diomeid and afterwards "went common amang the Grekis." Cullen draws on B. J. Whiting, "A Probable Allusion to Henryson's *Testament of Cresseid*."

[41]   *The Last Epistle of Creseyd to Troyalus*, in *The Works of William Fowler*, ed. Henry W. Meikle, James Craigie, and John Purves, 3 vols., 1:379–87. The poem is contained with others in a manuscript preserved with Fowler's papers. In his notes (3:31–34), Craigie concludes that the poems are probably by Fowler, and goes on to treat him as the author specifically of the *Last Epistle*. I will do the same, while admitting here that the matter is not certain. For a brief recent notice of the poem, see C. David Benson, "True Troilus and False Cresseid: The Descent from

Testament of Cresseid, but it is of course the *Testament* that he follows when telling of Diomeid's treatment of Cresseid and of the subsequent events. He has Creseyd tell it thus:

> He falsed hathe his faithe to me,
>   And light lied me, allas!
> Of force the court I left, and to
>   My fathers house did passe.
> The crewell godes not yet content
>   With me to make accordd,
> My luringe face they leaper made,
>   To se me men abhord.
> To hospitall by night I stole,
>   My self from sight to save,
> Wher me was given a clappinge dishe,
>   My wretched cromms to crave.[42]   (253–64)

In sum, to comprehend what Henryson means by tragedy in his solitary instantiation of the genre, we must try to see how he presents his tragic protagonist, both objectively, from others' viewpoints, and subjectively, from her own awareness and self-admission. McKenna finds the question of the heroine's identity to be "the most important, overriding concern in Henryson's poem."[43] I incline to agree with Fowler's reception of her as guilty, at this stage, only of changing her love from Troilus to Diomeid. Furthermore, in spite of Cresseid's own pessimistic assumption, which we have seen, that she lost her beauty before Diomeid rejected her, Fowler is more in accord with the subsequent development of the *Testament* in having her retain her beauty—she speaks of her alluring face—until she contracted leprosy. This matches Henryson's report of Saturn's sentence in the *Testament:*

Tragedy," pp. 169–70. He dates the poem *c.* 1604 and finds it the most sympathetic treatment of Criseyde in the period: "The sensitive, learned, though somewhat loose poem retells much of the love story in a clever blend of *Troilus* and the *Testament*, while powerfully expressing the emotion Peele saw as the heart of Chaucer's tale" (p. 169, referring to George Peele's *The Tale of Troy*, 1604, which he treats on p. 168).

[42] These lines can be edited thus:

> He falsed hath his faith to me and light lied me, alas!
> Of force the court I left, and to my father's house did pass.
> The cruel gods, not yet content with me to make accord,
> My alluring face they leper made; to see me, men abhorred.
> To hospital by night I stole, myself from sight to save,
> Where me was given a clapping dish, my wretched crumbs to crave.

Cresayd blames the gods for her leprosy and also, in effect, for her betrayal at the hands of Diomeid—which would correspond to her charge against the gods in Henryson's poem. Fowler gets around Henryson's disjunction of first portraying Cresseid as supported by her father in the leprosarium and then of showing her as completely bereft of aid by suggesting that she stole off to the lepers unknown even to her father.

[43] McKenna, "Henryson's 'Tragedie,' " p. 26. He goes on to deduce that Henryson's theory requires the tragic figure not only to discover but also to bear the burden of her identity; he traces "her downfall into enlightenment" and acceptance of responsibility (pp. 28–29).

> This duleful sentence Saturne tuik on hand,
> And passit doun quhair cairfull Cresseid lay,
> And on hir heid he laid ane frostie wand;
> Than lawfullie on this wyse can he say:
> "Thy greit fairnes and al thy bewtie gay,
> Thy wantoun blude, and eik thy goldin hair,
> Heir I exclude fra the for evermair."[44]   (309–15)

Cynthia, too, in speaking of her "lustie lyre" (339) confirms that she is still beautiful.

It seems, then, that Henryson thinks of Cresseid, at least in this part of the poem, of losing her beauty at a blow. The blow is not at first characterized as the sort of *ictus indiscretus* of Fortune spoken of in the *Consolation of Philosophy*, but rather as a divine punishment provoked by a specific act of blasphemy. Henryson devotes thirty of the eighty-six stanzas of the poem to illustrating this point, and reinforces it with Cresseid's immediate conclusion, "My blaspheming now have I bocht full deir" (354), and with the irony of Calchas's sentiment in the next stanza that long prayers are not necessary to inform the gods of what one desires (363–64).[45]

CRESSEID'S UGLY VISION: AN ACTION DREAM

Since the central third of Henryson's tragedy is taken up with the dream in which the gods inflict the leprosy, it has loomed large in readers' assessments of the poem, and it must be given a proportionate prominence in our attempt to appreciate his work as a tragedy. But first it will be necessary to devote an excursus to its nature and the traditions to which it belongs, which to my knowledge have never been recognized.

---

[44] At this point, we see, Saturn is not only *said* to give a sentence, but is also *depicted* as giving it. But much earlier, in line 151, he is introduced with the statement: "And first of all Saturne gave his sentence." I suspect that this is not a contradiction or a mistake on Henryson's part, but rather a textual error, and that for "sentence" in line 151 we should read "presence"; for the point being made is that Saturn is the first of the planetary gods to answer Cupid's summons. The *OED*, s.v. "presence," no. 4, gives an example of "showing one's presence," in Lydgate (the same example is also given in the *MED*, s.v., 1b), but the only instance of "giving presence" comes from 1630 (*OED*, no. 2b). I note further that the planetary gods are not summoned to act as judges of the accuracy of Cupid's charge; her commission of the crime is taken for granted, or perhaps considered judicially notorious, like a confession made in court, needing no proof. See my "Right to Remain Silent," pp. 1000–01. Their function is rather to assess a suitable punishment for her guilt. Cupid agrees to the suggestion of Mercury (who speaks for the other planets) that the sentence of punishment be left to a subcommittee consisting of Saturn and Cynthia. In normal medieval usage, when it is up to the judge or judges to determine guilt as well as punishment for guilt, the sentence encompasses both aspects; this is how the term is used in *The Sheep and the Dog* (see below). Both the *OED*, s.v., 3b-c, and the *MED*, s.v., 3a-b, note that the term can mean *either* a verdict or a punishment, but they should indicate that in the former case the verdict regularly *includes* the punishment.

[45] The lack of strong piety that Calchas manifests here fits well with the weak response that he gave to Cresseid when hearing of her divorce from Diomeid: "Peraventure all cummis for the best" (104).

Cresseid's dream has invariably been analyzed in terms of Macrobius's schemata: Ralph Hanna, for instance, sees it as a Macrobian *insomnium* or purely natural and nonprophetic dream.[46] But apart from the consideration that Henryson shows no direct knowledge of Macrobius, Cresseid's dream is a misfit in his system, for he, like later medieval dream analysts, deals with dreams from the point of view of information or knowledge, whether a matter of explaining or revealing present realities, or predicting future events, or imparting a warning or a command, or, in the case of *insomnia* and *phantasmata*, simply reflecting past events or present worries.[47] Cresseid's dream, on the contrary, is not primarily an information dream but a miraculous "action dream," in which a usually supernatural figure does something physical to the dreamer in the dream that stays with the dreamer when he or she awakes. Ordinarily, reasons for the action are given in the dream, but it would be wrong to interpret the dream merely as a prophecy that is fulfilled immediately on awaking. Cresseid does not become a leper after she wakes, but rather wakes to find herself a leper.

All biblical dreams are information dreams: for instance, Jacob's vision of the ladder in Genesis 28. But the episode in Genesis 32 in which Jacob wrestles with "God" and is left lame would be a typical action dream if it were stated, or construed, to have happened while he was asleep. The same would be true if, when God descended in a pillar of cloud and afflicted Miriam with leprosy for speaking against Moses, He had done so in a dream.[48]

Occasional instances of action dreams are to be found in secular works in the Middle Ages. For instance, in Machaut's *Fontaine amoureuse* a knight dreams of exchanging rings with his wife and wakes to find her ring on his finger in place or his own. Towards the end of John Gower's *Confessio amantis*, John swoons and witnesses an assembly of lovers, who discuss his case. Cupid removes the lance from his heart and Venus anoints the wound, and he wakes cured.[49] Another example is to be found in Christine de Pisan's *Dit*

---

[46] Ralph Hanna III, "Cresseid's Dream and Henryson's *Testament*." Pittock, "Complexity," pp. 203–4, accepts the diagnosis of *insomnium*, but reads it as an information dream telling of a present event: "It does not predict what happens but reveals what is already happening. When Cresseid regains consciousness she already has the leprosy she has dreamed about." In both of these analyses, the supernatural causation of the leprosy is discounted, which would seem to be at variance with Henryson's apostrophe to Saturn. McKenna, "Henryson's 'Tragedie,'" p. 33, also takes her dream as only a dream, and the leprosy as a venereal disease (accepting this, of course, means also accepting her promiscuous behavior).

[47] See Steven F. Kruger, *Dreaming in the Middle Ages*. He sees Cresseid's dream as an example of a true dream: her fall into leprosy is announced in the dream and confirmed by a mirror after she wakes (p. 136); the gods show their anger and "promise" to punish her: she "will be" a leper (p. 137).

[48] Numbers 12.1–10. God says here that He has two normal ways of communicating with His prophets, namely, in visions and in dreams; but with Moses He speaks directly and clearly (12.6–8). The Vulgate and Douai versions are: "Si quis fuerit inter vos propheta Domini, in visione apparebo ei vel per somnium loquar ad illum. At non talis servus meus Moses, qui in omni domo mea fidelissimus est; ore enim ad os loquor ei, et palam. Non per enigmata et figuras Dominum videt." "If there be among you a prophet of the Lord, I will appear to him in a vision, or I will speak to him in a dream. But it is not so with my servant Moses, who is most faithful in all my house; for I speak to him mouth to mouth and plainly, and not by riddles and figures doth he see the Lord."

[49] See my *Love and Marriage*, pp. 233 and 156 respectively.

de la Rose. The goddess Loyalty in a dream gives the poet a commission from the God of Love to publicize the Order of the Rose. She shows Love's letter of commission, and then disappears. When Christine awakes, she knows that her dream was not a lie, for she finds near her the letter exhibited by the goddess.[50]

Miraculous dreams of this sort are most frequently met with in hagiographic literature. As an example, let me cite a series of wonders attributed to St. Dominic in the Legenda aurea, three in the version edited by Graesse[51] and five in the expanded account in William Caxton's Golden Legend (1483). We are told of a girl "sick of the stone," whose mother prayed to St. Dominic, and, in the words of Caxton's translation, "the night following, St. Dominic came to the maid sleeping, and laid in her hand the stone with which she had been tormented. And then she awoke and found herself delivered of the pain, and delivered to her mother the stone, and told her vision." Caxton's two added miracles follow. First is the story of a woman whose son had scrofula. She prayed to God and St. Dominic, and the following night a man in a friar's habit appeared to her and instructed her how to concoct a remedy; "then she awoke and did so." The second added miracle is about a man with a belly swollen like that of a monster; he prayed to St. Dominic, who "appeared to him in his sleep and opened his belly without pain, and took out all the ordures, and anointed him with his holy hand and healed him perfectly." The original Legenda account is resumed with the story of a woman who was reproved by other women for spinning on the feast of the Translation of St. Dominic: "and she was angry and answered, 'Ye that be women of the friars, keep ye their feasts!' And anon the eyes of the woman swelled and there came out rotten matter, and there issued worms, so that one of the neighbors took eighteen worms out of her eyes." But she repented, went to the friars' church, vowed that she would never "missay" to St. Dominic again but would always keep his feast devoutly, "and anon she was made whole." There follows the story of a nun who "was smitten in the thigh so grievously that five months during they doubted that she would have died." Then, after tearfully praying for a long time to St. Dominic, "she slept, and saw St. Dominic with two friars, that opened the curtain that hung afore her bed, and entered." He asked her why she wanted to be healed, and she answered, "Sir, that I might more devoutly serve God." Dominic then took out ointment from under his cope and anointed her thigh, curing her instantly. He told her that it was the ointment of love, which could not be bought; none of God's gifts was more precious than charity, but it would be soon lost if not well kept. The saint then appeared to the nun's sister and told her of the cure. The sister rushed to the nun, and wiped off the sweet-smelling ointment with a bundle of silk and kept it with great reverence.[52]

[50]   Christine de Pisan, Dit de la Rose, Œuvres poétiques, 2:29–48.

[51]   James of Varazze, Legenda aurea, pp. 481–82.

[52]   William Caxton, The Golden Legend, 4:196–98. The first two miracles in the Legenda, that is, the first and the fourth miracles in Caxton's account, are in Vincent of Beauvais's Speculum historiale 30.120, which antedates James's work. The added miracles of Caxton's version are not to be found in the edition of John of Vignay's Legende doree that I have consulted, that published by Antony Verard, Paris, 20 May 1496; see fol. 163v. This edition seems to correspond to that of

The first, third, and fifth of these incidents involve miracle dreams, whereas in the second there is only an information dream, and in the fourth both the miraculous infliction of the malady and its miraculous cure take place in the waking state without visionary experience. But the different possible circumstances of the cure (or infliction) of disease are interchangeable or variable at will. Constance, daughter of the emperor Constantine, has leprosy (we are not told why or how), and she is cured in a dream-vision by St. Agnes.[53] But her father, whose life, as we saw in the last chapter, was treated as a glorious non-tragedy by Lydgate, was afflicted with leprosy by God as a punishment for persecuting Christians, according to the life of St. Sylvester, though the malady is not said to have come upon him in any obviously miraculous way. But because he virtuously refrains from resorting to an extreme remedy (bathing in the blood of 3000 infants), Sts. Peter and Paul appear to him in a dream and tell him how to be cured, namely by being converted and baptized by Pope Sylvester.[54] The actual cure, which takes place after baptism, is accompanied by a waking vision: Constantine sees Christ, but the onlookers see only a great light that descends upon the emperor.[55]

Visions that parallel the juridical setting of the dream in the *Testament of Cresseid* can also be found. In the life of St. Forsey, the saint apparently dies

---

Lyons 1485, described by Pierce Butler, *Legenda aurea—Légende dorée—Golden Legend: A Study of Caxton's Golden Legend with Special Reference to Its Relations to the Earlier English Prose Translation*, pp. 38–39, except for an added life of St. Roch at the end of the Verard edition. However, the additional Dominic miracles are to be found in some manuscripts of Vignay; see Warren F. Manning, "The Jean de Vignay Version of the Life of Saint Dominic," p. 33. Surprisingly, they are also in *The Golden Legend of Jacobus de Voragine*, translated and adapted by William Granger Ryan and Helmut Ripperger, p. 429, even though the translators claim to be following Graesse's edition, and to be making no use of previous English versions, having consulted only modern French and German translations (p. xvi). Ryan makes the same claim in his recent (1993) complete translation, but this time he omits the two miracles (2:56). I have not checked to see if the extra miracles are in the *Gilte Legende*, the earlier English prose translation that Caxton used. The life of St. Dominic is missing from some MSS, but it is to be found in Harley 630, Egerton 876, and an Ashburnham MS (now Brit. Lib. Add. 35298); see Butler, pp. 54, 62, 146, 149, 154, and Auvo Kurvinen, "Caxton's *Golden Legend* and the Manuscripts of the *Gilte Legende*," p. 361.

[53] Caxton, *Golden Legend*, 2:251–52; *Legenda aurea*, p. 116. Other dream-cures occur in the lives of St. Hippolytus (restoration of lost leg), Caxton, 4:232–33; Sts. Cosmas and Damian (thigh transplant), 5:176; St. Mark (cure of breast cancer), 3:139. In the life of St. James the Greater, a man dreams of being fed by the saint, and he wakes to find a freshly baked loaf of bread at hand (4:110). In the entry for Mary's Purification, a woman dreams of attending a celestially ministered mass and having her candle broken; she wakes and finds herself holding a piece of the candle (3:25–26).

[54] Constantine is able to identify his visionary advisors when St. Sylvester shows him pictures of the saints in a book. In a fourteenth-century German version of the story cited by Saul Nathaniel Brody, *The Disease of the Soul: Leprosy in Medieval Literature*, pp. 157–58, the disease is inflicted on Constantine by an angel while he is asleep at night, but it is not clear whether he witnesses the action in a dream. Compare Gower's account of the story, *Confessio amantis* 2.3187–3496, where the disease is not said to be inflicted supernaturally or as a punishment, even by implication (*pace* Brody, p. 158). The same is true of Lydgate's treatment; he says simply that Constantine was chosen to be emperor for his great nobility, and that he became a leper, as the chronicles testify (*Fall* 8.1182–83).

[55] Caxton, *Golden Legend*, 2:199–201; *Legenda aurea*, pp. 71–72. Both Gower and Lydgate omit the vision of Christ. For simple cures of "unmotivated" leprosy, see the lives of St. Martin (Caxton, 6:148) and St. Landry (7:188).

and his soul is conducted to trial by three angels; demons argue with the angels over their right to the soul, but though the Lord Judge declares himself on the side of the angels, the demons are able to punish Forsey, with the approval of the angels and of God Himself, for having received a usurer's donation; and when he is restored to life, "the token and trace of the stroke abode ever after." [56] The same sort of curious incident, in which a person suffers "clinical death," is brought to judgment, undergoes punishment, and is restored to life with marks of the punishment appearing on his body, occurs in the life of St. Jerome, where God as judge orders him whipped for being more of a Ciceronian than a Christian. [57]

In these examples, afflictions that are designated as punitive also have a reformative function. The same is true, at least implicitly, of the God of Love's vengeance against Troilus in the first book of Chaucer's poem: its effect is Troilus's repentance and conversion. Though we see Love directly only in his vindictive mood, we are meant to share Pandarus's optimism: "And now I hope / That thow the goddes wrathe hast al apesed" (1:939–40). Henryson, however, chose to limit the gods' intentions to retribution, in keeping with their *ad hoc* personalities. In so doing, he had abundant precedents in the *vitae sanctorum*, for often saints are shown to be content with punishing those who bear them enmity. [58]

Many readers of the *Testament,* especially those who conclude that Henryson is protesting against the unfairness of the universe or the Deity, are unable to see Cresseid's leprosy, or any such affliction, in anything but negative terms, say, as punishment for sin or as motiveless malignity or as mindless natural evil. It is true that sometimes Henryson treats affliction only negatively (though never blasphemously or skeptically); for instance, in *A Prayer for the Pest*, he regards the disease merely as punishment—justified punishment—for offenses committed. [59] But elsewhere, in *The Abbey Walk*, losses are caused by Fortune under God's direction. Sometimes, as in the case of Job and Toby, natural afflictions are temptations, which must be endured in patience. At other times, to be sure, adversity is recognized as deserved, but it is also corrective, and serves to save as well as to punish:

> God of His justice mon correct,
> And of His mercy petie haif;
> He is ane juge to nane suspect,
> To puneis synffull men and saif.   (33–36)

We have so far considered the ramifications of suffering only from the viewpoints of the sufferer and the inflictor or curer of the suffering, namely, God or some godlike supernatural spirit. But suffering has other dimensions and effects as well, notably in connection with the human witnesses of the suffering. It can serve not only as a monitory example ("this may happen to you as

---

[56] Caxton, 5:177–80; cf. *Legenda*, pp. 639–42.
[57] Caxton, 5:200–201; *Legenda*, p. 654. Other judgment-visions occur in the accounts of the Assumption (4:251–52) and the Nativity of the Virgin (5:109), and in the life of St. Denis (5:254).
[58] Giselle Huot-Girard, "La justice immanente dans la *Légende dorée*."
[59] See Douglas Duncan, "Henryson's *Testament of Cresseid*," p. 134.

well"), but also as an invitation to the exercise of virtue in alleviating the suffering, and as a source of edification. This is the way that Henryson presents Troilus as he rides by the group of lepers, at the culmination of the poem.

Henryson could have found a model for Troilus as charitable knight in the person of St. Louis of France. Here is Caxton's description:

> When he came in Paris, or in other cities, he visited the hospitals and other small houses where poor people lay in, and without abomination of deformity ne of ordure of filth or some patient or sick, administered, many times kneeling, giving meat to the poor with his own hands. In the abbey of Royalmont, which he founded and endowed with great revenue and rents, is showed notorily that such and semblable alms he made there many times. And yet greater marvel, a monk of the said abbey, a leper, an abominable, and as then deprived both of nose and eyes by corruption of the said sickness, the blessed St. Louis administered, humbly putting, kneeling, with his own hands both meat and drink within the mouth of the said leper without any abomination. The abbot there present which unnethe might see that, wept and sighed piteously.[60]

It is not hard to imagine that this picture of the saintly knight *par excellence*, more impressive than the descriptions of a hundred commonplace cures in other legends, might have influenced Henryson's portrayal of Troilus and provided him with at least a partial motivation in making Cresseid a leper.[61]

It would be a mistake, then, to limit Henryson to a narrow view of suffering. But it would also be a mistake to assume *a priori* that he had all of the traditional explanations for suffering in mind at all times. We must rather keep an open mind on the subject, and see where the poem leads us.

THE DISAPPEARANCE OF THE GODS
AND THE COMPLAINT AGAINST FORTUNE

In two of Chaucer's tragedies, as we have seen, divine intervention is taken against the wicked protagonists, with different results. In the *Tragedy of Nabuchodonosor*, God unilaterally removes the diseased condition, and Nabuchodonosor reacts gratefully, with due respect—thus effectively removing his story from the ranks of genuine Chaucerian tragedy. In contrast, in the *Tragedy of Antiochus*, Antiochus consciously repents and acknowledges

---

[60] Caxton, 7:209, translating Vignay, fols. 292v–293, expanded from a supplementary chapter in *Legenda*, p. 916.

[61] "Saint Loys" is also a candidate for the "Seint Loy" of Chaucer's Prioress and the carter of the *Friar's Tale* (see the note to *General Prologue* 120, *Riverside Chaucer*, p. 803). The French of Stratford atte Bowe, as opposed to that of Paris, could take advantage of "the rule of *s*," especially when looking for rhymes. As G. C. Macaulay, *The Complete Works of John Gower*, 1:xvii, puts it: "The poet has it in his power either to use or to omit the *s* of inflexion in the nominatives singular and plural of masculine nouns, according as his rhymes may require."

God's lordship, but God is adamant in having the punitive disease run its horrible course. What happens in Henryson's tragedy? It has often been noticed that Cresseid is not repentant for having offended the gods; she even comes close to blaspheming them again in calling them "craibit" (353), that is, irritable or ill-natured; she is only sorry for having been punished for offending them. The conclusion usually drawn from this reaction is that Henryson wishes to emphasize the weakness not only of her moral or philosophical outlook but also and most especially of her religious viewpoint: she does not yet have the proper respect for the gods.[62] But Henryson himself addresses Saturn in similarly disrespectful terms: "O cruell Saturne, fraward and angrie, /Hard is thy dome and to malitious!" (323–24).

We must consider the possibility that Henryson did not take them seriously as gods and did not intend his readers to do so; that he wished the gods to be seen not so much as representatives of divinity as representatives of the natural world. The question is important, of course, in determining the exact nature of Cresseid's tragic adversity.

Henryson's attitude toward the gods, I submit, is much like that of his master Chaucer. Both poets in their pagan settings make an attempt to show their characters acting in accord with the dictates of their polytheistic beliefs, but they also have them act as "natural monotheists" of the Boethian variety. They pray both to the gods and to God, but the two are not equivalent. They are most nearly alike when they are the recipients of prayers of petition, thanks, and praise, but not when they are addressed by disappointed votaries. The gods can be cursed, whereas God is never treated disrespectfully. Jupiter is a special case: he is sometimes cursed when considered as one of the gods, as, for instance, when Troilus thinks Criseyde is dead and he calls out: "O cruel Jove, and thow, Fortune adverse" (*Troilus* 4.1192), but not when treated as God, as at the end of Troilus's monologue on free will: "Almyghty Jove in trone" (4.1079), or in Criseyde's oath: "Or ellis se ich nevere Joves face" (4.1337). At times, the abused gods react vindictively, as in Chaucer's first account of how Troilus fell in love with Criseyde (though Cupid's vengeance here is actually benevolent, as I will point out below); but more often there is no response, as, for instance, when Troilus returns to Troy after delivering Criseyde to Diomede:

> He corseth Jove, Appollo, and ek Cupide,
> He corseth Ceres, Bacus, and Cipride,
> His burthe, hymself, his fate, and ek Nature,
> And, save his lady, every creature. (*Troilus* 5.207–10)

Troilus is not to be seen as guilty of a serious impiety here, for the gods are in effect treated as "creatures," not as the Creator; they are at the most "deificait," to use Henryson's word (288), deified in the eyes of men, and perhaps

---

[62] I should point out, however, that a good many critics tend to side with Cresseid in her low estimate of the gods. See the list of opinions given by Aswell, "Role of Fortune," p. 471 n. 1, and by Hanna, "Cresseid's Dream," p. 296 n. 1. Hanna says that the central question asked by most critics of the *Testament*, is, "Does Cresseid receive a just sentence and punishment for blaspheming Venus and Cupid?" (p. 288).

taken as stand-ins for the natural world and hence for the divine order, there-fore "participant of devyne sapience" (289), but not truly divine themselves. They are at times regarded as intermediaries between God and man, rather on the level of angels or saints in a Christian context. But they are unlike the saints in that they often lack the requisite sanctity, and their actions can be quite unjust or arbitrary. Furthermore, whereas the gods can be maligned with impunity, at the discretion of the poets, the same is rarely true of the saints, in stories where they appear as functioning characters.

With these thoughts in mind, let us see how the gods are dealt with in the rest of the *Testament*. After Cresseid tells her father of Cupid's vengeance (370–71), there is no further reference to the pagan deities, except for some largely decorative touches. Phoebus goes to rest (400); Cresseid remembers Flora's activities in May (426); she states that Fortune is fickle (469); and she looks forward to spending her afterlife with Diana (587–88). Elsewhere, she simply refers to "God," whether in soliloquy in her Complaint: "Under the eirth God gif I gravin wer" (414), or in concert with the other lepers: "Worthie lordis, for Goddis lufe of hevin, /To us lipper part of your almous deid!" (493–94). She talks also in terms of fate, echoing the "fatall destenie" that Henryson spoke of earlier (62), or in terms of her fortune, or both; for exam-ple, "Fell is thy fortoun, wickit is thy weird" (412). The substance of her Com-plaint combines both of these notions, fortune (fortuitous change) and fate (predetermined change) in lamenting the loss of the pleasurable things in life. Such loss can be either expected or unexpected, whether viewed as the result of arbitrary chance or ineluctable destiny. To the unreflective, of course, no change for the worse is expected, whereas to the reflective no disas-ter should come as a complete surprise.

When Cresseid addresses the ladies of Troy and Greece, she assumes that they, like her in the past, are unreflective. She says:

> O ladyis fair of Troy and Grece, attend
> My miserie, quhilk nane may comprehend,
> My frivoll fortoun, my infelicitie,
> My greit mischeif, quhilk na man can amend.
> Be war in tyme, approchis neir the end,
> And in your mynd ane mirrour mak of me:
> As I am now, peradventure that ye
> For all your micht may cum to that same end,
> Or ellis war, gif ony war may be.   (452–60)

In the preceding stanzas, she has stressed particularly the devastations caused by her leprosy, and she is clearly warning that others may come to a similar state or worse. But there is no suggestion here or elsewhere in the Complaint that she is thinking of the retributive action of the gods, whether for disrespect or for immoral behavior. She is not warning the ladies to take preventive action against change, but only to be aware that change will come. Chaucer's Criseyde does much the same when she learns that she must leave Troy: she calls on everyone to look on her as an example that all happiness must come to an end (4.837–40). Cresseid goes on in the next stanza to say, in effect, that if the change for the worse is not sudden, then it will be gradual: "Nocht is your fairnes bot ane faiding flour" (461), and so on. We can contrast this realistic notion of the way of the world with her earlier unrealistic and unreasonable expectation that by some sort of divine favor her beauty would never fail.

She ends these reflections on the inevitability of change by speaking of the Goddess of Chance: "Fortoun is fikkill quhen scho beginnis and steiris" (469). But Henryson sums up her whole complaint by referring to determined, not fortuitous, events, saying that she was "chydand with hir drerie destenye" (470).

In light of the consideration that there is no return in Cresseid's Complaint to the "crabbedness" of Cupid and the planetary gods, it would seem to be a mistake to find the main significance of Cresseid's dream in the personality disorders and vindictiveness of the gods. It would be more fitting to see them primarily as "pro-rated" causes or manifestations of sublunary mutability, of generation and corruption. This is the way Henryson introduces them:

> Quhilk hes power of all thing generabill,
> To reull and steir by thair greit influence
> Wedder and wind, and coursis variabill.   (148–50)

Looked at from a cosmological point of view, life-nourishing and life-destroying events must be regarded as morally neutral. But when mutability is personified in the goddess Fortune, these same events are often seen as beneficent or malevolent, and the same is true of the personified planets. In Henryson's depiction, Saturn presides over bad weather, whereas Jupiter, "nureis to all thing generabill" (171), runs interference against Saturn's activities. A similar contrast between good and bad events is observable in the next two pairs of gods. Mars causes the disasters of human conflicts, while Phoebus, like Jupiter, is a "tender nureis" (199) in meteorological matters. Venus is bad, for she destroys the love that she inspires, whereas Mercury is the source of all that is recreative and medicinal (though Henryson allows himself a Chaucerian slap at the avarice of physicians in his description). Cynthia, who is traditionally neutral and takes on the qualities of other planets with which she comes in conjunction, is portrayed as having both favorable and unfavorable elements, the reflected light of the sun and her own dark spots, one of which forms a picture of a thieving churl.

Fortune is often depicted as being as changeable as the moon, and Henryson could well have made the reverse equation. But instead he attributes Fortune-like changeableness to the other female deity, Venus; or it might be more accurate to say, as Duncan Aswell does, that he strips her of all but her fortunal aspects, and leaves her practically unrecognizable from an astrological point of view.[63] Venus resembles Fortune in what might be called her tragic guise, when she is seen as always bestowing prosperity first and then adversity. Though she laughs with one eye and weeps with the other (231), it

---

[63] Aswell, "Role of Fortune," p. 478. Florence Ridley, "A Plea for the Middle Scots," p. 188 n. 18, rightly rejects the a-religious aspect of Aswell's interpretation of Henryson's presentation of Cresseid's world.

is the weeping eye that receives the emphasis, in the sense that misfortune follows good fortune. The same trait in the present context is also indicative of typical female inconstancy or hypocrisy, and was applied to the forerunners of Cresseid, beginning with Benoit of Sainte-Maure and repeated especially by Guido of Le Colonne and John Lydgate.[64]

This picture of Venus is in direct contrast to the gentle view of her that Henryson gives at the beginning, where he says:

> For I traistit that Venus, luifis quene,
> To quhome sum tyme I hecht obedience,
> My faidit hart of lufe scho wald mak grene,
> And therupon wth humbill reverence
> I thocht to pray hir hie magnificence. (22–26)

If we decide that the contrast is deliberate and thematic, then we might wish to search for a logical explanation: perhaps Henryson portrays himself in the beginning as deluded about the true nature of Venus, which becomes apparent only in Cresseid's dream. But it may well be that no irony is intended, and that the contrast is due to the disjunctive mode that we have seen in operation at the beginning of the poem. It is to be observed in the setting itself: at one moment, showers of hail come from the north, then suddenly the sun is shining; only later are we informed that a wind coming from the same direction as the hail has purified the air of clouds. Henryson specifies that Aries brings the hail "in middis of the Lent" (5), whereas later he speaks of "the winter nicht" (39).[65] He gives the impression that the nights are still longer than the days, for he wishes to cut the night short by reading a book—which would also indicate that he has trouble sleeping, for sleep is naturally one of the best ways to make the night pass quickly. But when he picks up the other book, it is with the object of "breaking" his sleep (61).[66]

[64] See Gretchen Mieszkowski, *The Reputation of Criseyde, 1155–1500*; Fox B, pp. 359–360; and see my *Love and Marriage*, p. 116 n. 32.

[65] There is a clear contradiction here if "lent" means the season of spring, as it still did in the fifteenth century (see the *MED*), whether computed according to the older but still current systems of beginning it in February, or according to the more recent method of beginning it when the sun enters Aries at the vernal equinox—in Henryson's time, around March 11. See my *Chaucer and the Cult of St. Valentine*, pp. 15–18. If "Lent" refers to the forty days of fasting before Easter, the reference to Aries would still indicate that the vernal equinox was past. When one is not speaking of the four formal seasons, it is of course common to divide the year into winter and summer, with winter thought of as lasting quite late. Chaucer on several occasions indicates that it does not give way until May; see, for instance, *Troilus* 2.50–52; 3.351–53, 1062. But earlier in *Troilus* Chaucer states that April was the time of "lusty Veer the prime" (1.155–57). Henryson speaks of the four seasons in the fable of *The Preaching of the Swallow*: Spring (Ver), the secretary of Summer, comes when Winter is away (1706–07).

[66] Some readers have found a contradiction in Henryson's description of the planetary Venus: he says that she appeared ("uprais") and set her face to the west, in opposition to the setting sun (11–14); this should mean that the Evening Star rose in the east. However, Henryson could not have been unaware that this was impossible; anyone with even an elementary knowledge of astronomy knows that Venus is either obscured by the sun or very close to it, and can only appear in the east just before the sun rises or in the west just after the sun sets. Henryson must have intended to say that Venus appeared in the west as the sunset faded. Fox A, p. 87, rejects the suggestion of Charles Elliott in his edition of Henryson's *Poems* (1963) that "in oppositioun" is

Henryson's disjunctive Venuses, one beneficent and the other maleficent, may be the result of the sort of heedlessness that allows medieval poets to use the pagan gods as the spirit moves them without much thought for their feelings as "real persons."[67] We see this sort of thing in the *Knight's Tale* when Chaucer has the Theban suppliants first speak of Fortune in favorable terms: "Lord, to whom Fortune hath yiven / Victorie, and as a conqueror to lyven" (915–16), and a few lines later in unfavorable terms: "Thanked be Fortune and hire false wheel, / That noon estaat assureth to be weel" (925–26).

In Cresseid's dream, then, both beneficent and maleficent gods agree in the person of their speaker Mercury (himself beneficent) to punitive measures against Cresseid, and the bland Cynthia joins Saturn in afflicting her with leprosy. But once the fiction of the planetary gods is dropped, and with it the notion of divine vindictiveness, Cresseid's affliction can be seen from the aspect of neutral cosmology: there comes a time in the allotted span of every living creature when the life-enhancing forces must give way to the forces of decay.

Henryson had an important precedent for his temporary use of interacting planetary gods. In the *Knight's Tale*, such activity takes place only in the second half of the poem, in connection with the tournament between the forces of Palamon and Arcite. Palamon's earlier apostrophe,

> O crueel goddes that governe
> This world with byndyng of youre word eterne
> And writen in the table of atthamaunt
> Youre parlement and youre eterne graunt,   (1303–06)

has no more to do with the subsequent planetary tableau than Henryson's initial picture of Venus does with Cresseid's dream. When Palamon goes on to suggest that Saturn may have played a role in his misfortune, he is of course thinking of the god's planetary characteristics, but he joins him to the nonplanetary Juno and contrasts both with Venus in a nonplanetary context:

> But I moot been in prisoun thurgh Saturne,
> And eek thurgh Juno, jalous and eek wood,
> That hath destroyed wel ny al the blood
> Of Thebes with his waste walles wyde;

not to be taken in the astronomical sense, and Elliott in his second edition (1974) seems to agree with him; for he admits that a planetary meaning of opposition would create an "unnatural astronomy" (a phrase used by Fox) that "may well carry a thematic point." But I find a nonastronomical meaning of opposition to be the only plausible reading. I add that "uprais" in line 12 cannot mean "rose up"—unless, of course, we are to admit that Henryson is deliberately talking nonsense. Unlike Fox, however, I see nothing unnatural about Henryson's reference to the brightness of Venus. Venus can, in fact, be so bright as to cast a faint shadow, and one could certainly see by its light (and by residual sunlight and the light of other stars) that the sky was clear of clouds. I should note my agreement with Fox that the word "esperus" in line 48 makes no sense as a reference to the planet Venus as Evening Star (Hesperus), and that we should accept the Anderson and Kinaston reading of "esperance."

[67] This is not to say that Henryson intended no connections at all between his two references to Venus. For various possibilities, see MacQueen, *Robert Henryson*, pp. 51–54.

And Venus sleeth me on that oother syde,
For jalousie and fere of hym Arcite.   (1328–33)

When Mercury appears to Arcite a bit later, it is not as a planetary deity but as the divine messenger and courier; he is identified as the god who slew Argus (1385–90). Similarly, after the planetary gods have affected the outcome of the tournament and brought about Arcite's death (through the not-yet-planetary Pluto), we hear no more of them. The Jupiter that Arcite appeals to in his dying speech: "And Juppiter so wys my soule gye" (2786), "So Juppiter have of my soule part" (2792), is not the planetary deity but rather God, under which designation Arcite also prays: "for love of God" (2782). When Chaucer says, "Arcite is coold, ther Mars his soule gye" (2815), he is not speaking of the planetary god but of Mars as a psychopomp, like Mercury in *Troilus* (5.1827), and much like Diana in the *Testament of Cresseid*. Theseus sees Arcite's death as brought about not by the planetary gods, but by "the Firste Moever of the cause above" (2987), with whom is to be identified "Juppiter the Kyng, / That is prince and cause of alle thyng" (3035–36), and "God, that al this wyde world hath wroght" (3099).

To recapitulate, Henryson first depicts Cresseid's leprosy in the context of her dream as a god-inflicted torment, but then he translates it into a cosmic accident or fated event in the section formally titled "The Complaint of Cresseid."[68] This narrative disjunction by which he dismisses the gods as participants from his tragedy has not often been noticed, I think, but it needs to be noticed, because it means that Cresseid's affliction is reinterpreted as a natural malady, like that of the other lepers, a disease that one must accept and cope with as such.[69] In this way, and in the further effects her new condition have in her life, the malady is shown to have an important bearing on the reform of her character.

REASONS AND MORALS

We have noted that Cresseid did not point a moral in her address to the ladies of Troy and Greece. One could perhaps hold that it was not necessary, that the lesson to be drawn was obvious, though implicit: namely, that since present good fortune will disappear, one should not trust in blind Prosperity (to use the language of the *Monk's Tale* and Henryson's own *Moral Fables*); rather, one should be careful and try to avoid avoidable falls and not be too downcast by those that cannot be helped. But I think that the remainder of

[68] So Charteris; compare Thynne's rubric: "Here foloweth the complaynt of Creseyde." Mieszkowski, *Reputation*, p. 134, makes a similar analysis, but assigns a different meaning to it: she sees Cresseid in her Complaint as attempting to evade her guilt: "By shifting the blame for her situation from irritable gods to a fickle fortune, and characterizing that fortune as unaffected by human efforts to escape it, she implies that her punishment is morally neutral, a piece of bad luck, the kind of senseless trial that all human beings at times must endure, regardless of how they have lived."

[69] Compare MacQueen, *Robert Henryson*, p. 85, who says that "the law of lipper leid" (line 480) at this stage in the poem is Henryson's general image for the human situation.

the poem justifies us in concluding that Henryson deliberately refrained from having Cresseid think in this way at this point in her development.

Cresseid will come to a deeper, but not complete, understanding of her situation later. Then she will blame herself for being fickle. Now she blames only Fortune. She points out that the sort of sorry circumstances in which she finds herself can and will befall others who do not even advert to the possibility of such transformations in their lives. However, her warning does not seem to be motivated by solicitude for others, but rather, if anything, by a desire to make others miserable before their time. She does not indicate how the awareness of the inevitability of future misfortune can be of any conceivable benefit to those so warned. The advice that usually accompanies such warnings is to repent of wrongdoing. Examples can be seen in Henryson's *Thre Deid Pollis* and *Ressoning Betuix Deth and Man.* But Cresseid is not yet ready to admit that she brought her troubles, or some of them, on herself. Cupid's accusation to this effect did not strike home. And just as her rhetorical admonition to others ladies would be profitless to them, her lament does nothing for herself, not even as a palliative: "Hir cairfull cry / Micht not remeid nor yit hir murning mend" (472–73). It takes another person, a fellow leper, who has suffered the same affliction, to convince her to resign herself to her condition, and to make a virtue of necessity.[70]

It is only the appearance of Troilus that inspires Cresseid to a deeper realization of the nature of her misfortunes. This encounter and its aftermath have been uniformly judged to be the most effective parts of the poem, and they are worthy to stand with the account that Thomas Malory wrote at approximately the same time of the last meeting between Lancelot and Guinevere. But while Malory was reworking an older source,[71] Henryson invented his episode from his own imagination.

Chaucer had Troilus consider and then reject the idea of his visiting the Greek camp in disguise (5.1576–82). Henryson hit upon the notion of arranging a meeting between the undisguised Troilus and a disguised Cresseid near the field of combat.[72] He gives a skillful account in the tradition of Aristotelian psychology[73] of how the sight of Cresseid's ruined visage floods Troi-

[70] Spearing, *Criticism*, p. 188, suggests that Henryson was influenced by Theseus's urging of the same counsel at the end of the *Knight's Tale*, line 3042. Compare Patterson, "Christian and Pagan," p. 710.

[71] Malory used the episode contained in the *Stanzaic Morte Arthur,* which in turn was based on an addition to the French *Mort Artu,* now preserved only in a Vatican manuscript; it is edited by Jean Frappier, "Sur un remaniement de la *Mort Artu* dans un manuscript du XIVe siècle: Le Palatinus latinus 1967," and included as an appendix in his editions of *Mort Artu,* the first, pp. 239–40, and the second, pp. 264–66. The episode seems not to have been in Malory's copy of the *Mort Artu.*

[72] Henryson's geography is confused and is best ignored. We recall that Calchas's home and temple are far out of town, a distance immediately defined as a mile or two, and that the leper hospital is first said to be at the town's end, while in the next stanza it turns out to be in a village a half mile away. If the lepers do their begging in the vicinity of the hospital, and the Trojans encounter them on their way back to Troy, Calchas's establishment must be still further along the road to Troy. Henryson does not explain how Troilus would have been able to erect a marble tomb and place an inscription over Cresseid's grave.

[73] See Marshall W. Stearns, *Robert Henryson,* pp. 97–105; Fox A, pp. 123–24 (= Fox B, pp. 377–78).

lus with the memory of her beauty and renews his sorrow. Henryson is at fault
for not saying why Cresseid did not recognize Troilus, as another leper does,
even though "upon him scho kest up baith her ene" (498); he could easily
have given a reason, if he had thought of doing so—by saying, for instance,
that in her case her formerly crystalline eyes were now "mingit with blude"
(337), and their vision impaired.[74] Such an explanation would have reinforced
the impact of what follows. When Cresseid learns who it is who "hes done to
us so greit humanitie" (534), the eyes of her understanding are opened, as it
were, and she is able to acknowledge for the first time the true nature of her
downfall.

E. M. W. Tillyard notes that since the *Testament of Cresseid* is a tragedy in
the medieval sense (he should say, one of the medieval senses, or in the Chaucerian sense), Henryson cannot omit the aspect of prosperity, even though he
deals primarily with the subsequent adversity. He finds Henryson's means
simple and brilliantly effective, in having Cresseid recall her old life and
court in her formal Complaint.[75] Tillyard refers only to the two stanzas beginning "Quhaire is . . . ?" (416–33), though similar recollections are to be
found in the previous and following stanzas as well. But Cresseid's Complaint
does not contain her only summoning up of former prosperity, as we shall
see; and her selective memory here completely avoids any reference to what
must have been, or what should have been, her greatest source of happiness,
namely, her condition as Troilus's beloved. Instead, she pictures herself only
as a carefree and thoughtless enjoyer of good food, good clothes, good
weather, and the various pleasures of good society. Her only mention of Troilus thus far in the poem came in her angry rebuke to the gods of love, where,
though she called him noble, she linked him with Diomeid in saying that she
was "clene excludit" from them both (132–33). In a way, she is justified in
saying this, since she was removed from Troy and Troilus against her will;
but in the context she would seem to be implying that it was Troilus who had
given up on her and not the other way round.

At the end of the poem her recollection of former happiness is more complete. Just as the sight of her in her diseased state calls up in Troilus the painful
realities of the past, Troilus's presence and generous conduct, followed by
the realization of who he is, does the same for her. In her lament over her falseness, she refers to her prosperity (548), meaning by it exactly what she meant
by the things she listed in her Complaint as lost, but now at last she recognizes
that she wrongly valued them over Troilus's love, loyalty, gentleness, fidelity,
and other good and rare qualities.

Let us consider the nature of her relationship with Troilus. It is quite clear
that when Diomeid "received" Cresseid he married her, since he divorces
her. He gives her a *libellus repudii*, the biblical term for the document by
which a man according to the Mosaic Law could put away his wife. Henryson
has likened this process, which Jesus abrogated in the Gospels,[76] to the

---

[74] Fox B, pp. 378–79, adds to his earlier edition a discussion of Henryson's failure to account
for Cresseid's lack of recognition.

[75] E. M. W. Tillyard, "Henryson: *The Testament of Cresseid* (1470?)," pp. 10–11.

[76] Matthew 5.31–32: "Dictum est autem, 'Quicumque dimiserit uxorem suam det illi libellum
repudii.' Ego autem dico vobis quia omnis qui dimiserit uxorem suam, excepta fornicationis

pagan practice of divorce. I have shown elsewhere that Chaucer described the union of Troilus and Criseyde in their first night together at Pandarus's house in terms suggestive of a valid and binding marriage.[77] If it is true that Henryson was a canon lawyer[78]—his fable of *The Sheep and the Dog* shows an easy familiarity with canonistic literature and procedure[79]—he would have been especially alert to the legal implications of the situation. He may, that is, have concluded that Troilus was married to Criseyde, and that this is how he was able not only to "keep continence" for love of her, as Cresseid says, but also to be honest and chaste in his conduct (554–55). This conclusion would be certain if Henryson intended Cresseid to speak of the ruby ring that she returns to Troilus as the one that he sent to her "in dowry" (583), as the Thynne and Anderson texts read, but it is more problematic if the correct reading is that given by Charteris, "in drowrie." However, "drowry," which properly in this context should mean only "love-token," had come to mean "dowry" before the end of the fifteenth century.[80] But if Henryson had in mind the exchange of rings that occurred in Chaucer's story during the lovers' first night together, he changed the circumstances of the account, for he has Cresseid say that Troilus "sent" the ring to her. If he was thinking in matrimonial terms, he may have meant "drowrie" to signify the "morning-gift" made by the husband to the wife on the morning after the consummation

causa, facit eam mechari, et qui dimissam duxerit adulterat" ("And it hath been said, 'Whosoever shall put away his wife, let him give her a bill of divorce.' But I say to you that whosoever shall put away his wife, excepting for the cause of fornication, maketh her to commit adultery, and he that shall marry her that is put away committeth adultery"). Cf. Mark 10.4: "Moses permisit libellum repudii scribere et dimittere."

[77] See above, p. 144 n. 106.

[78] A Magister Robertus Henrisone, incorporated in Glasgow University in 1462, was said to be a licentiate in arts and a bachelor in decrees (that is, a bachelor of canon law). This record was first cited by David Laing in 1865, who, however, also noted that there were records of many Henrysons (and specifically Robert Henrysons) of that time and place. See Wood's edition, p. xiii, and Fox B, pp. xiii–xv.

[79] Particularly noteworthy is the procedure followed when the Sheep refuses Judge Wolf as suspect. In accord with standard practice in an ecclesiastical court, which was based both on canon law and Roman civil law, the judge has the parties each choose an arbiter. The great authority on judicial procedure was the "Speculator," William Durant, Bishop of Mende (late thirteenth century). See his *Speculum judiciale*, 1:157: lib. l, partic. l, *De recusatione* par. 4 no. 4: "Proposita autem causa suspicionis, eligentur a partibus arbitri." There is no appeal from the sentence of arbiters; see Ibid., 1:107: *De arbitro et arbitratore* par. 4: "Item a sententia arbitri non appellatur." According to lines 1214–15, the arbiters consult "mony decretalis off the law, / And glosis als," which probably refers to canon law, in contrast to the civil law of the next lines: "Of civile mony volum they revolve, / The codies and digestis new and ald." Mary E. Rowlands, "Robert Henryson and the Scottish Courts of Law," p. 224, notes that by canon law "another judge should have been appointed to replace the wolf regardless of the arbiters' decision, because the judge was likely to be angered by the rejection and so make an unjust judgment." See Fox B's notes, pp. 251–62, for more canonical references. Craig McDonald, "The Perversion of Law in Robert Henryson's Fable of *The Fox, the Wolf, and the Husbandman*," discusses the use of arbitration from records of the secular courts, including those of Drumferline. He notes that arbitration was commonly used in both ecclesiastical and secular courts in fifteenth-century Scotland, citing James J. Robertson, "The Development of the Law," p. 145.

[80] See the *Dictionary of the Older Scottish Tongue*, citing examples from 1497, 1500, 1503, 1513, etc.

of the marriage.[81] In the *Last Epistle*, Fowler puts the gift of the ring back into its Chaucerian setting, and seems to treat it as a matrimonial pledge:

> Except a ringe noght ells I have,
>   Which thou me gave that night
> That joyned was our hartes in one,
>   And faythe to others plight.[82]   (293–96)

If Henryson thought of Cresseid as married to both Troilus and Diomeid, he may also have been thinking of what Deuteronomy has to say of a woman who has received two libels of repudiation:

> If a man take a wife, and have her, and she find not favor in his eyes, for some uncleanness, he shall write a bill of divorce, and shall give it in her hand, and send her out of his house. And when she is departed, and marrieth another husband, and he also hateth her, and hath given her a bill of divorce, and hath sent her out of his house, or is dead, the former husband cannot take her again to wife, because she is defiled and is become abominable before the Lord. (Deut. 24.1–4)

In the case of Troilus and Cresseid, it was of course Cresseid and not Troilus who initiated the break, and her going to another husband forced him to write her off for unfaithfulness; but the final effect would be for all practical purposes the same. There seems to have been no question of a possible reconciliation with Troilus after she was dismissed by Diomeid. We should note also that Henryson shows Cresseid at the most as twice, not thrice, married, since he never refers to the fact that she is a widow in Chaucer's poem. The same will be true of Shakespeare.

But whether or not Henryson is to be taken as implying a marriage bond between Troilus and Cresseid, it is clear that the faith and love which Cresseid promised to Troilus (551) was meant to endure till death. She sees herself not as breaking her promise under great duress, but rather as having been frivolous and fickle when she made it and as having had a lecherous nature in contrast to Troilus's chastity.

We might expect her now to revise her previous apostrophe to fair ladies in the light of her new realization and confession, and warn them to avoid false-

---

[81] In the 1503 entry mentioned in the previous note, it may be that drowry is meant to be the equivalent of morning gift: James IV "confirmit ... the qwenis drowry and morwyngift."

[82] In an earlier account, the *Laud Troy Book*, Brixaida's decision to give up Troilus for Diomede is expressed, in part, thus:

> Sche wiste wel in hir thoght
> Off Troyle scholde sche nevere have noght;
> Sche hoped nevere of him mariage;
> Sche chaunged her wil and corage.   (13553–56)

Mieszkowski, *Reputation*, p. 114, interprets her to mean that she "cannot expect marriage from her men." But it seems to me that one cannot go beyond the obvious meaning expressed by the editor, Ernst Wülfing, that she is simply "giving up the hope of ever being able to marry Troilus." Breisaid says something similar in the *Gest Hystoriale of the Destruction of Troy*: "Ho trust never with Troiell, terme of hir lyve, / To mell with in mariage, ne more of hir lust" (9952–53).

ness in love if they do not want to share her fate.[83] It looks as if this may be
what she is doing when she begins, "Lovers, be war and tak gude heid" (561).
But instead she warns true lovers like Troilus to beware of false lovers like
her. She goes on to say that she was betrayed by the same sort of falseness in
another (that is, Diomeid) that caused her to betray Troilus,[84] though she
does not now blame Diomeid, much less the gods, or other women, but only
herself: "Nane but my self as now I will accuse" (574).

She offers hardly more hope in this apostrophe than she did in her previous
one. If one loves another faithfully and hopes for the like fidelity in return,
she says, one is likely to be disappointed. She implies that there are fewer
women than men who are worthy of trust, for she says, "Quha findis treuth,
lat him his lady ruse" (573), that is, if a faithful man finds reciprocal fidelity
in a lady, let him praise her.

It is only after Cresseid is dead that we are presented with the expected
moral, which Cresseid in her finally incurable short-sightedness and pessimism was not prepared to give, and it must be supplied by Henryson himself:

> Now, worthie wemen, in this ballet schort,
> Maid for your worschip and instructioun,
> Of cheritie, I monische and exhort,
> Ming not your lufe with fals deceptioun.
> Beir in your mynd this sore conclusioun
> Of fair Cresseid, as I have said befoir.
> Sen scho is deid, I speik of hir no moir.   (610–16)

A surprising number of critics ignore Henryson's conclusion, perhaps
classing it with the lame and often irrelevant morals that conclude his fables;
and many others find it ironic or excessively harsh.[85] But these reactions are,
I believe, as seriously mistaken as the view of many readers that Henryson
(or his narrator) is basically harsh in his attitude towards Cresseid.[86] Hyder

---

[83] McKenna, "Henryson's 'Tragedie,'" p. 30, says, "Implicit in her warning to other women at
the end of the poem is the belief that a reorientation of human character is possible, that the
tragic figure potentially and paradoxically has the god-like power to help prevent tragedies." I
find such a message not at all in Cresseid, but only in Henryson's concluding stanza, whereas
McKenna finds both Troilus and Henryson as Narrator more negative than Cresseid, less able to
recognize the possibility of reform—even when the Narrator warns the women of his audience
against Cresseid's kind of behavior, thereby assuming their ability to improve their character.

[84] See my translations of lines 568–72, above, n. 39.

[85] An exception is Jane Adamson, "Henryson's *Testament of Cresseid:* 'Fyre' and 'Cauld,'" pp.
59–60, who has high praise for Henryson's moral. See also Twycross-Martin, "Moral Pattern,"
pp. 32–33, 49, who notes that Henryson's moral ("Be faithful") differs from Chaucer's ("Avoid
love").

[86] For instance, Larry Sklute, "Phoebus Descending: Rhetoric and Moral Vision in Henryson's *Testament of Cresseid*," finds in Henryson a "dark moral vision . . . as stern as it is
orthodox, . . . as harsh as it is pessimistic," which is disguised by "the sympathy manifested on
the rhetorical surface" of the poem (pp. 190, 197), whereas Kevin J. Harty, "Cresseid and Her
Narrator: A Reading of Robert Henryson's *Testament of Cresseid*," says that "the poem's narrator, not its author, is the stern moralist" (p. 753). For other views, see Louise O. Fradenburg,
"Henryson Scholarship: The Recent Decades," pp. 79–82. Denton Fox, "The Coherence of Henryson's Work," pp. 275–81, says that Henryson is not a stern moralist, but he presents in his

Rollins is closer to the truth in holding that Henryson presents "the same sympathetic comprehension of the character of Creseyde that had made Chaucer pity her."[87]

The point Henryson makes in the last stanza is precisely the lesson that is called for. He is sincere in saying that he speaks out of charity, and he has a more benign view of women than Cresseid does. She believes that the world is divided into true women and false women, and that the former are a pitifully small minority. Henryson on the contrary believes, by implication, that all women are capable of worthiness if only they will take instruction and heed, by the example of such as Cresseid, the evils of falseness and deceit. He also indicates that some formerly worthy women, or potentially worthy women, have fallen through their own fault, and not because of their debased nature. He undoubtedly means to say that Cresseid herself was one of these, in spite of her dying opinion to the contrary, though he does not explicitly modify her self-assessment.

One might think it more gracious if Henryson had included men as well as women in his final admonition, without necessarily going so far as Chaucer did when he stated (a bit playfully but perhaps also sincerely) that men have in fact more often proved to be unfaithful than women. We have, after all, seen the instance of Diomeid. But Diomeid has not been prominent in the poem, and by the time Henryson comes to round off the tragedy, his bad example has been completely overshadowed by the light of Troilus's sterling character. Furthermore, the address to "worthie wemen" echoes Troilus's epitaph for Cresseid, which begins, "Lo, fair ladyis" (607).

Cresseid's death is presented rather abruptly, without much motivation or explanation. Her distress on learning of Troilus's identity is not made to seem different in kind from her nonfatal reaction to finding herself in a leper colony. We are left to assume that she feels death coming on when she takes paper and presumably writes out her testament. In describing how she makes her will, Henryson performs a disjunctive shift opposite to that which we observed in the opening stanza of Chaucer's *Troilus*, for by the time she finishes the short list of her bequests, she no longer seems to be writing it. One result is that it is not clear whether her address to Diomeid is part of the testament.[88] Henryson ends her statement by saying, "And with

three major poems "a world in which there is very little justice, and a world in which apparently trivial faults can bring the harshest of punishments" (p. 280). More recently, Jill Mann, "The Planetary Gods in Chaucer and Henryson," pp. 99–100, finds Henryson more compassionate towards Cresseid than Chaucer is towards Criseyde.

[87] Hyder E. Rollins, "The Troilus-Cressida Story from Chaucer to Shakespeare," p. 396. Mieszkowski, *Reputation*, p. 75, rightly faults Rollins for overlooking some earlier harsh treatments of Criseyde; but it remains doubtful that many of these treatments had come to Henryson's attention. Mieszkowski makes a case only for Lydgate's *Troy Book* (p. 136), but she holds that Criseyde's reputation for fickleness was proverbial—even in Chaucer's time.

[88] Fox A, p. 48 n. 1, assumes that it is not, no doubt relying on line 584 ("Thus I conclude schortlie and mak ane end"), which precedes the bequest of her spirit to Diana. Tillyard, "Henryson's *Testament*," p. 18, seems to make the same assumption when he says, "The thought that Diomede, who forsook her, still has the brooch and belt which Troilus, who was true, gave her and that she cannot restore them is too cruel and she dies." But if the lines are to be taken as part of her will, then she must be confirming Diomeid's possession of what she earlier, to her shame, bestowed on him.

that word scho swelt" (590). Troilus does not read but only hears of her legacy.

Henryson does not describe Cresseid's death, but only uses the word "swelt," which is the same expression he then applies to Troilus's reaction (599). The news of her death does not prove fatal to Troilus, any more than did his earlier recollection of her, though then, we were told, his sorrow was so great that "he was reddie to expyre" (515). Another narrative break can be seen in the disparity between Cresseid's material resources at the point of death and her lack of such goods both before and after she makes her testament. In keeping with the usual phraseology of wills, Cresseid makes provision for defraying the expenses of her burial:

> My cop and clapper and myne ornament
> And all my gold the lipper folk sall have,
> Quhen I am deid, to burie me in grave.   (579–81)

Henryson has us assume for the moment that she is still in possession of personal jewelry.[89] But this assumption immediately dissolves: when she dies, she clearly possesses only her ruby ring, and she is buried without expense: "And sone ane lipper man tuik of the ring, /Syne buryit her withouttin tarying" (593–94), and Troilus hears "how scho endit in sic povertie" (598).

When the leper comes to Troilus with news of Cresseid, his first thought is to remember the wrong that she did to him: he bursts out, "I can no moir, / Scho was untrew, and wo is me thairfoir" (601–02). He uncharacteristically blames Cresseid here, and perhaps we are meant to think that the sight of the ruby ring causes a momentary lapse in his generous spirit. In his earlier encounter with her, his sorrow seemed to be directed more towards her than towards himself, for it was inspired by his love for her: "Ane spark of lufe than till his hart culd spring" (512). He admitted no accusation against her to his thoughts, let alone to his words, and did nothing that could compromise her reputation, with the ironic result that Cresseid herself failed to recognize him: "And nevertheles not ane ane uther knew" (518). He was first drawn to the lepers, in keeping with his charitable nature, by "pietie" (496). When the sight of Cresseid renewed his old love for her, he gave alms, as he had already intended to do, but now more abundantly and for an additional motive:

> For knichtlie pietie, and memoriall
> Of fair Cresseid, ane gyrdill can he tak,
> Ane purs of gold, and mony gay jowell,
> And in the skirt of Cresseid doun can swak;
> Than raid away and not ane word he spak.   (519–23)

---

[89] Tillyard, "Henryson's *Testament*," p. 17, construes the meaning of the lines thus: "In sincere pity and unselfishness she bequeaths the gold Troilus gave her to the lepers." But if Henryson had in mind only Troilus's alms (which I think unlikely), he would logically have to mean only Cresseid's share of them, for the lepers had already seen to "the equall distributioun / Of the almous" (527–28), which Cresseid acknowledges when she asks who it is who "hes done to us so greit humanitie" (534).

His intention of honoring the memory of Cresseid remained entirely private. In so acting, he verified the characteristic recalled by Cresseid: he was "of all wemen protectour and defence" (556). He not only protected women physically, but also "helpit thair opinioun" (557), for love of Cresseid. If he did not help Cresseid's opinion after she betrayed him, at least he was careful to do nothing to injure it. He may have wavered when he received her dying bequest, though perhaps we are to understand that his exclamation over her falseness was heard by no one but himself. The messenger who brought the ring was in any case privy to Troilus's relationship with Cresseid, as was the whole leper community; for if they did not "hear" her testament, they did hear her preliminary confession.

Henryson shows Troilus as regaining his habitual control over himself by adding a report: "sum said" (603). Unlike in the case of the earlier report of Cresseid's going into the court common, here there can be no question about the narrator's not believing the report: it is the truth of what happened. It presents Troilus as giving in once more to the desire to memorialize Cresseid. This time, however, it is to be a public memorial, expressed in words, words not spoken but engraved in gold:

> Lo, fair ladyis, Cresseid of Troy the toun,
> Sumtyme countit the flour of womanheid,
> Under this stane, lait lipper, lyis deid.   (607–09)

The epitaph is characterized as a "ressoun" (606), that is, not simply a statement but an explanation; Cresseid is identified, her former estate is specified, and her subsequent malady, which can be inferred to be the cause of her death, is named.

When Cresseid asked her father to convey her to the leprosarium secretly to prevent her identity from being revealed, she would not have thought it a help to her reputation to have her disease known. But she soon changed her mind, if we can judge from her Complaint, for she addressed fair ladies in almost the same terms as the epitaph. She pointed out the contrast between her former condition, when she "was callit of eirdlye wichtis flour" (435), and her present misery. She had hoped to be the flower of love in Troy, and, according to Cupid, she was; and for Troilus she was "sumtyme his awin darling" (504). Troilus chooses his expression carefully: she was sometime counted the flower of womanhood. This was her reputation not only in the eyes of the world, but also in the estimation of Troilus and of Cresseid herself. Cresseid's opinion of what constituted the highest attributes of womanhood was superficial, and therefore she was right in her judgment: she was the flower of womanhood, in her limited understanding of the words. Troilus had a more profound notion of womanly perfection, and was sadly disappointed in thinking that it was verified in Cresseid. But the words of the epitaph do nothing to betray this disappointment. A passerby could assume not only that she was at one time reputed to be the flower of womanhood, but also that her reputation was and still is justified: that even now she is justly counted as having been an exemplar of perfect womanhood. Troilus does not reveal her betrayal of him or her shame at having been betrayed by Diomeid.

The "reason" of the epitaph is also a message to fair ladies. But like Cresseid in her Complaint, Troilus draws no useful moral. Cresseid failed to come up with a lesson because she was as yet incapable of it; Troilus does not spell one out because he is too generous, and does not wish to offend her memory in any way. Henryson, therefore, with fine tact, takes the task upon himself.

Henryson chose not to imitate Chaucer in interjecting a Christian overview at the end of his Trojan tragedy, but it could be said that in this decision he was following Chaucer's example in the *Knight's Tale*. Even in the *Troilus*, Chaucer does not bring Christian revelation to bear on the story itself. When Troilus's spirit rises to the eighth sphere, he receives no greater understanding of the divine economy than he could have worked out for himself by means of a pre-Christian natural theology, and it is still up to Mercury to assign him his place in the afterlife.

Perhaps Tillyard is right in saying that Cresseid's dedication of her spirit to Diana stands for her aspiration to the monastic life,[90] which would correspond to the kind of religious life that Chaucer first shows Criseyde as leaning towards in her widowhood. Tillyard may also be right in supposing that Cresseid's soul is to be thought of as going to purgatory, even though strictly speaking purgatory did not exist as such before Christ harrowed hell and opened the gates of heaven.[91] Other readers, who like Tillyard regard Diana primarily in her role as goddess of chastity, see Cresseid's purification as complete,[92] so that her joining Diana in the afterlife would be the equivalent of going to heaven rather than going to purgatory.[93]

[90]   Tillyard, "Henryson's *Testament*," pp. 17–18.

[91]   It is likely that Henryson would not be thinking so precisely here, and a similar lack of precision about the afterworld can be seen in his *Orpheus and Eurydice*. Orpheus finds in hell not only Herod and Pilate, but also many popes and cardinals, even though Orpheus presumably lived in pre-Christian times. Another nonrealistic presentation of the afterlife can be seen in *The Thre Deid Pollis*: the skulls await the decree of God on their souls at Doomsday, whereas according to standard medieval theology, souls are judged and assigned their fate at death. But compare the similarly primitive notion of sleeping in hope of the resurrection, or of the coming of Christ, in the lives of St. Stephen (Caxton, *Golden Legend* 2:157), St. Germain (3:208 and 4:147), and the Seven Holy Sleepers (4:126). I should note that in the *Fables*, Henryson has a dream of Aesop, a pre-Christian Roman and student of civil law who is now in heaven (lines 1373–74). Tim William Machan, "Robert Henryson and Father Aesop: Authority in the *Moral Fables*," p. 206, assumes that Henryson has converted him to a Christian; but this conclusion is not necessary.

[92]   For example, Del Chessel, "In the Dark Time: Henryson's *Testament of Cresseid*."

[93]   This is how Cresseid sees the matter, according to Fox A (p. 49), and Fox agrees with her (p. 56). Fox asserts that Henryson is taking for granted "an unquestioned belief in the culpability of sexual love" in his audience (p. 58). But even if one qualifies Fox's phrase to avoid heresy (sexual love was held to be good in itself, but bad when abused), it presupposes a monolithic rigorism among orthodox Christians in the Middle Ages. For a wide range of medieval views, see *Love and Marriage*, Index, p. 355, s.v. "sexual delight." A similarly harsh view is attributed to Henryson by C. David Benson, "Troilus and Cresseid in Henryson's *Testament*"; he agrees with Fox's estimate of Cresseid's moral improvement (while denying high moral standing to Troilus), but says she falls short of Christian knowledge and salvation. However, if one insists on the point that she is not saved in Christian terms (and therefore real terms), one must conclude that she goes to hell and stays there. But though it was perhaps the majority view in the Middle Ages that all pagans were damned because of their lack of Christian knowledge, we have seen that there was a strain of belief that salvation could be attained without such knowledge by virtuous non-Christians (above, p. 195).

But it may be that Henryson was thinking of Diana not so much as goddess of chastity (he does not refer to this function, nor to her role as moon-goddess), but as the huntress-goddess of the wilderness, "quhair scho dwellis" and where Cresseid will walk with her, "in waist woddis and wellis" (587–588). According to Boccaccio's *Genealogy of the Gentile Gods*, which Henryson may have used for his description of the planets,[94] Diana was called the goddess of mountains and woods, had a carriage drawn by stags, enjoyed the society and services of nymphs, and was considered to be the protector of paths.[95] Belief in Diana as a deity honored by women was denounced in the Carolingian capitulary *Episcopi eorumque*, which Gratian included as a canon in his *Decree*; and by its very appearance there it was put on prominent display in the Middle Ages.[96] If the identification of Henryson as a canonist is accurate, it is likely that he would have been familiar with the passage. But whatever specific connotations of Diana he had in mind, it is obvious that he does not have Cresseid envisage a particularly happy afterlife for herself. It is not the "pleyn felicite" that Chaucer's Troilus perceives and no doubt looks forward to at the end (5.1818), but rather a life of sad mourning like that set forth in the testament that Chaucer gives to Criseyde:

> Myn herte and ek the woful goost therinne
> Byquethe I with your spirit to compleyne
> Eternaly, for they shal nevere twynne.
> For though in erthe ytwynned be we tweyne,
> Yet in the Feld of Pite, out of peyne,
> That highte Elisos, shal we ben yfeere,
> As Orpheus with Erudice, his fere.   (*Troilus* 4.785–91)

Chaucer here makes reference, rare in the Middle Ages, to the "happy ending" of Ovid's story of Orpheus and Eurydice in the *Metamorphoses*, where Ovid shows them as finally reunited forever in the underworld; but in Crisyede's view, though there is no physical torment in the Elysian Fields, neither is there joy; there will, however, at least be the consolation of being with Troilus. She will later lose the right even to this hope, and it is perhaps a realization of this sort that Henryson's Cresseid reflects in her testament, something like the sense of permanent defilement attached to the twice-repudiated wife in Deuteronomy.

---

[94] So MacQueen, *Robert Henryson*, pp. 47–49; compare Fox B, pp. 357–58.

[95] Boccaccio, *Genealogia deorum gentilium* 5.2.

[96] Gratian, *Decretum* 2.26.5.12 (cols. 1030–31): "Episcopi eorumque ministri omnibus viribus elaborare studeant," etc. The relevant portion says that some women believe that they and an innumerable multitude of women ride with Diana, goddess of the pagans, at night on certain beasts, and obey her and attend her services ("Credunt se . . . cum Diana, nocturnis horis, dea paganorum, vel cum Herodiade, et innumera multitudine mulierum equitare super quasdam bestias, et multa terrarum spatia intempeste noctis silentio pertransire, ejusque jussionibus obedire velut domine, et certis noctibus evocari ad ejus servitium"). For a translation of the whole canon, see my *Devil, Demonology, and Witchcraft*, pp. 50–52 (rev. ed., pp. 53–54). The canon says that such women are the victims of diabolically inspired dreams, and what they think happens in the flesh really happens only in the spirit (that is, in their minds). We have here, then, another category of dreams, the "pseudo-action dream."

At the end of the *Troilus*, Chaucer chooses to lay a large share of the blame for the events of his tragedy on the religious rites and beliefs of paganism. But his ultimate message to would-be lovers entails a dour view not only of the pagan world but also of the world under the Christian dispensation: he advises his young readers to love only Christ, for He will not betray them. If betrayal by human lovers is not precisely inevitable in every instance, he implies that it is a painful possibility or likelihood for each of them. Earlier still, his advice is even starker, in his address to women: "Beth war of men, and herkneth what I seye!" (5.1785). This admonition corresponds to Cresseid's advice to men to beware of women, whereas Henryson's final advice is for women to beware of themselves. He has hope for them, if they will only keep their virtue. Chaucer professes to have more faith in female virtue than male, in general, but he is not at all hopeful for a winning combination of lovers, with fidelity on the part of both the man and the woman.

In sum, contrary to what many readers think who give primary emphasis to the nature and role of the planetary gods in the *Testament of Cresseid,* I find Henryson optimistic at the end of his poem, certainly more optimistic than Chaucer at the end of *Troilus*; but I also find that Henryson makes his Cresseid a lesser woman than Chaucer's Criseyde. I mentioned that Henryson had the advantage of relying on his readers' familiarity with Chaucer's version of the story. But, whether intentionally or not, he effectively distracts us from remembering the strong points of Criseyde's character and focusses on her weaknesses. We are not allowed to recall the obvious sincerity of Criseyde's love for Troilus or the remorse she suffers in our last view of her in the Greek camp. At the most we are likely to recall only the Criseyde reported to us in Chaucer's poem as we accompany Troilus through his last agonies, the Criseyde as seen through her feeble letters, through Troilus's dream of her kissing the boar, and through the evidence of her gifts to Diomede. But even these images, I think, are relegated to a barely conscious drawing room of memory. The whole context of Criseyde's tragedy in Chaucer's poem is subverted in the sequel. There is nothing in Henryson's poem to remind us of what really happened to her: that she was removed from Troy and from Troilus much against her will and to her great distress, that her scheme for returning was revealed to be hopelessly unworkable, that she despaired of ever being reunited with Troilus, and that only then did she give in, guilt-ridden and with great reluctance, to Diomede's suit. The alternative to throwing in with Diomede was to live alone, faithful but forever forlorn, with her father Calkas. There is not a hint of this situation or this alternative in the *Testament of Cresseid*; rather, the pervasive underlying assumption is that Cresseid of her free fickle will, without the "force and fear sufficient to sway a constant man or woman" that canonists recognized as invalidating matrimonial consent,[97] or excusing wrongful actions, abandoned Troilus and was received by Diomeid; and that she deliberately violated her promise to return to Troy.

---

[97] R. H. Helmholz, *Marriage Litigation in Medieval England*, pp. 90–94, 178, 220–28. Henry VIII used a variant of this argument to have his marriage to Anne of Cleves annulled; see my *Matrimonial Trials of Henry VIII*, pp. 272, 280; cf. 14 n. 15.

Henryson attempted to accomplish this feat, of changing Criseyde's character to that of Cresseid, primarily through the use of two sensationalistic diversionary tactics: first, the vague accusation that she turned to a life of promiscuity, and second the account of her petulant complaint against the gods and their punishing her with leprosy. As noted above, I think it likely that he wished to deny the promiscuity and also likely that he meant the leprosy ultimately to be regarded not as a divine punishment but as a natural misfortune.

If this is a fair account of Henryson's intentions and strategy, we must conclude that his plan largely backfired; that is, most of his readers have given too much, or the wrong kind of, weight to the promiscuity and blasphemy episodes, and have emerged with a distorted view of Cresseid. Hyder Rollins's judgment on Henryson's handling of Chaucer's Criseyde, that he "forever damned her as a loose woman,"[98] has turned out not to be true, since readers of *Troilus and Criseyde* do not usually filter their understanding of the earlier tragedy through their knowledge of the sequel; but it has proved true, for the most part, of his own Cresseid. For Rollins himself, along with most other readers, have understood Henryson as saying that Cresseid became sexually common, and many consider her punishment by the gods to be at least partially based on her licentious conduct.

If we accept Cresseid as not promiscuous but only shamed, and as not punished by God but only overwhelmed by the natural forces of mutability embodied in the planets and the figure of Fortune, we should accept her as no better and no worse than she appears in her Complaint: that is, as having been an essentially shallow woman from the beginning, one who can only be brought to a deeper realization of her limitations and failings by Troilus's kindness to her in her leprous condition. She then understands that her fall from prosperity did not begin with her expulsion from Diomeid, but with her failure to comprehend that Troilus's love for her comprised her true prosperity, and that she herself caused her first fall, a fall which led to all her other misfortunes. However, even at the end she is not able to see that she could have prevented her loss of Troilus; but her story, her tragedy, is told to teach this lesson to others.

Henryson's *Testament of Cresseid* is a Chaucerian tragedy because it is inspired by Chaucer's tragedy, *Troilus and Criseyde*. It also conforms to Chaucer's understanding of tragedy as explained in the *Boece* and *Monk's Tale*. It is a poem about a person of high standing who began in prosperity and ended in misery from which there was no recovery; it bewails this state of affairs, and it draws suitable lessons of mutability and caution. These elements are basically confirmed in McKenna's empirical assessment of Henrysonian tragic theory, which we can accept as a kind of "independent audit" to check against the above account. We have already noted that he sees the *Testament* as conforming to the Chaucerian fall from prosperity to adversity. The final self-awareness and acceptance of responsibility that he finds in Cresseid functions as part of the lamentation evoked by her fall, as do the comments of the narrator, who serves as a kind of choric figure: "He is emotionally torn by the complex of feelings evoked by her story, and he

---

[98] Rollins, "Troilus-Cressida Story," p. 397.

attempts to convey these emotions to his audience." Furthermore, "the Narrator-as-chorus specifically warns the women of his audience against such behavior as has brought Cresseid to her final disposition, cautioning them to shrink from these things too" (I do not find, as he does, a similar message in Cresseid's final warning, an implicit "belief that a reorientation of human character is possible"). He sees Henryson himself as more pessimistic than the Narrator, as possessing a tragic vision existing outside the strictly moral realm: "a pessimism in which categories of right and wrong, good and evil, do not always apply."[99] We can agree with this, and assimililate it to Chaucer's lesson that when Fortune flees, she flees, whether deserts are just or unjust. Other elements in McKenna's analysis correspond to the irreversibility of the final wretchedness: Cresseid's isolation from society and her estrangement from the gods. A final element, "the tragic figure's essential criminality,"[100] is true enough of Cresseid, but we should be cautious about saying that it is a necessary part of Henryson's notion of tragedy in general. Doubtless he would recognize the possibility of a tragic protagonist who was not guilty of violating any codes of conduct, and presumably he found such a tragedy in Chaucer's *Troilus and Criseyde*.

I have been at pains to point out the various verbal, thematic, and narrative disjunctions to be found in Henryson's poem, and I have generally given him the benefit of the doubt by placing them in a medieval tradition, or at least practice, of such abrupt changes of course. Undoubtedly, however, some of these reversals, shifts, or startings and stoppings of themes and motifs were not deliberate but were the result of inadvertance or lack of artistic control on Henryson's part. But even these should not be judged with undue harshness. Medieval authors were more tolerant of contradictions than most modern readers (though it is worth noting that a good many of the disjunctions noted above have either not been noticed or have not been "resented" by twentieth-century critics who have written on the poem). Sometimes in the Middle Ages there was a conscious effort to resolve discrepancies by eliminating opposing views, or by explaining them away, as Gratian did in his *Decree*, which he titled *Concordance of Discordant Canons*, or as the scholastics did in their *sic et non* method, in which they prefaced their discussions of a problem with pros and cons, and concluded their middle-ground solutions with responses to objections and qualifications of alternative solutions.[101] But at other times authors simply allowed one pole to replace its opposite, or diverted attention from one theme to a parallel or even contrary theme, without justifying or qualifying the result. They were used to such contrary side-by-side effects in the Pentateuch, where modern documentary critics have discerned the stitching together of different sources, notably the Jahwist, Elohist, and Priestly. One is not to look at such a work and all its parts simultaneously, from the single point in time of a Boethian eternity, but rather as it progresses

---

[99] McKenna, "Henryson's 'Tragedie,'" pp. 30–31.

[100] Ibid., pp. 31–33.

[101] See George Makdisi, "The Scholastic Method in Medieval Education: An Inquiry into Its Origins in Law and Theology"; S. T. Knight, "Some Aspects of Structure in Medieval Literature," p. 10.

from beginning to end.[102] If it works in this way, it must be judged a success, though sometimes only a qualified success.

Henryson's *Testament* is a case in point. It cannot always be analyzed in accord with postmedieval ideals of unity and coherence. For instance, Venus in the beginning is not to be completely harmonized with Venus in the middle; she is instead to be taken as she comes. We must remember particularly what Chaucer's Pandarus points out to Criseyde, that the end is every tale's strength (*Troilus* 2.260), and this must be especially true for the genre of tragedy, as Chaucer defined it for succeeding generations: its primary focus is on the conclusion in adversity. The *Testament of Cresseid* has a strong ending, which justifies much of what went before, and which must dispel any doubt about whether Henryson's initial intention of telling a tragedy was transmuted to some other intention along the way. Moreover, if one reads the work as Henryson intended it (in the way I have argued for above), one can hardly fail to be moved to compassion by his account of the fallen Cresseid. Even if some of his disjunctions are to be seen as awkward, this very awkwardness in attempting to come to grips with his story can be seen as a strength, in that it contributes to the emotions or attitudes of sorrow, sympathy, understanding, and forgiveness that he projects from the beginning. If such a conclusion could be reached in the case of a fallible *persona* manipulated by an infallible author, the same can readily be done for an imperfect narrator who is to all intents and purposes identical with the imperfect, and vulnerable, author.

---

[102] This way of reading medieval narrative is illustrated to good effect by A. R. Heiserman, "The Plot of *Pearl*," and in a different way by Ian Bishop, *Pearl in Its Setting*, pp. 95–98.

Conclusion

Boccaccio was a much more learned man than Chaucer, at least in the writings of Antiquity. Chaucer's awareness of classical literary traditions was extremely limited. But because of this very limitation, he had the good fortune to believe something that would not have occurred to Boccaccio, namely, that tragedy was a living genre, and a common one at that. And he set about writing tragedies of his own. What Chaucer actually found, in Boccaccio's *De casibus* and elsewhere, and identified as tragedies, were simply sad or disastrous stories, for which more or less appropriate morals were drawn, with no generic rationale or consistency beyond that of the moral exemplum, biographical sketch (both secular and sacred), and personal complaint. It was Chaucer's unconscious contribution, while consciously believing that he was simply adding entries to an existent literary form, to define and establish a new genre.

Chaucer was also fortunate in his idea of the nature and content of tragedy. He could easily have fallen heir to a much more restrictive and less promising definition, for instance, the fairly common Lactantian-Isidorian notion, which in fact is borne out in the surviving Roman tragedies, that tragedy specialized in the great crimes of wicked kings. Instead, he thought of tragedy as primarily a story beginning in prosperity and ending in adversity. This is a notion capable of encompassing everything that we have come to regard as tragic, whether "great tragedy" or run-of-the-mill tragedy. That is to say, our modern "instinctual" idea of tragedy was first introduced, both by definition and example, by Chaucer. And one of his examples, the *Troilus and Criseyde*, can lay claim to greatness; that is, it has made friends with the literary taste-makers of successive generations and has been received into their everlasting canons.

Chaucer's exemplifications of the genre were also generically influential. Henryson's *Testament of Cresseid* was directly inspired by the *Troilus*, while Lydgate's *Fall of Princes* was inspired by the *Monk's Tale*. In the long run, this latter, more pedestrian, avenue of influence was of greater importance, because it provided a wide and deep base for Chaucer's idea of tragedy, especially when supplemented by the monologues of *A Mirror for Magistrates*. It proved able to resist more specialized notions of tragedy that were imported to England from abroad, especially the bombastic horror-story paradigm of Senecan tragedy. In the event, Seneca's plays were a strong influence on Elizabethan drama, but, as I think almost everyone will admit, they were a largely deleterious influence. No one has pretended that Seneca's tragedies are great tragedies, and it is dubious whether a "Senecan formula" has ever produced, unaided, a play or other literary work that anyone would classify as a great tragedy, by whatever criteria.

In contrast, it is the virtue of Chaucer's formula that, while it has no recipe for success except for the general rule that it be well told, and even though in the event it has resulted in more bad tragedies than good—that is, more examples have been regarded as inartistic than artistic (but this is true of all non-qualitative genres)—it does not have built-in obstacles to success; and it was, I maintain, the principal generic influence on Shakespeare in his greatest tragedies. When Kenneth Muir says, "There is no such thing as Shakespearian Tragedy: there are only Shakespearian tragedies,"[1] he is right, in the sense that Shakespeare's tragedies cannot be contained in any restricted definition of tragedy, especially a definition of "great tragedy." But all of his tragedies fall within the genre of Chaucerian tragedy—including *The Tragedy of Troilus and Cressida*, which some modern critics exclude from the category of tragedy because of a supposed rule that a tragedy must end in death.[2] The simple generic notion of tragedy possessed by the Elizabethans and Jacobeans is well stated by Samuel Johnson, in speaking of Shakespeare's fellow-actors Hemings and Condell and their arrangements of the plays by genre in the First Folio: "Tragedy was not in those times a poem of more general dignity or elevation than comedy; it required only a calamitous conclusion, with which the common criticism of that age was satisfied, whatever lighter pleasure it afforded in its progress."[3]

What I call Chaucerian tragedy corresponds in many ways to Willard Farnham's "*De casibus* tragedy," and there is no need to repeat his documentation of the impact of this tradition leading up to Shakespeare, once we abstract from material that does not deal explicitly with tragedy.[4] I differ

---

[1] Kenneth Muir, *Shakespeare's Tragic Sequence*, p. 12

[2] The title and running titles call the play a tragedy in the First Folio of 1623, where it is printed between the Histories and the Tragedies. The title-page of the first version of the 1609 Quarto calls it a history, and the same is true of the second version, but the preface attached to the latter associates it with comedy (it is "full of the palm comical," born of the brain "that never undertook anything comical vainly"); perhaps the writer did not read the entire play, or perhaps he is referring only to the comic scenes in the play. One of the plays in the Histories section of the First Folio, *Richard III*, is called *The Tragedy of Richard III* on its title-page, but *The Life and Death of Richard III* in the table of contents; the latter form is used in both places for *Richard II*, but in Q1 it is called *The Tragedy of King Richard II*, and a similar title is given to *Richard III* in its Q1 printing.

[3] Samuel Johnson, *Johnson on Shakespeare*, 1:68 (*Preface*). Just before this, he characterizes their notion of comedy: "An action which ended happily to the principal persons, however serious or distressful through its intermediate incidents, in their opinion constituted a comedy. This idea of a comedy continued long amongst us, and plays were written, which, by changing the catastrophe, were tragedies today and comedies tomorrow."

[4] In chapters 5 and 6 of *Medieval Heritage*, treating "Tragedy and the English Moral Play" in the fifteenth and sixteenth centuries, the actual term tragedy is almost nonexistent in the texts, except in works written after the *Mirror for Magistrates*, notably *A New Tragical Comedy of Apius and Virginia*, by "R.B.," of 1567–68, based on Chaucer's *Physician's Tale* (pp. 251–58), and Thomas Preston's *A Lamentable Tragedy Mixed Full of Pleasant Mirth, Containing the Life of Cambises, King of Persia*, of 1569–70, based on Richard Taverner's *The Garden of Wisdom*, 1539 (pp. 263–70). Farnham treats the *Mirror* in chapter 7 and "The Progeny of the *Mirror*" in chapter 8, with chapters 9 and 10 devoted to "The Establishment of Tragedy upon the Elizabethan Stage."

with Farnham mainly in my perception and evaluation of the origins of medieval tragedy. I reject the designation "*De casibus* tragedy" because it perpetuates the false notion that Boccaccio considered the histories of his *De casibus virorum illustrium* to be tragedies. Farnham almost states the truth of the matter, belatedly, at the end of his chapter on Chaucer and Lydgate: "The Boccacesque tragical story quickly gained the name of tragedy, and under the sponsorship of Chaucer and Lydgate it bore the name with increasing assurance. However, we must remember that Boccaccio did not write his stories of the falls of princes in order to illustrate any learned medieval theory of tragedy. His purpose is never so stated, and his desire to follow his moral idea, let the form of his stories be what they may and let men call them what they may, is quite obvious."[5] Farnham leaves the door open to the assumption, and perhaps continues to make the assumption himself, that Boccaccio if asked would have readily classified his stories as tragedies, and that labeling them as tragedies added nothing essential to their meaning. He also assumes that there was a common movement among the readers of the *De casibus* to consider the book a collection of tragedies. But, apart from Chaucer and those who followed him, I know of only one person who came to this conclusion, namely, Iñigo López de Mendoza, Marquis of Santillana, a generation after Chaucer's death. Like Boccaccio, Santillana was familiar with Seneca's tragedies, but he was more impressed with the definitions of tragedy given in commentaries on Dante, especially that of John de Serravalle (which, as we have seen, was an English commission); he agreed with Serravalle in considering the *Inferno, Purgatorio,* and *Paradiso* to be not a single comedy taken together but three comedies.[6] As examples of tragedy, he named both Seneca's tragedies and Boccaccio's *De casibus,* and when he came to write a tragedy of his own, on the naval defeat of Aragon at Gaeta in 1435, he portrayed the grieving mother and wives of the royal captives as petitioning Boccaccio himself to recount the disaster.[7]

Laurence of Premierfait did not associate the *De casibus* with tragedy, nor did the scribes who copied his translations.[8] Nor did George Chastelain, who in his *Temple de Boccace* saw himself as continuing the *De casibus.*[9] This work, finished in 1465 and dedicated to Margaret of Anjou, Queen of England, received several generic characterizations from its various copyists, such as mirror for princes, complaint, and consolation, but tragedy was not one of them.[10]

The Latin and French reflexes of the term "tragedy" were rare when Chaucer introduced the term into the English language, and even his *Troilus* was

---

[5] Farnham, *Medieval Heritage,* p. 171.

[6] IDEAS AND FORMS, pp. 203–05.

[7] Santillana, *Comedieta de Ponça.* He was forced to convert his work from a tragedy to a minor comedy, a "comediette," because events took a turn for the better and the captives were ransomed.

[8] See Bozzolo, *Manuscrits des traductions françaises d'ouevres de Boccace.*

[9] George Chastelain, *Le temple de Bocace,* ed. Susanna Bliggenstorfer.

[10] See Bliggenstorfer, pp. *23–*24. She says, "Ainsi le *Temple de Bocace* devient à la fois un miroir de prince, un consolation, une complainte, le récit d'un cas et de *remoustrances,* une imitation ou bien un traité de fortune, selon l'importance que veut accorder un scribe à telle ou telle partie du texte."

not recognized as a specimen of a new, or old, genre called tragedy, but was rather referred to in more ordinary terms. John Gower, one of the two dedicatees to whom Chaucer's little tragedy was to "go," mines it for exempla: of Troilus as a sacrilegious lover (because he fell in love with Criseyde in a temple), and of Diomede as wrongly supplanting Troilus in Criseyde's affections.[11] The author of a treatise for women religious, *Disce mori*, composed in the 1450s, alludes to the poem as an example of fleshly love;[12] Thomas Usk considered it a treatise of noble love;[13] and the translator of the rule for Whittington's Hospital in 1442 took the reference to tragedy to be completely nongeneric, saying, in effect, "Go, little rulebook, go, little tragedy." Even Lydgate did not refer to *Troilus* as a tragedy, and perhaps he did not think of it as a tragedy at the time he told the story of Troilus and Criseyde in his *Troy Book*; at this point he was taken up with the obsolete genre of tragedy practiced in Old Troy, which involved masked pantomimists who acted out the story as the author recited it. Only Henryson is on record as having recognized *Troilus* for what it was, a genre of its own. He received it in kind and gave it what might be called an "early postmodern turn,"[14] for in place of the mainly conjunctive and unitary mode of the *Troilus* he used a disjunctive and paratactic approach in the *Testament of Cresseid*.

The last monastic chronicler in England, Richard Lavender, who was not himself a monk but a visitor to the Abbey of Croyland, in telling the story of the Yorkist dynasty, of Edward IV, his sons and daughters, and the usurping Richard III, did not imitate the knowledgeable St. Albans historian Thomas Walsingham in likening his account of the Peasants' Revolt to a tragedy. Rather he imitated another kind of monastic chronicler, John Lydgate, in dividing his history into tragedies, which Lavender understood to mean something like chapters.

Even though Walsingham as early as 1378 used the adjective *tragicus* to speak of a murder in Westminster Abbey, and three years later spoke of the English uprising as a tragic history, the first recorded use of "tragic" in English occurs in George Joye's *Exposition of Daniel the Prophet*, published at Antwerp in 1545, where he says: "Noble valeant princes . . . have there bene, which at last . . . have had a miserable tragik ende."[15] This is a conclusion

---

[11] Gower, *Confessio amantis* 2.2451–58; 5.7505–602; 8.2531–36.

[12] Lee Patterson, "Ambiguity and Interpretation: A Fifteenth-Century Reading of *Troilus and Criseyde*."

[13] Thomas Usk, *The Testament of Love* 3.4, p. 123; see my *Love and Marriage*, pp. 290–91.

[14] See Ihab Hassan, "Toward a Concept of Postmodernism," esp. pp. 267–68 (= pp. 91–92 in *The Postmodern Turn*).

[15] *OED* s.v. "tragic," no. 3. Under "tragical," the first listing is attributed to Caxton, *c.* 1489, referring to his *Blanchardyn and Eglantine*, but the passage in question, which refers to "the unfortunate report and tragicall tidings" of the captivity of Blanchardyn's father (chap. 54, p. 213) is not from Caxton's version but rather from that of Thomas Pope Goodwine, published in 1595 (see pp. 227–31 of Leon Kellner's edition). In promising a second volume, Goodwine uses tragedy in an "untragic" sense, equating it with "adventure": "Thus, gentlemen, to satisfie your expectations and performe my promise, I find you the second part of Blanchardine's adventures, whose succes, if I find as fortunate as his first, looke shortly, so soone as time and leasure will serve, for the finishing of all his tragidies" (p. 223). The earliest authentic entry for "tragical" is that in Nicholas Udall, *The First Tome or Volume of the Paraphrase of Erasmus upon the Newe Testamente*, published in 1548, on Mark 12, fol. 78, referring to a notion of acting tragedies: the

that one could well have come to from reading the *Fall of Princes*. The adjective seems to have become popular only at the end of the sixteenth century, and it is only then that we can safely assume that it was used with a sense of referring to "the tragic." The horizon of expectability was occluded, as far as tragedy was concerned, until long after Chaucer's time, but it was Chaucer's setting of the term tragedy that established its meaning, though it remained obscured from the view and the expectations of the literary populace in general for a very long time.

To sum up, it was Chaucer who first considered Boccaccio's stories to be tragedies. And unlike Boccaccio, who served a cautionary moralism and wished to stress retributive justice first and foremost, Chaucer aimed primarily at sympathy and empathy, and he had a generic theory that included all kinds of falls and misfortunes. His belief that he was writing in an established literary genre of tragedy gave him a new dimension and set him apart from writers who simply wrote ably on the theme of mutability, or who had a keen sense of *lacrimae rerum*.

With his *Troilus and Criseyde*, Chaucer wrote the first tragedy that has any claims to greatness since the Greeks. Any tragedy that is recognized today as great tragedy—which does not include Euripides's happily ending *Iphigenia Among the Taurians*, a favorite of Aristotle's, or another of his favorites, the potential tragedy derivable from the plot of Homer's *Odyssey*—can be seen to fit Chaucer's conception of tragedy. Not only did Chaucer introduce the term tragedy into the English language; not only was he the first author in any vernacular language who consciously composed tragedies; he was also the author who fixed the meaning of "tragedy" for subsequent generations: the untutored sense of the word that we all share to this day.

scribes and the Pharisees "counted Jesus for an ignorant person, and avaunted and set out themselfes among the simple and unlearned people, what with their magnifike and hye titles, and what with their tragicall and masking apparell, as though they had bene almost God almighties peeres."

Bibliography

MANUSCRIPTS

Bethesda
National Library of Medicine MS accession no. 146304, *see* Arderne.

Cambridge
Cambridge University Library MS Ii 3.21 (*c.* 1400–20), *see* Boethius, William of Aragon.

London
British Library, MS Harley 2693, fols. 131–202v, *see* Walsingham.
British Library, Royal MS 15 B.3, *see* William of Conches.

Oxford
Oxford University Library, Bodleian MS Laud Misc. 626, *see* Huguccio.

Paris
Bibliothèque Mazarine MS 1651, fols. 129–209bis, *see* Mézières.
Bibliothèque Nationale, MS lat. 14380 (14 c.), *see* William of Conches.

San Marino
Huntington Library MS 64 (15 c.), astrological-medical compilation.
Huntington Library MS 144 (*c.* 1480–1500), containing works of Lydgate and Chaucer's *Melibeus* (titled *Proverbis*) and *Monk's Tale* (running title: *The Falle of Princis*).

Vatican City
Bibliotheca Apostolica Vaticana, MS lat. 562 (14 c.), *see* Trevet.
—— MS lat. 5202, fols. 1–40v (13 c.), *see* William of Conches.
—— MS Ottoboni 1293 (16 c.), *see* William of Conches.
—— MS Urbinas lat. 355 (Seneca's tragedies and Trevet's commentary).

PRIMARY SOURCES

Accessus ad Querolum, Florence, Biblioteca Ambrosiana, MS Ambros. H. 14 inf., fol. 48, edited with other passages by Remigio Sabbadini, *Studi italiani di filologia classica* 11 (1903) 248–56, and included in his *Storia e critica di testi latini* (Catania 1914); in the second edition of the latter (Padua 1971), it appears on pp. 328–29.
Alger, Horatio, Jr., *Struggling Upward; or, Luke Larkin's Luck*, published serially in *The Golden Argosy*, 13 March–19 June 1886 (Philadelphia 1890; repr. New York 1984, intro. Ralph D. Gardner).
Alemannus, *see* Averroes.

Alighieri, Pietro, *Petri Allegherii super Dantis ipsius genitoris Comediam commentar-ium*, ed. Vincenzo Nannucci (Florence 1845) (the reprint in *Il "Commentarium" di Pietro Alighieri nelle redazioni ashburnhamiana e ottoboniana*, intro. Egidio Guidu-baldi [Florence 1978], has serious omissions and distortions, and should not be used).

Anthologia latina, part 2, ed. Alexander Riese (Leipzig 1906).

Arderne, John, *Practica*, Bethesda, National Library of Medicine MS (accession no. 146304).

—— *Treatises of Fistula in ano*, etc., ed. D'Arcy Power, EETS os 139 (1910).

Aristotle, *Poetics* (Greek text), ed. D. W. Lucas (Oxford 1968); Latin translation by William of Moerbeke, ed. Lorenzo Minio-Paluello, *De arte poetica*, Aristoteles lati-nus 33, ed. 2 (Brussels 1968); English translation: *The Poetics of Aristotle: Transla-tion and Commentary*, tr. Stephen Halliwell (London and Chapel Hill 1987).

Averroes, *Middle Comentary on Aristotle's Poetics*, English translation of the Arabic text, tr. Charles E. Butterworth, *Averroes' Middle Commentary on Aristotle's Poe-tics* (Princeton 1986); Latin translation by Herman Alemannus: critical edition, *Averrois Cordubensis Commentarium medium in Aristotelis Poetriam*, ed. William Franklin Boggess (University of North Carolina diss., 1965); edition from 5 MSS: ed. Minio-Paluello in Aristotle, *De arte poetica*, pp. 39–74; English translation by O. B. Hardison in *Classical and Medieval Literary Criticism*, ed. Alex Preminger *et al.* (New York 1974).

Balbus Januensis, John, *Catholicon* (Mainz 1460, repr. Farnborough, Hants. 1971).

Baldwin, William, *et al.*, *A Mirror for Magistrates*, ed. Lily B. Campbell, *The Mirror for Magistrates* (Cambridge 1938, repr. New York 1960).

Bible, Vulgate, ed. Robert Weber, *Biblia sacra iuxta vulgatam versionem*, 2 vols. (Stutt-gart 1969, corr. repr. 1975).

—— *Biblia sacra cum glossa ordinaria* (Douai-Antwerp 1617).

—— *Biblia latina cum glossa ordinaria*, editio princeps (Strassburg 1480/81); facsimile reprint, intro. Karlfried Froehlich and Margaret T. Gibson, 4 vols. (Turnhout 1992).

Boccaccio, Giovanni, *Tutte le opere*, general ed. Vittore Branca, 12 vols. (Milan 1964–).

—— *Comedìa delle ninfe fiorentine*, ed. Antonio Enzo Quaglio, *Tutte le opere*, vol. 2 (1964).

—— *Decameron*, ed. Vittore Branca, ed. 2 (Florence 1958? repr. 1965); *Concordanze del Decameron*, ed. Alfredo Barbina (Florence 1969).

—— *De casibus virorum illustrium*, first version = Text A (*c.* 1356–73), facsimile of the *c.* 1520 Paris edition, ed. Lewis Brewer Hall (Gainesville 1962); second version = Text B (*c.* 1374), ed. Pier Giorgio Ricci and Vittorio Zaccaria, *Tutte le opere*, vol. 9 (1983); abridged translation of Text A, *The Fates of Illustrious Men*, tr. Louis Brewer Hall (New York 1965).

—— *De mulieribus claris*, ed. Vittorio Zaccaria, *Tutte le opere*, vol. 10 (1967).

—— *Esposizioni sopra la Comedia di Dante*, ed. Giorgio Padoan, *Tutte le opere*, vol. 6 (1965).

—— *Filostrato*, ed. Vittore Branca, *Tutte le opere*, vol. 2 (1964); ed. Vincenzo Pernicone [1937] and tr. Robert P. apRoberts and Anna Bruni Seldis, *Il Filostrato* (New York 1986); tr. R. K. Gordon, *The Story of Troilus* (London 1934; repr. New York 1964), pp. 23–127.

—— *Genealogia deorum gentilium*, ed. Vincenzo Romano (Bari 1951); translation of books 14–15, *Boccaccio on Poetry*, tr. Charles G. Osgood (Princeton 1930, repr. New York 1956 and Indianapolis n.d.).

—— Glosses to Dante's *Eclogues*, ed. Giorgio Brugnoli and Riccardo Scarcia, *Le egloghe* (Milan 1980).

—— *Teseida delle nozze d'Emilia*, ed. Alberto Limentani, *Tutte le opere*, vol 2 (1964).

Bode, Georg Heinrich, *Scriptores rerum mythicarum latini tres*, 2 vols. (Zelle 1834, repr. Hildesheim 1968).

Boethius, *De consolatione Philosophiae*, LCL.

—— French translation by Jean de Meun, ed. V. L. Dedeck-Héry, "Boethius' *De consolatione* by Jean de Meun," *Mediæval Studies* 14 (1952) 165–275.

—— Latin text and glosses and Chaucer's translation (*Boece*), Cambridge, Cambridge University Library MS Ii 3.21, and the edition by Edmund Taite Silk, *Cambridge MS Ii.3.21 and the Relation of Chaucer's Boethius to Trivet and Jean de Meung* (Yale University diss., 1930; Ann Arbor, Xerox University Microfilms, cat. no. 70–23051–02800)

Bower, Walter, Continuation of John Fordun's *Scotichronicon*, ed. Walter Goodall, 2 vols. (London 1759).

Buti, Francesco da, *Commento sopra la Divina comedia,* ed. Crescentino Giannini, 3 vols. (Pisa 1858–62).

Calendar of Entries in the Papal Registers Relating to Great Britain and Ireland: Papal Letters, vol. 4, *A.D. 1362–1404*, ed. W. H. Bliss and J. A. Twemlow (London 1902, repr. Nendeln 1971).

Capgrave, John, *Abbreviation of Chronicles*, ed. Peter J. Lucas, EETS os 285 (1983).

Cato, Pseudo-, *Nomina Musarum* (Incipit: "Clio gesta canens transactis tempora reddit"), *Minor Latin Poems*, LCL, p. 634.

Caxton, William, *The Golden Legend, or Lives of the Saints* (1483), ed. F. S. Ellis, 7 vols. (London 1900).

—— *Caxton's Blanchardyn and Eglantine* (c. 1489), ed. Leon Kellner, EETS es 58 (1890).

Charles d'Orléans, *Poésies*, ed. Pierre Champion, 2 vols. (Paris 1923–27).

—— *The English Poems of Charles of Orleans*, ed. Robert Steele and Mabel Day, EETS os 215, 220 (1941–46, repr. with suppl., 1970).

Chastelain, George, *Le temple de Bocace*, ed. Susanna Bliggenstorfer, Romanica helvetica 104 (Bern 1988).

Chaucer, Geoffrey, *The Complete Works of Geoffrey Chaucer*, ed. Walter W. Skeat, ed. 2, 7 vols. (Oxford 1899–1907).

—— *The Complete Works of Geoffrey Chaucer*, ed. F. N. Robinson, ed. 1 (Boston 1933); ed. 2, *The Works of Geoffrey Chaucer* (Boston 1957).

—— *The Riverside Chaucer*, general ed. Larry D. Benson (Boston 1987). Unless otherwise noted, all citations of Chaucer will be from this edition.

—— *Boece*, ed. Ralph Hanna III and Traugott Lawler, *Riverside Chaucer*; for the text as given in the Croucher Manuscript, *see* Boethius.

—— *Monk's Tale*, ed. Susan H. Cavanaugh, *Riverside Chaucer*.

—— *Nuns' Priest's Tale*, ed. Derek Pearsall, *The Nun's Priest's Tale*, Variorum Edition vol. 2, part 9 (Norman 1984).

—— *Troilus and Criseyde*, ed. Stephen Barney, *Riverside Chaucer*; ed. Robert Kilburn Root, *The Book of Troilus and Criseyde* (Princeton 1926); ed. B. A. Windeatt, *Troilus and Criseyde* (London 1984).

Croyland Chronicle, ed. William Fulman, *Historia croylandensis,* in *Rerum anglicarum scriptorum veteres*, vol. 1 (Oxford 1684); *The Crowland Chronicle Continuations, 1459–1486*, ed. and tr. Nicholas Pronay and John Cox (London 1986).

Dante, *De vulgari eloquentia*, ed. Pier Vincenzo Mengaldo, *Opere minori*, vol. 2, ed. Mengaldo *et al.* (Milan 1979).

Dante, *Comedia*, ed. and tr. Charles S. Singleton, 3 vols. in 6 (Princeton 1970–75).

De nominibus Musarum, ed. F. J. E. Raby, *A History of Secular Latin Poetry*, ed. 2 (Oxford 1957), 2:85.

Deschamps, Eustace, *Oeuvres complètes*, ed. Auguste Queux de Saint Hilaire (vols. 1–6) and Gaston Raynaud (vols. 7–11) (Paris 1878–1903).

Dictionary of Medieval Latin from British Sources, ed. R. E. Latham *et al.* (Oxford 1975–).

Dictionary of the Older Scottish Tongue, A, ed. William A. Craigie *et al.*, 7 vols. to date (London 1937–).

Donatus, Aelius, *Commentum Terenti*, ed. Paulus Wessner, 2 vols. (Leipzig 1902–05, repr. Stuttgart 1963–66).

Douglas, Gavin, *The Shorter Poems of Gavin Douglas*, ed. Priscilla J. Bawcutt, Scottish Text Society 4.3 (Edinburgh 1967).

Dunbar, William, *Poems*, ed. James Kinsley, *The Poems of William Dunbar* (Oxford 1979).

Durant, William *Speculum judiciale*, 2 vols. (Basel 1574, repr. Aalen 1975).

Epistolae academicae Oxon., ed. Henry Anstey, vol. 1, Oxford Historical Society 35 (Oxford 1898).

Evanthius (Evanzio), *De fabula*, ed. Giovanni Cupaiuolo (Naples 1979).

Faral, Edmond, *Les arts poétiques du XIIe et XIIIe siècle* (Paris 1924).

Flamma, Galvano, *Chronicon extravagans de antiquitatibus Mediolani*, ed. Antonio Ceruti, *Miscellanea di storia italiana* 7 (1869) 445–505.

Fowler, William, *The Last Epistle of Creseyd to Troyalus*, in *The Works of William Fowler*, ed. Henry W. Meikle, James Craigie, and John Purves, 3 vols., Scottish Text Society 2.6, 3.7, 3.13 (Edinburgh 1914–40), 1:379–87; 3:31–34.

Freculph of Lisieux, *Chronicon*, PL 106.

Fulgentius, *Mythologiae*, ed. Rudolf Helm, *Opera* (Leipzig 1989).

Garland, John, *Parisiana poetria*, ed. Traugott Lawler, *The Parisiana Poetria of John of Garland* (New Haven 1974).

Geoffrey of Vinsauf, *Documentum de arte versificandi*, ed. Faral, *Les arts poétiques*, pp. 265–320.

—— *Poetria nova*, ed. Faral, *Les arts poétiques*, pp. 197–262.

Gest Hystoriale of the Destruction of Troy, ed. George A. Panton and David Donaldson, EETS os 39, 56 (1869–74).

Gower, John, *The Complete Works of John Gower*, 4 vols. (Oxford 1899); the two volumes comprising *The English Works* were reprinted as EETS es 81–82 (1900).

Gratian, *Decretum*, ed. Emil Friedberg, *Corpus iuris canonici*, 2 vols. (Leipzig 1879–81, repr. Graz 1959), vol. 1.

Greville, Fulke, *The Life of Sidney*, ed. Mark Caldwell, *The Prose of Fulke Greville, Lord Brooke* (New York 1987).

Guido da Pisa, *Expositiones et glose super Comediam Dantis*, ed. Vincenzo Cioffari (Albany, N.Y. 1974).

Horace, *Works*, LCL.

Henryson, Robert, *Poems*, ed. Charles Elliott (Oxford 1963; ed. 2, 1974).

—— *The Poems and Fables of Robert Henryson*, ed. H. Harvey Wood, ed. 2 (Edinburgh 1958).

—— *The Testament of Cresseid*, ed. Denton Fox:
   Fox A: *Testament of Cresseid* (London 1968);
   Fox B: *The Works of Robert Henryson* (Oxford 1981);
   Fox C: *The Poems* (Oxford 1987), with text identical to Fox B (with two minor exceptions noted on p. xii) and with pruned but updated notes.

—— *Works*, see Fox B above; all quotations from Henryson will be from this edition, unless otherwise noted.

Herbert, J. A., *Catalogue of Romances in the Department of Manuscripts in the British Museum*, vol. 3 (London 1910).

Higden, Ranulf, *Polychronicon*, ed. Churchill Babington and Joseph Rawson Lumby (with the translation of John Trevisa and an anonymous fifteenth-century translation), 9 vols., Rolls Series 41.1–9 (London 1865–86).

Huguccio, *Magne derivationes*, Oxford, Bodleian MS Laud Misc. 626.

Innocent III, Pope (Lotario dei Segni), *De miseria condicionis humane*, ed. Robert E. Lewis, Chaucer Library (Athens, Ga. 1978).

Isidore of Seville, *Chronica majora* and *Chronicorum epitome*, ed. Theodore Mommsen, *Chronica minora saec.* IV, V, VI, VII, vol. 2, Monumenta Germaniae historica, Auctores antiquiores 11 (Berlin 1894).

—— *Etymologiae, sive Origines*, ed. W. M. Lindsay, 2 vols. (Oxford 1911), to be used with the annotations of Faustino Arévalo's edition, PL 82.

James de Varazze (Jacobus a Voragine), *Legenda aurea*, ed. T. Graesse (Dresden 1846, repr. Breslau 1890); unreliable abridged English translation: *The Golden Legend of Jacobus de Voragine*, tr. and adapted by [William] Granger Ryan and Helmut Ripperger (New York 1941; repr. New York 1969); complete English translation by William Granger Ryan: Jacobus de Voragine, *The Golden Legend: Readings on the Saints*, 2 vols. (Princeton 1993).

Jean de Meun, *see* Boethius.

—— *Roman de la Rose*, ed. Félix Lecoy, 3 vols. (Paris 1965–70).

Jerome, Saint, *Adversus Jovinianum*, PL 23.

John of Salisbury, *Policraticus*, ed. C. C. J. Webb (Oxford 1909), following the column numbers of PL 199.

John of Vignay, *Legende doree* (Paris: Verard, 1496).

Johnson, Samuel, *Preface to Shakespeare*, in *Johnson on Shakespeare*, ed. Arthur Sherbo, 2 vols., vols. 7–8 of the Yale edition of Johnson's works (New Haven 1968).

Justinian, *Digesta*, ed. Theodor Mommsen, Paulus Krueger, and Wolfgang Kunkel in vol. 1 of *Corpus iuris civilis*, ed. 16, 3 vols. (Berlin 1954).

Lactantius, Lucius Caecilius Firmianus, *Diuinae institutiones*, ed. Samuel Brandt (Vienna 1890).

Langland, William, *Piers Plowman*, B Text, ed. A. V. C. Schmidt, *The Vision of Piers Plowman*, new ed. (London 1987).

Laud Troy Book, ed. J. Ernst Wülfing, EETS os 121–22 (1902–03).

Laurentius, *Accessus Terentii*, ed. Jenö Abel, *Az ó- és középkori Terentiusbiographiák* (Budapest 1887), pp. 40–46.

Le Neve, John, *Fasti ecclesiae anglicanae, 1300–1541,* vol. 4, compiled by B. Jones (London 1963).

Liber exemplorum ad usum praedicantium saeculo XIII compositus a quodam fratre minore anglico de provincia Hiberniae, ed. A. G. Little (Aberdeen 1908).

Lidia, ed. Edmond Lackenbacher, in Gustave Cohen, general ed., *La "comédie" latine en France au XIIe siècle*, 2 vols. (Paris 1931), 1:212–246.

Lydgate, John, *Fall of Princes*, ed. Henry Bergen, 4 vols., EETS es 121–24 (1924–27).

—— *The Minor Poems*, ed. Henry Noble MacCracken, EETS es 107, EETS os 192 (1911–34).

—— *Siege of Thebes*, ed. Axel Erdmann and Eilert Ekwall, EETS es 108, 125 (1911–30).

—— *Temple of Glass*, ed. John Norton-Smith, *John Lydgate: Poems* (Oxford 1966, corr. repr. 1968).

—— *Troy Book*, ed. Henry Bergen, EETS es 97, 103, 106, 126 (1906–35).

Machaut, Guillaume de, *La prise d'Alexandrie; ou, Chronique du roi Pierre Ier de Lusignan*, ed. L. de Mas Latrie (Geneva 1877, repr. Osnabrück 1968).

Macrobius, *Commentarii in somnium Scipionis*, ed. Mario Regali, *Commento al Somnium Scipionis*, 2 vols. (Pisa 1983–90).

Manuale ad usum percelebris ecclesie Sarisburiensis, ed. A. Jeffries Collins, Henry Bradshaw Society 91 (Chichester 1960).

Metham, John, *The Works of John Metham*, ed. Hardin Craig, EETS os 123 (1916).

Mézières, Philippe de, *Oracio tragedica seu declamatoria Passionis domini nostri Jhesu Christi*, Paris, Bibliothèque Mazarine MS 1651, fols. 129–209bis.

Middle English Dictionary, ed. Hans Kurath, Sherman M. Kuhn, Robert E. Lewis, *et al.* (Ann Arbor 1954–).

Miller, Robert P., *Chaucer: Sources and Backgrounds* (New York 1977).

Mort Artu, ed. Jean Frappier, *Le mort le roi Artu* (ed. 1, Paris 1936; ed. 2, Geneva, 1954).

Norton, Thomas, *Ordinal of Alchemy*, ed. John Reidy, EETS os 272 (1975).

Ordinary Gloss to the Bible, *see* Bible.

Orosius, *Historiae*, PL 31.

Osbern of Gloucester, *Liber derivationum*, ed. Angelo Mai, *Thesaurus novus latinitatis, sive Lexicon vetus* (Rome 1936).

Oxford English Dictionary, ed. 2, 20 vols. (Oxford 1989).

Ovid, *Works*, LCL.

Papias, *Elementarium doctrinae rudimentum* (*c.* 1045), ed. Bonino Mombrizio, *Papias vocabulista*, ed. 4 (Venice 1496, repr. Turin 1966), with a supplement for the missing section *pecus-placidus* from ed. 1 (Milan 1476).

Peter of Blois, *Epistulae*, PL 207.

Petrarch, Francis, *De viris illustribus*, ed. Guido Martellotti (Florence 1964).

—— *Compendium* = *Vitarum virorum illustrium epitome*, in *Opera omnia* (Basel 1554, repr. Ridgewood, N.J. 1965), 1:551 ff.

—— *Epistola senilis* 17.4, ed. J. W. Hales, *Originals and Analogues of Some of Chaucer's Canterbury Tales*, ed. F. J. Furnivall *et al.* (London 1888), pp. 151–72.

—— *Prose*, ed. Guido Martellotti *et al.* (Milan 1955).

Pisan, Christine de, *Dit de la Rose*, ed. Maurice Roy, *Œuvres poétiques de Christine de Pisan*, 3 vols. (Paris 1886–96), 2:29–48.

Placidus, *Glossae* (*c.* A.D. 500), ed. J. W. Pirie and W. M. Lindsay, *Glossaria latina*, vol.4 (Paris 1930, repr. 1965).

Premierfait, Laurence of, First translation of the *De casibus* of Boccaccio: *De la ruyne des nobles hommes et femmes*, ed. Collard Mansion (Bruges 1476, copy at the Huntington Library); compared also with the edition of Huss and Schabeler (Lyons 1483, microfilm of copy in Madrid, Biblioteca Nacional).

—— Second translation of Boccaccio: *Des cas des nobles hommes et femmes*, ed. Nicholas Couteau (Paris 1538); book 1, ed. Patricia May Gathercole (Chapel Hill 1968).

Promptuarium parvulorum, ed. A. L. Mayhew, EETS es 102 (1908).

Revised Medieval Latin Word-List from British and Irish Sources, ed. R. E. Latham (Oxford 1965, repr. with Supplement, 1980).

Robbins, Rossell Hope, *Historical Poems of the Fourteenth and Fifteenth Centuries* (New York 1959).

Santillana, Iñigo López de Mendoza, Marqués de, *Comedieta de Ponça*, ed. crit., ed. Maxim P. A. Kerkhof (Madrid 1987).

Seneca, *Apocolocyntosis* (*Ludus de morte Claudii*), ed. and tr. W. H. D. Rouse, LCL (with Petronius)

—— *Tragedies*, LCL; MS Vatican Urb. lat. 355 (with Trevet's commentary).

Shakespeare, William, *The Riverside Shakespeare*, ed. G. Blakemore Evans *et al.* (Boston 1974).

Silk, E. T., *see* Boethius, Trevet.

Statius, *Thebaid*, LCL.

Stoppard, Tom, *Rosencrantz & Guildernstern are Dead* (New York 1967).

Suetonius, *Works*, LCL.

Terence, *Comedies*, LCL.

The Towneley Plays, ed. Martin Stevens and A. C. Cawley, 2 vols., EETS ss 13 (1994).

Trevet, Nicholas, *Expositio super librum Boecii de consolatione*, Vatican MS lat. 562 (14 c.); ed. from eight other manuscripts by Edmund Silk, *Exposicio fratris Nicolai Trevethi anglici ordinis predicatorum super Boecio de consolacione* (uncompleted and unpublished; copies available from the Sterling Memorial Library, Yale University).

—— *Expositio super tragedias Senece*, partial editions: Introduction and commentary on *Thyestes*, ed. Ezio Franceschini, *Il commento di Nicola Trevet al Tieste di Seneca* (Milan 1938), pp. 1–8; commentary on *Hercules furens*, ed. Vincenzo Ussani jr, *L. Annaei Senecae Hercules furens et Nicolai Treveti Expositio*, vol. 2 (Rome 1959); commentary on *Agamemnon*, ed. Piero Meloni (Palermo 1961); commentary on *Hercules oetaeus*, ed. Piero Meloni (Palermo 1962); commentary on *Troades*, ed. Marco Palma (Rome 1977).

Trevisa, John, *see* Higden.

Udall, Nicholas, *The First Tome or Volume of the Paraphrase of Erasmus upon the Newe Testamente* (London 1548; facsimile repr., New York 1975).

Usk, Thomas, *The Testament of Love*, ed. Walter W. Skeat, in *Chaucerian and Other Pieces*, vol. 7 of *The Complete Works of Geoffrey Chaucer* (Oxford 1907).

Valerius Maximus, *Memorabilia*, ed. Karl Kempf, *Valerii Maximi Factorum et dictorum memorabilium libri novem* (Leipzig 1888, repr. Stuttgatt 1966).

Vatican Mythographers, *see* Bode.

Vincent of Beauvais, *Speculum quadruplex: naturale, doctrinale, morale, historiale*, 4 vols. (Douai 1624, repr. Graz 1964–65).

The Vision of Philibert, ed. J. O. Halliwell, *Early English Miscellanies* (London 1854).

Vitruvius, *De architectura*, LCL.

Walsingham, Thomas, *Archana deorum*, ed. Robert A. van Kluyve, *De archan[is] deorum* (Durham, N.C. 1968).

—— *Chronicon Angliae*, ed. Edward Maunde Thompson, Rolls Series 64 (London 1874).

—— *Prohemia poetarum Fratris Thome de Walsingham*, London, British Library MS Harley 2693, fols. 131–202v.

—— *Ypodigma Neustriae*, ed. Henry Thomas Riley, Rolls Series 28.7 (London 1876).

Walton, John, verse translation of Boethius, *De consolatione Philosophiae* (1410), ed. Mark Science, EETS os 170 (1927).

William of Aragon, *Commentum in Boethii Consolationem*, Cambridge Univ. Lib. MS Ii.3.21, part 2.

William of Conches, *Glose super librum Boecii de consolacione*, original short text: Vatican MS lat. 5202, fols. 1–40v (13 c.); Paris Bibl. Nat. MS lat. 14380 (14 c.); Vatican MS Ottoboni 1293 (16 c.); expanded version, London, Brit. Lib. Royal MS 15 B.3.

William of Malmesbury, *Gesta regum Anglorum*, ed. Thomas Duffus Hardy (London 1840, repr. Vaduz 1964).

SECONDARY SOURCES

Adamson, Jane, "Henryson's *Testament of Cresseid*: 'Fyre' and 'Cauld,'" *Critical Review* (Melbourne) 18 (1976) 39–60.

Aers, David, "Criseyde: Woman in Medieval Society," *Chaucer Review* 13 (1978–79)

177–200, revised as "Chaucer's Criseyde: Woman in Society, Woman in Love," in *Chaucer, Langland and the Creative Imagination* (London 1980), pp. 117–42, 218–22.

—— "Masculine Identity in the Courtly Community: The Selfloving in *Troilus and Criseyde*," in *Community, Gender, and Individual Identity: English Writing 1360–1430* (London 1988), pp. 117–52.

Aiken, Pauline, "Vincent of Beauvais and Chaucer's *Monk's Tale*," *Speculum* 17 (1942) 56–68.

apRoberts, Robert P., "Criseyde's Infidelity and the Moral of the *Troilus*," *Speculum* 44 (1969) 383–402.

Arthur, Ross G., Review of Robert Francis Cook, *The Sense of the Song of Roland* [Ithaca 1987], *Studies in the Age of Chaucer* 11 (1989) 202–04.

Aswell, E. Duncan, "The Role of Fortune in *The Testament of Cresseid*," *Philological Quarterly* 46 (1967) 471–87.

Axton, Richard, "Chaucer and 'Tragedy,'" *Chaucer to Shakespeare: Essays in Honour of Shinsuke Ando*, ed. Toshiyuki Takamiya and Richard Beadle (Cambridge 1992), pp. 33–43.

Babcock, R. W., "The Mediaeval Setting of Chaucer's *Monk's Tale*," *Publications of the Modern Language Association* 46 (1931) 205–13.

Baldwin, John W., *The Language of Sex: Five Voices from Northern France Around 1200* (Chicago 1994).

Barański, Zygmunt G., "*Comedìa*: Notes on Dante, the Epistle to Cangrande, and Medieval Comedy," *Lectura Dantis* 8 (Spring 1991) 26–55.

Barney, Stephen A., ed., *Chaucer's Troilus* (Essays) (Hamden Conn. 1980).

—— See Chaucer.

Barthes, Roland, *The Pleasure of the Text*, tr. Richard Miller (New York 1975).

Bayley, John, *The Characters of Love: A Study in the Literature of Personality* (London 1960).

Bennett, Bob, *Horatio Alger, Jr.: A Comprehensive Bibliography* (Mt. Pleasant, Mich. 1980).

Bennett, J. A. W., "Henryson's *Testament*: A Flawed Masterpiece," *Scottish Literary Journal* 1 (1974) 5–16.

Benson, C. David, "'O Nyce World': What Chaucer Really Found in Guido delle Colonne's History of Troy," *Chaucer Review* 13 (1978–79) 308–15, incorporated into his book, *The History of Troy in Middle English Literature: Guido delle Colonne's Historia destructionis Troiae in Medieval England* (Woodbridge 1980), pp. 144–50.

—— "Troilus and Cresseid in Henryson's *Testament*," *Chaucer Review* 13 (1978–79) 263–71, incorporated into *The History of Troy in Middle English Literature*, pp. 138–43.

—— "True Troilus and False Cresseid: The Descent from Tragedy," in Boitani, ed., *The European Tragedy of Troilus*, pp. 153–70.

Benson, Larry D., "The Alliterative *Morte Arthure* and Medieval Tragedy," *Tennessee Studies in Literature* 11 (1966) 75–87.

Bergen, Henry, *see* Lydgate.

Bieber, Margarete, *The History of the Greek and Roman Theater*, ed. 2 (Princeton 1961).

Bigongiari, Dino, "Were There Theaters in the Twelfth and Thirteenth Centuries?" *Romanic Review* 37 (1946) 201–24.

Billanovich, Guiseppe, *Petrarca letterato: Lo scrittoio del Petrarca* (Rome 1947).

—— "Pietro Piccolo da Monteforte tra il Petrarca e il Boccaccio," *Mediævo e Rinascimento: Studi in onore di Bruno Nardi* (Florence 1955), pp. 1–76.

Bishop, Ian, *Pearl in Its Setting* (Oxford 1968).

Bloomfield, Morton W., "Distance and Predestination in *Troilus and Criseyde*," *Publications of the Modern Language Society* 72 (1957) 14–26.

—— "*The Man of Law's Tale*: A Tragedy of Victimization and a Christian Comedy," *Publications of the Modern Language Association* 87 (1972) 384–90.

Blyth, Charles, "Virgilian Tragedy and *Troilus*," *Chaucer Review* 24 (1989–90) 211–18.

Boggess, William F., "Hermannus Alemannus' Latin Anthology of Arabic Poetry," *Journal of the American Oriental Society* 88 (1968) 657–70.

Boitani, Piero, "Eros and Thanatos: Cressida, Troilus, and the Modern Age," in Boitani, ed., *European Tragedy of Troilus*, pp. 281–305.

—— "The *Monk's Tale*: Dante and Boccaccio," *Medium aevum* 45 (1976) 50–69.

—— *The Tragic and the Sublime in Medieval Literature* (Cambridge 1989).

—— "Two Versions of Tragedy: Ugolino and Hugelyn," in *The Tragic and the Sublime*, pp. 20–55.

Boitani, Piero, ed. *The European Tragedy of Troilus* (Oxford 1989).

Botterill, Steven, Review of H. A. Kelly, *Tragedy and Comedy from Dante to Pseudo-Dante* [Berkeley 1989], *Italian Studies* 46 (1991) 117–18.

—— Review of Robert Hollander, *Dante's Epistle to Cangrande* [Ann Arbor 1993], *Italica* 72 (1995) 382–83.

Bouveresse, Jacques, *Wittgenstein Reads Freud: The Myth of the Unconscious*, tr. Carol Cosman from *Philosophie, mythologie et pseudo-science: Wittgenstein lecteur de Freud* (Paris 1991), Foreword by Vincent Descombes (Princeton 1995).

Bozzolo, Carla, "Le 'Dossier Laurent de Premierfait,'" *Italia medioevale e umanistica* 22 (1979) 439–47.

—— *Manuscrits des traductions françaises d'oeuvres de Boccace, XVe siècle* (Padua 1973).

Bradley, A. C., *Shakespearean Tragedy*, ed. 2 (London 1905).

Branca, Vittore, *Boccaccio: The Man and His Works*, tr. Richard Monges and Dennis J. McAuliffe (New York 1976).

Brennan, John Patrick, Jr., *The Chaucerian Text of Jerome, Adversus Jovinianum: An Edition Based on Pembroke College Cambridge MS 234* (University of California, Davis, diss., 1967; Xerox University Microfilms, Ann Arbor, cat. no. 68–6018).

Brewer, Derek, "Gothic Chaucer," in *Geoffrey Chaucer*, ed. Brewer (London 1974), pp. 1–32.

Bridges, Margaret, "The Picture in the Text: Ecphrasis as Self-Reflectivity in Chaucer's *Parliament of Fowles, Book of the Duchess*, and *House of Fame*," *Word and Image* 5 (1989) 151–58.

—— "The Sense of an Ending: The Case of the Dream-Vision," *Dutch Quarterly Review of Anglo-American Letters* 14 (1984) 81–96.

Brody, Saul Nathaniel, *The Disease of the Soul: Leprosy in Medieval Literature* (Ithaca 1974).

Brückmann, Patricia, "*Troilus and Criseyde* 3.1226–1232: A Clandestine Topos," *English Language Notes* 18 (1980–81) 166–70.

Butler, Pierce, *Legenda aurea—Légende dorée—Golden Legend: A Study of Caxton's Golden Legend with Special Reference to Its Relations to the Earlier English Prose Translation* (Baltimore 1899).

Camargo, Martin, "The Consolation of Pandarus," *Chaucer Review*, 25 (1990–91) 214–28.

—— *The Middle English Verse Love Epistle* (Tübingen 1991).

Capéran, Louis, *Le problème du salut des infidèles*, 2 vols. (Toulouse 1934).

Carruthers, Mary, "The Wife of Bath and the Painting of Lions," *Publications of the Modern Language Association* 94 (1979) 209–22.

Casella, Maria Teresa, "Nuovi appunti attorno al Boccaccio traduttore di Livio," *Italia medioevale e umanistica* 4 (1961) 77–129.

Cawley, A. C., ed., Geoffrey Chaucer, *Canterbury Tales* (London 1958).

Chambers, E. K., *The Mediaeval Stage*, 2 vols. (London 1903).

Chavannes-Mazel, Claudine A., *The Miroir historial of Jean le Bon: The Leiden Manuscript and Its Related Copies* (Cambridge 1991).

Chessel, Del, "In the Dark Time: Henryson's *Testament of Cresseid*," *Critical Review* (Melbourne) 12 (1969) 61–72.

Cloetta, Wilhelm, *Beiträge zur Literaturgeschichte des Mittelalters und der Renaissance*, vol. 1: *Komödie und Tragödie im Mittelalter*; vol. 2, *Die Anfänge der Renaissancetragödie* (Halle 1890–92).

Clough, Andrea, "Medieval Tragedy and the Genre of *Troilus and Criseyde*," *Medievalia et humanistica* 11 (1982) 211–27.

Coleman, Janet, *Piers Plowman and the "Moderni"* (Rome 1981).

Cook, Robert Francis, *The Sense of The Song of Roland* (Ithaca 1987).

Courtenay, William J., *Schools and Scholars in Fourteenth-Century England* (Princeton 1987).

Craik, Thomas W., "The Substance and Structure of *The Testament of Cresseid*: A Hypothesis," *Bards and Makars*, ed. Adam J. Ailken *et al.* (Glasgow 1977), pp. 22–26.

Craun, Edwin D., "Blaspheming Her 'Awin God': Cresseid's 'Lamentatioun' in Henryson's *Testament*," *Studies in Philology* 82 (1985) 25–41.

Cullen, Mairi Ann, "Cresseid Excused: A Re-reading of Henryson's *Testament of Cresseid*," *Studies in Scottish Literature* 20 (1985) 137–59.

Cunningham, J. V., "Tragedy as Essence," an appendix added to *Woe or Wonder: The Emotional Effect of Shakespearean Tragedy* (first published by the University of Denver Press in 1951) when reprinted in his *Collected Essays* (Chicago 1976), pp. 128–29.

Curry, Walter Clyde, "Destiny in Chaucer's *Troilus*," *Publications of the Modern Language Association* 45 (1930) 129–68; repr. in *Chaucer and the Mediaeval Sciences*, ed. 2, New York 1960, pp. 241–98, and in Schoeck and Taylor, *Chaucer Criticism*, 2:34–70 (cited from the latter).

David, Alfred, "Chaucerian Comedy and Criseyde," in Salu, ed., *Essays*, pp. 90–104, 137–39.

—— *The Strumpet Muse: Art and Morals in Chaucer's Poetry* (Bloomington 1976)..

Dean, Nancy, "Chaucerian Attitudes Toward Joy with Particular Consideration of the *Nun's Priest's Tale*," *Medium aevum* 44 (1975) 1–13.

Diekstra, F. N. M., *A Dialogue Between Reason and Adversity: A Late Middle English Version of Petrarch's De remediis* (Assen 1968).

Dinshaw, Carolyn, *Chaucer's Sexual Poetics* (Madison 1989).

Dobson, R. B., and J. Taylor, *Rymes of Robyn Hood: An Introduction to the English Outlaw* (Pittsburg 1976).

Doležel, Lubomír, "Narrative Worlds," *Sound, Sign, and Meaning: Quinquagenary of the Prague Linguistic Circle*, ed. Ladislav Matejka (Ann Arbor 1976), pp. 542–52.

—— *Occidental Poetics: Tradition and Progress* (Lincoln, Nebr. 1990).

Dollimore, Jonathan, *Radical Tragedy*, ed. 2 (Durham, N.C. 1989).

Donaghey, B. S., "Nicholas Trevet's Use of King Alfred's Translation of Boethius, and the Dating of His Commentary," *The Medieval Boethius: Studies in the Vernacular Translations of De consolatione Philosophiae*, ed. A. J. Minnis (Cambridge 1987), pp. 1–31.

Donaldson, E. Talbot, ed., *Chaucer's Poetry* (New York 1958).

Duncan, Douglas, "Henryson's *Testament of Cresseid*," *Essays in Criticism* 11 (1961) 128–35.

Durling, Robert M., *The Figure of the Poet in Renaissance Epic* (Cambridge, Mass. 1965).

Duffy, Eamon, *The Stripping of the Altars: Traditional Religion in England, c. 1400–c. 1580* (New Haven 1992).

Dunning, T. P., "God and Man in *Troilus and Criseyde*," *English and Medieval Studies Presented to J. R. R. Tolkien*, ed. Norman Davis and Charles L. Wrenn (London 1962), pp. 164–82.

Dwyer, Richard A., *Boethian Fictions: Narratives in Medieval French Versions of the Consolatio Philosophiae* (Cambridge, Mass. 1976).

Edwards, A. S. G., "The Influence of Lydgate's *Fall of Princes*, c. 1440–1559: A Survey," *Mediaeval Studies* 39 (1977) 424–39.

Eliason, Norman, *The Language of Chaucer's Poetry* (Copenhagen 1972).

Erzgräber, Willi, "Tragik und Komik in Chaucers *Troilus und Criseyde*," *Festschrift für Walter Hübner*, ed. Dieter Riesner and Helmut Gneuss (Berlin 1964), pp. 139–63.

Famiglietti, R. C., "Laurent de Premierfait: The Career of a Humanist in Early-Fifteenth-Century Paris," *Journal of Medieval History* 9 (1983) 25–42.

Farnham, Willard, *The Medieval Heritage of Elizabethan Tragedy* (Berkeley 1936).

Fisher, John H., *The Complete Poetry and Prose of Geoffrey Chaucer* New York 1977).

Fleming, John V., Review of Winthrop Wetherbee, *Chaucer and the Poets: An Essay on Troilus and Criseyde* [Ithaca 1984], *Studies in the Age of Chaucer* 7 (1985) 262–70.

Fox, Denton, "The Coherence of Henryson's Work," in Yeager, ed., *Fifteenth-Century Studies*, pp. 275–81. *See also* Henryson.

Fradenburg, Louise O., "Henryson Scholarship: The Recent Decades," in Yeager, ed., *Fifteenth-Century Studies*, pp. 65–92.

—— "'Voice Memorial': Loss and Reparation in Chaucer's Poetry," *Exemplaria* 2 (1990) 168–202.

Francis, W. Nelson, ed., *The Book of Vices and Virtues: A Fourteenth-Century English Translation of the Somme le roi of Lorens d'Orléans*, EETS os 217 (1942).

Frank, Robert W., Jr., *Chaucer and the Legend of Good Women* (Cambridge, Mass. 1972).

Frappier, Jean, "Sur un remaniement de la *Mort Artu* dans un manuscrit du xive siècle: Le Palatinus latinus 1967," *Romania* 57 (1931) 214–22. *See also Mort Artu.*

Friedman, John Block, *Orpheus in the Middle Ages* (Cambridge, Mass. 1970).

Frye, Northrop, *Anatomy of Criticism: Four Essays* (Princeton 1957).

Galbraith, V. H., *The St. Albans Chronicle, 1406–1420* (Oxford 1937).

Ganim, John, *Style and Consciousness in Middle English Narrative* (Princeton 1983).

Garbáty, Thomas J., "Chaucer and Comedy," in Ruggiers, ed., *Versions of Medieval Comedy*, pp. 173–90.

—— "*Troilus* 5.1786–92 and 5.1807–27: An Example of Poetic Process," *Chaucer Review* 11 (1976–77) 299–305.

Gardner, Ralph D., *Horatio Alger; or, The American Hero Era* (Mendota, Ill. 1964).

—— "The Return of Horatio Alger!" Introduction to Alger, *Struggling Upward*, pp. v–xii.

Gaylord, Alan T., "The Lesson of the *Troilus:* Chastisement and Correction," Salu, *Essays*, pp. 23–42, 128–30.

Godman, Peter, "Henryson's Masterpiece," *Review of English Studies* 2.35 (1984) 291–300.

Gray, Douglas, *Robert Henryson* (Leiden 1979).

Griffiths, Ralph A., "The Trial of Eleanor Cobham: An Episode in the Fall of Duke Humphrey of Gloucester," *Bulletin of the John Rylands Library* 51 (1968–69) 381–99.

Haas, Renate, "Chaucer's *Monk's Tale*: An Ingenious Criticism of Early Humanist Conceptions of Tragedy," *Humanistica lovaniensia* 36 (1987) 44–70.

—— " 'Kissing the steppes of Uirgile, Ouide,' etc. and *The Legend of Good Women*," *Proceedings: Anglistentag 1989 Würzburg*, ed. Rüdiger Ahrens, Proceedings of the Conference of the German Association of University Professors of English 11 (Tübingen 1990), pp. 298–309.

Hahn, Thomas G., *God's Friends: Virtuous Heathen in Later Medieval Thought and English Literature*, (University of California, Los Angeles, diss., 1974).

Haidu, Peter, "Romance: Idealistic Genre or Historical Text?" in *The Craft of Fiction: Essays in Medieval Poetics*, ed. Leigh A. Arrathoon (Rochester, Mich. 1984), pp. 1–46.

Hanna, Ralph, III, "Cresseid's Dream and Henryson's *Testament*," *Chaucer and Middle English Studies in Honor of Rossell Hope Robbins*, ed. Beryl Rowland (London 1974), pp. 288–97.

Hansen, Elaine Tuttle, *Chaucer and the Fictions of Gender* (Berkeley 1992).

—— "Irony and the Antifeminist Narrator in Chaucer's *Legend of Good Women*," *Journal of English and Germanic Philology* 82 (1983) 11–31.

Hardman, Phillipa, "Chaucer's Muses and His 'Art Poetical,' " *Review of English Studies* 2.37 (1986) 478–94.

Harty, Kevin J., "Cresseid and Her Narrator: A Reading of Robert Henryson's *Testament of Cresseid*," *Studi medievali* 3.23 (1982) 753–65.

Hassan, Ihab, "Toward a Concept of Postmodernism," *The Dismemberment of Orpheus: Toward a Postmodern Literature*, ed. 2 (Madison 1982), pp. 259–71, repr. in *The Postmodern Turn: Essays in Postmodern Theory and Culture* (Columbus 1987), pp. 84–96.

Heiserman, A. R., "The Plot of *Pearl*," *Publications of the Modern Language Association* 80 (1965) 164–71.

Helmholz, R. H., *Marriage Litigation in Medieval England* (Cambridge 1974).

Hemingway, Samuel B., "Chaucer's Monk and Nun's Priest," *Modern Language Notes* 31 (1916) 479–83.

Höltgen, Karl Josef, "König Arthur und Fortuna," *Anglia* 75 (1957) 35–54.

Hoffman, Richard L., "The Influence of the Classics on Chaucer," *Companion to Chaucer Studies*, ed. Beryl Rowland, rev. ed. (New York 1979), pp. 185–201.

Hollander, Robert, *Dante's Epistle to Cangrande* (Ann Arbor 1993).

Holley, Linda Tarte, *Chaucer's Measuring Eye* (Houston 1990).

Horney, Karen, *The Neurotic Personality of Our Time* (New York 1937).

Hornsby, Joseph Allen, *Chaucer and the Law* (Norman 1988).

Hortis, Attilio, *Studi sulle opere latine del Boccaccio* (Trieste 1879).

Howard, Donald R., Introduction to Geoffrey Chaucer, *Troilus and Criseyde and Selected Short Poems*, ed. Howard and James Dean (New York 1976).

Hunter, G. K., "Seneca and English Tragedy," *Seneca*, ed. C. D. N. Costa (London 1974), pp. 166–204, repr. in Hunter's *Dramatic Identities and Cultural Tradition* (Liverpool 1978), pp. 174–213.

Huot-Girard, Giselle, "La justice immanente dans la *Légende dorée*," in *Épopées, légendes, et miracles*, Cahiers d'études médiévales 1 (Montreal 1974), pp. 135–47.

Hussey, S. S., "The Difficult Fifth Book of *Troilus and Criseyde*," *Modern Language Review* 67 (1972) 721–29.

Imray, Jean, *The Charity of Richard Whittington: A History of the Trust Administered by the Mercers' Company, 1424–1966* (London 1968).

Janssen, Anke, "The Dream of the Wheel of Fortune," *The Alliterative Morte Arthure: A Reassessment of the Poem*, ed. Karl Heinz Göller (Cambridge 1981), pp. 140–52, 179–81.

Jauss, Hans Robert, "Theorie der Gattungen und Literatur des Mittelalters," *Grundriss der romanischen Literaturen des Mittelalters*, part 1: *Généralités*, ed. Maurice Delbouille (Heidelberg 1972), pp. 107–38; reprinted, with original pagination, in Jauss's collected essays, *Alterität und Modernität der mittelalterlichen Literatur* (Munich 1977), essay no. 10; translated as "Theory of Genres and Medieval Literature" (but mistakenly attributed to "volume 6" of the *Grundriss*) along with other of Jauss's essays, *Toward an Aesthetic of Reception*, tr. Timothy Bahti (Minneapolis 1982), pp. 76–109, 205–11. The French version that appeared in *Poétique* 1 (1970) 79–98 was translated from a preliminary or incomplete stage of the essay.

Jeudy, Colette, "L'abrigé de la *Thébaïde* de Laurent de Premierfait," *Italia medioevale e umanistica* 22 (1979) 413–38.

Jones, Peter Murray, "Four Middle English Translations of John of Arderne," *Latin and Vernacular: Studies in Late-Medieval Texts and Manuscripts*, ed. A. J. Minnis (Cambridge 1989), pp. 61–89.

Jones, Terry, *Chaucer's Knight: The Portrait of a Medieval Mercenary* (Baton Rouge 1980).

Jordan, Robert M., *Chaucer and the Shape of Creation* (Cambridge, Mass. 1967).

—— "Metafiction and Chaucer's *Troilus*," *Chaucer Yearbook* 1 (1992) 135–55.

Kamowski, William, "A Suggestion for Emending the Epilogue of *Troilus and Criseyde*," *Chaucer Review* 21 (1986–87) 405–18.

Kaske, R. E., "The Knight's Interruption of the *Monk's Tale*," *English Literary History* 24 (1957) 249–68.

Kaylor, Noel Harold, Jr., "Chaucer's Use of the Word *Tragedy*: A Semantic Analysis," *Language and Civilization: A Concerted Profusion of Essays and Studies in Honour of Otto Hietsch*, ed. Claudia Blank *et al.*, 2 vols. (Frankfurt 1992), 2:431–44.

Kearney, Milo, and Mimosa Schraer, "The Flaw in Troilus," *Chaucer Review* 22 (1987–88) 185–91.

Kelly, Douglas, "The Source and Meaning of *Conjointure* in Chrétien's *Erec* 14," *Viator* 1 (1970) 179–200.

Kelly, Henry Ansgar, "Aristotle-Averroes-Alemannus on Tragedy: The Influence of the *Poetics* on the Latin Middle Ages," *Viator* 10 (1979) 161–209.

—— "Cangrande and the Ortho-Dantists," *Lectura Dantis* 14–15 (1994) 61–95; reponse by Robert Hollander, pp. 96–110; reply by H. A. K., pp. 111–15.

—— *Canon Law and the Archpriest of Hita* (Binghamton 1984).

—— "Chaucer and Shakespeare on Tragedy," *Leeds Studies in English* 20 (1989) 191–206.

—— *Chaucer and the Cult of St. Valentine*, Davis Medieval Texts and Studies 5 (Leiden 1986).

—— "Chaucer's Arts and Our Arts," *New Perspectives in Chaucer Criticism*, ed. Donald M. Rose (Norman 1981), pp. 107–20.

—— "The Croyland Chronicle Tragedies," *The Ricardian* 7.99 (December 1987) 498–515.

—— "Croyland Observations," *The Ricardian*, 8.108 (March 1990) 334–41.

—— "The Devil at Large," *Journal of Religion* 67 (1987) 518–28.

—— *The Devil, Demonology, and Witchcraft* (New York 1968; rev. ed., 1974).

—— *Divine Providence in the England of Shakespeare's Histories* (Cambridge, Mass. 1970).

—— "English Kings and the Fear of Sorcery," *Mediaeval Studies* 39 (1977) 206–38.

—— *Ideas and Forms of Tragedy from Aristotle to the Middle Ages* (Cambridge 1993).

—— "Interpretation of Genres and by Genres in the Middle Ages," *Interpretation: Medieval and Modern*, ed. Piero Boitani and Anna Torti (Cambridge 1993), pp. 107–22.

Kelly, Henry Ansgar, "The Last Chroniclers of Croyland," *The Ricardian*, 7.91 (December 1985) 142–77

—— "Lawyers' Latin: *Loquenda ut vulgus?*" *Journal of Legal Education* 38 (1988) 195–207.

—— *Love and Marriage in the Age of Chaucer* (Ithaca 1975).

—— *The Matrimonial Trials of Henry VIII* (Stanford 1976).

—— "Medieval Relations, Marital and Other," *Medievalia et Humanistica* 19 (1992) 133–46.

—— "The Metamorphoses of the Eden Serpent During the Middle Ages and Renaissance," *Viator* 2 (1971) 301–27.

—— "The Non-Tragedy of Arthur," *Medieval English Religious and Ethical Literature: Essays in Honour of G. H. Russell*, ed. Gregory Kratzmann and James Simpson (Cambridge 1986), pp. 92–114.

—— Review of Piero Boitani, ed., *The European Tragedy of Troilus* [Oxford 1989], *English Language Notes* 30 (1992–93) 78–80.

—— "The Right to Remain Silent: Before and After Joan of Arc," *Speculum* 68 (1993) 992–1026.

—— "Sacraments, Sacramentals, and Lay Piety in Chaucer's England," *Chaucer Review* 28 (1993–94) 6–22.

—— "Shades of Incest and Cuckoldry: Pandarus and John of Gaunt," *Studies in the Age of Chaucer* 13 (1991) 121–40.

—— *Tragedy and Comedy from Dante to Pseudo-Dante* (Berkeley 1989)

—— "Tragedy and the Performance of Tragedy in Late Roman Antiquity," *Traditio* 35 (1979) 21–44.

—— "The Varieties of Love in Medieval Literature According to Gaston Paris," *Romance Philology* 40 (1986–87) 301–27.

Kindrick, Robert L., *Robert Henryson* (Boston 1979).

Klein, Robert, and Henri Zerner, "Vitruve et le théâtre de la Renaissance italienne," *Le lieu théâtral à la Renaissance* (Paris 1964), pp. 49–60, reprinted in Robert Klein, *La forme et l'intelligible* (Paris 1970), pp. 294–309.

Kluckhohn, Clyde, *Navaho Witchcraft* (Cambridge, Mass. 1944).

Knight, Stephen T., *Geoffrey Chaucer* (Oxford 1986).

—— "Some Aspects of Structure in Medieval Literature," *Parergon* no. 16 (Dec. 1976) 3–17.

Knowles, Michael David, *The Religious Orders in England*, 3 vols. (Cambridge 1948–59).

Koeppel, Emil, *Laurents de Premierfait und John Lydgates Bearbeitungen von Boccaccios De casibus virorum illustrium: Ein Beitrag zur Litteraturgeschichte des 15. Jahrhunderts* (Munich 1885).

Koff, Leonard Michael, "Ending a Poem Before Beginning It, or The 'Cas' of Troilus," in Shoaf, *Chaucer*, pp. 161–78.

Krook, Dorothea, *Elements of Tragedy* (New Haven 1969).

Kruger, Steven F., *Dreaming in the Middle Ages* (Cambridge 1992).

Kurvinen, Auvo, "Caxton's *Golden Legend* and the Manuscripts of the *Gilte Legende*," *Neuphilologische Mitteilungen* 60 (1959) 353–75.

Lawlor, John, *The Tragic Sense in Shakespeare* (London 1960).

Lawton, David, "Irony and Sympathy in *Troilus and Criseyde*: A Reconsideration," *Leeds Studies in English* 2.14 (1983) 94–115.

Leicester, H. Marshall, Jr., *The Disenchanted Self: Representing the Subject in the Canterbury Tales* (Berkeley 1990).

Lepley Douglas L., "The Monk's Boethian Tale," *Chaucer Review* 12 (1977–78) 162–70.

Lerer, Seth, *Boethius and Dialogue: Literary Method in the Consolation of Philosophy* (Princeton 1985).

—— Review of Gerard O'Daly, *The Poetry of Boethius* [London 1991], *Speculum* 68 (1993) 542–44.

Lewis, C. S., *The Allegory of Love* (London 1936).

Linder, Amnon, "The Knowledge of John of Salisbury in the Late Middle Ages," *Studi medievali* 3.18 (1977) 881–932.

Longo, Joseph A., "The Double Time Scheme in Book II of Chaucer's *Troilus and Criseyde*," *Modern Language Quarterly* 22 (1961) 37–40.

Lumiansky, Robert M., "The Alliterative *Morte Arthure*, the Concept of Medieval Tragedy, and the Cardinal Virtue Fortitude," *Medieval and Renaissance Studies* 3, ed. John M. Headley (Chapel Hill 1968), pp. 95–118.

McAlpine, Monica E., *The Genre of Troilus and Criseyde* (Ithaca 1978).

Macaulay, G. C., *see* Gower.

McCall, John P., "The Trojan Scene in Chaucer's *Troilus*," *English Literary History* 29 (1962) 263–75.

McDonald, Craig, "The Perversion of Law in Robert Henryson's Fable of the *Fox, the Wolf, and the Husbandman*," *Medium aevum* 49 (1980) 244–53.

Machan, Tim William, "Robert Henryson and Father Aesop: Authority in the *Moral Fables*," *Studies in the Age of Chaucer* 12 (1990) 193–214.

McKenna, Steven R., "Henryson's 'Tragedie' of Cresseid," *Scottish Literary Journal* 18.1 (May 1991) 26–36.

McKinnell, John, "Letters as a Type of the Formal Level, in *Troilus and Criseyde*," ed. Salu, *Essays on Troilus*, pp. 73–89, 135–37.

MacQueen, John, *Robert Henryson: A Study of the Major Narrative Poems* (Oxford 1967).

Magoun, Jr., F. P., "Chaucer's Summary of Statius's *Thebaid* II–XII," *Traditio* 11 (1955) 409–20.

Makdisi, George, "The Scholastic Method in Medieval Education: An Inquiry into Its Origins in Law and Theology," *Speculum* 49 (1974) 640–61.

Mann, Jill, "The Planetary Gods in Chaucer and Henryson," *Chaucer Traditions: Studies in Honour of Derek Brewer* (Cambridge 1990), pp. 91–106.

—— *Geoffrey Chaucer*, Feminist Readings (Atlantic Highlands, N.J. 1991).

Manning, Warren F., "The Jean de Vignay Version of the Life of Saint Dominic," *Archivum fratrum praedicatorum* 40 (1970) 29–46.

Marshall, Mary Hatch, "*Theatre* in the Middle Ages: Evidence from Dictionaries and Glosses," *Symposium* 4 (1950) 1–30, 366–89.

Martellotti, Guido, "La questione dei due Seneca, da Petrarca a Benvenuto," *Italia medioevale e umanistica* 15 (1972) 149–69.

Mazza, Antonia, "L'inventario della 'parva libraria' di Santo Spirito e la biblioteca del Boccaccio," *Italia medioevale e umanistica* 9 (1966) 1–74

Mazzoni, Francesco, "Guido da Pisa interprete di Dante e la sua fortuna presso il Boccaccio," *Studi danteschi* 35 (1958) 29–128.

Meech, Sanford B., *Design in Chaucer's Troilus* (Syracuse 1959, repr. New York 1969).

Meiss, Millard, *French Painting in the Time of Jean de Berry*, part 2: *The Limbourgs and Their Contemporaries*, 2 vols. (New York 1974).

Mieszkowski, Gretchen, *The Reputation of Criseyde, 1155–1500*, Transactions of the Connecticut Academy of Arts and Sciences 43.3, pp. 71–153 (New Haven 1971).

Minnis, Alastair, *Chaucer and Pagan Antiquity* (Cambridge 1982).

—— "'Glosynge Is a Glorious Thyng': Chaucer at Work on the *Boece*," *The Medieval*

280 *Chaucerian tragedy*

Boethius: Studies in the Vernacular Translations of De consolatione Philosophiae, ed. A. J. Minnis (Cambridge 1987), pp. 106–24.

Mogan, Joseph J., *Chaucer and the Theme of Mutability* (The Hague 1968).

Morse, Ruth, "Absolute Tragedy: Allusions and Avoidances," *Poetica* (Tokyo 1993) 1–17.

Muir, Kenneth, *Shakespeare's Tragic Sequence* (London 1972).

Murray, Henry A., "Proposals for a Theory of Personality," Murray *et al.*, *Explorations in Personality* (New York 1938), pp. 36–141.

Neuse, Richard, "*Troilus and Criseyde*: Another Dantean Reading," in Shoaf, ed., *Chaucer's Troilus*, pp. 199–210.

Newman, Barbara, "'Feynede Loves,' Feigned Lore, and Faith in Trouthe," in Barney, ed., *Chaucer's Troilus*, pp. 257–75.

Niebuhr, Reinhold, *Beyond Tragedy: Essays on the Christian Interpretation of History* (London 1938).

Nist, John, "The Art of Chaucer: *Pathedy*," *Tennessee Studies in Literature* 11 (1966) 1–10.

Nitecki, Alicia K., "'Fenȝeit of the New': Authority in *The Testament of Cresseid*," *Journal of Narrative Technique* 15 (1985) 120–32.

Norton-Smith, John, *Geoffrey Chaucer* (London 1974).

O'Daly, Gerard, *The Poetry of Boethius* (London 1991).

Opitz, Curt Richard, "De argumentorum metricorum latinorum arte et origine," *Leipziger Studien zur classischen Philologie* 6 (1883) 193–316.

Osberg, Richard H., "Between the Motion and the Act: Intentions and Ends in Chaucer's *Troilus*," *English Literary History* 48 (1981) 257–70.

Owen, Charles A., Jr., "*Troilus and Criseyde:* The Question of Chaucer's Revisions," *Studies in the Age of Chaucer* 9 (1987) 155–72.

Paris, Gaston, "Tristan et Iseut," *Poèmes et légendes du moyen-âge* (Paris 1900), pp. 113–80.

Parker, Deborah, Review of H. A. Kelly, *Tragedy and Comedy from Dante to Pseudo-Dante* [Berkeley 1989], *Speculum* 67 (1992) 704–05.

Parkes, Malcolm B., *English Cursive Book Hands, 1250–1500* (Oxford 1969).

—— and Elizabeth Salter, *Troilus and Criseyde: A Facsimile of Corpus Christi College Cambridge MS 61* (Cambridge 1978).

Parkinson, David J., "Henryson's Scottish Tragedy," *Chaucer Review* 25 (1991–92) 355–62.

Patch, Howard, "Troilus on Determinism," *Speculum* 6 (1929) 225–43, repr. in Schoeck and Taylor, eds., *Chaucer Criticism*, 2:71–85.

Patterson, Lee W., "Ambiguity and Interpretation: A Fifteenth-Century Reading of *Troilus and Criseyde*," *Speculum* 54 (1979) 297–330, slightly revised in *Negotiating the Past: The Historical Understanding of Medieval Literature* (Madison 1987), pp. 115–57.

—— *Chaucer and the Subject of History* (Madison 1991).

—— "Christian and Pagan in *The Testament of Cresseid*," *Philological Quarterly* 52 (1973) 696–714.

Pearsall, Derek, *John Lydgate* (London 1970).

—— *The Life of Geoffrey Chaucer: A Critical Biography* (Oxford 1992).

—— "The *Troilus* Frontispiece and Chaucer's Audience," *Yearbook of English Studies* 7 (1977) 68–74.

Perry, William, "Tragic Retribution in the 1559 *Mirror for Magistrates*," *Studies in Philology* 46 (1949) 113–130.

Pertile, Lino, "*Canto-cantica-Comedía* e l'Epistola a Cangrande," *Lectura Dantis* 9 (Fall 1991) 105–23.

—— Review of H. A. Kelly, *Tragedy and Comedy from Dante to Pseudo-Dante* [Berkeley 1989], *Medium aevum* 60 (1991) 139–40.

Pertusi, Agostino, "Il ritorno alle fonti del teatro greco classico: Euripide nell' Umanesimo e nel Rinascimento," *Venezia e l'Oriente fra tardo Medioevo e Rinascimento*, ed. Pertusi (Venice 1966), pp. 205–24.

—— "La scoperta di Euripide nel primo Umanesimo," *Italia medioevale e umanistica* 3 (1960) 101–52.

Pickens, Rupert T., Review of Robert Francis Cook, *The Sense of the Song of Roland* [Ithaca 1987], *Speculum* 65 (1990) 960–63.

Pittock, Malcolm, "The Complexity of Henryson's *The Testament of Cresseid*," *Essays in Criticism* 40 (1990) 198–221.

Power, Eileen, "The Lady," *Medieval Women*, ed. M. M. Postan (Cambridge 1975), pp. 35–52.

Pratt, Robert A., "'Joye after Wo' in the *Knight's Tale*," *Journal of English and Germanic Philology* 57 (1958) 416–23.

—— "A Note on Chaucer and the *Policraticus* of John of Salisbury," *Modern Language Notes* 65 (1950) 243–46.

—— "Some Latin Sources of the Nonnes Preest on Dreams," *Speculum* 52 (1977) 538–70.

Pratt, Robert A., ed., Geoffrey Chaucer, *The Tales of Canterbury* (Boston 1966).

Rajna, Pio, "Il teatro di Milano e i canti intorno ad Orlando e Ulivieri," *Archivio storico lombardo* 14 (1887) 5–28.

—— "Il titolo del poema dantesco," *Studi danteschi* 4 (1921) 5–37.

Reaney, P. H., *A Dictionary of British Surnames*, rev. R. M. Wilson (London 1976).

Reeve, M. D., and R. H. Rouse, "New Light on the Transmission of Donatus's *Commentum Terentii*," *Viator* 9 (1978) 235–49.

Ridley, Florence, "A Plea for the Middle Scots," *The Learned and the Lewed: Studies in Chaucer and Medieval Literature*, ed. Larry D. Benson, Harvard English Studies 5 (Cambridge, Mass. 1974), pp. 175–96.

Robertson, D. W., Jr., "Chaucerian Tragedy," *English Literary History* 19 (1952) 1–37, repr. in Schoeck and Taylor, eds., *Chaucer Criticism*, 2:86–121.

Robertson, James J., "The Development of the Law," *Scottish Society in the Fifteenth Century*, ed. Jennifer M. Brown (New York 1977), pp. 136–52.

Robinson, F. N., *see* Chaucer.

Rock, Daniel, *The Church of Our Fathers*, 3 vols. (London 1849–53).

Rollins, Hyder E., "The Troilus-Cressida Story from Chaucer to Shakespeare," *Publications of the Modern Language Association* 32 (1917) 383–429.

Root, Robert K., "The Monk's Tale," *Sources and Analogues of the Canterbury Tales*, ed. W. F. Bryan and Germaine Dempster (Chicago 1941, repr. New York 1958), pp. 615–44.

Rowlands, Mary E., "Robert Henryson and the Scottish Courts of Law," *Aberdeen University Review* 39 (1962) 219–26.

Ruggiers, Paul G., "Some Theoretical Considerations of Comedy in the Middle Ages," in Ruggiers, ed., *Versions of Medieval Comedy*, pp. 1–17.

—— "Towards a Theory of Tragedy in Chaucer," *Chaucer Review* 8 (1973–74) 89–99.

—— "A Vocabulary for Chaucerian Comedy: A Preliminary Sketch," *Medieval Studies in Honor of Lillian Herlands Hornstein*, ed. Jess B. Bessinger, Jr., and Robert R. Raymo (New York 1976), pp. 193–225.

Ruggiers, Paul G., ed., *Versions of Medieval Comedy* (Norman 1977).

Russo, Vittorio, "Il senso del tragico nel *Decameron*," *Filologia e letteratura* 11 (1965) 29–83.

Sabbadini, Remigio, "Biografi e commentatori di Terenzio," *Studi italiani di filologia classica* 5 (1897) 289–327.

Salter, F. M., "The Tragic Figure of the Wyf of Bath," *Proceedings and Transactions of the Royal Society of Canada* 48 (1954), part 3 section 2, pp. 1–3.

Salu, Mary, ed., *Essays on Troilus and Criseyde* (Cambridge 1979).

Scanlon, Larry, *Narrative, Authority, and Power: The Medieval Exemplum and the Chaucerian Tradition* (Cambridge 1994).

Schirmer, Walter F., *Der englische Frühhumanismus* (Leipzig 1931).

—— *John Lydgate: A Study in the Culture of the Fifteenth Century*, tr. Ann E. Keep from the German ed. of 1952 (London 1961).

Schoeck, Richard J., and Jerome Taylor, eds., *Chaucer Criticism*, 2 vols. (Notre Dame 1961).

Segert, Stanislav, "Syntax and Style in the Book of Jonah: Six Simple Approaches to Their Analysis," *Prophecy: Essays Presented to Georg Fohrer on His Sixty-fifth Birthday*, ed. J. A. Emerton (Berlin 1980), pp. 121–30.

Serafini, Mario, "Le tragedie di Seneca nella *Fiammetta* del Boccaccio," *Giornale storico della letteratura italiana* 126 (1949) 95–105.

Sewall, Richard B., "The Tragic Form," *Essays in Criticism* 4 (1954) 345–58, repr. in *Tragedy: Modern Essays in Criticism*, ed. Lawrence Michel and Sewall (Westport, Conn. 1963), pp. 117–29.

Shoaf, R. A., with Catherine S. Cox, ed., *Chaucer's Troilus and Criseyde: "Subgit to alle Poesye"; Essays in Criticism* (Binghamton 1992).

Skeat, *see* Chaucer.

Sklute, Larry, "Phoebus Descending: Rhetoric and Moral Vision in Henryson's *Testament of Cresseid*," *English Literary History* 44 (1977) 189–204.

Smalley, Beryl, *English Friars and Antiquity in the Early Fourteenth Century* (Oxford 1960).

Smith, James, "Chaucer, Boethius, and Recent Trends in Criticism," *Essays in Criticism* 22 (1972) 4–32.

Sowell, Madison U., Review of H. A. Kelly, *Tragedy and Comedy from Dante to Pseudo-Dante* [Berkeley 1989], *Journal of the Rocky Mountain Medieval and Renaissance Association* 11 (1990) 165–67.

Spearing, A. C., *Criticism and Medieval Poetry*, ed. 2 (London 1972).

—— "*Troilus and Criseyde*: The Illusion of Allusion," *Exemplaria* 2 (1990) 263–77.

Stäuble, Antonio, *La commedia umanistica del Quattrocento* (Florence 1968).

Stearns, Marshall W., *Robert Henryson* (New York 1949).

Stefanini, Ruggero, "Tenzone sì e tenzone no," *Lectura Dantis* 18–19 (1996) 111–28.

Steiner, George, *The Death of Tragedy* (London 1961).

Stevens, Martin, "The Performing Self in Twelfth-Century Culture," *Viator* 9 (1978) 193–212.

—— "The Winds of Fortune in the *Troilus*," *Chaucer Review* 13 (1978–79) 285–307.

Strange, William C., "The *Monk's Tale*: A Generous View," *Chaucer Review* 1 (1966–67) 167–80.

Stockton, Eric W., tr., *The Major Latin Works of John Gower* (Seattle 1962).

Strohm, Paul, "Middle English Narrative Genres," *Genre* 13 (1980) 379–88.

—— *Social Chaucer* (Cambridge, Mass. 1989).

Swanson, R. N., *Church and Society in Late Medieval England* (Oxford 1989).

Tatlock, John S. P., *The Complete Poetical Works of Geoffrey Chaucer Now Put into Modern English* (New York 1912).

—— *The Development and Chronology of Chaucer's Works* (London 1907).

Taylor, Ann M., "Troilus' Rhetorical Failure (4.1440–1526)," *Papers on Language and Literature* 15 (1979) 357–69.

Theiner, Paul, "The Medieval Terence," *The Learned and the Lewed: Studies in*

Chaucer and Medieval Literature, ed. Larry D. Benson (Cambridge, Mass. 1974), pp. 231–47.

Tillyard, E. M. W., "Henryson: *The Testament of Cresseid* (1470?)," chap. 1 of *Five Poems, 1470–1870* (London 1948), pp. 5–29.

Tinkle, Theresa, *Medieval Venuses and Cupids: Sexuality, Hermeneutics, and English Poetry* (Stanford 1996).

Todorov, Tzvetan, *The Fantastic: A Structural Approach to a Literary Genre*, tr. Richard Howard (Ithaca 1973), from *Introduction à la littérature fantastique* (1970).

—— *Introduction to Poetics*, tr. Richard Howard (Minneapolis 1981); originally published as *Qu'est-ce que le structuralisme: Poétique* in 1968 and revised in 1973; Todorov supplied a new preface, dated May 1980, to the English edition (pp. xx–xxxii).

Took, John, Review of H. A. Kelly, *Tragedy and Comedy from Dante to Pseudo-Dante* [Berkeley 1989], *Modern Language Review* 87 (1992) 216–17.

Twycross-Martin, Henrietta, "Moral Pattern in *The Testament of Cresseid*," *Chaucer and Fifteenth-Century Poetry*, ed. Julia Boffey and Janet Cowen (London 1991), pp. 30–50.

Villa, Claudia, *La "Lectura Terentii*," vol. 1: *Da Ildemaro a Francesco Petrarca* (Padua 1984).

Vitto, Cindy L., *The Virtuous Pagan in Middle English Literature*, Transactions of the American Philosophical Society, vol. 79, no. 5 (Philadelphia 1989).

Watson, Charles S., "The Relationship of the *Monk's Tale* and the *Nun's Priest's Tale*," *Studies in Short Fiction* 1 (1964) 277–88.

Werckmeister, Otto Karl, *Ende der Ästhetik* (Frankfurt 1971).

—— "Marx on Ideology and Art," *New Literary History* 4 (1972–73) 501–19.

—— Review of Meyer Schapiro, *Romanesque Art* [New York 1977], *Art Quarterly* 2.2 (1979) 211–18.

Wetherbee, Winthrop, *Chaucer and the Poets: An Essay on Troilus and Criseyde* (Ithaca 1984).

—— "The Context of the Monk's Tale," *Language and Style in English Literature: Essays in Honour of Michio Masui*, ed. Michio Kawai (Tokyo 1991), pp. 159–77.

Whiting, B. J., "A Probable Allusion to Henryson's *Testament of Cresseid*," *Modern Language Review* 40 (1945) 46–47.

Wickham, Glynne, *Early English Stages*, vol. 1 (London 1966).

Windeatt, Barry, "The Text of the *Troilus*," in Salu, ed., *Essays on Troilus*, pp. 1–22, 126–28

—— *Troilus and Criseyde*, Oxford Guides to Chaucer (Oxford 1992).

Windeatt, Barry, ed., *see* Chaucer, *Troilus*.

Wright, Dorene Allen, "Henryson's *Orpheus and Eurydice* and the Tradition of the Muses," *Medium aevum* 40 (1971) 41–47.

Yeager, Robert F., ed., *Fifteenth-Century Studies: Recent Essays* (Hamden Ct. 1984)

Young, Karl, "Chaucer's *Troilus and Criseyde* as Romance," *Publications of the Modern Language Society* 53 (1938) 38–63.

Zaccaria, Vittorio, "Le due redazioni del *De casibus*," *Studi sul Boccaccio* 10 (1977–78) 1–26.

Index

CHAUCER STUDIES